Reading the Epistles of
James, Peter, John, and Jude
as Scripture

Reading the Epistles of James, Peter, John, and Jude as Scripture

THE SHAPING AND SHAPE
OF A CANONICAL COLLECTION

David R. Nienhuis *&* Robert W. Wall

WILLIAM B. EERDMANS PUBLISHING COMPANY
GRAND RAPIDS, MICHIGAN / CAMBRIDGE, U.K.

© 2013 David R. Nienhuis and Robert W. Wall
All rights reserved

Published 2013 by
Wm. B. Eerdmans Publishing Co.
2140 Oak Industrial Drive N.E., Grand Rapids, Michigan 49505 /
P.O. Box 163, Cambridge CB3 9PU U.K.

Printed in the United States of America

18 17 16 15 14 13   7 6 5 4 3 2 1

Library of Congress Cataloging-in-Publication Data

Nienhuis, David R., 1968-
Reading the epistles of James, Peter, John, and Jude as scripture:
the shaping and shape of a canonical collection /
David R. Nienhuis & Robert W. Wall.
pages   cm
Includes bibliographical references and index.
ISBN 978-0-8028-6591-5 (pbk.: alk. paper)
1. Bible. Catholic Epistles — Criticism, interpretation, etc.
2. Bible. Catholic Epistles — Canon.
I. Wall, Robert W.   II. Title.

BS2777.N54   2013
227′.906 — dc23

2013022267

www.eerdmans.com

For Les Steele

Gifted Teacher,
Wise Mentor,
Generous Colleague,
and
Dear Friend

Contents

CONTENTS

Abbreviations

Ancient Texts

Act. Pet.	*The Acts of Peter*
Adum.	Clement of Alexandria, *Adumbrationes in epistolas catholicas (Comments on the Catholic Epistles)*
Adv. Haer.	Irenaeus, *Adversus omnes haereses (Against Heresies)*
Adv. Jud.	Tertullian, *Adversus Judaeos (Against the Jews)*
Adv. Marc.	Tertullian, *Adversus Marcionem (Against Marcion)*
Adv. Prax.	Tertullian, *Adversus Praxeas (Against Praxeas)*
Ant.	Josephus, *Antiquities of the Jews*
Apoc. Pet.	*Apocalypse of Peter*
1 Apol.	Justin, *First Apology*
2 Bar.	*Second Baruch/Syriac Apocalypse of Baruch*
Barn.	*Letter of Barnabas*
Bell.	Josephus, *Bellum Judaicum (Jewish War)*
b. Sanh.	Babylonian Talmud, tractate *Sanhedrin*
Carn.	Tertullian, *De carne Christi (On the Flesh of Christ)*
Catech.	Cyril of Jerusalem, *Catechetical Lectures*
CD	The Qumran Damascus Document
CE	Catholic Epistles
Cels.	Origen, *Contra Celsus*
Cher.	Philo, *De cherubim (On the Cherubim)*
1 Clem.	*First Letter of Clement*
Com. Apoc.	Victorinus of Pettau, *Commentary on the Apocalypse of John*
Com. Jn.	Origen, *Commentary on John*
Com. Mt.	Origen, *Commentary on Matthew*
Com. Rom.	Origen, *Commentary on Romans*

Conf.	Philo, *De confusione linguarum (On the Confusion of Tongues)*
Con. Nest.	Leontius of Byzantium, *Contra Nestorianos et Eutychianos (Against the Nestorians and Eutychians)*
Cult.	Tertullian, *De cultu feminarum*
De Trin.	Augustine, *De Trinitate* or Hilary of Poitiers, *De Trinitate*
Deus	Philo, *Quod deus sit immutabilis (That God Is Unchangeable)*
Dial.	Justin, *Dialogus cum Tryphone (Dialogue with Trypho)*
Doc.	Augustine, *De doctrina christiana (On Christian Doctrine)*
Dom.	Cyprian, *De Dominica Oratione (On the Lord's Prayer)*
1 En.	*1 Enoch*
Ep.	*Epistle*
Eph.	Ignatius, *To the Ephesians*
1-2 Esdr.	*1-2 Esdras*
Exhort.	Cyprian, *De Exhortatione Martyrium (Exhortation to Martyrdom)*
Fide	Augustine, *De Fide et Operibus (On Faith and Works)*
Fort.	Cyprian, *Ad Fortunatum (To Fortunatus: Exhortation to Martyrdom)*
H.E.	Eusebius, *Historia Ecclesiastica (Ecclesiastical History)*
Herm.	*Shepherd of Hermas*
Hom. Ex.	Origen, *Homilies on Exodus*
Hom. Jer.	Origen, *Homilies on Jeremiah*
Hom. Josh.	Origen, *Homilies on Joshua*
Hom. Lev.	Origen, *Homilies on Leviticus*
Hom. Num.	Origen, *Homilies on Numbers*
Hyp.	Clement of Alexandria, *Hypotyposes (Outlines)*
Iambi	Amphilochius of Iconium, *Iambi ad Seleucum*
Idol.	Tertullian, *De idolatria*
In Flacc.	Philo, *In Flaccum*
Jub.	*Jubilees*
Leg. ad Gai.	Philo, *Legatio ad Gaium*
Magn.	Ignatius, *To the Magnesians*
Mart. Pol.	*Martyrdom of Polycarp*
m. Kidd.	Mishnah *Kiddushin*
Mort.	Cyprian, *De mortalis (On Mortality)*
Mos.	Philo, *Vita Mosis (Life of Moses)*
Mut.	Philo, *De mutatione nominum (On the Change of Names)*
Neof.	Targum *Neofiti*
NT	New Testament
Op.	Cyprian, *De opera et eleemosynis (On Works and Almsgiving)*
Paed.	Clement of Alexandria, *Paedagogos*

PE	Pastoral Epistles
Phil.	Polycarp *To The Philippians*
Phild.	Ignatius, *To the Philadelphians*
Pol.	Ignatius, *To Polycarp*
Post.	Philo, *De posteritate Caini (On the Posterity of Cain)*
Praescr.	Tertullian, *De praescriptione haereticorum (Prescription against the Heretics)*
Prin.	Origen, *De principiis (On First Principles)*
Prob.	Philo, *Quod omnis probus liber sit (That Every Good Person Is Free)*
Ps-J.	Targum *Pseudo-Jonathan*
Pss. Sol.	*Psalms of Solomon*
Pud.	Tertullian, *De pudicia (On Modesty)*
Quir.	Cyprian, *Ad Quirinum testimonia adversus Judaeos (To Quirinus: Testimonies against the Jews)*
Quis	Clement of Alexandria, *Quis dives salvetur? (Who Is the Rich Man That Shall Be Saved?)*
Ref.	Hippolytus, *Refutatio omnium haeresium (Refutation of All Heresies)*
Rom.	Ignatius, *To the Romans*
Scorp.	Tertullian, *Scorpiace (The Scorpion's Sting)*
Sectis	Leontius of Byzantium, *De sectis*
Sel. Dt.	Origen, *Selections from Deuteronomy*
Sel. Pss.	Origen, *Selections from the Psalms*
Sent.	Cyprian, *Sententiae LXXXVII episcoporum*
Sib. Or.	*Sibylline Oracles*
Smyrn.	Ignatius, *To the Smyrneans*
Sobr.	Philo, *De sobrietate (On Sobriety)*
Strom.	Clement of Alexandria, *Stromata (Miscellanies)*
Symb.	Rufinus, *Commentarius in symbolum apostolorum (Commentary on the Apostles' Creed)*
T. Job	*Testament of Job*
T. Lev.	*Testament of Levi*
T. Mos.	*Testament of Moses*
T. Naph.	*Testament of Naphtali*
Tral.	Ignatius, *To the Trallians*
Vir.	Cyprian, *De Habitu Virginum (On the Clothing of Virgins)*
Viris	Jerome, *Liber de viris illustribus (Lives of Illustrious Men)*
Zel.	Cyprian, *De Zelo et Livore (On Jealousy and Envy)*

Modern Commentaries, Periodicals, Reference Works, and Serials

AB	Anchor Bible Commentary
ABD	*Anchor Bible Dictionary*
ABRL	Anchor Bible Reference Library
ABS	Approaches to Biblical Studies
ACCS	Ancient Christian Commentary on Scripture
AJT	*American Journal of Theology*
AnBib	Analecta biblica
ANF	*Ante-Nicene Fathers*
ANRW	*Aufstieg und Niedergang der römischen Welt*
ANTC	Abingdon New Testament Commentaries
ANTF	*Arbeiten zur neutestamentlichen Textforschung*
BDAG	W. Bauer, F. W. Danker, W. F. Arndt, and F. W. Gingrich, *Greek-English Lexicon of the New Testament and Other Early Christian Literature*, 3rd ed. Chicago: University of Chicago Press, 1999.
BECNT	Baker Exegetical Commentary on the New Testament
BETL	Bibliotheca ephemeridum theologicarum lovaniensium
Bib	*Biblica*
BibInt	*Biblical Interpretation*
BibSac	*Bibliotheca Sacra*
BJRL	*Bulletin of John Rylands Library*
BNTC	Black's New Testament Commentary
BR	*Bible Review*
BTB	*Biblical Theology Bulletin*
BWANT	Beiträge zur Wissenschaft vom Alten und Neuen Testament
BZ	*Biblische Zeitschrift*
CBC	Cambridge Bible Commentary
CBNTS	Coniectanea Biblica New Testament Series
CBQ	*Catholic Biblical Quarterly*
CBR	*Currents in Biblical Research*
CEB	Common English Bible
CH	*Church History*
CPNC	Crossway Publishing NIV Commentary
CPNivC	College Press NIV Commentary
CRBS	*Currents in Research: Biblical Studies*
CSS	Cistercian Studies Series
CurTM	*Currents in Theology and Mission*
DLNT	*Dictionary of the Later New Testament and Its Developments*
DTIB	*Dictionary for the Theological Interpretation of the Bible*
ER	*Encyclopedia of Religion*

ESV	English Standard Version
ETL	*Ephemerides theologicae Louvanienses*
EvQ	*Evangelical Quarterly*
ExAud	*Ex Auditu: An International Journal of Theological Interpretation of Scripture*
Exp	*Expositor*
ExpT	*Expository Times*
HC	Hermeneia Commentaries
HTR	*Harvard Theological Review*
IBS	*Irish Biblical Studies*
ICC	International Critical Commentary
IVPNTC	InterVarsity Press New Testament Commentary
JBL	*Journal of Biblical Literature*
JETS	*Journal of the Evangelical Theological Society*
JR	*Journal of Religion*
JSNTSS	Journal for the Study of the New Testament Supplement Series
JTS	*Journal of Theological Studies*
LSJ	H. G. Liddell, R. Scott, H. S. Jones, *A Greek-English Lexicon,* 9th ed. with revised supplement. Oxford, 1996
MNTC	Moffatt New Testament Commentary
NASB	New American Standard Bible
NCBC	New Century Bible Commentary
Neot	*Neotestamentica*
NIB	*New Interpreter's Bible*
NIBCNT	New International Biblical Commentary
NICNT	New International Commentary on the New Testament
NIGTC	New International Greek Testament Commentary
NIV	New International Version
NovT	*Novum Testamentum*
NovTSup	Novum Testamentum Supplements
NRSV	New Revised Standard Version
NTC	New Testament in Context
NTD	Das Neue Testament Deutsch
NTL	New Testament Library
NTOA	Novum Testamentum et Orbis Antiquus
NTS	*New Testament Studies*
PBR	*Patristic and Byzantine Review*
PNTC	Pillar New Testament Commentary
QR	*Quarterly Review*
RB	*Revue Biblique*
RSV	Revised Standard Version

RVV	Religionsgeschichtliche Versuche und Vorarbeiten
SB	*Sources bibliques*
SBLDS	Society of Biblical Literature Dissertation Series
SBLMS	Society of Biblical Literature Monograph Series
SBLSBS	Society of Biblical Literature Sources for Biblical Study
SBLSS	Society of Biblical Literature Symposium Series
SBS	Stuttgarter Bibelstudien
SE	*Studia Evangelica*
SecCent	*Second Century*
SJT	*Scottish Journal of Theology*
SNTSMS	Society for New Testament Studies Monograph Series
SNTSU	Studien zum Neuen Testament und seiner Umwelt
SP	Sacra Pagina
StudBib	*Studia Biblica*
TDNT	*Theological Dictionary of the New Testament*
THNTC	Two Horizons New Testament Commentary
TLZ	*Theologische Literaturzeitung*
TNTC	Tyndale New Testament Commentary
TU	*Texte und Untersuchungen zur Geschichte der altchristlichen Literatur*
TynB	*Tyndale Bulletin*
VC	*Vigiliae Christianae*
VL	*Vetus Latina*
WBC	Word Biblical Commentary
WUNT	Wissenschaftliche Untersuchungen zum Neuen Testament
ZNW	*Zeitschrift für die neutestamentliche Wissenschaft*

Preface

This is a book woven of many threads.

Surely one of the most prominent of these threads is our dissatisfaction with the way in which the Catholic Epistles are routinely treated in standard biblical studies surveys. As our introductory chapter will make clear, one gets a sense that modern criticism has effectively marginalized these letters and has even attempted to secure their relative unimportance when their theological contribution is weighed against the presentations of the Gospels or the Pauline corpus. We therefore entered into this project as evangelists with the hope of rehabilitating interest in the Catholic Epistles in the church and the academy. And we have attempted to produce a book primarily for readers in the firm hope that if we can awaken and capture their interest in these precious texts, they will in turn become evangelists for this collection and the sacred treasures found therein.

We also write as teachers who have learned from our teachers that the goal of instruction is the cultivation of "holy reason," as John Webster calls it, which awakens students to Scripture's powerful and persuasive vision of God's salvation. No other scholar has taught us more than Brevard Childs; we are deeply indebted to his holy reason. The title of this book recalls the title of his final book, one on the Pauline collection. Although we do not formalize a dialogue between these two books, we intend ours to be read with his to form the basis of a canonical introduction to the NT letters.

Surely not least among the threads is our common love of Scripture. Both of us are deeply troubled by the way in which modern scholarship continues to produce studies of the text that do not (and often cannot) connect with Scripture's target audience, the people of God who gather each week by the power of the Spirit to be sanctified as disciples of Jesus. We refuse to believe that the church is not hungry for a deeper, more intelligent, and even more demanding encounter with the biblical text. Indeed, our years of experience teaching in local churches have convinced us that many who populate the pews each week seek a far higher level of Christian education than what they are frequently offered. We write out of the humble hope that our book might find its place as one more provision toward that worthy end.

The central core of this study is the insistence that the Catholic Epistles collection is in fact a *canonical collection* and not a random grouping of "other" or "general" letters that emerged from communities not founded by the Apostle Paul. We are convinced that the rehabilitation of these seven letters is dependent on recognizing the canonical intent that they be read as a whole that is greater than the sum of its parts. After an introduction that describes the problematic current state of scholarship and proposes an alternate approach, the first part of the book will relate how the historical *shaping* (pp. 17-39) and the final *shape* of the collection (pp. 40-69) envisage a particular reading strategy for the whole. These chapters mark the opening frame for the second part of the book, which is made up of introductions to each of the seven letters. These are rather entry-level commentaries designed with the student in mind to introduce and illustrate our particular approach. Both the footnotes and the bibliography provide a portal for students to enter into a deeper conversation with scholarly materials. The book climaxes in part three with a theological reading of the collection as a whole and concludes with a brief epilogue which reflects on what we have produced and proposes a trajectory for further study.

Of course, a number of people deserve a word of thanks for their influence in the development of this book. Thanks are given first of all to our colleagues in the School of Theology at Seattle Pacific University for their unending support and encouragement. We consider ourselves blessed to be members of such a faithful and friendly assembly of teacher-scholars. In particular we would like to mention our associates in the Bible department who have acted as cherished conversation partners along the way — Frank Spina, Jack Levison, Sara Koenig, Bo Lim, and Laura Sweat — and also our dean, Doug Strong, and research librarian, Steve Perisho.

Thanks go to the students of our fall quarter 2011 Biblical Texts course who read early drafts of this book; their comments and contributions proved invaluable as tools that sharpened our writing for its intended audience.

Looking farther afield, we acknowledge a debt of gratitude to the members of the SNTS seminar on the Catholic Epistles, which Rob cochaired, and the SBL groups that have gathered around these letters and generated a renewal of interest in their study, if from different angles than our own.

Allen Myers, senior editor of biblical studies at Eerdmans, first approached us to write this book, and has supported us at every step. We thank him for his unfailing patience and generous spirit in seeing it to completion.

Finally, we dedicate this book as a modest tribute to our treasured friend Dr. Les Steele, Professor Emeritus of Christian Formation at Seattle Pacific University. Not only has Les helped each of us — at different times and in different ways — understand better our vocation as teachers and scholars, he has been our enthusiastic cheerleader and wise conversation partner along the way. Les exemplifies for us the "friend of God" we find in James, whose deep Christian faith is practiced and confirmed by acts of generous hospitality.

PART 1

Introduction to a Canonical Collection

Introduction: Chaos or Coherence?

Modern biblical scholarship has shown little interest in maintaining the boundaries of the Bible's own canonical collections when evidence unearthed by historical-critical investigation has suggested alternative gatherings. Indeed, the dominant historical orientation to the Bible has so privileged the interpretive control of reconstructed origins of individual compositions that the later assembling of the texts into a canonical whole has come to be deemed irrelevant at best or a dangerous ecclesial distortion of the writings' "original" truth at worst. According to Adolf von Harnack, "Canonization works like whitewash; it hides the original colors and obliterates all the contours," obscuring "the true origin and significance of the works" contained therein.[1] A generation earlier, Franz Overbeck said:

> It is in the nature of all canonization to make its objects unknowable, and one can also say of all the writings of our New Testament that at the moment of their canonization they ceased to be understood. They have been transposed into the higher sphere of an eternal norm for the church, not without a dense veil having been spread over their origin, their original relationships, and their original meaning.[2]

1. *Origin of the New Testament,* trans. J. R. Wilkinson (London: Williams and Norgate, 1925), pp. 140-41.

2. *Zur Geschichte des Kanons* (Chemnitz, 1880), 80, quoted by G. Luedemann, *Heretics: The Other Side of Christianity* (London: SCM, 1996), p. 270, n. 298. The concern to reconstruct historical origins is now the mainstay of biblical scholarship regardless of one's theo-

As a result of this rather rigid focus on the point of composition, introductory textbooks on the NT have come to take on a rather predictable form and structure. While there will always be a few such texts that simply address the biblical writings individually, text by text in canonical order, it is far more likely that a modern primer will analyze the apostolic writings according to "more appropriate" organizational rubrics reflecting the conventions of modern scholarly canonical reconstruction.

It is quite likely, for instance, that one will find prolegomena devoted to historical and methodological issues, followed by a substantial section on the social, political, and religious context of Jesus of Nazareth. Mark will likely be addressed first among the four Gospels, given the widespread affirmation that it has historical priority. Since preoccupation with historical point of origin is oriented toward an interest in authorship, it is almost certain that Acts will be removed from its canonical context to be treated alongside Luke's Gospel. The Gospel of John will likewise be removed to a later chapter (given its late provenance) to be read with the letters of John in an entirely separate section entitled "Johannine Literature," which may very well also include discussion of the Apocalypse.

The textbook will undoubtedly include a substantial section on the Apostle Paul. Again, given scholarly interest in historical origins, the author may begin with a chapter or two on Paul's life and thought. The book might then treat the Pauline epistles in canonical order, but it is far more probable that the letters will be separated like sheep and goats, with the blessed "authentic" writings on one side (reordered according to pre-

---

logical commitments. Consider the recent introduction to Hebrews and the "General Epistles" written by K. Jobes: "These are ancient books that were written in a time and place quite unlike the modern setting in which we read them today. To understand the books of the Bible as theological writings, we must understand the author's ideas within each book's original historical setting. . . . Without such knowledge, the risk of misunderstanding the biblical books is great" (*Letters to the Church: A Survey of Hebrews and the General Epistles* [Grand Rapids: Zondervan, 2011], p. 6). While we have no interest in denying the value of historical investigation into a text's point of composition, we reject the notion that an understanding of a biblical text is entirely predicated on the scholar's ability to reconstruct its "original historical setting." Put sharply, these texts were preserved not because of what their first readers thought of them but because, over time, the church discerned that they were vehicles of the Spirit's communication to faithful readers *regardless* of their sociohistorical locale. Indeed, the reception of these books as canonical provided them with a new setting, one grounded not in the social world of their first readers but in the historical phenomenon of canonization which resulted in the literary setting of the biblical canon.

sumed date of composition, of course) and the subcanonical "Deutero-paulines" on the other.

Despite the many rearrangements of this scholarly biblical canon, the introductory student will still get the sense that "the Gospels" and "the Pauline writings" represent a coherent body of NT biblical literature. But what will that student find in the chapters that follow? The answer is literally impossible to predict, for though every introductory textbook analyzes a gathering of NT writings that are not Gospels and do not come from the pen of Paul, no real agreement seems to exist for how to organize these remaining texts, or indeed, if what remains constitutes anything like a coherent "collection" at all.

The ancient church, of course, provided readers with a whole set of literary clues to indicate clearly that the seven letters of James, Peter, John, and Jude, called "the Catholic Epistles" (hereafter "CE"), should be read together as a distinctive and coherent witness alongside the Pauline corpus. The most obvious of these clues is found in the titles themselves: all of Paul's letters are addressed "to the" recipient (e.g. *pros Romaious, pros Galatas*) while the CE are set apart, titled "the letter of" the author (e.g. *Iakobou epistolē*). But only a very small handful of introductory texts present a collection under this title containing these seven letters[3] — and even among them, one is hard-pressed to find any who think of these texts as an intentionally constructed canonical unit of the NT. Even Brevard Childs, whose work has set the standard for canonical approaches to the NT, saw no compelling reason to read the letters together as a singular canonical witness.[4]

Indeed, in a survey of introductory works published in English since the 1980s we found a veritable kaleidoscope of options, with at least eight

---

3. D. Guthrie, *New Testament Introduction* (rev. ed.; Downers Grove: InterVarsity, 1990); L. M. McDonald and S. Porter, *Early Christianity and Its Sacred Literature* (Peabody: Hendrickson, 2000); R. A. Gundry, *A Survey of the New Testament* (4th ed.; Grand Rapids: Zondervan, 2003).

4. According to Childs, the canonical title "catholic epistles" "remains a useful one to designate a collection of New Testament writings which is distinct from the Gospels and the Pauline corpus. It is neither a precise canonical nor a modern genre classification. Its usage has no great theological significance other than to reflect the church's growing concern that the New Testament letters be understood as universal, even when, in their original form, they often carry a specific addressee (cf. II and III John)." *The New Testament as Canon: An Introduction* (Valley Forge: Trinity, 1985), p. 495.

different organizational rubrics in play that include at least seventeen different collections of writings among them. There seems to be basic agreement that at least James, 1-2 Peter, and Jude may be grouped in this "collection" of texts.[5] But should it include Hebrews, 1-3 John, and Revelation as well? Should we follow Davies, Theissen, and deSilva and include some or all of the so-called Deuteropauline texts, since they were, after all, also not written by Paul?[6] Or perhaps, since these are obviously all "later" writings, we should follow Ehrman and include some extracanonical early Christian texts?[7]

And how ought we to label this collection? Young calls them the "Non-Pauline Epistles" but leaves 1-3 John to be treated elsewhere, resulting in the confusing implication that the Johannine letters are somehow *not* "non-Pauline."[8] Thielman joins Young in this, creating a *nine-letter* "non-Pauline" collection that joins Hebrews and Revelation to the traditional seven.[9] Theissen[10] and Spivey, Smith, and Black[11] gather them together under the category of "pseudonymous" NT texts, even though scholarship remains in dispute over the authenticity of these writings (per-

---

5. Consider, e.g., D. Lockett, who wrote *An Introduction to the Catholic Epistles* for the Approaches to Biblical Studies series (New York: Clark, 2012) but was only able to address the letters of James, Peter, and Jude: "The epistles of John are omitted here because of historical-critical sensibilities that lead to reading each of these texts in isolation from one another and dictate that 1-3 John be studied under the rubric of their likely historical author, John. Along with much biblical scholarship, the ABS series has taken up the letters of John along with the Gospel of John" (p. 7).

6. So S. L. Davies, *The New Testament: A Contemporary Introduction* (San Francisco: Harper & Row, 1988); G. Theissen, *The New Testament* (London: Clark, 2003); D. deSilva, *An Introduction to the New Testament: Contexts, Methods and Ministry Formation* (Downers Grove: InterVarsity, 2004).

7. So B. D. Ehrman, *The New Testament: A Historical Introduction to the Early Christian Writings* (4th ed.; Oxford: Oxford University Press, 2007).

8. F. Young, "The Non-Pauline Epistles," in *The Cambridge Companion to Biblical Interpretation,* ed. John Barton (Cambridge: Cambridge University Press, 1998), pp. 290-304. Wall at one time was more amenable to the "non-Pauline" designation as a theological description of those writings that do not belong to the Pauline apostolate ("Introduction to the Epistolary Literature of the NT," in *The New Interpreter's Bible,* ed. L. E. Keck (Nashville: Abingdon, 2002), vol. 10, but his ideas on the subject have developed since then.

9. F. Thielman, *Theology of the New Testament* (Grand Rapids: Zondervan, 2005).

10. Theissen, *New Testament.*

11. R. A. Spivey, D. M. Smith, and C. Black, *Anatomy of the New Testament* (5th ed.; Upper Saddle River: Prentice-Hall, 2006).

haps the reason their "pseudonymous" collections differ). Maybe we should just follow the rather simple approach of Wilder, Charles, and Easley and treat the last eight NT writings as "The End of the New Testament"?[12] Or Davies, whose collection "The Concluding Letters" includes nearly *half* of the NT writings?[13] Or just come up with a new, creative organizing thematic that attempts to group writings according to reconstructed historical context or proposed subject matter?[14]

Though far from dominant, the most common designation one finds is "the General Letters." Unfortunately, scholars who use this title do not appear to agree on its exact meaning. A few employ the term as a translation of an ancient *title of a collection* (i.e., *katholikē*) and accordingly address the seven letters placed therein by the early church.[15] Most read it as a *genre designation,* that is, a term for encyclical letters addressed "generally"; they therefore include Hebrews, and sometimes exclude the Johannine letters.[16] Still others extend the genre designation beyond letters to include all *encyclical literature;* thus they include the Apocalypse of John,[17] and sometimes even texts like the *Didache.*[18] Tellingly, a great majority of scholars who do employ the title "General Letters" go immediately on to

---

12. So Terry L. Wilder, J. Daryl Charles, and Kendell Easley, *Faithful to the End: An Introduction to Hebrews through Revelation* (Nashville: Broadman and Holman, 2007).

13. Davies, *A Contemporary Introduction.*

14. See J. W. Drane, *Introducing the New Testament* (Oxford: Lion, 2000); W. M. Dunnett, *Exploring the New Testament* (Wheaton: Crossway, 2001); B. D. Ehrman, *A Brief Introduction to the New Testament* (Oxford: Oxford University Press, 2004); idem, *The New Testament: A Historical Introduction.*

15. So, e.g., Guthrie, *New Testament Introduction;* McDonald and Porter, *Early Christianity and Its Sacred Literature;* Gundry, *Survey.* Yet each of these treat the letters atomistically, one by one, and not as a coherent and meaningful *collection* of texts.

16. So, e.g., D. A. Fiensy, *New Testament Introduction* (CPNivC; Joplin: College, 1994); W. R. Ramsay, *The Westminster Guide to the Books of the Bible* (Louisville: Westminster John Knox, 1994); L. T. Johnson, *The Writings of the New Testament: An Interpretation* (Minneapolis: Augsburg Fortress, 2002); C. Cousar, *An Introduction to the New Testament: Witnesses to God's New Work* (Louisville: Westminster John Knox, 2006); K. Jobes, *Letters to the Church.*

17. Davies, *A Contemporary Introduction;* T. D. Lea and D. A. Black, *The New Testament: Its Background and Message* (2nd ed.; Nashville: Broadman and Holman, 2003); W. A. Elwell and R. W. Yarbrough, *Encountering the New Testament: A Historical and Theological Survey* (2nd ed.; Grand Rapids: Baker Academic, 2005).

18. Ehrman, *The New Testament: A Historical Introduction;* S. L. Harris, *The New Testament: A Student's Introduction* (Columbus: McGraw-Hill, 2008). The *Didache* is a first- or second-century church order.

insist that the designation is incorrect and unhelpful because several of the letters were not originally written to function as encyclicals![19]

Given the chaotic state of scholarly opinion, it is not surprising that many others find it acceptable simply to lump all the texts together under the label "other."[20] Note in this regard the rather honest assessment provided by McDonald and Porter in their book *Early Christianity and Its Sacred Literature:* "Hebrews, the General Epistles, and Revelation constitute their own category of writings in the NT, not because they have many features in common but because they do not fit conveniently into the other categories."[21] These texts are simply inconvenient for modern scholarship because they do not fit into the "other categories" — and this is the case, of course, because the "other categories" are organized according to modern historical-critical assumptions that are completely foreign to the theological concerns that shaped the biblical text in the first place.

Clearly, contemporary biblical scholarship does not know what to do with this particular subsection of the NT. The result is an embarrassingly disorganized and tentative scholarly presentation in comparison to the Gospels and Pauline writings. The CE are offered up as the leftovers of the NT, an optional plate of "other writings" to be consumed, should one desire, after the main courses of Gospel and Paul. Indeed, when one factors in the theological impact of the Pauline letters over the course of Christian history, is it any wonder that these other letters continue to be overlooked by scholar and layperson alike?

---

19. G. Krodel, ed., *The General Letters* (Proclamation; Minneapolis: Fortress, 1995), p. vii; R. Pregeant, *Engaging the New Testament: An Interdisciplinary Approach* (Minneapolis: Fortress, 1997), p. 454; P. Achtemeier, J. Green, and M. M. Thompson, *Introducing the New Testament: Its Literature and Theology* (Grand Rapids: Eerdmans, 2001), pp. 513-14; Ehrman, *The New Testament: A Historical Introduction,* p. 176; Fiensy, *New Testament Introduction,* p. 323; McDonald and Porter, *Early Christianity and Its Sacred Literature,* p. 517; Johnson, *Writings,* 455-56.

20. J. Blair, *Introducing the New Testament* (Nashville: Broadman and Holman, 1994); A. G. Patzia, *The Making of the New Testament: Origin, Collection, Text and Canon* (Downers Grove: InterVarsity, 1995); R. Brown, *An Introduction to the New Testament* (ABRL; New York: Doubleday, 1997); Johnson, *Writings;* I. H. Marshall, S. Travis, and I. Paul, *Exploring the New Testament 2: A Guide to the Letters and Revelation* (Downers Grove: InterVarsity, 2002); C. Blomberg, *From Pentecost to Patmos: An Introduction to Acts through Revelation* (Nashville: Broadman and Holman, 2006); A. M. Hunter, *Introducing the New Testament* (3rd ed.; Louisville: Westminster John Knox, 2006).

21. McDonald and Porter, *Early Christianity and Its Sacred Literature,* p. 517.

The Approach of This Study

It is precisely here that a close examination of the ancient canonical process that brought this collection into being offers real promise for the Bible reader committed to hearing the apostolic message as it is communicated through the integrity of the final, fixed form of the text. Unlike most modern treatments of the CE, which gather interpreters around their respective, reconstructive points of composition, this book targets their formation and final form as a discrete canonical collection. We contend that this is their *real* point of origin as Scripture, a perspective that proposes a different reading strategy — one that supplies additional observations about their meaning and application for today.

We admit at the outset that the proposed theological coherence of the CE collection is at odds with modern criticism's consensus, which underscores its literary diversity and theological incoherence and the original independence of each letter from the others, no matter what interpretive strategy is employed. Those who analyze texts from a largely historical point of view propose theological definitions retrieved from different points of origin where different authors respond to the spiritual crises of their different recipients shaped within different social and religious worlds. On the exegetical landscape of current biblical studies of these texts, then, the theological diversity found within the catholic corpus can be explained as the by-product of differing moments/places of origin and their respective trajectories/tradition histories.

Those who also treat the CE primarily as literature do not disagree with this conclusion. Their own explanatory constructions, however, explicate the same theological diversity as the by-product of different genres, textual structures, or rhetorical patterns — regardless of who wrote these texts, for whom, when, or where. In this light, then, the CE is no real collection at all but an arbitrary grouping of literary miscellanea gathered together and arranged during the canonical process at a non-Pauline address, without any thought of their theological coherence or canonical function *as a per se collection*. Even if one admits that their titles present these letters as the enduring deposit of Jerusalem's apostolic "Pillars" (see Gal. 2:9), the theological incoherence of the CE, and their independence from each other, has become a matter of critical dogma.[22]

---

22. We should note in passing how different the status of this question is when com-

Without denying the importance of this work, our book inclines the angle of approach toward the CE differently, admitting into evidence new findings from the canonical period when these seven books were formed into a second collection of letters "to provide a broader and more balanced literary representation of the apostolic witness than the letters of Paul furnished by themselves."[23] In doing so, we intend to challenge the critical consensus regarding the theological incoherence of the CE collection. Put simply, we contend that the canonical collection of four witnesses, James, Peter, John, and Jude ("the Pillars of Jerusalem"), be read together as the interpenetrating parts of a coherent theological whole. The historical process that formed them into a collection can also help guide the church's present use of its seven epistles as Scripture for spiritual wisdom and moral guidance. In fact, our thesis is that when this epistolary collection is embraced in the church according to the hermeneutics of the canonical process, both its theological coherence *and* its crucial role within the biblical canon will become more clearly understood.

As the backdrop for this new assessment of the CE, we observe that a central phenomenon of the canonical process is the purposeful formation of individual collections that eventually add up to form a single canon of collections that the church came to recognize as maximally effective in forming the one, holy, catholic, and apostolic church. That is, *the canonical process was vested in the importance of relationships among writings rather than in the authorization of individual writings in isolation from all the rest.*[24]

---

pared to the scholar's scruples regarding the Pauline corpus of letters. Biblical theologians typically approach the Pauline collection, even inclusive of its disputed membership, with the presumption of its essential theological unity. Whoever their real authors or implied readers are and no matter in what literary shape they have arrived at our canonical doorstep, the Pauline collection extends the thought of a particular person and the theological conception of each Pauline letter is measured by the theological dispositions of that particular person.

23. H. Y. Gamble, "The New Testament Canon: Recent Research and the *Status Quaestionis*" in *The Canon Debate*, ed. L. McDonald and J. A. Sanders (Peabody: Hendrickson, 2002), p. 288.

24. The fascinating intellectual history by M. C. Legaspi, *The Death of Scripture and the Rise of Biblical Studies* (Oxford: Oxford University Press, 2010), narrates the effects of early modernity on the study and use of Scripture, one of which is the detachment of Scripture from the church and the dismantling of the strategic relationships among canonical texts in order to treat each text alone. Our recovery of the use of "Scripture" (instead of "biblical studies") is an attempt to alert the reader to the theological and interpretive importance of the history of formation and the final literary form of the church's Scripture.

In this sense, both the final shape of each collection and the finality of the single biblical canon create an aesthetic that is substantively and functionally different than those alternate "shapes" of biblical writings created according to the interests of modern scholarship in an individual text's authorship, date, and social location. For example, the shape of Luke-Acts, an invention of modern criticism, differs from the shape of biblical canon received by the church, which locates the Gospel within a fourfold Gospel and Acts outside it (see below). Even though the canonical approach to Scripture's aesthetic should not be considered a substitute for critical constructions such as Luke-Acts, our project places significant historical interest in the *canonization* of biblical texts (and not their *composition*) as their real "point of origin" as the church's Scripture.

The deep logic of this shift of focus from composition to canonization, with its various additional claims of canonical rather than authorial intent, follows the epistemology of modernity's defense of a text's "original meaning." For example, J. Barton's reasonable definition of historical-critical orthodoxy[25] can be reappropriated for an interpreter's approach to a text's canonization, except now as a reader of a *canonical* text (rather than an authored one), which is located differently both in its postbiblical social world, in the reception of its intended audiences, and in relationship to other texts within an emerging biblical canon as an analogy of the church's apostolic Rule of Faith. In fact, in some cases we know far more about a text's postbiblical point of origin as *canonical* than we do about its origins as an authored composition, making that point of origin a more practical critical measure in protecting the sanctity of the church's text from interpretive abuse. But our primary justification project is, of course, meta-theological: *indexing a biblical text's "original meaning" by its initial reception as Scripture helps to illumine it within canonical context, which is how the church currently receives its apostolic witness as a source of wisdom and means of grace.*

Think of the canonical process as a type of evolutionary mechanism. New external threats during the early centuries of Christianity, provoked by ever-changing audiences, debates between rival Christianities, new responsibilities taken on to meet the internal pressures of an expanding religious movement, and even a history of using texts in the church's worship

---

25. J. Barton, "Historical-Critical Approaches," in *The Cambridge Companion to Biblical Interpretation,* ed. J. Barton (Cambridge: Cambridge University Press, 1998), pp. 9-20.

and mission — all forge a different social environment for the postbiblical reception of these sacred texts. The selecting and shaping of individual narratives or letters to form whole collections is a natural response to this environment. A piece of our canonical approach to the CE collection is cued by the reasons for the church's preservation, canonization, and continuing use of a second collection of letters, called "Catholic," which is predicated on this collection's adaptability to the social and religious exigencies facing the catholic, apostolic church at this second point of origin.

While the formation of the CE collection is profitably studied as a historical phenomenon — what we call "canonization from below" — it can also be mined for what this process implies for Bible practices in their intended ecclesial setting. Most scholars interested in the canonical process are historians who are not interested in explaining the choices made in theological terms. They do not assume a particular theology of Scripture, nor do they presume that the canonical process is one of spiritual discernment led by the Holy Spirit, what we call "canonization from above." The version of the canonical approach followed in this book is a species of theological interpretation that is vitally interested in a careful reconstruction of the canonical process as a deep reservoir of important interpretive clues for using Scripture to inform the witness and form the faith of today's church. The church's discernment of the Spirit's leading role in the production of the biblical canon is not predicated on the identity of a text's author but on its effect in forming a congregation that is wise for salvation and mature for good works.

Most modern constructions of the canonical process follow individual books through their earliest history, whether in the West or East, as evinced in the manuscripts, by allusions to and citations of the earliest Christian writings, or in the various canon lists. While useful in helping track the sociology and theology that attend the canonical process within antiquity, this kind of work largely ignores the phenomenology of the process itself: almost every individual book entered the biblical canon as an integral member of a whole collection (e.g., Torah, Psalter, Book of the Twelve, Fourfold Gospel, Pauline collection, Catholic Epistle collection, etc.). The final redaction of a collection, therefore, displays the aesthetic that is maximally effective for understanding the authorized roles of a biblical canon. In Pauline idiom, these particular roles combine to make believers wise for salvation and to bring them to maturity to perform the good works of God (2 Tim. 3:15-17). If a reader recognizes this theological dimension of the Bible's formation, instantiated in its final literary form, then the phenomena of canonization, and in particular the "canonical shaping" of discrete collections of biblical books and their placement within the final form of the biblical canon, will be mined for interpretive prompts that continue to guide how these texts are faithfully used as the church's Scripture.

We contend that the final literary form of the biblical canon is in this sense a work of aesthetic excellence. That is, the formation of a canonical collection or even of the biblical canon as a whole was fixed at the moment the church recognized that a *particular* literary shape had sufficient aesthetic excellence to function most effectively as Scripture. While certainly related to what the church affirms about the Bible's authority and holiness, *Scripture's formation into a textual analogue of the apostolic Rule of Faith* is the end result of a vast repertoire of choices spiritual leaders observed being made when individual texts were gathered into discrete collections, which were then put together to form a single biblical canon.

But this observation begs a more practical question that is more to the present point: what prompted the church to make those editorial decisions that put collections of individual sacred writings together into a particular shape and size? Even if we are to believe these decisions merely recognize the Spirit's will, Harnack observed that a century before the church discerned which way the wind was blowing its various canon lists and manuscript traditions evinced multiple different possible shapes and sizes.[26] This debate continues into our own day, whether to set aside the very idea of a biblical canon or to open it up to additional texts. The tenor of this debate calls forth this question: Why did the church settle on the biblical canon it did? Why this canonical shape and not some other?

From our routine experience as humans we might allow that how objects are formed is an important factor of their utility. How individual bits work together as a whole and for what purpose are decisive measurements

---

26. Harnack's principal thesis of course is that the NT canon was formed over an extended period of time and that books were *selected* from many possibilities; see, e.g., A. Harnack, *History of Dogma* (Boston: Little, Brown, 1901), 2:38-60. Different conditions shaped different selections; any change of bishop or circumstance would have led to different selections. Harnack's essential understanding of the phenomenology of a "canonical process" is right, even if we may contest his conclusions. That is to say, the notion of a selective process is important *theologically;* one must explain those selections theologically (or pneumatologically) and not just phenomenologically.

of an object's performance, whether it will be well received and well used. In objecting to what he calls "high art," what is valued momentarily for art's sake but is unused in any practical way and so is soon forgotten as a passing fad, Nicholas Wolterstorff advances a more functional conception of the aesthetic excellence of an enduring work of art.[27] In his view, any work of public art should be shaped and sized in a way that makes it accessible for ever-changing audiences, constantly performing in ways that inspire them to do good work or to live more virtuously as a result. While defining aesthetic excellence in this more activist direction, Wolterstorff allows for inherent properties of color and texture, shape and proportion that distinguish a good work of art from one of lesser quality.[28] People are naturally drawn to a particular work of art or a line of poetry or a landscape because it inspires them but also because they are able to recognize the sheer excellence of its nature.

Architect Moshe Safdie advances an "ethics of architecture" based on a similar idea. He claims the function of a building, which determines its form, must "uplift people's spirits so that it becomes a place for the community." For this to occur, the final form of a building must resonate with the culture of a particular place. Given these prerequisites, Safdie concludes, "there is a profound ethics to architecture which is different from the other areas. A painter, a sculptor, a writer can express freely. They don't

27. See Nicholas Wolterstorff, *Art in Action* (Grand Rapids: Eerdmans, 1980), especially his proposal of a distinctively "Christian aesthetic," pp. 65-174. Wolterstorff is therefore not primarily interested in whether art can be used as a source of Christian theology or as an auxiliary of divine revelation, although we take it he would allow that great art which deals with themes central to the Christian faith might better function in drawing people to God.

28. Typically, this recognition or intuition of the aesthetic excellence of a particular object is not immediate but occurs at the end of a long process of editing and reshaping that work of art. Professor R. Maddox, a leading scholar of John and Charles Wesley, reported in a private conversation that he is working on a multivolume critical edition of the poetry of Charles Wesley in which he will note all the words and lines that Wesley crossed out and changed when writing his lyrical lines, many of which are the most memorable in the history of Christian hymnody. The recognition of a text's aesthetic excellence often happens at the end of a protracted process of trial and error, when different versions of the same text are tested until one is found that is most effective in performing the role intended for it — in Wesley's case, for a congregation's worship. The canonical process unfolded in a similar way toward a similar end. The final redaction of a canonical collection, such as the thirteen-letter Pauline corpus, is fixed and finalized when the church recognizes that this is the version from among other options (e.g., the ten-letter Pauline corpus) that best performs the work Scripture is assigned to perform.

affect society as a whole. We build buildings that have a purpose, that stay there for hundreds of years." Against the "look at me" quality of some public art, he adds that "if there is an ethic, there's not a wonderful freedom. There are constraints about architecture. So [architects] have a responsibility to make buildings that have a timeless quality about them which is the ethics of our profession," which is better judged by taxi drivers who know how the public feels than by art critics![29]

In applying this more functional definition of aesthetic excellence to the literary architecture of the Christian biblical canon, we would argue for an "ethics of canonization" grounded in the church's deep sense of the Bible's aesthetic excellence — that is, its completeness and coherence — as a trusted witness to the word and ways of God.[30] The implications of such an ethic follow: First, the church discerned when the Bible had become shaped into that particular literary form which would more effectively enable the Spirit to use it in performing those religious roles that form a holy people who know and serve God. Every collection of texts was received and folded into the biblical canon on the basis of a résumé of ecclesial performances among rank-and-file believers that would commend its future productivity according to the purposes of God. The church's decisions, in this sense, were rational and based upon solid evidence of a text's spiritual utility. Before a text was received into the biblical canon, it was first used widely and well for congregational teaching and reproving, correcting, and training believers into the way of God. Our point is that the enduring excellence of a particular form is recognized from among other possibilities by its capacity to perform the work intended for a biblical canon. Scripture is a beautiful thing because it performs its public roles well.

Second, there are literary properties inherent to the biblical canon that might naturally draw readers to its wisdom or into its narrative world as a story of higher quality. For example, Scripture's diverse parts are noteworthy because of their rich texture. As a literary genre, the biblical canon is a collection of collections made up of artfully told stories, memorable lyrics, vivid poetry, exacting law codes, all of which direct us to ultimate meaning. Yet these diverse and discrete parts are nicely fitted together into

---

29. Jeffery Brown, interview with Moshe Safdie on PBS Newshour, October 14, 2011.

30. So, e.g., Christopher Seitz allows that the final literary form of the canonical text "bears the fullest witness to all that God has said and handed on within the community of faith." See his "Canonical Approach," in *DTIB*, pp. 100-102.

whole collections and then into a single biblical canon whose internal unity of theological and moral content renders a more coherent — and perhaps for this reason more compelling — word about God. Moreover, the effects of reading Scripture in the company of the Spirit and the worshiping community enable the reader to experience God's holy presence and the joy and peace, the conviction and judgment elicited by the divine word.

Finally, like the artist who changes the wording of a poem or a line of a painting because it makes the poem better or the painting's image more arresting, the indwelling Spirit forms a community's capacity to recognize which particular bits and what form are necessary in constructing a single biblical canon that is most effective in accomplishing its holy purposes. The church's decisions in forming the collections of the biblical canon, if they are directed by the Holy Spirit, will effectively help to accomplish God's redemptive desires for the world.[31] In other words, if a loving God has created us for loving communion with God and each other, then the church's production of Scripture in its present canonical form and so the church's practices of Scripture — its careful exegesis, its theological interpretation, its vibrant proclamation — must target this same holy end.

31. For a fascinating study of this phenomenon of collection building (in this case the OT's Book of the Twelve), which treats many of the same observations we have made about the CE collection, see *Reading and Hearing the Book of the Twelve*, ed. J. D. Nogalski and M. A. Sweeney (SBLSS 15; Atlanta: Society of Biblical Literature, 2000).

The Shaping of a Canonical Collection

In both structure and content, the Bible is reflective of a community's redactional act. The early church did not simply receive and transmit its diverse Scriptures in an ad hoc fashion, but carefully and prayerfully arranged them to forge evocative intertextual relations which, under the aegis of God's Spirit, would produce an inexhaustible font of interpretive insights useful for teaching, reproof, correction, and training in righteousness.

An overview of the centuries-long process of canonical shaping makes it plain that the formation of the CE collection took place well after that of the Gospel and Pauline canons. The latter are widely recognized to have been in broad circulation in something close to their current form by the end of the second century. As we are about to relate, however, the CE collection did not emerge until the mid to late third century and was not embraced across the Christian world until the late fourth. The CE collection can thus be seen to represent the final redactional act of the church's canon-constructing endeavor.

While the final *shape* of the CE collection may appear rather modest at first glance (for indeed, all seven letters combined take up less space than Paul's second letter to the Corinthians), attention to the *shaping* of the CE leads us to recognize that the collection is, in effect, the final piece of the canonical puzzle. This is in no way to be received as a random grouping of "other" texts from the ancient world gathered together here simply because they appear to bear a "general" address. From the perspective of the canonical process, the CE collection is revealed to be the pièce de résistance that determined the ultimate form of the NT canon. It is the final brushstroke of canonization, without which the masterwork of the NT would have been incomplete.[1]

This chapter seeks to review the story of that final redactional act.[2] Before we do so, however, we must underscore something we have just said regarding our perspective as narrators of this story. Brevard Childs has insisted that those attending to the canonical process hold *Historie* in appropriate tension with *Geschichte*. The former is "the attempt to understand events from an objective, scientific analysis, applying ordinary human experience, apart from any confessional content, as the measure of its credibility" — what we termed in the last chapter "canonization from below." *Geschichte*, by contrast, represents "historical reflections on events and conditions carried on within a confessing community of faith,"[3] that is, an account of canonization "from above" informed by theological convictions about the character of God, the purposes of Scripture, and the call of the church to produce and then submit itself to the canon it was led to create.

"Conservative" treatments of the canonical process tend to blur *Historie* and *Geschichte*, which in our opinion capitulates to the rather modernistic presumption that the theological truth of the latter depends entirely on the historiographical truth of the former (a presumption that, more often than not, results in rather thin accounts of both).[4] "Liberal" narrations of the process are equally modernist in their orientation, but typically insist on drawing a radical distinction between the two, viewing *Geschichte* as a pollutant to a right construal of truth in the form of *Historie*. This chapter will work hard to keep the tension in place by carefully tracking the historical phenomenon of canonization "from below" while mining that history for interpretive prompts that suggest how these

---

1. Gamble agrees: "it is very difficult to speak of a New Testament canon having taken any clear shape, whether in conception or in substance, prior to the appearance of this particular canonical collection." H. Y. Gamble, "The New Testament Canon: Recent Research and the *Status Quaestionis*" in *The Canon Debate*, ed. L. McDonald and J. A. Sanders (Peabody: Hendrickson, 2002), p. 288.

2. For a more thorough treatment of the canonization of the CE collection, see D. R. Nienhuis, *Not by Paul Alone* (Waco: Baylor University Press, 2007), pp. 29-97.

3. B. S. Childs, *The Church's Guide for Reading Paul: The Canonical Shaping of the Pauline Corpus* (Grand Rapids: Eerdmans, 2008), p. 165.

4. A recent example of this kind of treatment is M. J. Kruger, *Canon Revisited* (Wheaton: Crossway, 2012).

texts were intended, "from above," to inform the life and witness of today's church.

The story will unfold according to the following major plot points. After surveying the foggy landscape of the early to mid second century, we will focus on the work of Irenaeus of Lyon, whose *Against Heresies (Adv. Haer.)* represents the first major plot point in the development of the NT canon. We will then go on to consider the development of the collection in the late second and third centuries, first in the West, and then in the East. From there, we will turn to the canon lists of the fourth and fifth centuries and conclude with some reflections on the arrival of the collection and the significance of the final form.

Early to Mid Second Century: The Period before Irenaeus

A survey of the admittedly sparse documentary witness of the second-century church makes it fairly clear that among the CE only 1 Peter and 1 John were known and used, though the authority of Jude is overtly acknowledged by some at the end of that century. Indeed, the best evidence for use of 1 Peter and Jude in the second century is probably 2 Peter (assuming a late date for that letter), as it incorporates a good deal of the latter[5] and asks us to read it in self-conscious acknowledgement of the former (e.g., 3:1).

Though he never cites the letters outright, Polycarp of Smyrna (d. ca. 156) echoes enough of 1 Peter (e.g., his *Phil.* 1) and 1 John (e.g., *Phil.* 7) to allow most to conclude that he appealed to the letters as authoritative apostolic literature. Eusebius tells us that Polycarp's contemporary Papias also knew and used both letters.[6] Justin Martyr (d. ca. 165) also appears to know 1 John.[7] Indeed, we could list a number of apparent echoes of these two letters in the writings of this period, but it is not until Irenaeus that we hear them spoken of overtly.

---

5. Compare, e.g., 2 Pet. 2:1-18 and 3:1-3 with Jude 4-13 and 16-18. For a detailed discussion of the parallels between 2 Peter and Jude, see R. Bauckham, *Jude, 2 Peter* (WBC 50; Waco: Word, 1983), pp. 141-43.

6. *H.E.* 3.36.1-2; 3.39.3, 17.

7. E.g., *Dial.* 123.9; *1 Apol.* 32.7-8.

Late Second and Third Centuries: The West

The work of Irenaeus of Lyon (ca. 130-200) represents a seismic shift in NT canon history, for he was the first theologian of the church to make explicit appeal to proto-NT texts *as texts,* and thereby the first "catholic" leader to argue for a particular content and shape for the canon.[8] Irenaeus knew and used 1 Peter and 1 John consistently (as well as 2 John on at least one occasion[9]), though it is worth noting that his use of these texts pales in comparison to his reliance on the Pauline literature. Indeed, his writings make it clear that Paul was widely viewed as the most important apostolic authority in the second century.

This dominance of Pauline influence, however, clearly bore a number of problems for nascent Christian orthodoxy, since Paul was claimed as the central apostolic authority for a range of competing articulations of the faith, most dangerously the "Gnosticism" of individuals like Valentinus and the anti-Judaism of Marcion. Irenaeus's five-volume masterwork *Adv. Haer.* represents his attempt to ground emerging catholic orthodoxy in a firm, historic documentary witness of apostolic texts and ecclesial traditions.

Most important for our purposes is his strategic use of the Acts of the Apostles as an "anchor" text for locating Paul in harmonious relation to the larger Christian mission, against the Marcionites, who argued that Paul alone understood the identity and mission of the Lord.[10] As a westerner in full alliance with the Roman church, Irenaeus understood his task to be a

---

8. Chief among the "on the ground" realities that characterized the process is the community-specific nature of the text's development. Different groups claiming the name "Christian" (e.g., Marcionites, Montanists, various so-called "Gnostic" and "Jewish Christian" groups) championed different collections of texts. Our focus in this chapter is exclusively on the Bible we now possess, the Bible of the group that over the course of the second century came to call itself "catholic." For more thorough accounts of the patristic use of this term, see R. P. Moroziuk, "The Meaning of *katholikē* in the Greek Fathers and Its Implications for Ecclesiology and Ecumenism," *PBR* 4 (1985), pp. 90-104, and J. B. Lightfoot's discussion in his edition of the *Apostolic Fathers* (reprint, Grand Rapids: Baker, 1981), 2.1.413-15; 2.2.310-12. On the problematic use of the unqualified term "Gnostic," see M. A. Williams, *Rethinking "Gnosticism": An Argument for Dismantling a Dubious Category* (Princeton: Princeton University Press, 1996). For recent assessments of the various groups and emphases that made up ancient "Jewish Christianity," see J. Lieu, *Neither Jew Nor Greek: Constructing Early Christianity* (New York: Clark, 2002) and M. Jackson-McCabe, ed., *Jewish Christianity Reconsidered: Rethinking Ancient Groups and Texts* (Minneapolis: Augsburg Fortress, 2007).

9. *Adv. Haer.* 3.16.5-8.

10. *Adv. Haer.* 3.12.

defense of "the tradition derived from the apostles, of the very great, the very ancient and universally known church founded and organized at Rome by the two most glorious apostles, Peter and Paul."[11] He argues on this basis that any reading of Paul that seals him off from his colleagues in Jerusalem is untenable and unhistorical and leads ultimately to a heretical distortion of the apostolic message.

Though Irenaeus has the entire Jerusalem apostolate in mind, it is clearly Peter who is positioned as the counterpart to Paul. Indeed, Irenaeus makes this case by appealing to Paul himself:

> With regard to those who allege that Paul alone knew the truth, let Paul himself convict them, when he says that one and the same God wrought in Peter for the apostolate of the circumcision, and in himself for the Gentiles [Gal. 2:8]. Peter, therefore, was an apostle of that very God whose was also Paul; and him whom Peter preached as God among those of the circumcision . . . did Paul also among the Gentiles."[12]

In this manner Irenaeus establishes the ground of the earliest apostolic message in the two-sided mission to Jews and Gentiles, the former headed by Peter, the latter by Paul.

This Acts-inspired "missional" logic for receiving the apostolic message was developed by Irenaeus's theological heir, Tertullian of Carthage (ca. 160-223), most especially in his work *Against Marcion (Adv. Marc.)*. Like Irenaeus, Tertullian made extensive use of 1 Peter and 1 John and relied heavily on the Acts of the Apostles in support of a proper understanding of Paul against those who would isolate him from the wider apostolate. Unlike Irenaeus, however, Tertullian focused not just on Peter but on James, Peter, and John, the "Pillars" of the Jerusalem church as identified in Gal. 2:9. Indeed, Tertullian works hard to *demote* Paul's authority in this text, calling these three the "original" apostles and Paul a "later," *posterior* apostle: "Even if Marcion had introduced his Gospel under the name of Paul in person," Tertullian argues, "that single document would not be adequate for our faith, if destitute of the support of his predecessors."[13]

---

11. *Adv. Haer.* 3.3.1-2.
12. *Adv. Haer.* 3.13.1.
13. *Adv. Marc.* 4.2.4-5.

Tertullian makes much of Galatians 1 and 2, using this important Marcionite proof-text against them: it turns out that Paul needed to visit the Jerusalem Pillars because they were "apostles before him" and he, being "inexperienced in grace," was "anxious lest he had run or was running in vain" (*Adv. Marc.* 1.20.2). The meeting was required, in fact, "perchance he had not believed as they did or was not preaching the gospel in their manner" (4.2.5). Indeed, Paul's immaturity was to blame for his apparent condemnation of "Peter and those others, Pillars of the apostolate" in Galatians, driven as he was by "his zeal against Judaism" as a "neophyte," though soon enough he would adapt to their wisdom, since "he himself was afterwards to become in his practice all things to all men" (1.20.2-3). Throughout Tertullian conceives of the three Pillar apostles as a unit: it is James, Peter, and John who are condemned by Paul at Antioch, not just Peter, for all three are Paul's authoritative "predecessors."

Beneath the sharp anti-Marcionite rhetoric, Tertullian seeks to establish one key point: any apparent separation between Paul and the Jerusalem apostolate had to do with an intentional division of mission, not message — "they arranged among themselves a distribution of their spheres of work, not a division of the Gospel."[14] He repeatedly describes their harmonious relationship in this manner:

> [I]n respect of the unity of their preaching, as we have read earlier in this epistle, they had joined their right hands, and by the very act of having divided their spheres of work had signified their agreement in the fellowship of the Gospel: as he says in another place, "Whether it were I or they, so we preach" [1 Cor. 15:11]. (*Adv. Marc.* 1.20.4)

> At length, when he had conferred with the originals, and there was agreement concerning the rule of the faith, they joined the right hands, and by the very act of having divided their spheres of work had signified their agreement in the fellowship of the gospel; as he says in another place, "Whether it were I or they, so we preach." (4.2.5)

> Well it is therefore that Peter and James and John gave Paul their right hands, and made a compact about distribution of office, that Paul should go to the Gentiles, and they to the circumcision. (5.3.6)

14. *Praescr.* 23.9.

Against those who would extricate Paul as the apostle par excellence, then, Tertullian follows his predecessor Irenaeus in insisting that Paul be received as an important representative of a larger group of apostolic bearers of the earliest Christian message. Tertullian's advancement of Irenaeus's argument is in his expansion of the Jerusalem leadership beyond Peter to include his fellow Pillars, John and James the brother of Jesus. Thus, Tertullian was the first to provide the full *logic* behind the ultimate form of the apostolic letter collection: it is a two-sided collection of writings rooted in the ancient apostolic missions to Jews and Gentiles. Tertullian was clearly unaware of a letter from James, however, so he nowhere attempts to ground this logic in an actual apostolic letter collection.

Before we move on from Tertullian it must also be noted that he is the first western writer to confirm the authority of the letter of Jude. After tracing the roots of feminine ornamentation to the fallen angels in the book of Enoch (*Cult.* 1.3.1-3) he felt the need to offer an extensive justification for his use of the text. After several supports for its authenticity, Tertullian concludes with the decisive argument to end all arguments: the text can be trusted by "the fact that Enoch possesses a testimony in the Apostle Jude."[15] Tertullian is thus able to assume that his readers know and accept Jude as an authoritative apostolic writing.

Other western church witnesses confirm the presence of 1 Peter, 1-2 John, and Jude in the West, and the corresponding absence of James, 2 Peter, and 3 John. The so-called Muratorian Fragment, which likely dates from around the year 200,[16] knows letters of John and Jude, and both Hippolytus of Rome (d. 235)[17] and Cyprian of Carthage (d. 258)[18] know 1 Peter and 1-2 John. While 2 Peter was likely known by the authors of the *Apocalypse of Peter* (early second century) and the *Acts of Peter* (later sec-

---

15. *Cult.* 1.3.1-3.

16. The Sundberg-Hahnemann theory that the Muratorian fragment is in fact a fourth-century product of the eastern church fails to convince us; see A. C. Sundberg, "Canon Muratori: A Fourth-Century List," *HTR* 66 (1973), pp. 1-41; G. Hahnemann, *The Muratorian Fragment and the Development of the Canon* (Oxford: Clarendon, 1992), and the discussion in Nienhuis, *Not by Paul Alone*, pp. 46 and 76.

17. Some have argued that Hippolytus knew and used 2 Peter; see *Ref.* 9.7.16-17; 10.33.11. In our opinion, the evidence is inconclusive (see *Not by Paul Alone*, p. 45).

18. Though Cyprian never quotes 2 John, it was quoted in his presence at the Council of Carthage in 256 (see J. Lieu, *The 2nd and 3rd Epistles of John: History and Background* [Edinburgh: Clark, 1986], p. 9).

ond century),[19] it was not explicitly cited by anyone until Origen articulated doubts about its authenticity in the early third century. There is no clear sign anywhere that anyone knows the letter of James. All this is to underscore the point already made that the end of the second century knew of a Jewish-Gentile "missional logic" when speaking of early apostolic authority but clearly lacked the documentary witnesses to instantiate this logic in an apostolic letter collection.

Late Second and Third Centuries: The East

A turn to the fathers of the eastern church from the same period reveals both agreement with their western counterparts and development of the traditions they maintained. Clement of Alexandria, who flourished between 190 and 215, likewise made use of 1 Peter, 1-2 John, and Jude. Clement differed from his western brethren, however, in his willingness to appeal to a far wider set of ancient sources as authoritative for theological reflection; he happily quoted from noncanonical and pagan sources alike if they served the purposes of his argument. This makes his lack of direct reference to the letter of James all the more powerful: he certainly would have appealed to the letter had he known of its existence, for he is well aware of traditions surrounding the brother of the Lord. In particular it is worth noting how, like Tertullian, Clement is aware of a "Pillars" tradition that links James, Peter, and John together as a kind of apostolic unit in relation to Paul. Fragments of his *Hypotyposes* preserved by Eusebius tell us the following:

> Peter, James and John [of Zebedee] after the ascension of the Lord did not struggle for glory, because they had previously been given honor by the Savior, but chose James the Just as Bishop of Jerusalem. (*Hyp.* 6 in *H.E.* 2.1.3)

> After the resurrection the Lord gave the tradition of knowledge to James the Just and John and Peter, these gave it to the other apostles

---

19. For an analysis of the apparent references, see Bauckham, *Jude, 2 Peter*, p. 148. For an argument in the opposite direction — that the author of 2 Peter was literarily dependent on *Apoc. Pet.*, see W. Grünstäudl, *Petrus Alexandrinus. Studien zum historischen und theologischen Ort des Zweiten Petrusbriefes* (WUNT; Tübingen: Mohr-Siebeck, 2013).

and the other apostles to the seventy, of whom Barnabas was one. (*Hyp.* 8 in *H.E.* 2.1.4)

Again, Clement's awareness of traditions surrounding James's authority makes it even more difficult to understand how he could avoid referring directly to the letter of James if he were aware of its existence.[20]

It is with the great biblical scholar Origen of Alexandria (d. ca. 253) that we enter a new phase in the development of the CE collection, for Origen is the first church father to offer some overt comment on all twenty-seven writings that are now part of the NT canon. It will come as no surprise that he makes extensive use of 1 Peter and 1 John. The situation was different for 2 Peter and 2-3 John, however. Indeed, it is doubtful that he accepted them as authentic; Eusebius at least records his doubts about all three of them (*H.E.* 6.25.8-9), and Origen does not appeal to the letters in any of his writings that have come down to us in Greek.[21]

Of greatest importance for us is the fact that Origen is the first church father to champion the letter of James. Though he is well aware of the fact that the letter is not accepted by everyone,[22] he nevertheless quotes it extensively as an authoritative apostolic letter. Strikingly, Origen found James most useful for its help in protecting a right reading of Paul's teaching on faith and works. For example, against those who argue by appeal to Romans 4 that Abraham's one key work of righteousness was his faith in God, Origen appeals to John 8:39, where Jesus challenges the Jewish leadership by saying, "If you were Abraham's children, you would be doing the *works* of Abraham." If Jesus had used the singular "work," Origen insists, then faith alone would be required, but this "would not be conceded by those who accept the saying as authoritative, 'Faith without works is

20. See Nienhuis, *Not by Paul Alone* pp. 48-50, for a more detailed argument against Clement's knowledge and use of the letter of James.

21. The majority of Origen's writings have not survived in Greek. Most have come down to us through fourth-century translations by Jerome and Rufinus. When these Latin texts are compared to the extant Greek texts, it becomes apparent that they are more akin to edited paraphrases than careful translations. Indeed, it is not uncommon for these translators to add scriptural citations where none existed in the original. Origen's appeals to 2 Peter are found only in the Latin translations, not in the Greek — and appeals to 2-3 John are not found in either the Latin or the Greek texts. See G. W. Butterworth's discussion in his introduction to *Origen: On First Principles* (London: SPCK, 1936), p. xxx.

22. See, e.g., *Com. Jn.* 20.10.66.

dead'" (*Com. Jn.* 20.10.66). No, believers must do *all* the works of Abraham and not just the singular work of believing in God, for being justified by faith does not exempt one from the obligation to perform good works.

It is in his commentary on Paul's letter to the Romans that we find the fullest expression of Origen's appreciation of James for its ability to shape a right reading of the Pauline teaching on justification by faith. While discussing Paul's comments on the value of circumcision, he quotes Ezek. 44:9: "No son of a foreigner, uncircumcised in heart and uncircumcised in flesh, of all the sons of the foreigners who are among the house of Israel, shall enter my sanctuary."

> This would mean that the one who does not have faith would be uncircumcised in the heart and the one who does not have works would be uncircumcised in the flesh. For one without the other is condemned, seeing that also faith without works is called dead [Jas. 2:17, 26] and that no one is justified before God by works without faith [Rom. 3:20; Gal. 2:16]. . . . Doubtless this is what the Lord also says in the Gospel, "He who believes in me keeps my commands" [John 14:15, 21, 23]; and again, "he who hears these words of mine and does them" [Matt. 7:24]; and likewise, "why do you say to me 'Lord, Lord' and do not do what I say?" [Luke 6:46]. You see, then, that everywhere faith is joined with works and works are united with faith. (*Com. Rom.* 2.9.396-408)

In a brilliantly unifying intertextual reading, Origen argues against a fideistic reading of Pauline justification, reconciling it with Jesus' call to join belief and discipleship, by appealing to the distinctive faith-works perspective found in the letter of James. Indeed, in numerous commentary passages Origen shows a deep concern to keep believers from concluding that Paul is advocating justification by "faith alone" without the corresponding evidence of a holy life. Commenting on Paul's discussion of Abraham's faith in Romans 4, Origen insists:

> Now you should not imagine that if someone has such faith . . . he would be able at the same time to have unrighteousness with it as well . . . the proof of true faith is that sin is not being committed, just as, on the contrary, where sin is being committed, there you have proof of unbelief. For this reason then it is also said of Abra-

ham in another passage of scripture that he was justified by the
works of faith. (*Com. Rom.* 4.1.63-73)[23]

James provided Origen with a useful corrective foil to such readings of
Paul. By appeal to James, Origen could offer a more thoroughly
intertextual, "catholic" reading of the larger apostolic witness, most particularly by reconciling the justification by faith passages of Paul with the
ethical injunctions of the Gospels. It is extremely significant that the earliest known tradent of the letter of James employed the letter in this particular fashion, for it suggests that James was led to its canonical home by being read as a corrective to distortions of the Pauline message.

Before we leave Origen, we must note one further significant development: apart from being the first church father to reflect knowledge of all
seven CE, Origen is also the first witness to use the word "catholic" in reference to some of them. The term is used primarily in reference to
1 John,[24] but it is also applied occasionally to 1 Peter[25] and, significantly,
the *Letter of Barnabas.*[26] Though Origen nowhere explains what he means
by that title "catholic," his regular use of it in regard to 1 John in particular
suggests he is thinking along the lines of contemporary secular usage, that
is, in reference to a letter that is addressed "generally" in distinction from
one addressed to a particular person or group. Though he nowhere refers
to a *collection* of letters by that name, Origen offers witness to the development of a *category* of letters falling under a genre called "catholic."

The Emergence of the Collection:
Eusebius and the Fourth-Century Eastern Church

The *Historia Ecclesiastica (H.E.)* written by Eusebius of Caesarea represents the third major plot point in the story of the shaping of the CE, for
two reasons. To begin with, Eusebius is our first witness to the fourth-
century practice of producing "canon lists" that advocate a particular content and sequence for the collection of NT texts. Though previous church

23. See also his appeal to James at 4.8.22-37, 64-69.
24. E.g., *Com. Jn.* 1.138 and 2.149.
25. *Sel. Pss.* 3; *Com. Jn.* 6.175.9.
26. *Cels.* 1.63.9.

fathers may have offered comment on the *canonicity of individual books,* Eusebius is the first to present groups of books in *categories of canonicity,* and in doing so he tells us much about the state of the NT canon in the early 300s. Second, Eusebius is important for our study because it is in this well-known church history that we hear for the first time of a seven-letter collection called "the Catholic Epistles."

Eusebius ranked apostolic writings in circulation according to four major categories, the middle two of which are somewhat confusingly presented as subcategories of a single set (*H.E.* 3.25). Twenty-two books are grouped into the first category, the "accepted" or "recognized" *(homolegoumenois)* books: the four Gospels, Acts, Paul's fourteen letters (including Hebrews), 1 John, 1 Peter, and the Revelation of John (though Eusebius admits that others do not accept the latter). The fourth category contains rejected texts, those "put forward by heretics under the name of the apostles" — books like the *Gospel of Peter,* the *Gospel of Thomas,* the *Acts of John,* and others.

The second and third categories are the "disputed" *(antilegomena)* and the "illegitimate" *(notha).* In contrast to the heretical writings of the fourth group, these are all orthodox texts accepted by some and rejected by others — and indeed, in other areas of the *H.E.* where he is speaking more generally, he lumps them all together as "disputed." When treating the matter more carefully, however, he divides them into these subcategories. Eusebius tells us of five "disputed books which are nevertheless known to most": James, Jude, 2 Peter, and 2-3 John. In the "illegitimate" category we find other books that were popular among some catholic Christians, such as the *Acts of Paul,* the *Shepherd of Hermas,* the *Apocalypse of Peter,* and the *Letter of Barnabas.*

One immediately notices that the five "disputed" texts are the remaining CE that, when added to the "accepted" books, comprise the ultimate twenty-seven book canon. Indeed, Eusebius *has* to separate these five out from the other disputed texts because, by his day, they belonged to a widely acknowledged collection of letters called "the Catholic Epistles." Earlier in the *H.E.,* when he is telling the story of the Lord's brother James, he concludes:

> Such is the story of James, whose is said to be the first of the so-called Catholic Epistles. But it is to be observed that it is disputed; at least, not many of the ancients have mentioned it, as is the case like-

wise with the epistle that bears the name of Jude, which is also one of the seven so-called Catholic Epistles. Nevertheless we know that these also, with the rest, have been read publicly in very many churches. (*H.E.* 2.23.25)

He says something rather similar about 2 Peter: "the so-called second epistle [of Peter] we have not received as canonical, but nevertheless it has appeared useful to many, and has been studied with the other scriptures" (*H.E.* 3.3.1).

In these comments Eusebius provides us with a snapshot of the penultimate moment in the shaping of the NT. *As a historian*, Eusebius observed concerns about the authenticity of James, 2 Peter, 2-3 John, and Jude, for they were not mentioned very often by his predecessors. As a historian *of the church*, however, Eusebius acknowledges that these writings had already been recognized as "useful" by the church of his day, regardless of whatever concerns the authorities might have had. Indeed, they were already in circulation with 1 Peter and 1 John as a collection called "the Catholic Epistles."

Because of the witness of Eusebius we can say with some confidence that the CE collection emerged from somewhere in the eastern church, some time *after* the work of Origen in the third century but *before* the work of Eusebius in the early fourth. Indeed, after Eusebius's day the canon lists of the eastern leaders speak in near uniformity in their acceptance of the seven-letter CE collection.

The points of similarity and dissimilarity among their statements are instructive and worthy of brief comment. First, we find a great deal of uniformity regarding the *title* of the collection, the *sequence* of the letters within the collection, and, for most, the fixed *number* of letters involved, namely, "the seven Catholic Epistles" in the order James–Peter–John–Jude. This is the case with Cyril of Jerusalem (ca. 350), the Synod of Laodicea (ca. 365), Athanasius of Alexandria (367), Epiphanius of Salamis (ca. 375), Gregory of Nazianzus (390), and Amphilochius of Iconium (ca. 390). Hence we would rightly conclude that the CE collection as we now know it had clearly "arrived" in the East. What was not yet entirely fixed was the *sequence of collections* within the larger NT. Nearly everyone throughout the third- and fourth-century Christian world began the NT with the fourfold Gospel and the book of Acts, but most Easterners listed the CE immediately *after* Acts and *before* the writings of Paul. Bruce Metzger has pointed out that "virtually all Greek manuscripts" of the NT follow this sequence.[27] The exceptions are Eusebius, Gregory, and Amphilochius, who follow what has now become the "received" sequence, Acts–Paul–CE.

Comments by some of the eastern fathers help us to understand the sequence James–Peter–John–Jude within the collection and Acts–CE–Paul within the NT. Cyril of Jerusalem says:

> Receive also the Acts of the twelve apostles; and in addition to these, the seven Catholic Epistles of James, Peter, John, and Jude; then, as a seal upon them all, and the last work of the disciples, the fourteen epistles of Paul. (*Catech.* 4.36)

Receiving Paul's letters as the final "seal" representing "the last work of the disciples" makes no sense historically, for we now know that Paul's letters are among the earliest writings of the NT. Referring to Paul as "last" only makes sense in light of the Acts narrative, which begins in Jerusalem with the ministry of James, Peter, and John to Jews, and ends with the ministry of Paul to the Gentiles. One is reminded here of Tertullian's concern to locate Paul in a *posterior* position in relation to the Jerusalem Pillars as related in Acts and indeed as Paul himself does in Gal. 1:17 (where he speaks of the Pillars as "those who were apostles before me") and in 1 Cor. 15:8 (where he notes that the risen Christ revealed himself to Paul "last of all"). Placing James first comports both with his character portrait in Acts, where he is leader of the Jerusalem church (12:17; 15:13-21; 21:17-26), and with Paul's identification of the "Pillars" of the Jerusalem church in Gal. 2:9, which names them in the order "James, Cephas, and John."

Somewhat similarly, Athanasius's list advocates the reception of the "Acts of the Apostles and seven letters, called Catholic, by the Apostles." After listing the seven CE by name, Athanasius says, "After these are fourteen letters by Paul" who, importantly, is not called an "apostle" (*Ep.* 39). This can also be seen to have been inspired by Acts, where the name "apostle" is typically reserved for the original disciples of the historical Jesus associated with the Jerusalem mission to the Jews (see especially Acts 9:27; ch. 15; 16:4). It seems likely that this sequence of texts and collections was meant to instantiate the narrative of Acts, where the Gentile mission

---

27. B. M. Metzger, *The Canon of the New Testament* (Oxford: Clarendon, 1987), pp. 295-96.

emerges out of the Jewish mission. As Paul himself insisted, salvation is "to the Jew first and also to the Greek" (Rom. 1:16; 2:9-10). Placing the CE first is a way of instantiating this theological claim in literary form.

A Word on the Ancient Eastern Syrian Churches

While the Greek-speaking churches of western Syria (centered at Antioch) were in association with the larger eastern Christian world, the Syriac-speaking churches of Eastern Syria (centered around the cities of Edessa and Arbela) were separated not only linguistically but also politically and geographically, such that they developed independently of the major Christian traditions of their day. This isolation is evident especially in their canon history.[28] While we have no real canon lists from this region before the turn of the fifth century, we do know that no extant manuscripts of the Old Syriac include any of the CE, and the fifth-century Peshitta version of the Bible included only the "major" CE, namely, James, 1 Peter, and 1 John.

The *Doctrine of Addai,* traditionally dated around the year 400 (before the circulation of the Peshitta), includes a proscription against reading anything other than "the Law and the Prophets and the Gospel . . . and the epistles of Paul which Simon Peter sent us from the city of Rome, and the Acts of the Twelve Apostles which John the son of Zebedee sent us from Ephesus." While we find use of James, 1 Peter, and 1 John in the writings of John Chrysostom (d. ca. 407) and Theodoret (d. ca. 466), there is no evidence that either of them accepted any of the minor CE, and we possess nothing to suggest that Theodore of Mopsuestia (d. 428) ever accepted any of the CE at all.[29]

The Arrival of the CE in the West

While there was a CE collection operative in some eastern churches in the later 200s, it would be the middle 300s before we find evidence of western

28. See J. A. Brewer, "The History of the New Testament Canon in the Syrian Church II: The Acts of the Apostles and the Epistles," *AJT* 4 (1900), pp. 345-63; J. Siker, "The Canonical Status of the Catholic Epistles in the Syriac New Testament," *JTS* 38 (1987), pp. 311-40.

29. Indeed, Leontius of Byzantium (d. ca. 620) accused Theodore of having rejected "the epistle of James and the other Catholic Epistles that followed it" (*Con. Nest.* 3.14).

leaders using James and 2 Peter, and the turn of the next century before we can consider the CE collection to be relatively "fixed" in the western churches.

The Latin West produced far fewer canon lists than did the East, so tracking the shaping process with complete clarity is not possible. It is quite plausible, however, to assume that the eastern CE collection was carried westward because of increased contact between eastern and western church leaders due to the Arian crisis.[30] Chief among these is Athanasius of Alexandria, who spent the years between 339 and 346 in exile in Rome for his anti-Arian stance. There he had a profound impact on the westerner Hilary of Poitiers, who was himself exiled to the East for the same reason between 356 and 360. Hilary's eastern influences are apparent in his post-exilic work: against the dominant western opinion he championed the letter to the Hebrews as Pauline, cited 2 Peter as an authentic writing of the Apostle Peter (*De Trin.* 1.18.3), and was the first theologian in the West to cite the letter of James as Scripture (4.8.28).[31]

It is not until Jerome's day (d. 420) that we can confirm the arrival of the CE in the West. Though trained in the Latin tradition, Jerome spent significant periods of residence in the East, and his comments on the canon reflect this cross-fertilization. In a letter written from Bethlehem in 394, Jerome lists the NT texts in the order Gospels–Paul–Acts–CE–Revelation. Though he places Paul before the CE with the westerners, he still links the CE with Acts and lists them in the order James–Peter–John–Jude in accordance with the eastern tradition (*Ep.* 53.9). In that letter Jerome praises all seven letters and makes no mention of any dispute, though in his *Lives of Illustrious Men* he speaks quite frankly of such things.

> Peter . . . wrote two epistles which are called Catholic, the second of which, on account of its difference from the first in style, is considered by many not to be his. (1.3)

---

30. See J. P. Yates's "The Reception of the Epistle of James in the Latin West: Did Athanasius Play a Role?" in *The Catholic Epistles and the Tradition*, ed. J. Schlosser (BETL 176; Leuven: Leuven University Press, 2004), 273-88.

31. Indeed, the form of the James citation does not correspond to any known Latin translation, suggesting that Hilary was translating the text himself from the Greek. So J. Ropes, *The Epistle of St. James* (ICC; Edinburgh: Clark, 1916), p. 101, and J. B. Adamson, *James: The Man and His Message* (Grand Rapids: Eerdmans, 1989), pp. 149-50.

James . . . wrote a single epistle, which is reckoned among the seven Catholic Epistles, and even this is claimed by some to have been published by someone else under his name, and gradually as time went on to have gained authority. (2.2)

Jude, the brother of James, left a short epistle which is reckoned among the seven Catholic Epistles, and because in it he quotes from the apocryphal book of Enoch it is rejected by many. Nevertheless, by age and use it has gained authority and is reckoned among the Holy Scriptures. (4.1-2)

John . . . wrote also one epistle . . . which is esteemed by all who are men of the church or of learning. The other two . . . are said to be the work of John the presbyter in whose memory another sepulcher is shown at Ephesus to the present day, though some think that the two memorials belong to this same John the evangelist. (9.4-5)

One immediately notices that Jerome's concept of canonicity differs from that of some of his forebears in that he appears to have been untroubled by doubts over authorship. He can mention such doubts without care, for "by age and use" these letters were able to gain authority *apart from* clear evidence of authorial origin. That is to say, these letters' canonical authority derives not from the person who *wrote* their words, but by the Spirit of God who made *use* of their words in the spirit-filled communities of the church.

Though Jerome followed western tradition in placing Paul before the CE, it is easy to see the influence of eastern Christianity on Jerome's canon when it is placed alongside the canons of other western leaders. First, almost everyone in the West follows the tradition of listing Peter first among the CE due to his honor of being the first bishop of Rome. This is the case with Augustine of Hippo (ca. 396),[32] Filaster of Brescia (ca. 397), the North African Canons (393, 397, 419), Rufinus of Aquileia (404), Junilius Africanus (ca. 545) and Cassiodorus (d. ca. 565). Second, Jerome is the only westerner of the period to use the eastern title "Catholic Epistles" *(katholikē epistolē)*. The preferred Latin title, when one was used, was "Canonical Epistles" *(epistulae canonicae)* — so Augustine, Junilius, and Cassiodorus.[33]

---

32. *Doc.* 2.13.

33. See the detailed lists in B. F. Westcott, *A General Survey of the History of the Canon of the New Testament* (6th ed.; Grand Rapids: Baker, 1980), pp. 539-79.

Jerome's Vulgate translation of the Bible appears to have fixed the final NT book sequence for the West insofar as it follows the eastern ordering within the CE collection (James–Peter–John–Jude) but the western ordering of collections within the NT (Gospels–Acts–Paul–CE–Revelation). This order retains the sense that the two letter collections represent the two ancient missions of the early Christian apostolate, but it downplays the narrative logic of Acts, where Christian salvation emerges from the Jew first (CE) and then goes to the Greek (Paul). What accounts for this shift?

Though no one from the ancient world has left us with a clearly stated historical rationale for the move, the following points can be made with confidence. First, we note the smooth "canonical link" created when Acts, the last line of which describes the imprisoned Paul proclaiming the kingdom of God in Rome (28:31), is followed immediately by Paul's letter that proclaims the gospel to the Romans.[34] Second, ancient patristic citation statistics make it unambiguously clear that the Pauline writings were *always* first in authority, even among those who championed the sequence that placed the CE before his letters. Thus, the decision to embrace Paul's writings with the Acts of the Apostles on one side and the CE on the other appears attributable to the overriding theological concern that Paul be interpreted *within* the particular theological framework afforded by Acts and the CE. Paul is thus handed down to us in the full embrace of his apostolic colleagues.[35]

That such a concern existed is made clear not only by most of the church fathers we have considered in this chapter, but also by Augustine, who is the only ancient authority to leave behind an accounting for why the CE were included in the NT canon. His *De fide et operibus (On Faith and Works)* was written around 413 at the very end of the canonical shaping process. Here he addresses several contemporary errors associated with a misunderstanding of the proper relation between faith and works in the Christian life. Among them, "the most dangerous" was attributable to a "perplexing problem in the writings of the Apostle Paul" (*Fide* 27).

> Therefore, let us now see what must be torn away from the hearts of the God-fearing to prevent the loss of salvation through a treacher-

---

34. See R. W. Wall, "Romans 1.1-15: An Introduction to the Pauline Corpus of the New Testament," in *The New Testament as Canon,* ed. R. W. Wall and E. E. Lemcio (JSNTSS 76, Sheffield: Sheffield Academic, 1992), pp. 142-60.

35. So Childs, *Church's Guide for Reading Paul,* pp. 65-78 and 219-36.

ously false security, if, under the illusion that faith alone is sufficient for salvation, they neglect to live a good life and fail by good works to persevere in the way that leads to God. Even in the days of the Apostles certain somewhat obscure statements of the Apostle Paul were misunderstood, and some thought that he was saying this: "Let us now do evil that good may come from it" [Rom.3:8] because he said "Now the law intervened that the offense might abound. But where the offense has abounded, grace has abounded yet more" [5:20]. . . . Since this problem is by no means new and had already arisen at the time of the Apostles, other apostolic letters of Peter, John, James and Jude are deliberately aimed against the argument I have been refuting and firmly uphold the doctrine that faith does not avail without good works. (*Fide* 21)

The essay goes on to offer an intertextual reading of the apostolic letters, balancing passages from Paul with those of James and others as Origen had done two hundred years previously in his commentary on Romans, in order to arrive at a wholly apostolic understanding of the relation between faith and works. Augustine's primary Pauline text in the essay (repeated ten times) is Gal. 5:6, which insists on the priority of "faith working through love." This is interwoven with almost thirty references to the CE. Peter, says Augustine, "urged his readers to holiness in living and character" (*Fide* 22), while "James was so severely annoyed with those who held that faith without works avails to salvation that he compared them to evil spirits" (23). When one comes across Pauline passages that suggest one can be saved apart from evidence of a transformed life, "another interpretation assuredly must be sought for them, and these expressions of the Apostle Paul must be counted among the passages in his writings which Peter says are difficult to understand and which men must not distort to their own destruction [2 Pet. 3:16]" (26).

According to Augustine, then, the CE collection was added to the canon in order to keep readers from falling into a Paulinist fideism. This conclusion bears up with the evidence we have considered from the collection's historical development: from Irenaeus and Tertullian against Marcion, through Origen, and on to Augustine, at nearly every turn we find the insistence that Paul be placed in an appropriate interpretive frame lest his readers contract the spiritual sickness of heresy. Reading him in the embrace of Acts and the CE is the ancient canonical inoculation against this disease.

Conclusion: Hebrews? Jude? Catholic?

To conclude our historical overview of the shaping process, let us offer a few final comments on matters not directly addressed in the story just related. First, a preliminary word on the letter to the Hebrews to anticipate further comments in the next chapter.

Though today Hebrews is almost universally treated alongside some or all of the CE as one of the so-called "General Epistles," it is noteworthy that there is absolutely no support for this imprecise designation in antiquity, much less for placing Hebrews within its bounds. Though one does find a good deal of disagreement over the letter's proper *placement* in the canon (i.e., should it be placed *within* the Pauline letter-group according to stichoi-length, or at the *end* of the collection to designate its uncertain authorship?), both this disagreement and its distinctively Pauline title ("to the Hebrews," *pros Hebraious*) clearly designate its association with the Pauline collection. More will be said about Hebrews in the next chapter, but for now, one point must be made absolutely clear: antiquity knows nothing of a "General Epistles" collection, and the letter to the Hebrews is clearly *not* included in the canon in order to be read as a member of the CE collection.

Thus far we have focused almost exclusively on the development of the "Jerusalem Pillars" tradition in the CE as distinct from the Pauline. But what of Jude? Given its brevity, the extent of its early attestation is remarkable: though it was not appealed to extensively per se it was known and acknowledged as authoritative widely and from a very early period indeed. Given the logic behind the structure of the CE, Jude's inclusion makes perfect sense. As a brother of the Lord, his letter fits among the others originating from the Jerusalem mission headed by his brother James. Its inclusion at the end of the collection thus forms an inclusio with James, providing the sense that the letter collection comes wrapped in the embrace of Jesus' holy family according to the flesh. Precisely how Jude functions in this regard will be explored in subsequent chapters.

Interestingly, the inclusion of Jude turns the CE into a seven-letter collection. With this realization one immediately discerns a pattern in the final form of the NT: Paul's letters are written to seven churches (Rome, Corinth, Galatia, Ephesus, Philippi, Colossae, and Thessalonica); this is followed by the CE's seven letters, which precede the Revelation to John, which begins with seven letters to seven churches. Is there any significance to the "sevenness" of the CE collection?

The historical witness suggests there may very well be, for the church fathers made much of the symbolic significance of seven-letter collections. According to the author of the Muratorian fragment:

> . . . since the blessed apostle Paul himself, following the example of his predecessor John, writes by name to only seven churches . . . it is clearly recognizable that there is one church throughout the whole earth. For John also in his Apocalypse, though he writes to seven churches, nevertheless speaks to all.[36]

The sevenfold shaping of this letter collection somehow indicates a *whole* communication to the *whole* church. Similarly Cyprian of Carthage, speaking of the seven martyred Maccabbean brothers as a "sacrament of perfect fulfillment," goes on to comment on virtually every instance of the number seven in Jewish Scriptures before turning to the apostolic writings:

> And the apostle Paul, who is mindful of this lawful and certain number, writes to seven churches. And in the Apocalypse the Lord directs his divine mandates and heavenly precepts to the seven churches and their angels. The number is now found here in the brothers, that a lawful consummation [*consummatio legitima*] may be fulfilled.[37]

The presence of strikingly similar comments by Victorinus of Pettau,[38] Amphilochius of Iconium,[39] and Jerome[40] make it plain that this is not an isolated esoteric tradition. The presence of seven letters represents a "legitimate completion," a whole communication of the apostolic message.

All this emphasis on the wholeness and completion provided by the achievement of a seven-letter collection leads us to reconsider the significance of the assigned title "Catholic" for this particular group of letters. Most scholars assume, with the sixth-century theologian Leontius of By-

---

36. Muratorian Fragment, lines 47-60. For a recent, complete study of the text, see Hahnemann, *Muratorian Fragment*.

37. *Fort.* 11.101-8.

38. *Com. Apoc.* 1.7.

39. *Iambi* 289-31.

40. *Ep.* 53.9.

zantium, that "they are called catholic because they were not written to one group, as those of Paul, but generally to everyone."[41] This is a sensible conclusion given the prior secular use of *katholikē* to mean "general" or "universal." But as many of those same scholars have noted, the designation is not an entirely accurate description of these seven letters. James, 2 Peter, and Jude are often taken to bear "general" addresses, and 1 John (which bears no address at all) was the first of the group to be identified as a "general" epistle, but even then each of these letters clearly have specific audiences in mind, and 1 Peter and 2 and 3 John are each actually addressed to particular churches and individuals. Is it possible that the title of this collection was meant to convey more than just the nature of its address?

It must be remembered that before the church canonized a collection of letters by this name, the term was commonly used to describe a particular *community* of Christians. Its first known appearance in this regard is found in the letter of Ignatius of Antioch to the church in Smyrna (ca. 110). There Ignatius famously proclaims: "flee divisions as the beginning of evils . . . Let the congregation be wherever the bishop is; just as wherever Jesus Christ is, there also is the catholic church" (*Smyrn.* 6.2). Similar use in the *Martyrdom of Polycarp* (ca. 155) makes it clear that the term is associated with the *unity of the church* in opposition to the *divisions brought about by false doctrine*.[42] At the end of that century Clement of Alexandria says:

> It is evident that these later heresies and those which are still more recent are spurious innovations on the oldest and truest church. From what has been said I think it has been made plain that unity is a characteristic of the true, the really ancient church. . . . For God being one and the Lord being one, that also which is supremely honored is the object of praise, because it stands alone, being a copy of the one First Principle: at any rate the one church, which they strive to break up into many sects, is bound up with the principle of unity. We say, then, that the ancient and Catholic Church stands alone in essence and idea and principle and preeminence. (*Strom.* 7.17.107)

As these ancient witnesses make clear, by the time the CE collection arrived in the late third century, it is highly unlikely that a seven-letter collec-

---

41. *Sectis* 2.
42. *Mart. Pol.* 8.1; 16.2; 19.2.

tion titled "catholic" would have simply connoted a "general address." The ancients would have likely received these letters as a kind of *whole* and *complete* apostolic witness from the earliest church; as the last piece of the NT canon to be formed, it would have been received as a *legitimate completion* of the canon, both aesthetically and doctrinally; and, given the pervasive concern about protecting a right, "catholic" reading of Paul against his many heretical champions, they would have received this collection as a kind of *unifying* safeguard against the many aspects of Paul's letters that are "hard to understand, which the ignorant and unstable twist to their own destruction, as they do the other Scriptures" (2 Pet. 3:16).

Of course the historical witness cannot tell us *precisely* how the collection performs this function. In order to ascertain that we must turn from a consideration of the historical *shaping* of the collection to ponder the significance of its final literary *shape* — and to this end we now turn.

The Shape of the Canonical Collection

At the center of this chapter, and building on the contributions of the previous two, are two interpenetrating observations about the final literary form of the CE collection that are laden with hermeneutical promise. First, when the CE finally became a sevenfold collection suitable for the church's biblical canon, the letter of James functioned as its "frontispiece" to introduce the collection's core theological agreements. Second, when the church recognized this sevenfold form as canonical and so fixed it there, it did so in the company of Acts — a biblical narrative already received and used as Scripture a generation earlier by the church's great Apologists. As the last chapter demonstrated, Acts initially traveled with this collection to supply a context for reading and hearing its witness to God's word.[1] To pick up and use the CE with the narrative of Acts, as the canonical process compels, at the very least vests the seven letters and their implied apostolic authors with religious authority; but it also cues readers to the special importance of James for the church's future (especially in relationship to Paul's mission and message), and so also to the canonical letter written under his name. We will return to this prospect later in the chapter.

The question is reasonably asked why modern Bible readers should el-

---

1. We find little evidence to prove B. M. Metzger's assertion that "the Acts of the Apostles was added chiefly to prove Paul's apostolic character and to vindicate the right of his Epistles to stand alongside the Gospels." *The Canon of the New Testament* (Oxford: Clarendon, 1987), pp. 257-58. This more likely is an anachronistic construction of modern Protestant scholars, including B. S. Childs (*The Church's Guide for Reading Paul: The Canonical Shaping of the Pauline Corpus* [Grand Rapids: Eerdmans, 2008], pp. 223-37), to support a variety of claims about the canonical Paul, his Gentile mission, and his message.

evate the hermeneutical importance of the *canonical* moment, when texts were first recognized as sacred and received as Scripture to help form the church's theological understanding. This shift of interest is, of course, counterintuitive to the interpretive practices of modern criticism, which press hard after the *compositional* moment when texts were written and first read and heard. Although the theological and ecclesial reasons for doing so are often obscure to us, the "original" meanings of texts once delivered to their first readers have achieved a kind of normative quality for modern readers. But if one's angle of approach lines up with the properties of the canonical process, then one should expect that canonical collections, even one as variegated as this one, are best received and read as coherent wholes that are greater and more effective for their intended use than the sum of their collected parts.

To examine whether our expectation is credible, we first observe that the biblical canon is for the most part a collection of completed collections, fixed and then placed in theologically suggestive relationships with one another that are often cued by the canonical process itself. During this process individual writings were first preserved and edited, and then reproduced, circulated, read, and canonized in combination with other individual writings *as canonical collections.*[2] Indeed, the earliest history of canonizing the two collections of NT letters would seem to indicate that they were first formed and subsequently placed side by side within an emergent NT canon to facilitate a constructive ("self-correcting and mutually-informing") conversation between them.[3] In fact, we suggest that such a *chronology of canonization* illuminates the meaning and use of biblical texts more than speculations about the chronology of their composition featured in modern biblical criticism.

Quite apart from analyzing the semiotics of a textual whole (which is also useful), we first approach a canonical collection as the literary by-product of a historical process, a final literary redaction that logically reflects the commitments of the process itself. For example, the hermeneutics of the canonical process were not those of conflict but of consolidation, by which common ground rather than irreconcilable differences was

---

2. D. Trobisch, *Die Endredaktion des Neuen Testaments* (NTOA 31; Vandenhoeck & Ruprecht, 1996) pp. 40-43.

3. For a fuller description of this project and illustrations of it see R. W. Wall and Eugene Lemcio, *The New Testament as Canon* (JSNTSS 76; Sheffield: JSOT, 1992).

sought. The theological perspicuity of every part of the whole was measured by an ecumenical *regula fidei* ("Rule of Faith") to insure the unity of the canonical whole by this common theological referent.[4] While critical exegesis of the sevenfold CE collection demonstrates its pronounced theological and literary diversity — a diversity that aptly reflects what might be found within the church catholic — the inclusion of each writing to form a "catholic" collection, and its inclusion within a single biblical canon, assumes a general theological coherence to all other parts within itself and with other collections that constitute the canonical whole. That is, the product should instantiate the core properties of the process that produced it: we should expect the theological goods collected from a canonical collection's various parts not only to cohere as a whole, but to work together as a whole to form a distinctive and effective witness to the word of God.

In this sense, then, the formation of the CE collection is the endgame of an intentional, deliberate movement. Its sevenfold shape does not follow a mechanistic pattern of arrangement according to the length of its individual parts,[5] the perceived dates of their composition, or as a matter largely determined by the technology of a codex format.[6] In fact, we are aware of no scholar who denies that the formation of the NT served mostly religious aims and theological reasons, whether epistemic or sacramental. This intention is easily observed in the canon lists recovered at the conclusion of the canonical process and from different regions of the church catholic, which reflect the theological judgments made by different ecclesial traditions. Different groupings of writings were arranged according to their perceived usefulness or theological priority when performing a variety of religious tasks (liturgical, educational, missional, etc.). The

---

4. For the idea that the biblical canon as a whole and each part in it are judged as roughly analogous to an ecclesial (and ecumenical) Rule of Faith, see R. W. Wall, "Rule of Faith in Theological Hermeneutics," in *Between Two Horizons,* ed. J. Green and M. Turner (Grand Rapids: Eerdmans, 2000), pp. 88-107.

5. James has 1749 words and 247 stichoi, 1 Peter has 1678 words and 237 stichoi, and 1 John has 2137 words and 269 stichoi. Adding 2 John, with 245 words and 32 stichoi, and 3 John, with 219 words and 31 stichoi, to 1 John and 2 Peter (166 stichoi) to 1 Peter does not alter this arrangement, especially when throwing Jude (71 stichoi) into the mix.

6. Trobisch, for example, seems to posit a great deal of importance to the production of codices in the "final redaction" of the NT canon. See also E. J. Epp, "Issues in the Interrelation of New Testament Textual Criticism and Canon," in *The Canon Debate,* ed. L. McDonald and J. A. Sanders (Peabody: Hendrickson, 2002), pp. 503-5.

larger point is this: the final shape of collections instantiates value judgments regarding their enduring role as Scripture in forming a community's theological understanding and moral practices.

Wall's 2004 study of the formation of the Pauline canon, for example, argues that Paul's apostolic witness, which was initially maintained by a nine- or ten- letter corpus, was brought to completion and "fixed" by the late arrival of a small collection of three so-called "Pastoral Epistles," probably toward the end of the second century. The rubric he uses to consolidate his historical reconstruction is *the aesthetic principle,*" by which he seeks to capture the importance of that postbiblical moment when the faith community recognized the enduring excellence of a Pauline deposit fixed in the "shape" of a thirteen-letter corpus inclusive of the "Pastoral" three.[7]

A more general application follows from that study to this one: the phenomenon of collection-building within the bounds of the canonical process appears to follow a general pattern by which a body of individual writings or smaller collections, perhaps already in circulation here and there, is finally stabilized, completed, and arranged as a whole collection. Moreover, the community's recognition of a collection's final shape is functional, measured by the overall effectiveness of its performances as a biblical canon in the formation and practice of Christian faith.

We suggest that the aesthetic excellence of the CE collection, perhaps symbolized by its sevenfold membership, is evinced by several properties

---

7. R. W. Wall, "The Function of the Pastoral Epistles within the Pauline Canon of the New Testament: A Canonical Approach," in *The Pauline Canon,* ed. S. E. Porter (Leiden: Brill, 2004), pp. 27-44. We find no compelling objection to D. Trobisch's thesis that Paul himself may have placed a collection of his "major" letters into circulation, which were then added to and recognized as "Scripture" (if not also as "canonical") shortly after his death by important Pauline tradents; see his *Paul's Letter Collection* (Minneapolis: Fortress, 1994). Marcion did *not* create a Pauline canon, then, but simply valorized one already in circulation. What is more important than the early fact of a Pauline canon is the church's realization early on that Paul's teaching also supplied biblical warrants to "heretical" teaching, especially for various second-century "Gnostic" movements including that of Marcion. Given this internal threat to the church, need for a second collection of letters to bring balance and constraint to the letters of the canonical Paul was readily apparent — perhaps a collection similar in emphasis to the concerns voiced by James to the Paul of Acts according to Acts 21:20-21 (see below). In any case, we take it that Marcion is an important symbol of a canonical process that forms or edits collections of writings as necessary correctives in order to function more effectively analogically to the church's Rule of Faith.

inherent in its final redaction that would seem to suggest its theological coherence and anticipated use within the biblical canon. Of general importance to the overall shape of the collection, besides the late addition of James as its frontispiece and Acts to provide its narrative setting, is the role of 2 Peter to pull together the diverse CE into a Pillars collection.[8] What follows now is a catalogue of more particular findings that point the reader toward the collection's aesthetic excellence.

2 Peter 3:15-16. This passage, especially given the mediating role performed by 2 Peter within the collection in its final form, is a pivotal text for understanding the relationship between the CE and Pauline corpora within the NT canon. In particular, this text suggests two properties about the extant Pauline canon in play when the CE collection was received by the church as canonical. While 2 Peter claims that the Pauline witness is a fount of spiritual "wisdom" (3:15), sharing the same effect Israel's Scripture has on the community made "wise for salvation in Christ Jesus" (2 Tim. 3:15), it also indicates that the lack of clarity of Paul's letters opens their witness to potential abuse by the very teachers 2 Peter castigates. This passing reference to a Pauline collection, then, hints at a hermeneutical crisis that might threaten the future of the community. The addition of the CE collection to the NT canon may be understood as the church's response to such a worry.

James 2:22. Without proposing a theory of the book's date of composition, especially if related to its author's identity,[9] we suggest that the eventual reception of a canonical James came with a theological judgment about the ongoing function of the CE collection within the biblical canon

---

8. A forthcoming book by D. R. Nienhuis, currently titled *A Crucial Letter: The Canonical Function of the Second Letter of Peter,* promises to offer a thorough articulation of 2 Peter's role in the NT canon. In particular, the study claims that 2 Peter's historic marginalization has primarily to do with a failure to approach it in light of its *canonical* performance, which is to function as a "literary anchor" through which the various texts of the CE are linked both lexically and thematically.

9. This is, of course, one of the tasks of D. R. Nienhuis's *Not by Paul Alone: The Formation of the Catholic Epistle Collection and the Christian Canon* (Waco: Baylor University Press, 2007). While that book presented a composition hypothesis involving a second-century author of James whose goal, at least in part, was to compose a lead letter to establish an epistolary collection to counterbalance the Pauline collection, our focus in this chapter is on the final literary shape of the collection.

and its relationship with the Pauline corpus in particular (see below). Unlike the case for 2 Peter, which was added (and probably even composed) to extend the theological conception of 1 Peter, James was added to an emergent *collection* much later, probably toward the end of the third century, to help delimit its working relationship with a Pauline collection, which was already a fixed property within an otherwise still fluid biblical canon.

The catholic tendencies of the canonical redaction, by which an aesthetic of theological wholeness is pursued, are reflected by what is arguably the controlling text of the book's famous essay on "faith and works," Jas. 2:22.[10] Read canonically, this verse stipulates that "faith alone" (i.e., professed faith without works) — what had become the somewhat troubling hallmark of the Pauline tradition — cannot stand alone but is rather "brought to completion by the works" *(ek tōn ergōn hē pistis eteleiōthē)* — a phrase that both captures the moral inclination of the entire CE collection and sounds a cautionary note that any reductionistic reading of the Pauline corpus may well degenerate into a *sola fideism*.[11]

2 Peter 3:1-2. At a relatively early and more fluid stage in the formation of the CE collection, 2 Peter was added to 1 Peter in order to complete a Petrine theological conception.[12] Again without proposing a theory of 2 Peter's composition as a pseudepigraphon, whether as 2 Jude (as critical

---

10. For this argument, see R. W. Wall, *Community of the Wise: The Letter of James* (NTC; Valley Forge: Trinity, 1997), pp. 148-52. Most of our subsequent comments about the meaning of James are found in expanded form in that book.

11. Even though, as many contemporary scholars have opined, Jas. 2:14-26 does not carry the same hefty weight for its author that it has borne during its (especially Protestant) *Wirkungsgeschichte*, it is probably this one text more than any other — precisely *because* of its "anti-Pauline" correction and not in spite of it — that attracted the canonizing community to it: it captures well the intent of the canonical process if not then of the letter's authorial motive. Indeed, many understand Pauline tradition (rather than the traditions of a first- or second-century Judaism, which are rarely mentioned in any case) as the book's primary conversation partner. In any case, from a perspective *within* a NT setting, James now responds to what Paul might become or how Pauline traditions might be used as a canon within the canon. It is from its profoundly Jewish ethos that canonical James corrects canonical Paul. But to focus attention on 2:22 (rather than 2:21) reminds the reader that the canonical motive is not adversarial but complementary of a closer analogy to the church's Rule of Faith.

12. See R. W. Wall, "The Canonical Function of 2 Peter," *BibInt* 9 (2001); pp. 64-81.

orthodoxy would have it) or as 2 Peter (as the canonical redaction would have it), we contend that 2 Peter was added to the CE collection in light of its relationship to 1 Peter (rather than to Jude). The importance of this composition within Scripture, then, is as a "second letter" written "that you should remember the words spoken in the past . . ." (3:1-2) in order to complete a more robust Petrine witness to better form the theological understanding of subsequent generations of believers.

2 Peter and 1 John 1:1-3. We will argue that 1 John responds to an epistemic crisis within the community occasioned by the emerging influence of teachers whose gospel is at odds with the church's apostolic testimony. They are called "antichrists" because their Christology and its moral implications do not square with the "word of life" observed and heard "from the beginning" and then proclaimed to others by the apostles.

This occasion is precisely the same addressed by 2 Peter. This second Petrine letter's address introduces Peter as an "apostle of Jesus Christ" (though as *Simeōn* rather than *Simōn*!) and his intended readers as those "who have received a similar faith" (1:1). The author subsequently claims to have inside information about Peter's death from Jesus himself (1:14; cf. John 21:18) and more importantly to possess knowledge of Jesus based on eyewitness experience of the Lord's magnificence and auditory experience of God's proclamation of his Sonship (1:16-18). This testimony is the criterion by which competing claims of truth are measured and condemned. The canonical effect of this common concern for the authority of an apostolic tradition and of its attendant themes in both 2 Peter and 1 John is to include the Johannine epistles more securely within the network of materials brokered by 2 Peter.

The coherence of the three Johannine epistles and the church's recognition by the fourth century that they form a single witness.[13] The intertextuality of the three Johannine letters is clear from even a cursory reading (see the introduction to our chapter on the Johannine letters). We argue, for example, that 2 John "epitomizes" 1 John and that 3 John interacts with 2 John's prior instruction of hospitality to bring to completion the Johannine wit-

---

13. For this point, see J. Painter, *1, 2, and 3 John* (SP; Collegeville: Liturgical, 2002), pp. 51-58, whose interpretive strategy is to read the three letters together; also C. C. Black, *1-3 John* in NIB (Nashville: Abingdon, 1998), 12:365-78, especially p. 366.

ness and secure its role within the CE collection. Painter's recent commentary is helpful in this regard, not only by reading the three epistles together but then by locating them within the CE collection and so resisting the tendency to read them either as bits of a Johannine corpus or as a written response to problems created by the Fourth Gospel, in a manner, that is, decidedly not prompted by the final form of the NT canon itself.

Jude's placement within the CE collection. Painter's reading strategy agrees with the motive of the canonical redaction that placed Jude where it is, separating the three Johannine letters from the Apocalypse. That is, as a canonical metaphor, the inference is that John's letters are to be read together and within the context of the CE collection and not as members of a NT Johannine corpus.

It should be noted that the memorable benediction that concludes Jude (vv. 24-25), which some contend is reason alone for its preservation and canonization, is also a suitable ending to the entire collection, not because of its doxological argot but because of its practical interest in safeguarding those who might "stumble" into false teaching or immoral lifestyle (cf. v. 4). Significantly, James concludes with a similar statement that to rescue believers who "stray from the truth" is to save their "souls from death" (Jas. 5:19-20); and in fact this orientation to the congregation's internal spiritual welfare will become an organizing theme of the entire collection. Accordingly, then, Jude's benediction, when reconsidered in the context of the final redaction of the CE, is apropos to the collection's motive and role within the biblical canon.

Jude and James — books named after brothers of the Lord — *forming the literary brackets of the entire collection,* thereby guaranteeing their religious authority and importance for the future of the church catholic. What must be said, however, is that the authority of this collection is due not only to its connection with the Jerusalem Pillars, whose authority is defined and defended by Acts and whose order within the collection is cued by Paul's reference to them in Gal. 2:9, but also to its connection to the holy family.[14] The importance of this relationship between "the broth-

---

14. R. Bauckham's study of members of Jesus' family, in particular James and Jude, makes a compelling case for their lasting influence in the Jewish church in Palestine. *Jude and the Relatives of Jesus in the Early Church* (Edinburgh: Clark, 1990). They sought to preserve the Jewish legacy of the church and in particular the importance of a Jewish way of salvation that elevates the church's moral obligations as a condition of life with God against a

ers of the Lord" in the sociology of the canonical process has less to do with the hagiography of persons and more to do with the authoritative traditions linked to their names.

The intertextuality of James and Jude, which makes clear their literary relationship as the collection's inclusio, is cued by the address of Jude. Not only is the letter's authorship attributed to "the brother of James," who is also Christ's "servant," but the conclusions of both letters call the church to rescue its members who have wandered from the truth (Jas. 5:19-20; Jude 22-23). This thematic connection, which defines the church's vocation according to this collection, underwrites the famous benediction of Jude, which assures the reader that "God our Savior" is not responsible for the disaffection of those believers but is an active participant in securing their future salvation.

Sharply put, then, each of these various "properties" of a final redaction evinces historical moves that in some sense "complete" and make more effective (with respect to the church's intentions for its Scripture) an earlier form of the collection. At different moments along the way 2 Peter, 2 and 3 John, and Jude are added as constitutive elements of a more theologically robust whole — a historical phenomenon that may reasonably be explained as evidence of the church's recognition of the importance of this second collection of letters within its biblical canon. Such an "aesthetic principle" is similar to that which measures the integrity of other biblical collections as well; in this sense, religious authority is a property of canonical *collections* rather than of individual writings. For example, the authority of 2 Peter is recognized in relationship to 1 Peter or of James in relationship to the CE collection. Or a roughly parallel case is the fourfold Gospel, which Irenaeus said has an inherent integrity much like the "four corners of the earth" and which according to most canon lists of antiquity is placed first within the NT to recommend its formative value, with Matthew's Gospel typically given priority among the four as the most relevant continuation of the Tanakh's narrative of God's salvation.[15] Following Irenaeus, who pays close attention to the precise shape and particular role

---

"Paulinism" (but not necessarily Paul's idea) that "faith alone" liberated believers not only from sin's consequence but from any moral responsibility to flee from sin. In our mind, the final redaction of the CE, which encloses them by James and Jude, reifies this point within the canon and in self-correcting conversation with the Pauline corpus.

15. See D. Moody Smith, "When Did the Gospels First Become Scripture?" *JBL* 119 (2000), pp. 3-20.

of the fourfold Gospel collection, we contend that the theological integrity of the final redaction of a biblical collection, its placement with the NT, or even of an individual composition within the collection "signs" a role appropriate to the motives of a biblical canon.

James as the Collection's Frontispiece

When the sevenfold CE collection became Scripture is not an easy question to answer. Evidence in hand suggests that the letter of James was necessary in completing the pages of a Peter–John epistolary catalog.[16] Perhaps the first decisive question from a canonical perspective, then, is what motivated the late arrival of James to this catalog and then its extraordinary placement as the frontispiece of the collection's final redaction.[17] Surely the early grouping of letters from the two leading apostles (and friends) of the risen Lord, especially if read with the Acts story of their apostolic succession, makes perfect sense for a community that confesses itself to be an "apostolic" church.

Moreover, according to Acts 15, Peter comes to the defense of Paul's mission before a suspicious Jewish church led by James, even using Pauline terms in doing so (Acts 15:6-29; cf. 21:19-26). It would seem reasonable, then, that the canonical process would produce an epistolary collection that reflects the close working relationship between Peter and Paul, especially for a community where Paul's legacy had triumphed but was also being used to promote non-apostolic Christianities. To read Paul with Peter and John would enable the church to hear its Pauline witness without distortion. But why broker their ongoing canonical conversation by adding a letter from James?

Given the importance of James in Acts, where his résumé includes

16. We all recognize that informal "canons with the canon" delimit which books have "real" authority by their actual use by different readers. For this reason, it might be argued that the "1 Peter–1 John" canon survives to this day, since the other CE are typically neglected in worship and instruction.

17. This is a principal thematic developed in R. W. Wall, "Acts and James," in *The Catholic Epistles and Apostolic Tradition,* ed. K.-W. Niebuhr and R. W. Wall (Waco: Baylor University Press, 2009), pp. 127-52, although our interest here is largely rhetorical (the role of a "frontispiece" within a canonical collection) rather than historical. Without doubt the fathers from Eusebius forward vested theological value in the proper ordering of the letters.

leadership of the Jerusalem church, being a brother of Jesus, and having an important leadership role in the missions of both Paul and Peter (15:4-29; 21:17-25; cf. Gal. 2:1-15), the addition of a book written under his name to a collection that already included Peter and John makes good sense.[18] This very logic is evinced by Eusebius who recalls the narrative of Hegesippus (*H.E.* 2.23.3-18) regarding the martyrdom of "James the Just (or 'Righteous One')" as testimony to his courageous fidelity and Jewish piety and as the apparent reason why his "disputed" book should be included in the so-called "catholic" collection (2.23.25). While the connection between these traditions about the Jewish piety of James and his "catholic" letter appears to underwrite the authority of his "disputed" letter, our suspicion is that the "canonical" portrait of James found in the Book of Acts (rather than those found in other noncanonical Jewish and "Gnostic" writings) is more decisive for understanding the origins and ultimate canonization of the letter of James.[19]

It should therefore puzzle scholars, especially those who admit to the evident importance of James reported by Acts and in traditions that tell of his legacy as exemplar and leader, that no second- or third-century Christian writer quotes from or clearly alludes to the letter of James. Traditions about the legacy of James are pivotal to several writings outside the main-

18. In this regard, we should note the debates over the apostolicity of James and his "biological" relationship to Jesus, given the church's belief in Mary's perpetual virginity. The subtext of both debates was the ongoing authority of the Jacobean legacy within the broader church. In fact, Acts seems to legitimize the continuing importance of James on different grounds than his apostolicity or his relationship to Jesus, namely as the leader of the Jerusalem church. In this regard, we note that in the preface to his early commentary "On the Seven Catholic Epistles" (ca. 700) Bede the Venerable writes, "Although in the list of the apostles Peter and John are accustomed to be ranked as more important, the Letter of James is placed first among these for the reason that he received the government of the church of Jerusalem, from where the source and beginning of the preaching of the Gospel took place and spread throughout the entire world" (trans. D. Hurst, O.S.B. [CSS 82; Kalamazoo: Cistercian, 1985] p. 3).

19. Note for example the close linguistic and conceptual relationship between Acts 15:13-29; 21:17-26 and the letter of James. We should mention that the addition of the dominical "do unto others" saying to the all-important Acts 15:20, 29 (but strangely not to 21:25!) in Codex Bezae may well intend to draw a close linguistic connection between Jesus' teaching and James's teaching in order to underwrite the latter's religious authority for the future of the church. This is an important datum as the motive of this second version of Acts is primarily canonical, as we have suggested; cf. R. W. Wall, Acts in *NIB* (Nashville: Abingdon, 2002), 10:17-18.

stream ("Jewish Christian" and "Gnostic"), in which he is depicted as the pious pastor of the Jewish church and key strategist of the church's universal mission, in particular as the sometimes opponent of Paul's law-free mission to the nations. These same writings, however, do not refer to a letter, nor does their portrait of James comport with the core themes of the canonical letter written under his name.[20]

Most who offer explanations of this haunting silence appeal to the social world of the second-century church, where negative press of those Jacobites engaged in anti-Pauline bashing and efforts to conserve Jewish convictions and practices (in some cases heretical inclinations) led to the letter's suppression. Only later is a letter from James mentioned, perhaps reclaimed in edited form and put back into circulation as suitable reading material for the apostolic church. We find this explanation rather dissatisfying. Indeed, this same rationalization could be used of the Pauline canon, which was exploited by marginal and even heretical movements within the church, yet was already fixed and used by the end of the second century. And this supposed suppression of a letter from James also fails to explain why a similar silence is found among more marginal Jewish and so-called "Gnostic" writings of the second century for whom the legacy of James was valorized.[21] Again, the present text offers no alternative theory

---

20. These texts portray the personal piety of James, his reception of special revelation from God, his political importance in Jerusalem, and his martyrdom; however, whether or not fictitious, these personal characteristics do not carry over directly to the letter of James, whose themes are more "practical" and whose Jewish ethos and beliefs are not cast in overtly personal terms (for details, see Nienhuis's study of the second-century portrait of James in *Not by Paul Alone,* pp. 121-61). We do find the repeated references to a priestly James — as the Aaron to Jesus' Moses — fascinating, given the letter's emphasis on purity; cf. S. McKnight, "A Parting within the Way: Jesus and James on Israel and Purity," in *James the Just and Christian Origins,* ed. B. Chilton and C. A. Evans (Leiden: Brill, 1999), pp. 83-129. In the same volume Chilton offers the suggestive hypothesis that the practice of Nazirite vow-keeping within primitive Christianity "has been underestimated, and that James' deep influence is perhaps best measured by the extent to which other prominent [Christian] teachers fell in with his program [of Nazirite purity]" (p. 252).

21. The Ebionites followed such a "canon," which included Jesus traditions found in Matthew's Gospel; see Wall and Lemcio, eds., *NT as Canon,* pp. 250-71. A more precise articulation of this same point would distinguish between the legacy of James the Christian leader and the letter of James. In absence of a quotation or clear allusion to a textual tradition — a "letter of James" — in their writings, one must assume that these Jewish Christian groups were tradents of a Jacobean legacy rather than students of a Jacobean letter, even though the legacy is doubtless the principal source of the letter.

of the origins and transmission of James in earliest Christianity; our thesis about the performance of James as the frontispiece of a canonical collection of CE does not *depend* on a particular theory of its production.

Pastoral and Catholic Epistles:
The Shape of an Inter-Canon Dialogue

If we agree on evidence that the CE collection was formed during the third century and canonized sometime in the fourth, we should also agree on evidence that this process occurred after the fourfold Gospel and thirteen-letter (fourteen if Hebrews is included) Pauline canon was completed and already in wide circulation. The primary purpose anticipated for this new letter corpus, then, would likely have been to forge a more viable use of the biblical canon, which was still under construction. In this sense, any new reading of the life of the canonical Jesus narrated in the fourfold Gospel or the Pauline witness safeguarded in the thirteen- or fourteen-letter corpus would have been thickened by the addition of the CE collection.

At the very least, this added collection promises to prevent a distorted reading of the Pauline gospel by the church. Given the history of heretical currents emanating from Pauline traditions in the early church, one should not be surprised that a substantial Pauline criticism, an important hallmark of the James tradition within the early church (e.g., the Pseudo-Clementines, the *Gospel of the Hebrews*), is largely retained in the letter of James, especially (but not exclusively) in 1:22–2:26. Moreover, the Jewish roots of these traditions are hardly obscured in the letter.[22] The viability of such an inter-canon conversation between Pauline and Catholic, then, would not rest on the prospect of an easy *conceptual harmony* but on a *mutual criticism* — one that does not subvert the purchase of the Pauline

---

22. The Jewish background of James has been constructed by modern criticism but has more to do with maintaining a distinctively Jewish "ethos" than with ongoing performance of elements of a Judaic religion, whether from the Second Temple or the Diaspora. In this sense, James's rejection of supersessionism is neither formalistic nor legalistic but adheres in a principled way to a Jewish way of life — a way of life that James contends is threatened in part by certain tendencies of the Pauline tradition. We would add that the addition of the CE collection to the NT canon serves this "canonical" function of delineating the boundary between Christianity and Judaism not sharply but by underwriting the continuity between them.

canon but rather insures that its use by the church coheres to its own Rule of Faith.[23]

By the same token, the internal calculus of a catholic collection consisting only of 1 Peter and 1-2 John, when viewed through the lens of Acts, merely supplemented (rather than adding anything distinctive to) the extant Pauline canon. With the addition of James as its frontispiece and Jude as its conclusion, also of 2 Peter to 1 Peter and 3 John to 2 John, the initial Peter–John grouping was recalibrated into a more robust (some might say "louder"!) conversation partner for the canonical Paul. The relationship between these "Pillars" and Paul, recalled from Gal. 2:1-15 and hinted at elsewhere in his letters and Acts, is transferred differently to gauge the relations between the two epistolary corpora regulated by the canonical motives of the catholicizing church and by the theological grammar of the Rule of Faith — as textual representatives of partners engaged in a self-correcting and mutually-informing conversation. The first element of a unifying theology of the CE is thus conceived in more functional terms. The reception of James cues the church's critical concern about a reductionistic use of Pauline tradition that edits out the church's Jewish legacy, especially an ethos that resists any attempt to divorce a profession of orthodox beliefs from active obedience to God's law in a pattern of salvation (see below).[24]

An intriguing aspect of this emerging inter-canon dialogue, which has not yet been fully explored, is the relationship between the three Pauline "Pastoral Epistles" (hereafter PE) and the CE collection. We can only introduce our hunch in broad brushstrokes, and it begins at the point of canon-

---

23. Ironically, Luther's negative appraisal of James — that it fails a Pauline test of orthodoxy — illustrates this same methodological interest in reading James and Paul together, but Luther fails to engage the two according to the hermeneutics of the canonical process. To do so would have led him to recognize that the CE collection as a whole might actually render a Pauline "justification by faith" gospel more faithful to the church's Rule of Faith for the very reasons that he rejected James!

24. Our formulation of the relationship between the Pauline and catholic witnesses draws on an insight of James A. Sanders, who long ago commented that the Pauline witness concentrates on the "mythos" — or unifying narrative — of God's salvation as articulated and promised in the Torah and fully articulated and fulfilled in Christ. J. A. Sanders, "Torah and Paul," in *God's Christ and His People: Studies in Honour of Niles Alstrup Dahl,* ed. J. Jervel and W. A. Meeks (Oslo: Universitets forlaget, n.d.). In our opinion, it is the *ethos* of the Torah — obedience as loving response to God's saving mercies — that the CE collection concentrates on. The result of reading both groups of letters together, then, is a fuller presentation of God's gospel. See Wall and Lemcio, eds., *NT as Canon,* pp. 232-43.

ization. Toward the end of the second century, the same pressures that prompted the church to add the three PE to complete the canonization of the Pauline corpus also prompted the church to add a second letter corpus to its emerging NT canon.[25] Particular themes distinctive to or emphasized in the PE, which help to reconceive the Pauline witness in canonical terms for future readers, are apropos for the study of the CE collection as well. Each theme may be considered as a response to a crisis in the church that threatened its apostolic message and evangelical mission and prompted the church to delineate its witness for future generations. Our hunch is that the common ground occupied by the PE and the CE, the canonization of each occasioned by similar social forces and theological questions, may help readers better understand the roles and interplay between the two canonical corpora of letters.

Church as the "household of God" (1 Tim. 3:15). The Muratorian canon list adds that the PE are "for the ordering of ecclesiastical discipline." The use of the "household" metaphor in the PE is primarily concerned with the protocol and importance of Christian formation: the congregation functions as a household comprised of believers where Christian tradition is passed on to the postapostolic generation wherever Christian instruction is practiced in a disciplined, orderly manner.[26]

Thus Paul's understanding of a missionary church steadfastly guards its vocation of truth-telling against all sorts of intramural opposition in order to maintain theological purity. Even instructions given in supervision of liturgical prayers, found in 1 Timothy 2:1-15, are justified by an evangelical intent: the Christian congregation prays for everyone, including secular rulers and outsiders (vv. 1-2), which is exemplified by the practices of conventional social decorum in worship (v. 8) and the public square (vv. 9-15), because God our Savior desires that all the nations come to faith through a knowledge of the truth (vv. 3-4, 7).

But even here, as everywhere else in the PE, this redemptive calculus is extended to Paul's appointment as "preacher and apostle" (2:7b) for the express purpose of clarifying the theological foundations on which the

25. For a fuller discussion of the canonization of the Pauline corpus and the role of the Pastoral Epistles within it, see the Introduction to R. W. Wall with R. B. Steele, *1 and 2 Timothy and Titus* (THNTC, Grand Rapids: Eerdmans, 2012), pp. 15-36.

26. See F. Young, *The Theology of the Pastoral Epistles* (Cambridge: Cambridge University Press, 1994), pp. 79-85.

congregation worships in this manner (vv. 5-7a). In letters occasioned by his departure/absence (1:3), the instructions given to his successors indicate there is no falloff in the congregation's practices: what began with Paul's reception of God's word (cf. Tit. 1:1-3) and apostolic calling continues on in the disciplined formation of Christian congregations. In fact, 1 Timothy concludes (6:20) and 2 Timothy begins (1:13-14) with strong exhortations to safeguard Paul's apostolic memory and message. This is the endgame of "the ordering of ecclesiastical discipline."

This same theme of "ecclesiastical discipline" is supported by the CE collection. As introduced by James, the community's internal discipline extends to what is said and what is done, elaborations of which are found everywhere in the CE. Instructions to maintain church order are similarly attached in both the Petrine and Johannine letters to the prospectus of apostolic succession. In fact, the metaphor "household" is explicitly used in 1 Peter (2:5; 4:17) and "church" in 3 John (vv. 9, 10) in response to different threats to congregational life that may subvert the congregation's reception of and perseverance in the truth. For James the reception of "the implanted word" clearly depends on a humility instantiated by the community's spiritual leaders, who are quick to defend the poor (cf. 2:1-7, 15-16) and who use their teaching office wisely to build up rather than to tear down (3:1-17).

"Good works" as the hallmark of real Christians. The repetition of an exhortation to engage in "good works" in the PE underscores that "there is an indissoluble connection between beliefs and behavior."[27] Conversely, where this connection appears broken apart, where moral chaos is found, there is evidence of opposition to the core claims of Paul's gospel. Thus, for every virtue list found in the PE there is a contrasting vice list, together delineating the real difference between embodied truth and falsehood — this is also consistent with both Jewish theology and Greco-Roman moral philosophy. There is also clear continuity between the evangelical purpose of Paul's mission and this "indissoluble connection" between "healthy (i.e., Pauline) doctrine" and virtuous character (so 1 Tim. 1:8-11).

The stress on "good works" as the effective moral yield of receiving God's grace brings out in bold relief a point made elsewhere in the Pauline canon, most effectively in Rom. 12:1; 2 Cor. 9:8; and Eph. 2:8-10. The net result is to correct a dangerous misreading of Paul, which demonizes good

27. J. Bassler, *1 Timothy, 2 Timothy, Titus* (ANTC, Nashville: Abingdon, 1996), p. 34.

works as somehow subversive of the sinner's dependency on Christ's death for salvation. Further, the PE stress on the formation of a "godly" character as the distinguishing mark of the faithful believer, who is then morally competent to perform "good works," corrects another misreading of Paul: namely, the emphasis on teaching a saving orthodoxy to the exclusion of any instruction in a practical divinity that embodies confessed truth in the hard work of Christian charity and virtue. In this regard, too, the emphasis of the Pastoral Epistles brings a necessary balance to the whole of Scripture's Pauline teaching.

The keen emphasis of the CE on a community's covenant-keeping practices, introduced by Jas. 2:14-26, complements this same emphasis and so helps to correct the church's use of Paul to promote a false sola fideism. The community's confession of faith is embodied and so confirmed by its moral practices. Faith alone does not work with God, and so the Christian who claims faith but does not live it cannot be befriended by God. This is the deep logic of the second collection: faith is confirmed by faithfulness. We would argue that the theme of "good works" — the performance of God's will (1 Pet. 2:20; 3:17) — is a necessary condition of the believer's final salvation. While faith and not works alone is covenant-initiating, works and not faith alone are covenant-keeping.

A key emphasis of the Christology of the CE collection is the role of Jesus as messianic exemplar of good works. He demonstrates that faithfulness to God saves human lives. Those saved lives are in James those of the poor and powerless (2:5), in the Petrine witness non-believers (2 Pet. 2:18–3:7), and in the Johannine witness confessing believers (1 John 2:3-6). The messianic mission of Jesus is extended beyond his atoning death, appropriated by faith, to include an obedient life, followed in faithfulness.

The portrait of the canonical Paul. A final theme is the expanded résumé of the apostle Paul in the PE. Even though it is commonplace these days to suggest the letters convey propaganda about Paul that supports his legitimacy as exemplar and apostle, at the moment of their canonization rival Christian groups were embroiled in a debate over Paul's identity and legacy. In this postbiblical setting, the portrait of Paul that emerges by the addition of the PE (and Acts) helps to secure his "official" or canonical identity for subsequent generations of Christians.[28]

---

28. For this see Wall, *1 and 2 Timothy and Titus,* pp. 36-40.

Against alternate claims about the Pauline apostolate suggested in other letters (e.g., Galatians 1–2 and 2 Corinthians 11–12), there is no more expansive definition of his authority and religious purchase for the church than Tit. 1:1-3. Even a cursory comparison between this greeting and the equally lengthy one that begins Romans and so the Pauline corpus evinces that while in addressing the Romans Paul is concerned to set out the core beliefs of his gospel, which is preached to empower the salvation of the nations, in Titus the core concern is the importance of Paul himself for the salvation of God's elect. It is not the risen Christ that sets out the terms of the gospel, as in Romans, but God's word delivered directly to Paul at a *kairos idios,* "God's own timing." On this basis a "knowledge of the truth" is delivered to fashion the faith of God's elect so that God's promise to them, made in ages past, might now be fulfilled. Paul is now front and center in the outworking of God's promised salvation!

Even more crucially, this portrait and its various bits underwrite the importance of the Pauline apostolate that is now passed on to others to safeguard, with the Spirit's help, and to transmit to still other teachers (1 Tim. 6:20; 2 Tim. 1:13-14; 2:1-2) after the departure of the Lord's apostle. A peculiar eschatology emerges in these letters that is linked to the apostle, which concerns not only the eternal destiny of certain individuals but also of the (especially Gentile) church. Even as Jesus was concerned what choices his disciples would make in his absence, since these choices concerned eternal life, Paul is similarly concerned in these letters that their readers and hearers follow his example and instruction.

The importance of the apostolic witness as recipient of God's word and then the importance of receiving it from trusted others is a critical feature of the CE collection — one that we will develop in our comments on the individual letters. The addition of 2 Peter to 1 Peter and the Johannine letters to the CE collection has the overall effect of securing this apostolic impress for the entire corpus. In an epistemology necessarily different from that of the Pauline witness but having the same ends, both 2 Pet. 1:12-21 and 1 John 1:1-4 ground what is preached and written in the memory of those who were ear- and eyewitnesses of Jesus. This apostolic memory establishes an epistemic criterion of truth, and every departure from it is condemned. False prophets are exposed by the church's faithful proclamation of the truth (2 Pet. 2:1-3; 1 John 4:1-6), Christian faith is secured and formed according to the instruction of the truth (2 Pet. 1:12; Jude 3-4), and God's future judgment is measured by the truth (2 Pet. 2:2-3; cf. 3 John 12).

Simply put, salvation results from coming to knowledge of this apostolic-shaped truth (cf. 1 Tim. 2:4).

The Problem of an Orphaned Letter:
A Canonical Approach to "To the Hebrews"

The superscription "to the Hebrews" locates this anonymous letter within or alongside the Pauline corpus and so as part of Paul's canonical witness. This canonical location and its theological implications are easily affirmed by the letter's earliest reception history, which considered Hebrews part of the Pauline corpus. Although the studied ambivalence regarding where to locate Hebrews in the canon was already felt by its early interpreters, its modern reception by the academy (less so by the modern church) has hardened this sense. In fact, today's consensus among scholars, reflected in every critical introduction to the NT, is that Hebrews is a non-Pauline letter (i.e., neither written by Paul nor in line with his narrative of salvation). Most other bits of its critical prolegomena — its date and location, whether social or canonical, and its occasion and intended audience — remain contested and, most would say, indeterminate or unimportant.

Years ago one of us chaired a Society of Biblical Literature section that included Hebrews in a collection of other non-Pauline letters (including deutero-Paulines) under the rubric "The General Epistles." In this case, "general" is the academy's rubric for "miscellaneous" without any of the theological impress of the church's rubric "catholic." Naturally, each of these epistles, including Hebrews, was studied in isolation from the others, an independent broker of religious meaning from God-only-knows what authors for God-only-knows what audiences in God-only-knows what places in antiquity.

A canonical approach to Hebrews would surely disagree with this assignment. But this then begs the question: What about "To the Hebrews"? How does it function within the biblical canon, and what relationship does it enjoy with its Pauline and Pillars neighbors in the NT canon? Any detailed response to these important questions will need to await a future study. But the following suggestions are programmatic of a path forward.

First, the evidence from the point of its canonization suggests that Hebrews must be approached and first read within the NT as part of the Pauline witness. It was received and preserved as such, and its title confirms that. Whatever conclusions a consensus of modern criticism forwards about the letter, the church must use it as a member of the Pauline canon, if only on its margins. Indeed, the long and steady struggle to find a place for it in the sequence of Pauline letters is at the least suggestive of its importance: everyone (in the East, and eventually in the West) agreed that the Pauline canon was in some way incomplete — less than "excellent" to use aesthetic language — without the arresting presence of Hebrews.

Second, just the same, the ambivalence intensified by the reception of Hebrews within the modern academy has an ancient antecedent. Most early canon lists simply say "the fourteen epistles of Paul" simply to avoid listing them all (e.g., Eusebius, Cyril, Epiphanius, the Apostolic Canons, Rufinus, and Innocent), and other lists name and place Hebrews between the Pauline letters to churches and letters to individuals (Laodicea, Athanasius, Jerome, and probably also Claromontanus). Its final placement *within but at the end of the Pauline canon* suggests the church's ambivalence: Hebrews is "in but not of" the Pauline corpus.

Third, in closer consideration of this ancient aesthetic, however, we suggest two other possible roles for the letter. The first is as an appendix to the Pauline canon. If the rhetorical function of an appendix is to add information that is non-essential to a proper understanding of the collection but that nonetheless clarifies its presentation, then one might imagine the final shape of Scripture's Pauline witness as excluding Hebrews because it was deemed aesthetically complete within its thirteen-letter corpus but included Hebrews as a canonical appendix because it "further clarifies" a point in the Pauline witness that would be left more ambiguous without it. What that point is remains another topic for discussion, but almost certainly would include its robust dialogue between Christology and ethics as well as its potential gloss on the Acts portrait of Paul's conflict with the Diaspora synagogue, which is mostly lacking in the Pauline letters. Perhaps the interplay of Jewish and Hellenistic materials as well as the peculiar nature of the theological crisis that occasions the reading of Hebrews fills in a narrative gap that teases out more the theological implications and its fallout when Jesus is preaching among the Jews. Good material for an appendix!

Fourth, another possible role suggested by the final placement of Hebrews between the two letter corpora, however, is that of a canonical bridge that facilitates a mutually informing conversation between the two witnesses, Pauline and Pillars. In this case, the argument of Hebrews supplies a working glossary of themes that engages Scripture's reader with a living "word of God" that envisions a manner of discipleship that resists either a Pauline or Pillars reductionism. Its distinctive and complex portrait of a priestly Christ, for example, has this capacity. Although bits of this portrait recall and interpret a Pauline Christology, especially the centrality of Jesus' atoning death for putting the faith community into covenant with God, other bits prepare the reader for the Christology of the CE, which depicts his exemplary life — and his suffering in particular — as the pattern of the community's covenant-keeping.

Acts and the CE Collection

The keen emphasis placed on the community's reception of the apostolic tradition by the CE collection responds to an epistemic crisis provoked by rival teachers who parade a non-apostolic message among its membership (cf. 1 John 2:21-27). In the commentary portions of this book we will sometimes note that these "false prophets" seem to trade on a misreading of Paul's gospel to sound their contrary note about Jesus. The canonical edition of the CE collection is shaped to locate its internal hinge where 2 Peter meets 1 John and in their common emphasis on a gospel message built on an apostolic foundation of eyewitnesses who traveled with the historical Jesus. That is, *the epistemic crisis occasioned by rival claims to the gospel truth is solved in favor of those who have a direct line-of-sight to the real Jesus* and to the memories of what he actually did and said which is revelatory of the "word of life" (2 Pet. 1:16–2:3; 1 John 1:1-5).

But that is Paul's epistemological problem: his knowledge of Jesus was indirect since he did not know the historical Jesus. According to Acts, his "apostolate" is grounded on visionary experiences of the risen Lord and on traditions received from others who knew Jesus in the flesh, including the Jerusalem Pillars, the very ones he distances himself from in Galatians 1 and 2! And so among the various problems Acts tackles is an epistemic one: given that Paul did not accompany Jesus from the beginning (cf. Acts 1:21-22), in what sense might the catholic and apostolic church agree that Paul's letters (the fixed and portable instantiation of his gospel message) are important resources for its future? Moreover, since Paul's witness to the Lord's resurrection is a visionary one (9:3-6; 22:17-21; 26:12-19; cf. 1:22), how might the church discriminate his message from others who also claim that they received their "gospel" through similar media (e.g., visions and charismatic episodes)?

We suggest that the creation and reception of the so-called *Apostolos* (Acts and the CE collection) attends to these questions in different but complementary ways. Acts defends the importance of Paul by lining up the narrative of his ministry as continuous with that of the Pillars. While he does not qualify to be an apostle in a technical sense, since he was not an eyewitness of the historical Jesus (cf. Acts 1:21-22), he is nonetheless chosen by the risen Jesus and empowered by God's Spirit to continue what Jesus began to do and say (cf. v. 1) as a prophet-like-Jesus. We trust Paul because we first trust Peter and John and the brothers of the Lord (v. 14), whose line to Jesus as his immediate successors cannot be impugned. Irenaeus and Tertullian's advance against the heretics, who sometimes appealed to Paul to secure their version of the gospel truth, made this same point: you get to use Paul only *with* Peter, since it is evidently dangerous to use Paul otherwise. And if you use Peter and John, then you must locate your claims about Jesus in an apostolic tradition forged by the memories of what was heard, seen, and touched of the historical Jesus, and not in some reimagined Jesus mystically encountered on one's very own "road to Damascus" or revealed by one's very own Holy Spirit! Sharply put, *the epistemology of the Pillars tradition is superior to the epistemology of the Pauline tradition.* And so the addition of the CE collection to the extant Pauline canon and the lines of continuity between them help to secure Paul's apostolic tradition in the firmer soil of the Pillars' witness of the historical Jesus.

For this reason (and others we note below), we think D. Trobisch's observation that Acts played a strategic hermeneutical role in the canonical process is almost certainly correct.[29] But the application of a reading of Acts as an "early catholic" narrative, written to moderate the conflict between Paul and the "Jerusalem Pillars" articulated in Gal. 2:1-15, to the canon project is mistaken in our view. We remain unconvinced that Acts is "early catholic" in either its theological or sociological sensibility, but our

---

29. See D. Trobisch, "The Book of Acts as a Narrative Commentary on the Letters of the New Testament," in *Rethinking the Unity and Reception of Luke and Acts,* ed. A. Gregory and K. Rowe (Columbia: University of South Carolina Press, 2010), pp. 119-27. Although his desire is to rehabilitate Acts as a historical source for studying the NT letters, his observations are highly suggestive of the role Acts performs in establishing a canonical context for relating the missions of Paul and the Pillars and so the two canonical collections gathered in their names.

primary concern is that this perspective undermines the special relationship between Acts and the CE collection evinced during the fourth century, when they circulated together and appeared together in canon lists. Moreover, such a harmonistic reading of Acts fails to recognize the substantial role of James in the narrative world of Acts in moving the plotline of Paul's mission to the nations. In fact, our growing conviction is that the Acts narrative (rather than Galatians 2) best explains the importance of a final redaction of the CE collection, which posits the Letter of James as its frontispiece and therefore as central for its theological definition and canonical responsibility — especially if Acts and James arrived together at this same canonical moment.

For this reason, the relevant question for our project is not the historian's "Is the letter of James a letter from James?" but "What does the James of Acts have to do with the letter of James?" Our deep suspicion is that the portrait of James in Acts not only underwrites the authority of a letter of James but shows why it should function as frontispiece to a second corpus of letters when read as elements of a "self-correcting and mutually-informing" conversation within the biblical canon.

Acts narrates a story whose central characters are the same authors (e.g., Peter, Paul, James) and audiences/sources (e.g., Jerusalem, Timothy, Corinth, Ephesus, Rome) referred or alluded to in the subsequent NT letters.[30] NT readers naturally make associations between these common elements, noting as well a common concern for important topics of Christian discipleship (e.g., sharing goods, purity, suffering, the performance of the word of God, congregational unity). Literary intertexts of this sort suggest a logical relationship as members of the same conceptual universe; from a perspective within the NT, Acts supplies the "authorized" narrative behind the NT's most important epistolary texts.

Considered from this angle of vision, then, the critical orthodoxy of reading only the Pauline collection (Knox, Goodspeed, Bruce, Delatte, and many others) by Acts seems misplaced — even though the rehabilitation of Acts (perhaps even in a "new and improved" version) during the second half of the second century and then a renewed interest in Acts criticism during the second half of the twentieth century may well have been

---

30. While the logical relationship between Acts and the NT letters is reflected by the canonical process (see below), the narrator's own claim (Acts 1:1) is that Acts is better related to the preceding Gospel probably for christological rather than literary reasons.

prompted by the evidently strategic relationship between the Paul of Acts and certain Pauline letters (e.g., Romans, Ephesians, Galatians).[31] During the canonical process, Acts came to supply a narrative introduction for the entire epistolary canon, Pauline *and* Catholic; in fact, from a canonical perspective, the relationship between Acts and the CE is elevated in importance because Acts and the CE "came into life" together during the canonical process. In any case, the interpreter approaches the NT letters with the orienting concerns of Acts in mind and, in light of its story, more wakeful when negotiating between the NT's two different epistolary corpora as theological complements.

Given the reemergence of Acts as a text of strategic importance for underwriting the hermeneutics of the canonical process, we consider it highly likely that its narrative portraits of the church's earliest leaders — Peter and John, Paul and James — drawn as they are from early traditions of their teaching and ministry concurrent to the earliest stage of the canonical process — envisage a particular account of their religious authority,[32] of the nature of their ministries (e.g., prophetic, pastoral, missionary), and of the subject matter of their preaching. This supplied the canonizing community with both an explanatory context and a religious warrant for considering these NT writings together as formative of Christian theological understanding.[33]

We especially think Acts provides the impetus for the circulation (and perhaps even composition) of James, which led to the formation of a "Pil-

---

31. As an exercise in a recent "Acts" class, we had our students reflect on the importance of studying a particular Pauline text (e.g., Ephesians, 2 Timothy) in light of their prior study of related pericopes in Acts (e.g., 18:24–19:41; 20:17-38). The purpose of their project was more than identifying common Pauline traditions; it was to explore the meanings of a Pauline text that were brought to clearer light by its intracanonical relationship with Acts.

32. For an argument that the church's title for this composition, "Acts of the Apostles," cues its interest in the religious authority of the church's "apostles" (including Paul and James), see R. W. Wall, "The Acts of the Apostles in the Context of the New Testament Canon," *BTB* 18 (1988), pp. 15-23.

33. We are mindful of H. Räisänen's probing historicist response to the question in the title of his *Neutestamentliche Theologie? Eine religionswissenschaftliche Alternative* (SBS 186; Stuttgart: Katholisches Bibelwerk, 2000), which distinguishes more precisely between first and subsequent readers within faith and academic communities. The canonical approach presumes that biblical theology is a theological rather than historical enterprise, that its aims are determined by the church's rather than the academy's intentions, and that it is therefore religiously formative more than intellectually informative.

lars" collection. Acts also cultivates a sense of their personal relationships and in doing so provides a distinctive angle into the nature of the literary relationships between the Pauline and Pillars letters. Similarities and dissimilarities in emphasis and theological conception between the two letter collections may actually correspond to the manner by which Acts narrates the negotiations between reports from different missions and the theological convictions and social conventions required by each (e.g., Acts 2:42-47; 9:15-16; 11:1-18; 12:17; 15:1-29; 21:17-26). The relations between James and Paul or between Peter and James as depicted at strategic moments on the plotline of Acts are generally collaborative rather than adversarial and frame the interpreter's approach to their biblical writings as essentially complementary (though certainly not uniform and sometimes in conflict) in both meaning and function. If the critical consensus for a late first-century date of Acts, roughly contemporaneous with the earliest pre-canonical stage in the formation of the New Testament,[34] is accepted, then it is likely that its collection of portraits of early Christian leaders provides an important explanatory model for assessing the relationship between (and even within) the two emergent collections of canonical letters: the form and function of these Christian writings and their relationships to each other are another articulation of the early church's "sense" of the collaborative relationships among individual leaders and interpretative traditions, which is reflected then in Acts. So that, for example, if Peter and John are partners in Acts, then we should expect their written traditions to be conjoined in an emergent Christian Bible and their intracanonical relations to represent the church's perception of their theological coherence. Likewise, the more difficult although finally collegial relationship between James and Paul as narrated in Acts 15 and (especially) 21 may well represent their partnership in ecclesial formation in a manner that Protestant interpretation has sometimes subverted.

Because both the narrative world and its central characters are the lit-

---

34. D. Trobisch, *Die Endredaktion des Neuen Testaments. Eine Untersuchung zur Entstehung der christlichen Bibel* (NTOA 31; Göttingen: Vandenhoeck & Ruprecht, 1996). But now see the recent studies by R. I. Pervo and J. B. Tyson, both published in 2006, who date the earliest version of Acts to the early second century, and of Strange, who follows Cadbury and Lake in dating the canonical version of Acts to the late second century. But none of these reconstructions, even if accurate, undermine our essential claim. R. I. Pervo, *Dating Acts: Between the Evangelists and the Apologists* (Santa Rosa: Polebridge, 2006); J. B. Tyson, *Marcion and Luke-Acts: A Defining Struggle* (Columbia: University of South Carolina Press, 2006).

erary constructions of the storyteller and are shaped by his theological commitments, the interpreter should not expect a more precise connection between, for example, the kerygma of the Peter of Acts and the Petrine theology of 1 and 2 Peter. Nevertheless, there is evidence that Luke did indeed draw on important traditions common to the Petrine letters when composing his narrative of the person and work of Peter. In particular, 1 Peter's interpretation of Jesus as Isaiah's "Servant of God" (1 Pet. 2:21-25; cf. 1:10-12), the evident core of Petrine christology, is anticipated by four references to Jesus as "servant" in Acts (and only there in the NT), the first two in speeches by Peter (Acts 3:13, 26) and the others in a prayer by the apostles led by him (4:27, 30).[35] Moreover, the God of the Petrine epistles, who is known primarily through Jesus' resurrection (1 Pet. 1:3, 21; 3:21; cf. Acts 2:22-36) and as a "faithful Creator" (1 Pet. 4:19; cf. Acts 4:24), agrees generally with Luke's traditions of the Petrine kerygma. Even Peter's claim that the central mark of Gentile conversion is a "purity of heart" (Acts 15:9) is strikingly similar to 1 Pet. 1:22. Finally, the most robust eschatology found in Acts, famous for its sparseness of eschatological thought, is placed on Peter's lips (Acts 3:20-23), thereby anticipating the stress on salvation's apocalypse in 1 and 2 Peter (cf. 2 Pet. 3:1-13).[36] A second example may be the far thinner portrait of John in Acts, who, though depicted as Peter's silent partner, uses his one speaking role in Acts 4:19-20 to sound a key note of the Johannine epistles: "we cannot but speak of what we have seen and heard" (cf. 1 John 1:1-3).[37]

When these thematic connections are rooted in the narrative world of Acts — a world in which these characters have enormous religious authority and purchase for the church's future — the epistolary expression and development of these core themes is underwritten as also important for the church's future and formation. Moreover, the impression of kerygmatic continuity between the Lord's apostolic successors (Peter and John)

---

35. Cf. O. Cullmann, *Peter: Apostle-Disciple-Martyr* (London: SCM, 1953), pp. 63-69.

36. See Wall, "Canonical Function of 2 Peter," pp. 77-79.

37. See P. N. Anderson, *The Christology of the Fourth Gospel* (Valley Forge: Trinity, 1996), 274-77, who suggests that at the one point in Acts where Peter and John speak with one voice (4:19-20; Peter alone speaks when they are teamed elsewhere in Acts) the narrator has constituted a saying that combines Petrine (v. 19) with Johannine (v. 20) traditions. Their pairing in Acts in both work and speech may well envisage an emerging consensus within the ancient church that their traditions, both personal and theological, are complementary parts of an integral whole.

and Paul, cultivated by Acts, would seem to commend a more constructive relationship between their writings. Acts performs an interpretive role, not so much to temper the diversity envisaged by the two different collections of letters but to prompt impressions of their rhetorical relationship within the NT. According to Acts, the church that claims its continuity with the first apostles tolerates a rich pluralism, even as the apostles do within Luke's narrative world, although not without controversy and confusion. What is achieved at the pivotal Jerusalem Council (Acts 15) is confirmation of a kind of theological understanding rather than a more political theological consensus. The divine revelation given to the apostles according to Acts forms a "pluralizing monotheism" (so J. A. Sanders) which in turn contextualizes Paul's idiom of two discrete missions and appropriate proclamations, Jewish and Gentile, in Gal. 2:7-10. The variety of theological controversies Paul responds to in his letters, with whatever rhetoric he employs in doing so, is roughly analogous to the "Cornelius problem" in Acts.

Of course, Acts portrays Peter (rather than Paul) as first initiating and then explaining the admission of uncircumcised (therefore unclean) Gentiles into the church. Furthermore, the Peter of Acts finally defends Paul's mission and its spiritual results in a speech that is remarkably Pauline in theological sensibility (15:7-11) — perhaps reflecting Luke's familiarity with the Petrine and Pauline traditions used in the letters and the perceived unity of those traditions, as many modern interpreters have noted.[38] More remarkably, however, the question of whether to "Judaize" repentant Gentiles is settled in Acts 11:1-18 *before* Paul comes back into the narrative to begin his mission to the nations. In fact, Peter's second rehearsal of Cornelius's repentance at this "second" Jerusalem Council responds to a different problem altogether, one posed by the church's Pharisaic contingent, which is concerned (as evidently is James) about a normative *halakhah* for mixed Christian congregations (15:4-5). Peter's response concentrates — presumably agreeing with Paul's initial proclamation (cf. 13:38-39) — on an internal "purity of the heart" (15:9).

James, however, expands this Pharisaic concern for religious purity to include socio-religious *practices* (15:20). In fact, his *halakhah* reflects the more "traditional" worry of Jewish religion regarding syncretism — the "gentilizing" of repentant Israel (15:20; see also 21:17-26) — and in particu-

---

38. Although we think this critical conclusion is typically overstated since there are fundamental differences between Scripture's Petrine witness and the Pauline kerygma.

lar the possible weakening of the church's Jewish legacy in the Diaspora as Paul's mission to the nations takes the word of God farther from Jerusalem, the epicenter of the sacred universe (15:21). It is in response to James's Jewish concerns that the narrative of Paul's mission to the nations is shaped in Acts. Therefore, the Paul of Acts provokes and responds to a different set of theological controversies than does the epistolary Paul, who responds to internal opponents who want to "Judaize" repentant Gentiles. According to Acts, this issue is settled by Peter at the earlier Jerusalem council (11:1-18), and, even though it resurfaces in Antioch (15:1-2), those who raise it again are summarily dismissed by James as "unauthorized" teachers who do not represent the position of the Judean church (so 15:24). In fact, the entire narrative of Paul's European mission in Acts (Philippi, Thessalonica, Athens, Corinth, Ephesus) is simply not shaped by the same theological controversies that Paul stakes out in his letters as provoked by his Gentile mission.

In general, the Paul of Acts is exemplary of a more Jewish definition of purity (cf. 24:16-21). Thus, he is arrested in Philippi for being a Jew (16:20-21) and earlier circumcises Timothy (16:3; cf. Gal. 2:3!), not only to testify to his personal loyalty to the ancestral religion (cf. 21:23-26) but more critically to symbolize the importance of James's concern to preserve it in consecrated form. Consider, for example, the role Timothy performs in Acts in contrast to Titus in Galatians. Timothy is of mixed parentage, Jewish and Gentile, and, in prospect of the Diaspora church, Paul circumcises him in order to preserve his mother's Jewish inheritance.[39] He stands as a symbol of Paul's missiological intent in Acts, which is to found Christian congregations in the Diaspora with a mixture of Jewish and Gentile converts whose faith and practices are deeply rooted in the church's Jewish legacy.

From this canonical perspective, then, it may well be argued that a principal concern of the second collection of epistles, the CE, is to bring balance to a tendency toward religious syncretism by which the pressures of the surrounding pagan culture may distort if not then subvert the church's substantially Jewish theological and cultural legacy. The repetition of familiar Pauline themes in the CE, then to problematize them, acquires a thickened meaning when read in context of the antecedent Acts narrative: that is, a prior reading of Acts alerts the reader of CE that an in-

---

39. The Jewish cast of Paul's story in Acts is a principal exegetical interest of Wall, Acts in *NIB;* see pp. 213-15 for an introduction to this narrative theme.

creasingly Gentile (= Pauline) church must consider its religious and public purity as God's people according to the redemptive calculus of their
Jewish canonical heritage (Scriptures, practices, prophetic exemplars, etc.).
As such a Christian congregation's profession of faith must be embodied
in its public and internal practices in keeping with the ethos of its Jewish
legacy.[40] The full experience of God's righteousness is by performance of
works pleasing to God and neighbor and not merely by *sola fide* — no
matter how orthodox or sincerely confessed.

Conclusion: From Chaos to Coherence

Our emphasis on the precise shape of the CE as a discrete collection of
Scripture and its placement within the final form of the NT canon intends
to move beyond the current discussion of these epistles as individual (and
independent) compositions to the constructive proposal of reading them
together as a coherent literary whole. Conventional interpretive strategies
approach each letter to examine its distinctive literary form and theological perspective, including compositional prehistories and postbiblical histories. These studies have produced important insights and we remain in
their debt. Nonetheless, this book will comment on each letter as part of a
single canonical collection that is the deliberate production of the church,
whose reception and use of it within the bounds of Scripture intends to
deepen its theological understanding and moral practice.

Put sharply, *the markers of canonical shaping provided in this chapter
and the preceding chapter recommend a reading strategy that considers
intertextual allusions within the collection as instances of theological magni-
fication.* There is insufficient evidence to suggest that this intertextuality is
intended by the authors and editors of the CE, even though the late date of
both James and 2 Peter, and each a "canon-conscious pseudepigraphon,"

---

40. Of course, the Pauline letters would not disagree with this conclusion. We would
argue, however, that for the Pauline tradition these social, moral, and religious practices that
mark out a people as "Christian" are the natural yield of "being in Christ" and that "being in
Christ" is the result of profession that "Jesus is Lord." A Pauline redemptive calculus,
whether understood politically or personally, is concentrated by the beliefs of the Pauline
gospel rather than by the practices of the Pauline churches. It is this essential difference of
logic that fashions — we think from the early church — a different spirituality, one centered
on orthodox confession rather than found in the congregations of the CE traditions.

may well underwrite our contention that the important "intertextual" role each performs within the collection is deliberate. But our more basic point is this: the robust intertextual allusions within this collection — linguistic and thematic — commend a unified reading strategy. In both the commentaries on each letter and in our final chapter the theological importance of this unity will be explored.

PART 2

Introduction to the Catholic Epistles

The following chapters offer a canonical reading of each of the seven CE. While most modern commentaries focus almost exclusively on issues associated with the historical point of composition, we will be working to shift attention to critical issues surrounding the letters' reception at the historical point of canonization. Accordingly, each chapter will be introduced with an exploration of the identity of the canonical author (not the "actual" author of modern scholarly reconstruction). From there we will offer comment on key issues surrounding the literary composition of the letter, and conclude with an overview of its canonization. A brief commentary will follow, and each chapter will conclude with an articulation of that letter's theological witness.

In an earlier treatment of "the unifying theology of the CE collection,"[1] Wall proposed the following sequence of agreements, introduced by James, as distinguishing the theological conception of this collection:

> Human suffering tests the faith community's love for God.
> In response to the suffering of God's people, God discloses a "word of truth" to map the only way of salvation.
> In obedience to this word, the community must practice "pure and undefiled" behavior as the public mark of friendship with God.
> Theological orthodoxy by itself is inconclusive of friendship with God and is made effective only when embodied in loving works.

1. R. W. Wall, "A Unifying Theology of the Catholic Epistles: A Canonical Approach," in J. Schlosser, ed., *The Catholic Epistles and the Tradition* (BETL 176; Leuven: Leuven University Press, 2004), pp. 43-71.

Finally, the reward of steadfast obedience to God's word is eternal life with God.

Our attempt at a revised synthesis for the present study aims at a somewhat different purpose. While our primary intention remains to describe the theological conception of the CE collection as a whole, we also have our eye on how this result might be used in relating the theological goods of this collection to other biblical articulations of God's word. For this secondary purpose we will use a somewhat different sequence of agreements cued by Tertullian's Rule of Faith in his *Prescription against Heretics*.[2] Since every apostolic tradition is analogical to and ordered by this same Rule of Faith, not only are we better able to bring order to the diverse theological goods retrieved from the CE, we will also more easily compare those goods with those found among Scripture's other apostolic witnesses.

We have decided to adapt Tertullian's bold expression of this apostolic rule in producing this new synthesis for two reasons. First, the great Apologist's theological grammar is Trinitarian, thereby placing it more firmly on a trajectory beyond Irenaeus's precedent in a way that targets Nicene orthodoxy. Second, Tertullian's articulation of the apostolic rule reflects the version in play in the third century, when the church formed the CE collection to add to an inchoate NT canon that included the fourfold Gospel and the Pauline corpus. If we mine the interpretive cues at the point of canonization, then, it seems to us that Tertullian's account of the apostolic rule may better facilitate the continuing intracanonical conversations among Scripture's different but complementary theologies.

Here, then, is our translation of Tertullian's Rule of Faith, which we will use as our "rule of thumb" in organizing our theological reflections:

1. The Creator God is one God, who produced all things out of nothing through God's own word sent forth.[3]
2. Christ Jesus is this word sent forth into the world to redeem God's creation, disclose God's truth, and exemplify God's love.[4]

---

2. *Praescr.* 13.

3. According to Tertullian, *Praescr.* 13, "There is only one God, and He is none other than the Creator of the world, who produced all things out of nothing through His own Word, first of all sent forth."

4. Tertullian, *Praescr.* 13: "This Word is called His Son, and, under the name of God, was seen 'in diverse manners' by the patriarchs, heard at all times in the prophets, at last brought

3. The community of the Spirit forms loving fellowship with God as members follow God's word.[5]

4. Christian disciples follow God's word when responding to various trials, thus purifying themselves of sin and proving their love for God.[6]

5. The consummation of God's promised salvation at Christ's coming will restore God's creation, reveal God's victory over death, and reward the community's obedience to God's word.[7]

As a whole, the CE collection functions strategically to curb the church's tendency to read and use Paul's witness as its canon within the canon. It is our confidence that this collected witness to God's word will establish a more fully formed biblical theology informed by the full breadth and depth of the ancient apostolic witness.

---

down by the Spirit and Power of the Father into the Virgin Mary, was made flesh in her womb, and, being born of her, went forth as Jesus Christ; thenceforth He preached the new law and the new promise of the kingdom of heaven, worked miracles; having been crucified, He rose again the third day; (then) having ascended into the heavens, He sat at the right hand of the Father."

5. Tertullian, *Praescr.* 13: "Christ sent instead of Himself the Power of the Holy Ghost to lead such as believe." The idea of a "church" is not yet used by Tertullian; rather his sense is more congregational than catholic in force. Our preference for the rubric "community" is a nod to Tertullian, but also retains the emphasis of the NT witnesses on the practices and struggles of local congregations of believers.

6. Tertullian, this time from *On the Flesh of Christ* 16: "For in putting on our flesh, Christ made it his own; and in making it his own, he made it sinless . . . because in that same human flesh he lived without sin."

7. Tertullian, *Praescr.* 13: "Christ will come with glory to take the saints to the enjoyment of everlasting life and of the heavenly promises and to condemn the wicked to everlasting fire, after the resurrection of both these classes shall have happened, together with the restoration of their flesh."

The Catholic Epistle of James

Introduction

1. The Canonical James

The interpretive strategies of modern criticism typically assign meaning to the intentions of a text's real author. If the study of the letter of James is approached as the work of the historical James, one is quickly frustrated for lack of reliable evidence about him. Despite the fine work of John Painter and the consultation convened in 1996 under the direction of Bruce Chilton and Craig Evans to begin a quest of the historical James, most scholars either remain suspicious of the results or detach the portrait of this historical figure from the study of the much later pseudepigraphical letter, supposing one has nothing to do with the other.

While the historical James continues to elude us, it seems incontrovertible that the canonical status of the letter of James is linked to the church's historical memory of the brother of the Lord and leader of the Jerusalem congregation. The details of the person and his spiritual résumé during the church's turbulent first century are recalled and recalibrated by later tradents into a "canonical James" who then continued to exert influence in the church, especially in those communions that desired to preserve Christianity's Jewish heritage for the future.

In fact, the most salient features of the canonical James already are found in the NT itself. Although this witness to James is sparse and diverse, it suggests why he was venerated by the early church as a trusted carrier of God's truth. In stark contrast to the fourfold Gospel, which depicts the

Lord as at odds with his unnamed brothers, Paul cites an Easter tradition that actually names James as an early witness to Jesus' resurrection (1 Cor. 15:7). This may well explain the prominence of the James of Acts, who is evidently among those filled by his brother's Spirit on Pentecost (Acts 1:14) and who then succeeds Peter (12:17) as the spiritual leader of Christianity's mother church in Jerusalem (15:4-35; 21:17-26). While there are evident tensions between Paul and James (Gal 2:11-14), which are extraordinarily difficult to nail down as a historical matter, the James of Acts takes the initiative to settle these intramural conflicts by appealing to Israel's sacred traditions in the company of the Spirit.

Significantly, this canonical James of Acts is securely located in the Holy City as the pastor of its principal (Aramaic-speaking) Christian congregation and an observant Jew who remains deeply concerned with matters of public purity. Not only does he resist Peter's bid to define covenant-keeping purity as a matter exclusively of the heart — the effect of divine grace in response to the convert's profession of faith — but he extends its scope to include matters of religious practice and table fellowship (Acts 15:20, 29; 21:25). In fact, James's insistence that Paul complete his Nazirite vow when he arrives in Jerusalem for *Shavuot* should be recognized as a rabbi's admonition to complete a vow of purity. In his third-century masterpiece, Eusebius recalls the second-century testimony of Hegesippus, who remembered James as a "righteous" man by Torah's definition. Especially in second-century groups that sought to preserve a more Jewish form of Christianity against its supersessionist (and typically Pauline) varieties, "James the Righteous" was venerated as the very personification of authentic Christianity.

Quite apart from vague memories of a historical figure, mentioned here only in brief, the image that begins to emerge of a canonical James is more clear and thickened with lasting importance for the church that goes well beyond his membership within the holy family: James is an Easter witness to the risen Jesus, whom he serves with Torah piety and effective pastoral leadership. He is a "pillar" of the Jerusalem congregation, which is the custodian of Christianity's Jewish heritage and its mission to the circumcised (Gal 2:9). This résumé of his religious authority and ecclesial status makes it natural for biblical readers to transfer their trust in him to the letter attributed to him.

2. *The Composition of the Letter*

No scholarly consensus has been reached on any detail of this letter's point of origin, in large part because its hortatory idiom and lack of specific background information make it difficult to pin down a particular provenance and date. The unmistakable Jewish character of James and its measured use of Hellenistic literary conventions (e.g., parenesis, diatribe) have led some to suggest "the twelve tribes in the Dispersion" (1:1) is the actual address of a Jewish Christian community living somewhere outside Palestine. The absence of any mention of circumcision suggests a date prior to Paul's Gentile mission. This evidence coupled with images from first-century Palestine has led to the conclusion that the letter's author (or source) is likely James, the Lord's brother and the leader of the Jerusalem church, whose exhortation — perhaps to dislocated former congregants living outside Palestine — is an exercise of his pastoral office.

When considering the book's correspondence with the ideas and language of a Pauline canon already in circulation, however, others place James in a post-Pauline era when the earlier controversies of the Gentile mission were replaced by other conflicts between Pauline and non-Pauline Christianities. In this case, the letter's address may recall a Jewish (i.e., non-Pauline) Christianity represented by the figure and teaching of the venerated James the Just.

Theological considerations may prompt a shift of interest altogether from the letter's origins to its subsequent reception as the first of seven Catholic Epistles (CE). This interpretive angle considers the role of James within the final redaction of the NT. The setting apropos for using a biblical book as Scripture is not authorial but ecclesial, when within the bounds of the canonical process the religious importance of James for its faithful readers and hearers is clarified.

In this regard, James's role as the frontispiece of the CE collection intimates its indispensability as Scripture. Whatever circumstances occasioned the composition of each of the CE, their subsequent formation into a discrete and coherent collection some time during the fourth century was in some sense a response to the church's use (or misuse!) of its extant Pauline canon (cf. 2 Pet. 3:15-16). This fresh combination of catholic and Pauline letter collections provides the church with a more "apostolic" conception of Christian discipleship, and the repeated insistence of the CE on a practiced "faith that works" reminds the faith community that a professed "faith without works" forged by a myopic reading of Paul alone is an insufficient condition for maintaining a congregation's covenant relationship with God.

The Pauline index of the Jerusalem "Pillars" (Gal. 2:9) finally frames the relationship between the two epistolary collections, Pauline and Pillars, aptly introduced by Jas. 2:22: "faith [in Christ: Pauline] is made complete by works [like Christ: Pillars]." This more robust conception of Christian discipleship is the principal characteristic of friendship with God (v. 23). Whenever the gospel is distorted by the appropriation of one to the exclusion of the other — whether as faith without works or works without faith — the community's friendship with God is seriously threatened.

3. The Canonization of the Letter

The letter of James can only be called a "late bloomer" when compared to most other New Testament texts. Slowly but surely, however, it did achieve authoritative status in the churches, and as we have already described in our opening chapters, its blossoming into full canonical authority can rightly be seen as a defining moment in the development of the New Testament canon.

The origin of the letter is deeply shrouded in the fog of history. Scholars continue to debate its provenance, some confidently naming it the earliest of NT texts (dating it to the late 40s) and others the latest (with dates ranging well into the second century). This vast continuum of historical hypotheses is due in part to the evidence of the letter's reception in the early church. While apparent "echoes" of the epistle abound in the writings of the second-century church fathers, none "sound out" loudly enough for us to be sure the writer in question is actually referring to the letter itself. Commentators have long noted, for instance, the material James shares in common with texts like *1 Clement* (ca. 96) and *The Shepherd of Hermas* (ca. 130-40).[1] The parallels in these texts are strong at points, but unfortunately the mere presence of common material is not enough to determine literary dependence, for it is impossible to know which text is in the prior position (is *Hermas* alluding to James or James echoing *Hermas?*) or whether indeed both texts are themselves alluding to some other source we no longer pos-

---

1. See, e.g., L. T. Johnson, *The Letter of James* (AB 37A: New York: Doubleday, 1995), pp. 66-80.

sess.[2] At best, all we can safely say is that the letter shares a number of affinities with known second-century texts.

One thing that is unmistakably clear is the fact that the letter first emerged in the eastern Church. The fog clears in the third century with Origen of Alexandria (d. ca. 250) who used James extensively in his writings. By the time Eusebius wrote his early drafts of the *H.E.* (ca. 300), James was "known to most" (3.25.3) in the East as "the first of the epistles called catholic" (2.23.25). From that time forward James had "arrived" in the Eastern Church, for every major church father (Cyril, Athanasius, Epiphanius, Gregory, and Amphilochius) and codex of the NT (Sinaiticus, Vaticanus, and Alexandrinus) place James as the lead letter in a collection of seven called "catholic."

James took much longer to be received in the West, however. It is not listed in either the Muratorian Fragment (ca. 200)[3] or the "Cheltenham Canon" of the mid-late 300s, and there are no clear references to the letter in the writings of any major churchman working in the period between the formation of these two lists (i.e., Irenaeus, Tertullian, Hippolytus, or Cyprian). It is possible that the letter was carried westward through contact between Athanasius and western church leaders instigated by the Arian crisis, for the first western writer to make clear use of James is the anti-Arian disciple of Athanasius Hilary of Poitiers (d. ca. 368).[4] The letter makes brief appearances after this in the writings of pseudo-Ambrose and Filaster of Brescia, but it was the influence of Origen that assured its acceptance and use by Rufinus, Jerome, and Augustine. By the time of Augustine, James's place in the NT canon was secure throughout the Christian world.

But what made the letter of James useful *as Scripture* for the churchmen who received it as authoritative? The clearest indications of its value are in the works of Origen and Augustine. Both celebrated the letter for its ability

---

2. O. J. F. Seitz, "Relationship of the Shepherd of Hermas to the Epistle of James," *JBL* 63 (1944), pp. 131-40.

3. As noted earlier, the Sundberg-Hahnemann theory that the Muratorian Fragment is in fact a fourth-century product of the eastern church fails to convince us. See A. C. Sundberg, "Canon Muratori: A Fourth-Century List," *HTR* 66 (1973), pp. 1-41; G. Hahnemann, *The Muratorian Fragment and the Development of the Canon* (Oxford: Clarendon, 1992); and the discussion in D. Nienhuis, *Not by Paul Alone* (Waco: Baylor University Press, 2007), pp. 46 and 76.

4. See J. P. Yates's "The Reception of the Epistle of James in the Latin West: Did Athanasius Play a Role?" in Schlosser, ed., *Catholic Epistles and the Tradition*, 273-88.

to bridge the ethical injunctions of the Gospels with Pauline teaching on justification by faith. In his *Commentary on Romans*, Origen consistently weaves in passages from James to demonstrate the commensurability of the two writers, at one point going out of his way to protect against an antinomian reading of Paul by linking James's "faith without works is dead" with a series of Gospel texts that insist on good works, concluding with "You see, then, that everywhere faith is joined with works and works are united with faith."[5] In like manner Augustine frequently joined Gal. 5:6 ("the only thing that counts is faith working through love") with Jas. 2:19-26 to resolve the faith-works divide created by the Pauline message.[6] His *On Faith and Works* describes salvation apart from good works as a "treacherously false security" received from a misunderstanding of Paul's teaching and goes on to insist, "other apostolic letters of Peter, James and Jude are deliberately aimed against the argument I have been refuting and firmly uphold the doctrine that faith does not avail without good works."[7] As far as we can tell, the very text that became a problem for Luther's Paulinist critique of the medieval church was celebrated in the ancient church for the role it played in producing a fully biblical articulation of the role of good works in the life of faith.

Commentary

1. Greetings (1:1)

James follows the form of most Hellenistic letters by beginning with an author's salutation of his audience. The attribution to James recalls two earlier traditions that help to contextualize the reading of this letter (see above): Paul mentions the story of James's conversion by the risen Jesus on Easter (1 Cor. 15:7; cf. Jas. 2:1) and Acts portrays him as the leader of the Jewish church (Acts 15:13-21; 21:18-26; cf. Gal. 2:11-12). His pastoral concern is aimed at the corporate effect of saving grace embodied in a congregation's purity practices (Acts 15:20, 29; 21:25; Jas. 1:26-27), and his only appearances in Acts are to resolve intramural conflicts provoked by his church's misunderstanding of Paul's mission (Acts 15:1-21; 21:21-26; cf. Jas. 2:14-26).

The letter's recipients are greeted as "twelve tribes in the Dispersion."

---

5. *Com. Rom.* 2.9.396-408.
6. See, e.g., *Fide* 14.23; *De Trin.* 14.18.
7. *Fide* 41.61-62.

This address is symbolic of a religious location in which "twelve tribes" are believers whose spiritual "dispersion" *(Diaspora)* within a hostile world unsettles their faith and tests their allegiance to God. James proffers wisdom that will help secure this community's embattled faith.

2. The Source of the Community's Wisdom (1:2-21)

The main body of James is introduced by a powerful vision of Christian discipleship. Central to this vision is the believer's routine experience of "trials of any kind" (1:2), which tests a faith in God (v. 3) but to which thoughtful believers respond with "nothing but joy." This response is possible when trials are "considered" against the horizon of a coming age when human existence will be "mature and complete, lacking in nothing" (v. 4b). Restated as a beatitude: God promises to bless those who "endure temptation" with "the crown of life" (cf. Rev. 2:10) as reward for their devotion to God (1:12).

But hardship also occasions a theodicy that tests the devotion of immature believers who are "unstable in every way" (1:8). Because "trials" and "temptation" (v. 13) translate the same Greek word, *peirasmos,* readers readily connect suffering with the potential of spiritual failure. According to James, hardship can either produce a steady allegiance to God or "give birth to sin . . . and death" (vv. 14-15). Although demonic impulses (cf. 3:15; 4:5, 7) and external factors (cf. 2:2-7; 5:1-6) may tempt the believer to failure, James stresses the individual's responsibility to make wise choices since the inward "desire" is "one's own" (1:14) to control.

But the believer enjoys heavenly support in controlling his self-centered desire. When God is trusted as generous and impartial (1:5), God is petitioned for the necessary wisdom or know-how one may lack to pass the spiritual tests that trials occasion. Rather than doubting God's goodness (vv. 6-8) or being deceived by the belief that God is responsible for one's misfortune (v. 16), the knowing response is to petition "the Father of lights with whom there is no variation" (v. 17b) for wisdom and God will invariably respond with "generous acts of giving every perfect *(teleios)* gift" (v. 17a). The perfect gift is "the word of truth" (v. 18) because it is God-given and because it supplies the wisdom necessary for a life that is "mature *(teleios)* and complete" (v. 4).

The stated content of "the word of truth" is a stock synthesis of proverbial wisdom — "let everyone be quick to listen, slow to speak, slow to anger" (1:19b), but the primary role of the letter's main body is to provide the reader with a fresh and elaborate commentary on this "implanted word that has the power to save your souls" (v. 21).

3. An Essay on the Wisdom of "Quick Listening" (1:22–2:26)

The letter's main body consists of three essays that comment on the nature of a wise response that passes the test of faith. The sequence of these essays is indexed by the proverbial triad of 1:19. Accordingly, the first concerns the wisdom of "quick listening." Simply put, to listen quickly means to obey the "perfect law of liberty" promptly (vv. 22-25), which commands merciful treatment of the poor neighbor (1:26–2:7). "Orphans and widows" (1:27) is a biblical metaphor for society's most vulnerable members, and their presence in a congregation occasions a spiritual test that requires a fresh application of heavenly wisdom. To care for poor and powerless is the hallmark of God's covenant-keeping people (cf. Exod. 22:22; Deut. 24:17-21; Ps. 146:9; Isa. 1:17; Jer. 5:28; Acts 2:45; 4:32-35; 6:1-7; 9:36-42), and to abandon them risks God's displeasure (cf. 2:12-13).

Two case studies of "quick listening" are mentioned. The first concerns the community's leaders who discriminate against the poor in favor of the rich, giving them the best seats in the house while inviting the poor to sit "at my feet" (2:2-4). These practices are foolish in an assembly of the "glorious Lord Jesus Christ" (v. 1), who exemplifies God's preferential option for the poor (cf. Luke 14:7-14). The second case is that of discrimination in the civil court; it draws a damning analogy between the community's leaders and the very rich they foolishly privilege, who "drag you into court . . . and blaspheme the excellent name" of Jesus (2:6-7; cf. Luke 18:1-8).

Two congregations are differently appraised by God (1:26-27). Those who "hear the word but are not doers" and so delude themselves since what they profess but fail to enact is worthless to God (v. 26; cf. 1:22-23; 2:15-16). Rather the "pure and undefiled" religion is approved by God because of what it does: it cares for its own poor without being contaminated "by the world" (1:27).

The word that is heard is "the perfect (*teleios*; cf. 1:4, 17) law of liberty" (1:25). While this law is "perfect" because its source is divine (cf. Ps 18:7 LXX), the prior uses of "perfect" in 1:4, 17 forge a still thicker meaning of perfection that relates the law to the congregation's moral practices. "Perfect" signifies the goal of Christian discipleship, formed in faithful reception of God's gifts (vv. 17-18) and in response to spiritual tests (vv. 3-4). A "perfect law," then, is a "word of truth" that "saves your souls." The wise response, then, is to obey such a law and live. Moreover, this phrase trades on Torah's Jubilee legislation: the "law of liberty" concerns "the year of liberty" (Lev. 25:8-24), which became important especially during the Second Temple period for fashioning a sociological model of God's coming kingdom (cf. Luke 4:16-21; Jas. 2:5). The promise of future blessing introduced in 1:12 is here repeated to link enduring temptation/trials with the wisdom of law-keeping.

The economic practices of the "glorious Lord Jesus Christ" (2:1) establish the criterion by which God measures the community's treatment of its poor (cf. 2:12-13). While the Lord's expansive title used here alerts the reader to the letter's Easter ethos, more significant is the interrogative related to his faithfulness, better translated "Do you have the faith of our Lord Jesus Christ?" This phrase recalls the similar phrase used by Paul in which "the faith of Jesus Christ" (cf. Rom 3:22; Gal 3:22) is a subjective genitive of the crucified Christ's faithfulness that secures the world's salvation from sin. Jas. 2:1 is aimed differently, to Christ's ministry to the poor in obedience to the "royal law" (v. 8) rather than to the cross.

The reception of the wisdom of quick listening is profusely illustrated by both positive and negative example. God's appraisal that "you do well if you really do the royal law" (2:8) contrasts sharply with the "senseless person" who supposes that "you do well" by merely professing orthodox faith (vv. 19-20) without a complement of works (vv. 14-17).

Besides the example of Jesus, two other biblical figures, Abraham and Rahab, are mentioned as wise exemplars of caring for the poor in their distress. Their cases are introduced by the commonsense assertion that profession does not save. For example, if the pious benediction "go in peace" is given to the hungry and naked without also feeding and clothing them, nothing redemptive happens either for the poor or for the community not on God's side (cf. 2:14-17). The believer who claims to have the faith of Jesus apart from following his example is no different from the shuddering demon who does the same (cf. vv. 18-20).

The final example combines patriarch Abraham (2:21-24) and prostitute Rahab (v. 25) to make a universally valid claim: a profession of "faith without works is dead" (v. 26). According to rabbinic tradition, Isaac's binding is Abraham's final exam. Whether he passes or fails his spiritual test secures the promises God makes regarding Israel's destiny. According to James, Abraham is befriended by God because his faith is "brought to completion by works" (v. 22).

Rahab's biblical story (Josh. 2:1-15) makes this same point by what it does and does not mention. Hardly another biblical figure offers a more impressive profession of faith than Rahab (Josh 2:8-11), yet James does not mention that. Only her hospitable and courageous actions toward "the messengers" are noted. The rhetorical effect is to impress on the reader that the wise believer understands that God befriends people on the basis of their merciful "works and not by faith alone" (2:24).

4. An Essay on the Wisdom of "Slow Speaking" (3:1-18)

The wisdom of "slow speaking" is directed at those who aspire to become teachers (3:1). The letter has already noted that even believers sometimes lack the wisdom necessary to control the inward desires that incline them toward doubt and sin (1:5-6, 7-8, 13-15). That is, "all of us make many mistakes" (3:2). This realism is deepened by the bracing awareness that God will judge believers on the basis of what they say and do (1:12; 2:12-13).

To slow down what one says is not a matter of better diction; it concerns the careful choice of words the teacher uses. The difficulty of controlling what is said is illustrated by three examples from everyday life with increasing tension. The teacher controls the tongue (= speech) much as the rider controls the bit that guides the movement of a horse (3:3) or the pilot controls the rudder to maneuver a ship through strong winds to safe harbor (vv. 4-5a). The teacher's failure to control the tongue is likened to the "small fire" (literally "spark") that can destroy a great forest (vv. 5b-6a).

James applies the problem of a teacher's careless speech with damning effect (3:6): careless speech is a "world of iniquity (that) stains the whole body" (cf. 1:27) and directs the community's destiny — its "cycle of nature" — away from God's reign toward a future "inflamed by *Gehenna*" (cf. Mark 9:45, 47; *1 Enoch* 26–27). *Gehenna* is the Hellenized form of Hinnom, the name of a valley on the south side of Jerusalem used as a garbage dump. Over time this site became an important metaphor for evil and even envisaged as a possible location for the great eschatological battle when God's good will triumph over the devil's evil (cf. Isa. 66:23-24). No doubt this is the subtext of James's use in v. 6.

The more positive application of talking the walk is framed by the practical question "Who is wise and understanding among you?" (3:13). The question alludes to the instruction of Moses for Israel to search for "wise and understanding" leaders to broker disputes that might threaten the tribal confederacy (Deut. 1:12-13). The readers of this letter, faced with their own search for congregational leaders/teachers, are guided by a sharply worded contrast between two different kinds of wisdom with very different outcomes.

The wise and understanding teacher has a skill set learned not from experience or education; rather its source is a "wisdom from above" (3:17; cf. 1:17-18). Unlike the foolish teacher, whose selfish character (cf. vv. 14, 16a) is formed by a wisdom that "does not come down from above, but is . . . devilish" (v. 15) and whose résumé chronicles "disorder and wickedness of every kind" (v. 16b), the wise and understanding teacher is formed by "the wisdom from above" and mediates "a harvest of righteousness sown in peace" (v. 18).

The catalogue of virtues in v. 17, which characterizes the peacemaking speech of the wise and understanding teacher, has many parallels in antiquity. Even though consisting of universally upheld virtues, such lists are carefully fitted into their writings to perform particular roles for their audiences. The Pauline letters, for example, include similar lists of virtues that characterize those in Christ (e.g., Gal. 5:22-23). Central to Pauline anthropology is the profile of a new creature whose existence is the effect of divine grace made possible by the faithfulness of Christ and mediated by his life-giving Spirit. The anthropology of James assumes that believers must take responsibility for their destiny with God by making wise choices that resist doubt or their desire for worldly evils.

5. An Essay on the Wisdom of "Slowing Anger" (4:1–5:6)

Anger toward others stems from an inward desire for material pleasure and threatens the community's internal life (4:1-3). This text uses images of strife, both military — "conflicts" and "war" — and interpersonal — "disputes" and "murder" — to characterize its seriousness. The experience of being poor can provoke the impulse to covet the worldly goods of others (vv. 4-5), which tests the believer's friendship with a God who resists the arrogant and exalts the pious poor (vv. 6-12; cf. 2:5). To slow down anger requires one to resist "friendship with the world" (4:4; cf. 1:27; 3:6) and submit to God. James follows rabbinic teaching that human nature consists of two competing "spirits" or *yeṣārîm* — one inclined toward evil, the other toward good: to engage the one is to resist the other (4:7).

In response to this spiritual reality, v. 5 is better translated to pose a pair of rhetorical questions that expect a negative answer: "Or do you think Scripture says foolish things? Does the spirit that God made to dwell within us incline us intensely toward envy?" The wisdom of Scripture rather discloses that the promise of divine exaltation (vv. 6. 10) is rather aimed at a congregation that worships God by purifying its heart (vv. 7-9). The sanctified sinner no longer covets the goods of others but is a doer of God's law (vv. 11-12), which forbids coveting one's neighbor's possessions.

The opening invocative "Come now" (4:13a; 5:1a) links together two examples of friendship with the world to illustrate how a passion for things can subvert the believer's devotion to God and relations with others. The first example is the arrogant merchant (4:13-17) whose single-minded pursuit of financial profit takes him "to such and such a town" to "do business" (rather than God's law; cf. v. 15) and "make money" (rather than receive God's grace; cf. v. 6). The shift of pronoun to "you" (v. 14) suggests that this merchant typifies the kind of arrogance opposed by God (v. 6). Such people are functional atheists who plan their lives as though God does not exist (cf. vv. 14, 16) instead of making choices that please God (cf. vv. 15, 17).

The related illustration is of the rich farmer whose practices embody the foolishness of those who choose friendship with the world rather than with God and so "wail for the miseries that are coming" (5:1). The choice against God rests on two catastrophic mistakes. The first is a misappraisal of the long-term worth of material goods: "riches rot . . . clothes are moth-eaten . . . gold and silver rust" (5:2-3; cf. Matt. 6:19-21). The second is a faulty assessment of theodicy and God's sense of justice: such a person's luxurious lifestyle, purchased at the expense of mistreated and underpaid workers, is the hard evidence of guilt that will be used in the heavenly court convened by "the Lord of hosts" (v. 4). In a vivid reminder of the coming "great reversal," their death sentence will be carried out in "the last days" (v. 3) as a "day of slaughter" (v. 5).

The antecedent of James's curious reference to the murder of a single "righteous one" in 5:6 is much debated. In Christian tradition, the phrase fulfills the promise of the Isaianic servant, whose suffering on behalf of the world is marked out by his "righteousness" before God (Isa. 53:11; cf. Luke 23:47). In a letter that emphasizes God's vindication of the pious poor and indictment of the rich (cf. Jas. 1:9-11; 2:2-7; 4:4-6), however, the metaphor more likely functions here as a metonymy for poor laborers who are starving for lack of food because of either neglect (especially during famine) or juridical injustice (cf. 2:6-7). If the intended readers are believers whose marginal existence is characterized by these kinds of financial trials, then they might rightly hope — and so make their choices — for a future of reversed fortune, when the last will be first and the first last.

6. The Future of the Wise Community (5:7-20)

The letter's conclusion recalls important catchwords from its opening to form an inclusio that frames the three wisdom essays between. But this repetition more than repeats what has already been written. It supplies the principal motivation for following the letter's exhortation to make wise choices when faith is tested by tribulation: the coming triumph of the Lord is near (5:7-9). God's epic battle against and eventual victory over the evil forces that provoke human suffering is among Scripture's principal responses to the problem of suffering. The farmer's experience of waiting for "the early and the late rains" (v. 7) to water the crops before harvest exemplifies the kind of intelligent patience that awaits God's ultimate victory. This exhortation is made more urgent by the pointed assertion that the Lord's *parousia* is imminent (v. 8): "see, the Judge is standing at the doors" (v. 9).

The exhortation not to engage in "grumbling against one another so that you may not be judged" (v. 9) recalls the story of Job (v. 11), who endured to the end despite his complaining friends. James places him among the prophets who suffered with patient confidence when they "spoke in the name of the Lord" (v. 10; cf. Luke 11:47-54). The background for this exemplary Job is the LXX, followed by the *Testament of Job*, which unlike his portrait in the Hebrew Bible links his famous patience with his merciful treatment of the poor and that to his eventual restoration by a "compassionate and merciful" God (*Testament* 51–53; cf. Jas. 1:26–2:26). To care for the poor without complaint is to deal with life wisely.

This exhortation for patience is complemented by another to pray for healing (5:13-16a). Patience and prayerfulness are the twin dispositions of an apocalyptic worldview, which views Christian existence before the

Lord's arrival through the lens of suffering and powerlessness. The opening imperative to pray for wisdom (cf. 1:5-6), which when "implanted" and acted on is able to "save the soul" (1:21), is here recast as "the prayer of faith will save the sick" (5:15). The elders are summoned because they "implant" the saving word in the community's life and so now lead in a liturgy of healing that "prays over (the sick)" and "anoints them with oil" (v. 14). The olive oil administrated "in the name of the Lord" can be understood as either medicinal or, more likely in a worship practice, invocative of the powerful presence of the risen Lord who "will raise them up" (v. 15; cf. Mark 6:13; 9:38; Acts 3:6, 16) — whether at the end of the age or in physical healing is uncertain (cf. Acts 3:19-21). The logical connection between the healing of the sick and the forgiving of the sinner is thematic of the gospel tradition (vv. 15b-16a; cf. Matt. 6:12).

The earlier uses of "righteous/-ness" in James suggest that the "prayer of the righteous" (5:16) is "powerful and effective" because it coheres with God's pattern of salvation (cf. 2:23-24; 3:18). According to Jewish and Jesus traditions, the prophetic exemplar of effective prayer is Elijah (5:16b-18), whose words on Mt. Carmel produced rain because they aligned with God's words for Israel (cf. 1 Kings 18; Sir. 48:1-11; Luke 4:25). That is, prayer offered by the righteous for healing or forgiveness is a practice of wisdom because it produces "powerful and effective" results.

The final verses of James (5:19-20) form a benediction that enlists readers for a mission to "save the sinner's soul from death" (cf. 1:21). These sinners are lapsed believers who have "wandered from the truth" of God's word (cf. 1:18, 21). Without this sacred compass, doubt and inward desire "give birth to sin" and sin to death (1:14-15). The practice of the wisdom of James, then, concludes on these final words of hope: the repentance and restoration of those believers who have failed their test of faith is mediated by the community made wise for salvation by the instruction of this letter (cf. 2 Tim. 3:15).

Theology

1. The Creator God

The God disclosed by James is the one and only true God (2:19), the Creator of all things who has made every person in God's own likeness (3:9; cf.

1:17-18). God is therefore personal, to whom the believer turns when lacking in wisdom needed to pass daily spiritual tests (1:5). God is heavenly Father (1:17, 27; 3:9), from whom the wise humbly receive (1:21) good and perfect gifts (v. 17) which are generously provided by God, in every case (v. 17) and without discrimination (v. 5). Therefore, this generous God sends forth the "word of truth" to reveal the Creator's perfect plan of salvation in order to guide redeemed humanity into the age to come (v. 18), which is a restored creation, made complete, perfect, and lacking in nothing (v. 4).

In particular, God has chosen those out of this broken and corrupted world who are its last, least, lost, and lame to be enriched by their love for God (2:5): as Scripture teaches, "God gives grace to the humble" (4:6b). Thus, not only are the sick healed and the sinners forgiven by the Lord in the present age (5:14-16), their worship of God (v. 13) will be vindicated at God's coming triumph, when those who oppress them will be destroyed (vv. 5-6) and their own material fortunes will be reversed (1:9-11). Indeed, God promises future blessing, "the crown of life," to all those who love God (v. 12).

To love God is to do God's will, for life is granted to those who do God's will (4:15). In that God is also our Judge (4:11-12; 5:9), with the authority to save and destroy (4:12), humanity is obliged to do God's will. A concrete record of God's will is transmitted by the gift of the biblical Torah, which is the rule of faith for the faith community (2:8-13). God will save those who obey the law (1:25; 2:13) and will destroy those who live foolishly and disobey the law of God. As Scripture also teaches, "God resists the arrogant" (4:6a). The apocalypse of God's triumph over God's enemies (the deceived, the slanderous teacher, the arrogant rich, the impatient complainer, the sinner and apostate) is imminent (5:7-8), at which moment creation will be purified and restored (1:4; cf. 5:17-18), the reign of God will be secured on earth (2:5), and blessing will be dispensed to all those who evince by their wise responses to their spiritual tests a robust love for God (1:12; 2:5), such as Abraham, who is called a "friend of God" (2:23).

2. Christ Jesus

God sends forth "the word of truth" into the world (1:17-18) to fulfill the promise of blessing (v. 12) and to save God's people (v. 21) from the result of their deception and sin (vv. 13-16), which is death (5:19-20). This "word" from God reveals the plan and purposes of God's promised salvation (1:18) and as such is a "good and perfect gift" (v. 17). The word comes down from heaven as a revelation of divine wisdom (1:5; 3:17) and is especially apropos for believers during a season of spiritual testing (1:2-3). As with every article of divine revelation, this word of divine wisdom is trustworthy (v. 18) and effective (v. 21) in enabling people to pass the spiritual test because it accords with God's promise and plan of salvation (v. 18; cf. v. 12). As such, the way of wisdom is a "word on target" pointing humanity toward the complete restoration of human existence so that it lacks nothing (v. 4). Toward this end, then, the word is the instrument by which God creates an eschatological community which will receive God's promised blessing in the age to come (v. 18; cf. v. 12; 2:5).

This heavenly word is "implanted" within the faith community (1:21) by the word of its faithful teachers (3:1), who are "wise and understanding" (v. 13). Only within this community of the wise is the divine word "received" by believers who are both "receptive" to it (1:21; 5:12) and "pure" (i.e., spiritually mature; 1:21; cf. v. 27). They promptly do what the word requires (vv. 22-24) and are saved as a result (v. 21), ultimately receiving the blessing promised to those who love God (1:12, 25; 3:18).

The subject matter of the word is summarized in 1:19 as being "quick to hear" (i.e., to obey the biblical Torah; cf. 1:22–2:26), "slow to speak" (i.e., using "purifying" language toward and about others; cf. 3:1-18), and "slow to anger" (i.e., resisting one's innate passion for pleasure; cf. 4:1–5:6). To refuse this wisdom because of duplicity (1:6-8; 3:9-12) or deception (1:16, 22), and then to substitute a false wisdom (3:15), will only result in spiritual failure and social chaos (v. 16), personal evil (1:13-15), and ultimately death (5:19; 1:15). On the other hand, to apply divine wisdom to our spiritual tests results in life (1:12; 3:18; 4:15; 5:20). Of this the community's sacred tradition supplies many notable exemplars such as Jesus (2:1), Abraham (vv. 21-24), Rahab (v. 25), Job (5:9-11), and Elijah (vv. 16b-18).

In particular, Jesus received divine approval as the "glorious Lord Jesus Christ" (2:1) because of his obedience to the "royal law" (v. 8): he loved his poor neighbors, who are the chosen of God (v. 5), and resisted discrimination by the rich (vv. 1-4). Unlike the decisive "faith(fulness) of Jesus Christ" in Pauline preaching (Rom. 3:22; Gal. 2:20; 3:22), which formulates Christ's cooperation with God in forgiving those who trust in them for salvation, this same phrase presents Jesus to the community as moral exemplar to follow. Jesus "did well" and so gained God's approval (cf. 2:8), as also did Abraham (vv. 21-24) and Rahab (v. 25). Their obedience to God's rule of love is exemplary of an observed wisdom that is quick to do (rather than merely memorize) "the perfect law of liberty" (1:22-25; cf. 2:12), which heralds the "royal (or kingly) law" (2:8) of God's coming kingdom (v. 5). In this light, the realization of God's promised blessing (1:25) in the coming kingdom extends to all those who "hold to the faith of our glorious Lord Jesus Christ" (2:1) by caring for the marginal poor and resisting worldly evils (1:27).

3. The Community of the Spirit

The community of the wise is created anew by this "word of truth" (1:18). According to God's will, the community is constituted by the "poor of the world" who are chosen to be "rich in faith" (2:5); and those pious poor who persist in their love for God will ultimately be blessed (1:12) and vindicated (5:4-6) at the coming triumph of God's reign (2:5; 5:7-11).

Members of this congregation are displaced within the world order (1:1) and face many trials as a result (v. 2). A life of constant hardship and heartbreak, perhaps the result of their poverty and displacement, tests their love for God (v. 3). Indeed, some of the members have failed their test and have "wandered from the truth" in sin and error; and the prospect of their eternal life is imperiled (5:19-20).

The trials that threaten the community's relationship with God come from a variety of places (1:2). The principal source is within each person, where a spiritual struggle rages. The evil "spirit of envy" (4:5), fashioned by the Creator but directed by the evil one (v. 7), inclines even the believer toward "friendship with the world" and hostility toward the purposes of God (v. 4). Interpersonal strife, leading even to murder, results from an inward "passion for pleasure" (vv. 1-2), which corrupts the petitioner's address to God (v. 3) and understanding of God's will (vv. 13-17). As such, the believer's desires for an easy life or vile thoughts of a rival give birth to sin and so death (1:14-15; 3:14-16) rather than to wisdom and life (3:17-18).

Without spiritual maturity, the community also falls prey to "deception" about the nature of a "true and approved religion" (1:16, 22, 26; cf. v. 27) rooted in a faulty understanding of God and of God's requirements for God's people. Thus, for example, a congregation may come to believe that God approves of religious orthodoxy (2:19; cf. v. 8) that is merely confessed but never embodied (1:26; 2:14-17). But the requirements of God's covenant partner are more morally demanding and active than this (2:21-26).

Clearly, the congregation is the object of hostile forces outside itself. Not only are there rich and powerful outsiders who undermine the community's faith (2:6-7) in order to exploit poor members for their own advantage (2:2-4; 5:1-6), the congregation is "surrounded" by a "world," which is God's enemy (4:4). Living in an anti-God society leads naturally to accommodation of its "impurity" which threatens to contaminate the congregation's life together (1:27), specifically its caring treatment of the poor, whom friends of the "world" neglect and exploit (2:2-4, 6-7; 5:3-6); its members' language about one another (3:6); and the resigned contentment with one's lot in life (4:4-6, 14-15) that is necessary to resist a concern for mammon and serve the interests of God (vv. 7-10).

Whether besieged by the forces of evil within the individual believer or outside the believing community, the exhortation is the same: know God's spiritual/inward and social/external requirements, and be wise in response to spiritual testing. Christian formation is directed by "wise and understanding" teachers (3:13; see "elders" in 5:14), by whom the revelatory word is "implanted" and from whom it is humbly "received" (1:21). These leaders are summoned by the sick to administer healing "prayer in faith" (5:15) in expectation of God's imminent healing of all creation (1:4) in accordance with the Creator's ultimate purposes (v. 18).

The sources for the idea of wisdom in James remain contested among scholars. However, they clearly include the *topoi* and rhetorical patterns of Hellenistic moral culture.[8] In keeping with this intellectual tradition, the wisdom that guides the faith community through its spiritual testing is applied to an internal moral world which calls the believer to accountability for wise or foolish actions. Yet, the overarching conception of this "way of wisdom" remains largely biblical. Thus, with Scripture, James pairs wisdom with Torah (1:22-25; 2:8-10): doing the law of God (essentially moral rather than cultic) is wise because it results not only in purity but in God's blessing for the coming age. The test of faith, then, is an observed wisdom, exemplified by Jesus and Job, Abraham and Rahab. It is a way of wisdom that fairly summarizes the biblical proverbs to love the poor neighbor (2:1-

---

8. See, e.g., D. F. Watson, "James 2 in Light of Greco-Roman Schemes of Argumentation," *NTS* 39 (1993), pp. 94-121.

8), to speak well of others (3:17), and to resist coveting worldly pleasures that the mature believer can ill afford (4:1-5).

The character of this community for James is unrelated to its cultural or cultic identity as Jewish believers. Rather, the theological crisis is whether their poverty and powerlessness and the spiritual test they naturally provoke, incline them toward a more pious devotion to God (1:2-3). The status of their election (2:5) and their historic relationship to Abraham (vv. 21-24) are not primarily ethnic but sociological and moral in emphasis: these believers are the marginal heirs of Abraham's promise (1:12; 2:5) and friends of God (2:23) rather than of the world (4:4) because they perform merciful works like those of exemplary Abraham (2:24). In this sense, the sort of Christianity that is approved by God is an ethical religion: its witness to God is measured by the purity of collective and personal life (1:27; 2:14-26). That is, God's eschatological requirement is for an embodied wisdom that commends the community characterized by its merciful treatment of its own poor (1:22–2:26), the purity of speech among its word-brokers (3:1-18), and the denial of worldly affections among its aspiring middle class (4:1–5:6).

4. Christian Discipleship

The community addressed by James is in a "Diaspora" — a place of dislocation where its marginal existence occasions a testing of its faithfulness to the ways of God. James addresses immature believers in particular who are especially vulnerable to the vicissitudes of a difficult life. They must obey this "word of truth" — heavenly wisdom — and practice "pure and undefiled" behavior as the public mark of friendship with God.

Rather than a code of right conduct that demands rigorous compliance, the most important element of the moral universe shaped by James consists primarily of congregational purity practices. While the interior life of the individual believer is surely an important feature of this same moral universe, the community must resist the moral pollutants of the surrounding "world" (or anti-God) order (1:26) and care for the needy neighbor in accordance with God's "perfect law of liberty" (v. 27; cf. 2:1-13). There is a sense in which the rest of the composition articulates more fully what practices a "pure and undefiled" congregation performs as acceptable to God (cf. 2:24).

We note four purity practices mentioned in James that are consistent with the idealized portrait of the church in Acts: 1) The legacy of the Jewish piety personified by legendary James is articulated in the letter as a piety of poverty and powerlessness, of which the Lord Jesus himself is exemplary (2:1) and which may occasion suffering that tests the community's devotion to God. In fact, according to James the hallmark of religious purity is protecting and caring for the poor (1:27; 2:2-7) in keeping with Torah's stipulation (2:8; cf. 1:25). This practice of a community of goods reflects an asceticism — a world-denying ethos — that has replaced the world's preoccupation for material goods with a heartfelt devotion to God (4:1–5:6; cf. 1 John 2:15-17). 2) The concern of a community of goods for a radical social purity extends also to speech (3:17) as a principal element of good human relations, which identifies a collective interest in healthy speech patterns as a fundamental moral property of Christian discipleship (cf. 1 Pet. 3:13-17; 2 Pet. 2:3; 1 John 3:18; 3 John 10). 3) The literary inclusio of James (1:1 and 5:19-20) delineates a kind of spiritual Diaspora that frames another practice of the community's ethos: a commitment to the practice of rescuing wayward believers from theological and moral error not only to preserve doctrinal purity but also to insure their end-time salvation (cf. 2 Peter 2; Jude 17–25). 4) The virtue of hospitality especially to the poor and powerless members of one's own congregation (Jas. 1:27; 2:14-17) introduces a theme that is central to the CE discourse on Christian life (cf. Jas. 2:14-17; 1 Pet. 1:22; 4:9-11; 1 John 3:17-20a; 2 John 9-11; 3 John 5-8). In fact, hospitality toward other believers is an effective means for maintaining a congregation's solidarity against external threats and is also the concrete demonstration of its separation from the world order (cf. Jas. 1:27).

5. Consummation in a New Creation

The community's hope is concentrated by the event that concludes the story: the coming triumph of the Lord at the end of this age (5:7-9). At this climactic and cosmic "any moment," the eschatological community will be confirmed and vindicated, even as their enemies are judged and destroyed (vv. 4-6), for God will judge the foolish and bless the wise (1:12; 2:12-13; 4:11-12; 5:5-11).

On this apocalypse of God's salvation all NT witnesses substantially agree. All assent that divine judgment and blessing are finally creational activities that bring about the renewal of God's way of ordering all creatures (1:4, 18; 3:18; 5:17-18). All agree with James that the Lord's *parousia* is imminent and that the time for repentance is short because the day of judgment is close at hand (5:7-9, 19-20).

The Catholic Epistles of Peter

Introduction

When it comes to identifying key characters in the gospel story apart from the Lord himself, pride of place is typically given to the apostle Peter. Celebrated by ancient Christians as one of "the two most glorious apostles" (the other being Paul, of course),[1] Simon Peter was remembered as the chief of the apostles, the "rock" upon whom the church would be built, and a faithful early martyr for Christ.[2] Despite the weight of his prominence in Christian memory and tradition, however, the church received only two relatively short letters passed down in his name (and positioned them after the letter of James in the CE collection). Though both Petrine letters were ultimately canonized and placed side-by-side in the corpus, they are in many ways strikingly different from each other. The intensity of embrace for each has differed as a result, in the ancient world as well as our own.

While 1 Peter was widely known and loved by early Christians, 2 Peter floundered in obscurity and struggled to find its place among the canonical Scriptures. Both letters have had their traditional authorship ques-

---

1. The quotation is from Irenaeus, *Adv. Haer.* 3.3.2.

2. Numerous studies of the life and character of Peter have been produced. See, e.g., O. Cullmann, *Peter: Apostle, Disciple, Martyr* (London: SMC, 1953); R. E. Brown, K. P. Donfried, and J. Reumann, eds., *Peter in the New Testament* (Minneapolis: Augsburg Fortress, 1973); F. Lapham, *Peter: The Myth, the Man, and the Writings* (JSNTSS 239, Sheffield: Sheffield Academic, 2003); M. Hengel, *Saint Peter, the Underestimated Apostle* (Grand Rapids: Eerdmans, 2010).

tioned. The issues raised for 1 Peter are well-known and rehearsed in all the commentaries:[3] chief among them is the fact that the letter is written in a form of Greek considered to be far too elegant for that of an untrained Galilean fisherman (see Acts 4:13),[4] and the content of the letter often appears to be dependent on earlier traditions of the Greek church (and the traditions of Pauline literature in particular). Further, ancient Christianity remembered Peter's martyrdom as occurring sometime in the middle-60s, but the letter is addressed to Christian churches spread over the whole of Asia Minor, a situation deemed highly unlikely prior to the last quarter of the first century. Indeed, the author claims to be writing from "Babylon" (5:13), a known Christian cipher for the city of Rome (also in Revelation and 1 Clem.), but evidence for identifying Rome by this name can only be found after the destruction of the Jerusalem temple in 70 (and the historical parallel with the first exile truly works only if the temple has been destroyed). Despite this evidence, a number of recent scholars have produced strong counterarguments and continue to support authorship by Peter, most often by means of an amanuensis.[5]

2 Peter, by contrast, has very few contemporary advocates for its traditional authorship.[6] Even ancient authors did not hesitate to note the differences between the two letters, and several made sure their concerns about 2 Peter were recorded for posterity (see below, under "Reception of 2 Peter"). The language issues raised for 1 Peter are equally applicable here (how could a simple fisherman write so well?) and made even more troubling by the fact that an analysis of the linguistic differences makes it clear that the two letters could not have been written by the same person. The evidence against 2 Peter being authored by the historical Peter is often considered conclusive by appeal to its testamentary genre and its apparent knowledge of other authoritative apostolic letters (see below, under "Composition of 2 Peter").

---

3. See P. Achtemeier, 1 Peter (HC; Minneapolis: Fortress, 1996), pp. 1-43 for a thorough and helpful review of the evidence.

4. But see K. Jobes, 1 Peter (BECNT; Grand Rapids: Baker Academic, 2005), pp. 6-8 and 325-38, who offers an extensive argument, against the majority opinion, that the author was not a native Greek speaker.

5. E.g., P. H. Davids, The First Epistle of Peter (NICNT; Grand Rapids: Eerdmans, 1990) p. 10; I. H. Marshall, 1 Peter (IVPNTC; Downers Grove: InterVarsity, 1991), p. 20; R. A. Gundry, A Survey of the New Testament (4th ed.; Grand Rapids: Zondervan, 2003), p. 480.

6. The best review of the authorship issues for 2 Peter remains that of R. Bauckham, Jude, 2 Peter (WBC 50; Waco: Word, 1983), pp. 131-62.

Given the differences between the two letters, their uneven history of canonical reception, and modernity's myopic focus on the prehistory of the text, it is no wonder that contemporary critical scholarship sees little reason to read the two letters as two parts of a single correspondence. Indeed, most twentieth-century studies focused so narrowly on 1 Peter's apparent use of Pauline traditions that the letter was effectively approached as a somewhat redundant *2 Paul*. Happily this state of affairs has changed in the last twenty-five years, and the letter once called an "exegetical step-child"[7] now attracts significant scholarly interest as a text to be studied in its own right. By contrast, the critical consensus that 2 Peter is dependent on the earlier letter of Jude continues to lead most scholars to treat it not as the second letter of Peter, but as *2 Jude*. In the end, both letters are routinely pulled out of canonical context and interpreted against other backdrops than the one provided by their location among the CE.

1. The Canonical Peter

As we have said elsewhere, the modern quest to authenticate ancient authorship with anything approaching certainty obviously eludes us; indeed, it appears to have turned into a dead-end debate, with scholars on opposite sides of the theological spectrum simply rehearsing evidence that has been known for at least a generation. A canonical approach to the letters, by contrast, will turn attention away from reconstructing the historical point of a text's composition to consider instead a series of interests surrounding the point of a text's canonization, that moment when it was first taken up as Scripture useful for the formation of the faithful. Chief among these interests is the need to keep in mind the canonical portrait of the apostle as the frame through which these letters were received and interpreted by the ancient canonizing community.

As we take time now to construct this portrait, it must be recalled that this is not done in the service of historical ends, culling evidence from among these ancient texts in an attempt to verify or deny the authenticity of their authorship or the integrity of their scriptural authority. Canonically speaking, we are relatively disinterested in questions about the *his-*

---

7. So J. H. Elliott, "The Rehabilitation of an Exegetical Step-Child: 1 Peter in Recent Research," *JBL* 95 (1976), pp. 243-54.

torical Peter. We *are* interested in how Scripture itself prepares readers to read the letters of Peter, so to this end we begin the construction of a *canonical* Peter as an interpretive frame to render a fully biblical reception of Peter's apostolic message.

Peter in the Gospels. The tone for the entire NT is set by the weight of Peter's presence in the Synoptic tradition, which portrays Simon Peter as the preeminent disciple in terms of both calling (Matt. 4:18-22; Mark 1:16-20; Luke 5:1-11) and rank (Matt. 10:2; Mark 3:16; Luke 6:14). Many aspects of this priority can and should be addressed here. First and foremost is Peter's role as the *representative disciple* of Christ Jesus, both in leadership and example.

As an *example of discipleship* it is noteworthy that Peter is second only to Jesus as the acting subject in the Gospel pericopes; if anyone besides Jesus is speaking or acting in the narrative, it is most frequently Peter. From the heights of his faithfulness (e.g., Matt. 14:28-29) to the murky depths of his misunderstanding (e.g., Mark 8:32b-33; John 13:6-9) and disloyalty (e.g., Luke 22:54-62; John 18:15-18, 25-27), Peter is cast in the gospel story as a fully human disciple and leader who is truly "one of us" in his struggle to follow the Lord. In terms of *leadership,* his name can "stand for" the disciples as a whole (e.g., Matt. 26:40; Mark 16:7; Luke 9:32), and he is frequently portrayed as the spokesman for the group, voicing the questions and confessions of the entire apostolic band (e.g., Matt. 17:24; 26:35; Mark 8:29; Luke 18:28). This preeminence is solidified in the tradition preserved by Matthew that Jesus gave him the name Peter, saying "I tell you, you are Peter *(Petros),* and on this rock *(petra)* I will build my church."

But Peter's leadership, though *preeminent,* is in no way *solitary.* He may be "the rock" on which the church is built, but the authority that position affords him (Matt. 16:19) is in fact conferred on the church as a whole (Matt. 18:18-20). His authority in the Synoptics is repeatedly framed by his close relationship with the brothers James and John of Zebedee, who are together depicted as having distinctive insight into both the majestic power (Matt. 17:1; Mark 5:37; 9:2; Luke 8:51; 9:28) and the wretched suffering (Mark 14:33) of the earthly Jesus. The Gospel according to John, by contrast, knows of no disciples named "James" or "John," but ecclesial tradition is surely correct in associating the "beloved disciple" of that Gospel with the apostle John. Though that character is frequently depicted as being in a somewhat superior position in relation to Peter (13:23; 19:26-27; 20:1-10; 21:7), we find nevertheless that these two men more than any other are portrayed as closely associated in apostolic authority (13:23-24; 21:7, 20-23).

Peter in Acts and the non-Petrine Letters. The Gospel of John's focus on Peter and John prepares the way for Acts, which similarly reduces the Synoptic triad "Peter, James, and John" to simply "Peter and John." These two leaders walk in solidarity throughout the opening chapters of the book (1:13; 3:1-4, 11; 4:13, 19; 8:14), speaking and acting as one in heading the mission of the earliest church in Jerusalem. Nevertheless, between the two of them Peter remains the primary apostolic spokesperson, as evidenced especially by several speeches performed at key turning points in the narrative (Acts 2:14-42; 3:11-26; 10:34-43; 15:7-11).

Both characters fade out of the story halfway through Acts to allow Paul to take center stage, but before Peter departs from the narrative Luke goes out of his way to reveal that leadership in the Jerusalem church has been transferred to James the Lord's brother (Acts 12:17; 15:12-21). Thus, the whole picture of leadership in Jerusalem painted by Acts is that of an authoritative triumvirate of Peter, John, and James the Lord's brother. While James appears to act as bishop of the Jerusalem church, it is noteworthy that Peter is frequently cast as an ambassador of Jerusalem to churches abroad to check in on them and report what he finds to those in the mother church at home (see 8:14-25; 9:32–11:2; 12:19; 15:7).

This picture of Peter as both leader and collaborator is confirmed when we turn to the letters of Paul. On the one hand, his priority is clearly sustained. After Paul's calling by God, the first apostolic authority he sought out was "Cephas" (Gal. 1:18, with Paul using the Aramaic name translated in Greek to "Petros"). When Paul recounts the resurrection appearances of the Lord, he goes out of his way to note that the Lord appeared first to Peter, and then to the twelve (1 Cor. 15:5). When he describes the mission to Jews already in place when he began his ministry to Gentiles, he places Peter at its head (Gal. 2:7). In all this, we see that Peter, in effect, "stands for" the disciples of Jesus in a representative fashion.

Despite this clear authority, Peter is nevertheless described as an apostolic leader among leaders, based in Jerusalem as one of three "Pillars" of that church (Gal. 1:18–2:10, especially 2:9) but ministering abroad in places like Corinth (with Paul and Apollos, 1 Cor. 1:12) and Antioch (with Paul,

Gal. 2:11). Thus, Peter inhabits a "middle way" between the Jewish and Gentile missions; in his speeches and his actions he is revealed to be a spirit-filled interpreter of Israel's Scriptures who preaches the gospel to both Jew and Greek alike. As the conflict recounted in Gal. 2:11-14 indicates, this via media was a difficult road for Peter to maneuver.

The Canonical Portrait and 1-2 Peter. So the canonical portrait of Peter beyond his letters presents him as an example of discipleship and the figurative leader of the apostolic band who nonetheless stands alongside other apostolic leaders in ministry. The letters uphold and extend this canonical portrait in a number of fascinating ways. Some of these will be explored below, and others will be raised in the commentary.

As an *example* of discipleship, we note in the letters that the renowned authoritative leader (1 Pet. 1:1; 5:1; 2 Pet. 1:12-15, 16-18; 3:1-2) is nevertheless a fellow believer (1 Pet. 1:3; 4:17; 2 Pet. 1:1, 3-4) participating in the exile of faith (1 Pet. 2:11; 5:13) who "shares" with all believers "in the glory about to be revealed" (1 Pet. 5:1). The Gospel of John ends with Jesus beseeching Peter to "feed my lambs" and "tend my sheep" (John 21:15-17), and the letters depict Peter tending his flock and calling others to do the same (1 Pet. 5:2). The Gospel of Luke has Jesus telling Peter "when once you have turned back, strengthen your brothers" (22:32b), and thus the letters of Peter depict him pursuing the task of strengthening suffering fellow believers. This latter point is particularly striking in canonical perspective, for the same Peter who resisted Jesus' proclamation of the cross (Matt. 16:21-23; Mark 8:31-33) and denied Jesus at the point of his persecution (Matt. 26:69-75 and parallels) went on to receive spiritual empowerment that enabled him to witness faithfully when he suffered persecution himself (Acts 4:1-22; 5:17-32). Indeed, by the power of the Spirit he was delivered from persecution in order to continue his proclamation of Christ (Acts 12:1-18). On the basis of these trials (cf. 1 Pet. 1:6-7; 5:1) Peter is now able through his letters to offer believers one of the most compelling theologies of Christian suffering to be found in all Scripture.

In terms of *leadership,* we have noted that Peter "stands for" the disciples of Jesus in a representative fashion. It is only appropriate that this leader of the apostles offers in his letters authoritative witness to the full range of Christian orthodoxy as handed down by the earliest witnesses to Christ. We are not surprised, therefore, when we find in his letters as thorough a rendering of the apostolic Rule of Faith as can be found anywhere in the NT.[8] Here the first person of the Trinity is named both "Father" (1 Pet. 1:2-3; 2 Pet. 1:17) and "Creator" (1 Pet. 4:19; 2 Pet. 3:5). Christ's identity as Son of God (1 Pet. 1:3; 2 Pet. 1:17) is proclaimed, along with his death (1 Pet. 1:19; 3:18), descent to the dead (4:6), resurrection (3:18-21), ascent into heaven to sit at the right hand of the Father (v. 22), and eventual return (1 Pet. 1:7, 13; 2 Pet. 1:16; 3:10) to judge the living and the dead (1 Pet. 4:5; 2 Pet. 2:9; 3:7). The Spirit who proceeds from God (1 Pet. 1:12) is identified as the one who has spoken through the prophets (1 Pet. 1:10-12; 2 Pet. 1:20-21) and the one who gives life (1 Pet. 3:18) through the resurrection of the dead (v. 21) and the forgiveness of sins (v. 18).

Note that this robust presentation of the whole Rule of Faith is "thickened" by the presence of *both* letters. This intended function of the Petrine epistles is pressed home in 2 Peter's persistent concern with *memory*. The letter is written "to remind" (see 1:12-15) and clearly seeks to bind itself to 1 Peter:

> This is now, beloved, the *second letter* I am writing to you. *In them* I am trying to arouse your sincere intention by reminding you that you should remember the words spoken in the past by the holy prophets and the commandment of our Lord and Savior Jesus Christ spoken through your apostles. (2 Pet. 3:1-2)

The very real differences between 1 and 2 Peter may indeed be viewed as problematic on purely historical grounds, but from a canonical perspective the differences serve to strengthen and extend the NT witness to Peter's legacy as chief of the apostles.[9]

Peter's speeches in Acts also prepare the way for our reception of the letters. For instance, 1 Peter is addressed to believers in five Roman provinces of Asia Minor — "Pontus, Galatia, Cappadocia, Asia, and Bithynia" (1:1). The only other place in the NT where some of these same regional names appear grouped together is Acts 2:5-11, where we find "devout Jews

---

8. Indeed, "nowhere in the New Testament are so many components of the later creeds . . . brought together in so close a space as 1 Peter." P. Feldmeier, *The First Letter of Peter: A Commentary on the Greek Text* (Waco: Baylor University Press, 2008), pp. 44-45.

9. So R. W. Wall, "The Canonical Function of 2 Peter," *BibInt* 9 (2001), p. 67: "the biblical canon puts these two writings together, even though they address different theological crises by different theological conceptions, so that these two integral and complementary parts may complete a fully biblical Petrine witness to the Christian gospel."

from every nation under heaven" gathered in Jerusalem to celebrate Pentecost, some of who had come from "Cappadocia, Pontus, and Asia" (2:9). These Diaspora Jews become witnesses to the outpouring of the Holy Spirit on believers and hear the first public proclamation of the apostolic message as proclaimed by Peter (2:14-36). Some scholars have attempted to bolster the argument for Peter's authorship of 1 Peter by comparing the vocabulary and themes of the letter with Peter's speeches in Acts.[10] Though these attempts have proven largely unsuccessful on *historical* grounds, from a canonical perspective these Petrine speeches can be seen to form a *literary* backdrop for our reception of Peter's letters.[11]

Apart from the many points of thematic and lexical contact between the two texts, what emerges most clearly in the Acts narrative is the sense that Peter's apostolic authority is uniquely manifested in his capacity to serve as a Spirit-filled interpreter of Israel's Scriptures (see Acts 2:14-21, 25-28, 30, 31, 34-35; 3:21-23, 24-25). This spiritual competence is equally evident in his letters, both of which are rich with appeals to the OT. In fact, "only in Hebrews and the Apocalypse do we find a comparable density of Old Testament citations and allusions" to that of 1 Peter, which quotes mostly from Isaiah, Psalms, and Proverbs.[12] Though 2 Peter does not cite the OT as frequently, it does so consistently and with a particular emphasis on the value of OT *narrative* as a trustworthy guide to life with God in the present (e.g., 2:4-10).

Finally, the canonical portrayal of Peter as a *partner in leadership* is likewise maintained in his letters. He presents himself as an elder among elders (1 Pet. 5:1-2). His teaching stands in agreement with that of "our beloved brother Paul" (2 Pet. 3:15b-16), and his intention to leave behind a testament of his own particular witness (1:12-15) is grounded in the collective witness of his fellow apostles: "*we did not* follow cleverly devised myths when we made known to you the power and coming of our Lord Jesus Christ, but *we had been eyewitnesses* of his majesty. . . . *We ourselves* heard this voice . . . while *we were with him* on the holy mountain" (vv. 16-18). This collaborative presenta-

---

10. See, e.g., E. G. Selwyn, *The First Epistle of St. Peter* (London: Macmillan, 1947), pp. 33-36, followed by J. P. Love, "First Epistle of Peter," *Interpretation* 8 (1954), p. 67.

11. Indeed, see Jobes, *1 Peter*, pp. 27-28, on the possibility that the intended recipients of 1 Peter are the actual "Pentecost Pilgrims" who heard Peter's first sermon in Acts 2. While we find this unlikely, it seems quite plausible that the many thematic and lexical links between 1 Peter and Peter's speeches in Acts are rooted in the church's early memory of Peter. See the helpful discussion in J. H. Elliott, *1 Peter* (AB 37b; New York: Doubleday, 2000), pp. 25-27.

12. Feldmeier, *First Letter of Peter*, p. 25.

tion is inscribed in the structure of the letter collection itself; just as Peter stood alongside John in the Gospel and James the Lord's brother in Acts, so also Peter's letters are grouped together with James on one side and John on the other (more on this below, under "Canonical Reception").

But though the apostolic leaders proclaimed the gospel in harmonious unity, readers should not expect their messages to be perfectly uniform. Paul wrote to Gentiles in a manner appropriate for a pagan world, and James likewise to ethnic Jews in distinctively Jewish terms, but 1 Peter especially inhabits the middle way we have been prepared to expect from his canonical portrait. His description of the recipients' pre-Christian life indicates he is writing primarily to Gentiles (1:14, 18; 2:9-10; 4:2-4), but he nevertheless addresses them throughout in distinctively Jewish terms, generously applying the appellatives of Israel to them as though they were themselves ethnic Jews (see below, under "Composition"). Paul's letters may leave readers wondering about the ongoing validity of the old covenant and its Scriptures (cf. Acts 21:21; 2 Pet. 3:15-16), and James may conversely leave others wondering if his Christian message applies to Gentiles at all! But 1 Peter interlaces both worlds, carefully weaving together "Old Testamental, early Jewish, and early Christian traditions in a frequency that is without parallel in the New Testament."[13] Paul writes to Gentiles, and James to the twelve tribes of Israel, but in 1 Peter Israel functions as the "controlling metaphor"[14] for a Gentile church in need of a faith identity capable of keeping them faithful as resident aliens suffering in a pagan world.

2. The Composition of the Petrine Epistles

1 Peter. Though form-critical analyses from the first half of the twentieth century concluded that 1 Peter is a composite of ancient baptismal homilies with epistolary features added later,[15] contemporary scholars tend to view such theories as too speculative to be sustained.[16] 1 Peter is now generally approached as a coherent and unified "real letter."

---

13. Feldmeier, *First Letter of Peter*, p. 26.

14. So Achtemeier, *1 Peter*, pp. 69-73.

15. E.g., R. Perdelwitz, *Die Mysterienreligion und das Problem des I. Petrusbriefes. Ein literarischer und religionsgeschichtlicher Versuch* (RVV 11.3; Giessen: Töpelmann, 1911); F. L. Cross, *I Peter: A Paschal Liturgy* (London: Mowbray, 1954); Selwyn, *First Epistle of St. Peter.*

16. See the useful summary and critique of these theories in W. J. Dalton, *Christ's Proc-*

But what *kind* of letter is 1 Peter? The ancient church designated it a "catholic epistle" addressed to churches spread across five Roman provinces of Asia Minor north of the Taurus Mountains.[17] Recent studies have enabled many scholars to define its genre more narrowly as that of an ancient Jewish *Diaspora* letter.[18] The prototypes for this letter tradition are the letters of Jeremiah to the exiles in Babylon (Jer. 29:4-23; 2 *Bar.* 78–87), but other examples include the letters in 2 Macc. 1:1–2:18, the letter written from the Jerusalem council in Acts 15:23-29, and the letter of James. These letters took the form of encyclicals written from authorized persons in Jerusalem to Jews suffering spiritual hardship living as exiles away from their homeland. They offered consolation, directions on worship and ethics, and admonitions motivated by the hope of future restoration to the homeland. 1 Peter bears a number of striking affinities to this letter group, not least of which are the opening address to believers in the Diaspora (1:1), the persistent identification of the readers as "exiles" (1:1-2, 17; 2:11), and the closing description of the author's church as coexiles residing in "Babylon" (5:13).

In fact, the Diaspora theme is but one element in a richly drawn web of references to Israel's history and literature. One finds ongoing references to election (1:2, 15; 2:4, 6, 9, 21; 3:9; 5:10, 13) and obedience (1:2, 14, 22), to the Passover (1:13, 19), to the sacrificial system (1:2), and to significant figures from OT history (1:10-12; 3:6, 20). Indeed, the reader may compile a long list of quotations and allusions to the OT, which is far and away the most cited source in 1 Peter.[19] According to Schutter, "few early Christian documents incorporate as much of [OT] material in proportion with their size."[20] But 1 Peter reveals more than just a pattern of Christological prooftexting: as Achtemeier put it, 1 Peter uses Israel as the "controlling metaphor" for Christian life as a whole.[21]

---

lamation to the Spirits: A Study of 1 Peter 3:18–4:6 (AnBib 23; Rome: Pontifical Biblical Institute, 1989), pp. 69-75.

17. It has been argued that the sequence of regional names in the address reflects the route a courier would have run in delivering the letter. E.g., Elliott, *1 Peter,* pp. 84-93.

18. See especially K.-W. Niebuhr, "Der Jakobusbrief im Licht frühjudischer Diasporabriefe," *NTS* 44 (1988), pp. 420-42, and L. Doering, "First Peter as Early Christian Diaspora Letter," in *The Catholic Epistles and Apostolic Tradition,* ed. K.-W. Niebuhr and R. W. Wall (Waco: Baylor University Press, 2009), pp. 215-36.

19. See the list in Elliott, *1 Peter,* pp. 12-17.

20. W. L. Schutter, *Hermeneutic and Composition in 1 Peter* (WUNT; Tübingen: Mohr, 1989) p. 3; he finds forty-six OT quotations and allusions in 1 Peter.

21. Achtemeier, *1 Peter,* pp. 69-73. T. Martin, *Metaphor and Composition in 1 Peter*

1 Peter identifies itself as a short letter of encouragement and testimony (5:12) for believers who are suffering a "fiery ordeal" (4:12) of suffering. Readers are described as experiencing both discrimination (2:12; 3:16; 4:4, 14) and the charge that they are subversives (2:12, 15, 19-20; 3:10-11, 16; 4:15-16, 19). Earlier scholarship sought to associate the setting of the letter with one of the official imperial persecutions under Nero, Domitian, or Trajan, but such attempts have largely been set aside. Now most scholars agree that "the persecution of 1 Peter is local, sporadic and unofficial, stemming from the antagonism and discrimination of the general populace."[22] The believers suffer, it seems, because they are Christians (3:16; 4:14-16) who live according to a set of values and practices that puts them out of step with the dominant society (1:18; 4:3-4). From the content of the letter, one surmises that the recipients are also struggling internally over why they are suffering (e.g., 4:12) and how they ought to respond.

Peter's "encouragement and testimony" invite the reader to reconsider their situation theologically: the fiery ordeal they experience is actually a spiritual test designed specifically by God for the strengthening of their faith (1:6-7; 3:17; 4:19) in preparation for Christ's glorious return (1:8-9, 13; 4:13; 5:4) and God's final judgment (1:17; 2:12; 4:5, 17-19; 5:6, 10). Indeed, despite their pagan ancestry (1:14, 18; 4:3-4) they should reimagine themselves as Israel, the elect (1:1; 2:4-10; 5:13) and holy (1:2, 15-16; 2:5-10) people of God (2:9-10), struggling to remain faithful to God as they live as exiles (1:1, 17; 2:11) in a foreign land. God's great mercy (1:3) has provided believers with all the tools necessary to pass the test: they have trustworthy Scriptures (e.g., 1:10-12; 2:2-3, 22-25; 3:10-12), a model of faithful suffering in Jesus (2:4-5, 12, 18-25; 3:17-22; 4:1-2, 12-16), the empowering presence of the Spirit (1:2, 11-12; 3:18; 4:14), the testimony of the apostles (1:12, 23-25; 5:1), and a community of unfailing love for support (1:22; 2:1; 3:8; 4:8-11). Despite God's powerful assistance, believers must nevertheless discipline themselves (1:13; 2:11; 4:7) and keep faith by abstaining from the "passions of the flesh" that will cause them to stumble on the journey to salvation

---

(SBLDS 131; Chico: Scholars, 1992) argues that the use of OT metaphors divides the body into three sections: 1:14–2:10, united by the "household of God" metaphor; 2:11–3:12, united by the "aliens" metaphor; and 3:13–5:11, united by the "sufferers of the exile" metaphor.

22. M. Dubis, "Research on 1 Peter: A Survey of Scholarly Literature since 1985," *CBQ* 4 (2006), p. 203. See also the especially useful discussion in Achtemeier, *1 Peter*, pp. 23-36.

(2:11; 4:1-2). They must follow the pattern of life set forth in Christ Jesus (especially 2:13–3:12), not simply in the interest of saving their own souls, but to participate in God's work of redeeming the world (2:5, 9, 12, 20-25; 3:1-2, 14-22).[23]

2 Peter. Though 2 Peter is clearly also a letter, its striking difference from 1 Peter is immediately recognizable, most particularly in the language it employs. It has the highest occurrence of *hapax legomena* of any book in the NT: fifty-seven of the words it uses are not found elsewhere in the NT, and thirty-two of these are not found in the Greek OT either. By contrast, fifteen have significant parallels in contemporary Hellenistic Jewish Greek, and seventeen are paralleled in the second-century writings of the Apostolic Fathers. We have here a writer who is fond of literary and obscure terminology, one who has clearly sought to link his letter to 1 Peter[24] but has made no attempt to imitate its linguistic style.

2 Peter begins as we might expect with a prescript identifying the sender and recipients. Though the address is about as "catholic" as one could imagine ("To those who have received a grace as precious as ours"), the content targets a relatively specific audience that has already received 1 Peter and some letters of Paul. In place of a typical proem we find an "ex-

23. The precise nature of their response has been the subject of much debate (for a helpful overview, see Dubis, "Research," pp. 212-15). Is Peter advocating an ethic of accommodation to Roman culture (so D. L. Balch, *Let Wives Be Submissive: The Domestic Code in I Peter* [SBLMS 26, Chico: Scholars, 1981]) or an ethic of nonconformity (so J. H. Elliott, *A Home for the Homeless: A Sociological Exegesis of 1 Peter, Its Situation and Strategy* [Philadelphia: Fortress, 1981])? While most now argue the latter, that Peter is advocating a kind of "holy nonconformity" to strengthen community coherence and purify its witness to the gospel, others have tried to make the case that the author is attempting to chart a creative middle way between the two; see especially M. E. Boring, "Interpreting 1 Peter as a Letter [Not] Written to Us," *QR* 13 (1993), pp. 89-111; C. H. Talbert, "Once Again: The Plan of 1 Peter," in C. H. Talbert, ed., *Perspectives on First Peter* (Macon: Mercer University Press, 1986), pp. 141-51; and M. Volf, "Soft Difference: Theological Reflections on the Relation between Church and Culture in 1 Peter," *ExAud* 10 (1994), pp. 15-30.

24. Each is addressed from Peter, and they share similar greetings (1 Pet. 1:2; 2 Pet. 1:2) and closing doxologies (1 Pet. 4:11; 2 Pet. 3:18). 1 Peter is written to readers designated "the elect" (1:1), and 2 Peter follows this up by exhorting readers to "confirm their call and election" (1:10). Both also seem to be linked by a shared purpose: in the first letter, Peter says, "I have written this short letter to encourage you and to testify that this is the true grace of God" (5:12); in the second, Peter says, "This is now, beloved, the second letter I have written to you; in them I am trying to arouse your sincere intention by reminding you" (3:1-2).

ordium" which functions rhetorically as a kind of "solemn decree"[25] or "opening homily"[26] representing the definitive summary of the apostolic testimony to be remembered (1:12-15). Because most of the typical epistolary clues are missing, there is little agreement as to the precise structure of the letter — though the literary subunits are clear enough to follow the train of the argument. Finally, in place of a closing farewell we find a concluding exhortation and doxology. While 2 Peter is clearly a letter, it reads like a highly stylized encyclical.

In fact, scholars have long recognized that 2 Peter bears multiple literary marks of an ancient genre known as the "testament" or farewell discourse.[27] While the tradition is rooted in the OT (Jacob in Genesis 48–49, Moses in Deuteronomy 32–33; Joshua in Joshua 22–24; David in 1 Chronicles 28–29) and was taken up by NT writers (John 13–17, Acts 20), the primary examples of the genre include the *Testaments of the Twelve Patriarchs*, the *Testament of Moses*, the *Apocalypse of Baruch*, and the Enoch literature. 2 Peter is marked as a testament by its opening exordium (1:3-11), its announcement of Peter's imminent death (vv. 12-15), its prediction of coming threats (2:1-3; 3:3-4), its warning against deception (3:1-3, 14-17), and the summary-defense of apostolic teaching which proceeds by way of a series of proofs from Scripture. Striking in this regard is the manner in which the prophecy of coming false teachers occasionally slips out of future tense into the present: compare, for example, 2:1-3 with 2:10b, 13-14, 18-19 and 3:1-4 with 3:5.

From our perspective, the far more pressing feature of scholarly work on 2 Peter is the way in which focus on the text at the point of composition has led to its effective de-canonization as the second letter of *Peter*. Indeed, the letter is now routinely read as a kind of second letter of *Jude* because of its literary dependence on that text (compare especially Jude 4-13, and 16-18 with 2 Pet. 2:1-18 and 3:1-3).[28] Nevertheless, both the letter itself (3:1) and

---

25. So H.-J. Klauck, *Ancient Letters and the New Testament* (Waco: Baylor University Press, 2006), p. 410.

26. So Bauckham, *Jude, 2 Peter*, p. 132, who identifies the exordium as a component of the testament genre.

27. For a thorough overview of the genre and its application to 2 Peter, see Bauckham, *Jude, 2 Peter*, pp. 131-35.

28. Again, Bauckham, *Jude, 2 Peter*, pp. 141-43, offers a detailed presentation of the ways scholarship has accounted for the similarities between the two letters and why concluding that 2 Peter is dependent on Jude makes the most sense. For a challenge to the consensus, see

its canonical placement insist that we read it not as 2 Jude but as 2 Peter, that is, as an intentional extension of the NT Petrine apostolic witness. The commentary and theological analysis which follow will seek to read the letter in this light.

3. The Canonical Reception of the Petrine Epistles as Scripture

The reception of these two letters in the earliest church can be appropriately described as uneven. While the Fathers celebrated 1 Peter, most had little at all to say about 2 Peter. In fact, the acceptance of the latter appears to have taken place almost entirely "from below," that is, from its common use by Christians in the churches and not from its embrace by the leading churchmen and scholars of the day.

The Reception of 1 Peter. "Aside from the four Gospels and the letters of Paul, the external attestation for 1 Peter is as strong, or stronger, than that for any NT book. There is no evidence anywhere of controversy over its authorship or authority."[29] The earliest possible evidence for the letter's reception derives from other documents emerging out of its apparent place of composition, the city of Rome (1 Pet. 5:13). The evidence is not as unambiguous as one might hope, however. While the letter known as *1 Clement* (ca. 96) shares many striking commonalities in vocabulary and theme, not all scholars are willing to assert the probability that the author used 1 Peter.[30] We are on somewhat stronger ground with 2 Peter, which refers to itself as "the second letter that I have written to you" (3:1). Though the author clearly wants the reader to receive both letters as part of a single correspondence ("in *them* I am trying to arouse your sincere intention by reminding you that you should remember," vv. 1-2), most scholars have focused instead on the *lack* of correspondence between the two letters, and a few have wondered whether the author might have had in mind something other than 1 Peter as the *first* letter. It seems quite likely that the author had 1 Peter in mind, however, given

F. Lapham, *Peter: The Myth, the Man and the Writings* (JSNTSS 239; Sheffield: Sheffield Academic, 2003), pp. 152-58.

29. J. R. Michaels, *1 Peter* (WBC 49; Waco: Word, 1988), p. xxxiv.

30. E.g., Selwyn (*First Epistle of St. Peter*, p. 37) and Elliott (*1 Peter*, p. 140) argue in favor of *1 Clement's* dependence on 1 Peter, but Michaels (*1 Peter*, p. xxxiii) and Achtemeier (*1 Peter*, p. 45) argue against it.

the early and widespread acceptance of 1 Peter, the lack of any viable alternative, and the fact that our earliest Greek textual witness to 1 Peter is a papyrus codex with 2 Peter following immediately thereafter (P72).

More solid evidence emerges from the point of initial reception in Asia Minor (1 Pet. 1:1). Apart from numerous possible parallels in the works of Melito of Sardis and Eusebius's claim that Papias of Hieropolis used the letter (*H.E.* 3.39.17), the clearest early indication of use comes from Polycarp's letter to the Philippians, written early in the second century. Though 1 Peter is never identified directly by name, Polycarp's dependence on the letter has been noted since the time of Eusebius (*H.E.* 4.14.9). Two aspects of this relationship are deserving of our attention. First, the opening section of Polycarp's letter contains several allusions to the opening of 1 Peter, suggesting that Polycarp sought to loosely pattern his epistle after Peter's and expected his readers to catch the echoes. We note that the greetings are quite similar: Polycarp has "may mercy and peace from God Almighty and Jesus Christ our Savior be yours in abundance *(plēthyntheiē)*"; 1 Peter reads "may grace and peace be yours in abundance *(plēthyntheiē).*" Similar greetings using *plēthynein* are also found in 2 Peter, Jude, *1 Clement,* and the *Martyrdom of Polycarp.*[31]

Soon thereafter we find two direct references to 1 Peter:

> *Though you have not seen him, you believe in him with an inexpressible and glorious joy* [1 Pet. 1:8] which many desire to experience, knowing that by grace you have been saved, not because of works, but by the will of God through Jesus Christ. *Therefore prepare for action* [1 Pet. 1:13] and serve God in fear." (*Philippians* 1.3–2.1).

These opening parallels suggest that Polycarp valued 1 Peter for the way it exhorted believers to translate Christian belief into distinctively Christian behaviors. This interest is made all the more clear by the subsequent accumulation of allusions to 1 Peter in sections 8-10. Section 8 begins:

> Let us, therefore, hold steadfastly and unceasingly to our hope and the guarantee of our righteousness, who is Christ Jesus, *who bore*

---

31. This particular greeting form is also associated with several Jewish Diaspora letters (Dan. 6:26 in Theodotion and LXX; *2 Bar.* 78:2; *b. Sanh.* 11b) written to encourage people suffering exile; see Elliott, *1 Peter,* p. 321.

our sins in his own body upon the tree [1 Pet. 2:24], who *committed no sin, and no deceit was found in his mouth* [Isa. 53:9, cited in 1 Pet. 2:22]; instead, for our sakes he endured all things, in order that we might live in him. Let us, therefore, become imitators of his patient endurance, and if we should suffer for the sake of his name, let us glorify him [cf. 1 Pet. 4:16]. For this is the example he set for us in his own person [cf. 1 Pet. 2:21], and this is what we have believed.

Section 9 then extends this Christological model of faithful suffering to apostolic and post-apostolic figures, concluding, "be assured that all these did not run in vain but in faith and righteousness, and that they are now in the place due them with the Lord, with whom they also suffered together." Section 10 draws the exhortation to a conclusion, saying

Stand fast, therefore, in these things and follow the example of the Lord, firm and immovable in faith, *loving the brotherhood* [cf. 1 Pet. 2:12], cherishing one another, united in the truth, giving way to one another in the gentleness of the Lord, despising no one. When you are able to do good, do not put it off, because charity delivers from death. All of you *be subject to one another* [cf. 1 Pet. 5:5], and *maintain an irreproachable standard of conduct among the Gentiles, so that you may be praised for your good deeds* [cf. 1 Pet. 2:12] and the Lord may not be blasphemed because of you. But woe to him through whom the name of the Lord is blasphemed. Therefore teach to all the self-control by which you yourselves live.

Polycarp's use of 1 Peter indicates it was valued for its insistence that those who hold *the faith of Jesus* must imitate *the faithfulness of Jesus* in their day-to-day lives.

Patristic evidence from the second and third centuries shows widespread acceptance of 1 Peter without a hint of controversy about its authority. Irenaeus of Lyon (writing ca. 180) is the first to quote 1 Peter by name, and his use of the letter indicates he valued it primarily for its careful articulation of the coherence of the old and new covenants as the single work of God. In this regard, his favorite verse from 1 Peter appears to have been 1:12;[32] on each occasion Irenaeus uses it to demonstrate the coherence

---

32. See *Adv. Haer.* 2.17.9; 4.34.1; 5.36.3.

of salvation history as it has been foretold by prophets, fulfilled in Jesus, and proclaimed by the apostles. Likewise, in a section underscoring the ongoing validity of the Torah for Christian faith, Irenaeus insists that "the new covenant of liberty" canceled the "bondage" of the law but

> increased the feeling of reverence . . . that we may know that we shall give account to God not of deeds only, as slaves, but even of words and thoughts, as those who have truly received the power of liberty, in which [condition] a man is more severely tested, whether he will reverence, and fear, and love the Lord. And for this reason Peter says *that we have not liberty as a cloak of maliciousness* [1 Pet. 2:16], but as the means of testing and evidencing faith. (*Adv. Haer.* 4.16.5)

This interest in 1 Peter's witness to a fully biblical Christian ethics continues in other writers from the period. Tertullian alludes to 1 Peter on several occasions, but his most frequent reference is to the teaching on honoring the emperor (2:13-17).[33] Clement of Alexandria clearly valued 1 Peter for its ethical instruction; this is especially evident in his great moral treatise *Paedagogus* ("The Instructor"). The eleventh and twelfth chapters of the third book, which are devoted to an extended discourse on every aspect of Christian moral piety, are introduced with a reference to 1 Pet. 2:12: "We keep in mind these holy words particularly: 'Keep your conduct excellent among the heathens, so that, whereas they slander you as evildoers, they may, by observing the nobility of your actions, glorify God'" (3.11.53.3). Numerous quotations and allusions to 1 Peter follow; the most important passage appears to have been 4:8 ("love covers a multitude of sins"), which Clement cites as a saying of the Lord himself.[34]

Origen quotes 1 Peter repeatedly; he quotes or alludes to his favorite verses, 2:5 and 2:9, at least thirteen times each. His love of these verses is unsurprising since they offer the kind of typological reading of the OT that Origen championed. He refers to 2:5 whenever he seeks an allegorical interpretation of the Jerusalem temple (e.g., *Com. Jn.* 10.229; *Cels.* 8.19.23ff.). Frequently this linkage is used by Origen to find moral instruction for the Christian "priesthood" hidden in the OT descriptions of

---

33. See *Scorp.* 2.6; 14.13; *Idol.* 15.8.
34. 3.12; see also *Strom.* 1.27; 2.15; 4.17; *Quis* 38.

priestly duties in the temple cult (e.g. *Hom. Lev.* 9.9; *Hom. Num.* 4.3; *Hom. Josh.* 1.5).

By the turn of the fourth century Eusebius states, "Of Peter, one epistle, that which is called his first, is admitted, and the ancient presbyters used this in their own writings as unquestioned" (*H.E.* 3.3.1). We have seen that the letter was valued most especially for its instruction in Christian discipleship and its compelling articulation of the unity of the old and new covenants.

The Reception of 2 Peter. 2 Peter did not enjoy the same reception history as 1 Peter. Indeed, though we are able to track its slow welcome into the collection of canonical texts, its lack of use by the church fathers even upon its reception makes it extremely difficult for us to offer any precise claims about how it functioned as Scripture in those days.

Scholars have offered up possible echoes of the letter in a number of writings from the second century, but the only ones that can be substantiated are from the *Apocalypse of Peter* and the *Acts of Peter*.[35] On this basis we can say that the letter appears to have been associated with the burgeoning collection of Petrine pseudepigrapha in this period. It is in the third century that we find the earliest overt evidence of 2 Peter's existence. Our most ancient manuscript of the letter, P72, dates from this period; it is a codex of writings bound together for private use somewhere in Egypt. The book included, in the following order, the *Nativity of Mary*, the pseudo-Pauline *3 Corinthians*, *Odes of Solomon* 11, Jude, Melito's *Homily on the Passover*, a hymn, the *Apology* of Phileas, Psalms 33 and 34, and 1 and 2 Peter. The three proto-canonical texts appear to have come from different scribal hands, and the fact that they appear here out of sequence with a diverse collection of noncanonical texts strongly suggests that their authority was not yet fixed enough to render them incapable of semi-independent movement.

The first clear patristic witness to 2 Peter is Origen. In a fragment of his *Commentary on John* preserved by Eusebius, he says that Peter "has left one acknowledged epistle, and, it may be, a second also; for it is doubted" (*H.E.* 6.25.8). He does not quote or mention the letter in any of the writings that have come down to us in their original Greek, which is significant because the ancient Latin translations of Origen's works (which do include

---

35. See Bauckham, *Jude, 2 Peter*, p. 149.

a couple of references to 2 Peter) are widely believed to have been augmented by later writers.[36]

It is in the fourth century that the historical fog around 2 Peter finally begins to clear. Eusebius ranks 2 Peter, along with James, 2 and 3 John, and Jude, in the category of "disputed books which are nevertheless known to most" (*H.E.* 3.25.3). Though he will argue that these writings are "not canonical" (3.25.6), he also knows that they are widely used in the churches, circulating as part of a seven-letter collection called "the catholic epistles" (2.23.25). Hence, he can say of 2 Peter, "we have not received [it] as canonical, but nevertheless it has appeared useful to many, and has been studied along with the other scriptures" (3.3.1).[37] Its "usefulness to many" is indicated by its canonical place in the major fourth-century codices (Sinaiticus and Vaticanus), which show it was used in the worship life of the church even if the scholars of the day retained their doubts. Indeed, even a century later Jerome could approach the letter as fully canonical but still feel obliged to remind his readers that it "is considered by many to be not by [Peter]."[38] His discussion of similar concerns about the letter of Jude ends with him saying "by age and use it has gained authority and is reckoned among the Holy Scriptures."[39] No doubt he would have said exactly the same about 2 Peter.

All this makes it clear that the reception of 2 Peter took place "from below": it was its spiritual utility in the ancient churches that secured its canonical status, not the opinion of the churchmen and scholars of the day, who would have rejected it on the basis of its uneven record of use by

---

36. In his introduction to his critical edition of Origen's *de Principiis*, G. W. Butterworth notes that what has been passed down in Latin, when it is compared to the extant Greek, often seems more like edited paraphrases than careful translations (*Origen: On First Principles* [London: SPCK, 1936], p. xxx).

37. Evidence of this disputed status abounds in this period: though the eastern writers of the fourth century uniformly list it among the CE, the western Mommsen Catalog includes a scribal note saying "one only" as a protest against accepting 2 Peter. Likewise, Amphilochius of Iconium (ca. 396) notes that some churches accept all seven CE but others only James, 1 Peter, and 1 John (*Iambi.* 289-319). Though Hilary of Poitiers (d. ca. 368) could refer to the letter unambiguously as coming directly from the hand of Peter (*De Trin.* 1.18.3), his limited use does not provide enough material to allow us to make claims regarding its function as Scripture.

38. *Viris* 1.3. Elsewhere he defended the possibility of Petrine authorship by suggesting that different amanuenses were used (*Ep.* 120).

39. *Viris* 4.1-2.

earlier theologians. An understanding of *why* it was eventually recognized as Scripture, however, can only be inferred from its preservation among the seven CE. Thus our understanding of its theological function must await the canonical reading of the letter.

Commentary: 1 Peter

Letter Prescript: Peter to the Elect Exiles of the Dispersion (1:1-2)

The opening lines of 1 Peter follow the standard letter writing conventions of the day by identifying the author and recipients and culminates in a distinctively Petrine greeting (cf. 2 Pet. 1:2). It breaks with convention, however, in abbreviating the identity of the author and elaborating the identity of the recipients. Rhetorically, elaboration follows honor; one would expect the famous Peter to receive the extended introduction (compare, e.g., Rom. 1:1-7; Gal. 1:1-2; 1 Tim. 1:1-2), but this letter begins with Peter bestowing honor on his struggling recipients by means of a theologically rich identity statement.

The recipients[40] are initially identified by three terms that combine to stunning theological effect: they are the *elect exiles* of the *Diaspora*. The twelve occurrences of *Diaspora* in the Greek OT all refer in some way to God's scattering of Israel into exile among the nations as a punishment for unfaithfulness.[41] By locating the reader as a participant in the Diaspora, the address of 1 Peter links up with that of the letter of James and underscores the orientation of the entire CE collection as an address to believers who are called to reimagine their existence as a people residing in a hostile world that unsettles their faith and tests their allegiance to God.

In striking contrast to the OT backdrop of Diaspora as punishment, however, 1 Peter identifies these exiles as the "elect": they are not punished with dispersion in a foreign land but "chosen" for the task because of their honored standing before God. This identity statement describing their situation "from below" is immediately paired with a description "from

40. D. E. Hiebert, "Designation of Readers in 1 Peter 1:1-2," *BibSac* 137 (1980), pp. 64-75.

41. Deut. 28:25; 30:4; Neh. 1:9; Ps. 146:2 (147:2); Isa. 49:6; Jer. 15:7; 41:17; Dan. 12:2; Jdth. 5:19; 2 Macc. 1:27; *Pss. Sol.* 8:28; 9:2. Cf. W. C. van Unnik, "'Diaspora' and 'Church' in the First Centuries of Christian History," in *Sparsa Collectica* III: *The Collected Essays of W. C. Unnik* (NovTSup 31; Leiden: Brill, 1983), pp. 95-103.

above" that utilizes a Trinitarian framework to locate their existence firmly within the salvific purposes of God (1:2). Their status as a struggling minority is established according to the foreknowledge of God the Father and empowered by the sanctifying Spirit (literally "in the holiness of the Spirit") so that they may be obedient to Jesus, who was likewise elected by God to suffer for the redemption of the world (cf. 1:20).

This arresting portrayal of the recipients recalls the narrative of Acts, where persecution results in a scattering that has the counter-intuitive effect of extending the church's evangelistic mission (Acts 8:1ff.). In similar fashion, 1 Peter seeks to counter a natural intuition of suffering as evidence of divine punishment or indifference with a conceptualization that infuses their distress with theological significance. Believers suffer social hostility not meaninglessly or in spite of their relation to God but precisely because they are God's holy people, set apart as different for the express purpose of directing the world back to God (cf. 2:9).

Proem: Praise Be to God! (1:3-12)

The typical epistolary proem which praises the recipient is here exchanged for a eulogy to God that follows the prescript in gathering readers up into the unfolding plan of the Trinitarian God. Again, counter-intuitively, suffering readers are called to give praise to God for the honor bestowed on them (cf. Acts 5:41): by God's great mercy they have been "born anew" into their current state of being. This new existence is "into a living hope" (1:3) made known through the resurrection of Jesus from the dead, for a future inheritance that is already ready and kept in heaven by God for disclosure at the culmination of history (1:4-5).

The process by which human souls are saved (1:9; cf. Jas. 1:20) conforms to the pattern of thought that dominates the entire letter: suffering now leads to glory later. Trials, it turns out, are the mechanism God uses to cleanse and purify believers (1:6-7). In a world that strives after glory now and avoids suffering at all costs, believers will follow the route established by Jesus, embracing suffering now in the knowledge that such spiritual tests have the capacity to reshape them into people fit for praise, glory, and honor when Jesus Christ is revealed (1:7).

This plan of God for suffering followed by glory is rooted deep in Israel's history, foretold by faithful prophets who were empowered by the

Spirit to testify in advance concerning the suffering of Christ and the glory that followed for him (1:10-12). Believers are especially privileged in this regard, for the Spirit who revealed this in part to Israel's prophets has announced the whole story to them through the inspired preaching of the apostles (1:12). This spiritual knowledge, it turns out, works both ways: just as the OT reveals the truth of the Gospel in advance, so also the Spirit uses the Gospel to shed light retrospectively on the OT, enabling believers to clearly discern God's purposes in and through the holy literature of Israel so that it might continue to function as Christian Scripture.[42]

Body Opening: On Being God's Holy People (1:13–2:10)

The opening of the letter body is signaled by v. 13, a grammatically complex sentence that takes the praise in 1:3-12 into an exhortation to take up the identity of God's holy people. The initial phrase, literally "having girded the loins of your understanding," draws the reader's mind back to Moses' directions for celebrating the first Passover at the start of the exodus from Egypt:

> This is how you shall eat it: your loins girded, your sandals on your feet, and your staff in your hand; and you shall eat it hurriedly. It is the Passover of the LORD. For I will pass through the land of Egypt that night, and I will strike down every firstborn in the land of Egypt. . . . The blood shall be a sign for you on the houses where you live: when I see the blood, I will pass over you. . . ." (Exod. 12:11-13)

---

42. So J. B. Green, *1 Peter* (THNTC; Grand Rapids: Eerdmans, 2007), p. 31: "Peter finds an essential unity in the outworking of God's purpose, from the Scriptures of Israel to the community of Christ's followers — a unity that coheres in the one God, Yahweh, who raised Jesus from the dead; and in the Holy Spirit, who inspired the prophets of old and the evangelists who proclaim the message of the prophets as good news . . . Peter thus provides a particular way of articulating the beginning, middle, and end of the biblical story. The story of salvation finds its locus here: the prophets, who prophesied in advance, testified to the sufferings destined for Christ and the subsequent glory. How do we know this is a 'true' story? How do we know that this reading of the story is true? They prophesied through the Spirit, and the gospel message, which embodies the story, was brought by means of the Spirit. In short, Peter presents the Holy Spirit . . . as the enabler and guarantor of authentic exegesis of Israel's story, Israel's scriptures."

God's people Israel ate this meal hurriedly, under the protection of the lamb's blood, with their mind on a journey and their eyes on the Promised Land. So also Christians who are sprinkled with the blood of Christ (1:2, 18-20) must focus all their life's hope on the goal of the glory that comes at the end of a faithful journey of suffering with him (vv. 6-9).

This new life will require disciplined vigilance on their part (cf. 5:8-9). As Paul Achtemeier memorably summarizes, "Drunken people in long garments are not very good at hard labor."[43] Believers must set aside the sluggish practical reasoning of their former ignorance (cf. Rom. 12:2) and reimagine themselves as obedient children of a holy Father whose primary criterion of judgment is the performance of an obedient life (1:14-17). The emphasis on works (see also 2:12) draws our minds back to the faith and works discussion in James 1:2-4 and 2:14-26, but rather than speak extensively of works specifically, Peter elaborates by using words having to do with "doing good"[44] by means of right Christian "conduct." James introduced this latter word as well: "Who is wise and understanding among you? Show by your good conduct that your works are done with gentleness born of wisdom" (Jas. 3:13). 1 Peter will use the noun and verb forms seven times (1:15, 17, 18; 2:12; 3:1, 2, 16), and 2 Peter three times (2:7, 18; 3:11). Synonyms ("living," 4:3) and antonyms ("wander," 2:25) also contribute to this prominent Petrine motif.

The reference to Leviticus ("You shall be holy, for I am holy," Lev. 11:44-45; 19:2; 20:7) invites the reader to turn to that ancient manual of holiness to gain understanding of what kind of conduct is required of children who wish to conform to the pattern of the Parent.[45] Though this pattern of holy living will leave them feeling like strangers in a strange land ("exiles," 1:1, 17; 2:11), believers may gain confidence through the example of Christ, whose single-minded devotion to the will of God carried him through his suffering and death into a resurrection to glory (1:21).

The preeminent evidence of holiness is a life of genuine, unrelenting communal love (1:22). Indeed, a society of people suffering exile must bond together in protective love or risk losing their distinctive habits and

---

43. Achtemeier, *1 Peter*, p. 118.

44. Peter has a liking for the "doing good" word-group: *agathopoios* (2:14), *agathopoieō* (2:15, 20; 3:6, 17), *agathopoiia* (4:19).

45. E.g., love of neighbor (Lev. 19:13-18) and stranger alike (19:33-34), the pursuit of justice for the poor (19:13-15) and elderly (19:32), and concern for appropriate personal adornment (19:27-28).

being reassimilated into the dominant pagan culture. But the power of their resistance does not derive from their perishable and frail selves; no, they have been re-created by "the living and abiding word of God," which "abides forever." Note how the images from vv. 3-4 are remixed here: those born anew "through the *resurrection*" in v. 3 are here born "through the *word of God*." Similarly the "living *hope*" is now the "living *word*," and the "imperishable *inheritance*" is now the "imperishable *seed*" sown by the word of God. The point is clear: the new birth into hope for salvation is directly connected to the word of God proclaimed long ago by Isaiah (Isa. 40:6-8, quoted in 1:24-25a) and mediated to believers through the preaching of the apostles (v. 25b).

Once again, the spiritual reading of the OT described in 1:10-12 is modeled out for us in the instructive parallels between the word of Isaiah and message of our letter. Isaiah 40 begins with a prophecy of "comfort" (40:1) and future deliverance (v. 2) for God's people living in exile in Babylon. It announces triumphantly that God's "glory" is about to be revealed (v. 5, as in 1 Pet. 1:5-9). The prophet contrasts temporal human hardship and perishability with God's eternal power and plan expressed in his word (40:6-8), and goes on to call forth a "herald of good news" (v. 9) to proclaim this good word to God's people. Readers of 1 Peter are invited to reimagine their existence using Israel's story as a personal and communal metaphor for life in the world. With this new self-understanding at the forefront of their minds, believers must strip off old vices as they would throw away rotten clothes (2:1). Having "tasted that the Lord is good" (v. 3),[46] they must consider themselves vulnerable and hungry newborns crying out for more spiritual nourishment from Scripture[47] to help them grow up into the alternative identity that leads to salvation (cf. 1:9).

The next section shifts gears to weave together a tapestry of OT "stone" imagery (2:4-8) to describe Jesus as the pattern for the new life to which believers have been called. He is the "living stone" (cf. "living hope" in 1:3 and "living word" in 1:23) who is rejected by the world (like the read-

---

46. Ps. 34:8 is echoed; the whole Psalm substantiates the themes of the letter. Peter will return to this Psalm at 3:10-12. For the influence of Psalm 34 on 1 Peter, see F. W. Danker, "1 Peter 1:24–2:17: A Consolatory Pericope," *ZNW* 58 (1967), pp. 93-102, and K. Snodgrass, "1 Peter 2:1-10: Its Formation and Literary Affinities," *NTS* 24 (1977), pp. 97-106.

47. "Pure spiritual milk" (NRSV) is literally *logikon adolon gala*, with *logikon* echoing the *logou zōntos theou* of 1:23. This *logos* is mediated by the "word" (*rhēma*) proclaimed by the apostles (1:25b).

ers) but in God's sight is "chosen" (cf. 1:1) and "precious" (cf. 1:7). Believers follow his pattern by becoming living stones joined together in a new, spiritual temple of worship where acceptable sacrifices are offered to God (2:5; cf. v. 9). Once again, we return to a string of Scripture citations that interpret OT stone imagery christologically (Isa. 28:16 in 2:6; Ps. 118:22 in 2:7; Isa. 8:14 in 2:8) enabling a people shamefully dishonored by their culture to seek a different kind of honor through their association with Jesus. Viewed "from below," they are strangers and misfits, but in God's eyes they are what Israel was called to be when its people were likewise redeemed from slavery (2:9): "a chosen race, a royal priesthood, a holy nation, a people of God's possession" (Exod. 19:4-6), called out of dark ignorance to announce the light of God's salvation to the world (Isa. 42:16). A final reference to Hos. 1:6-9 confirms all that has been said thus far: the bestowal of this new, difficult identity-task is a gift from the God of mercy, whom the Holy Spirit reveals through the word written and proclaimed.

Body Middle: The Honorable Conduct of the Christian Resident Alien (2:11–4:11)

The transitions to the next two major sections of the letter are signaled by the warm direct address "beloved" (2:11; 4:12). After describing their new identity, Peter turns to a lengthy exhortation: God's born anew people must live accordingly. What that entails is spelled out in the sections that follow.

First and foremost, the maintenance of a life lived as an "alien and exile" among "Gentiles"[48] requires abstinence from the cravings that attack the newly purified soul (2:11; cf. 1:9 and 22) with the intention of drawing it back into the ways of the believers' former worldly life. This "resistance living" will draw slander and mockery from outsiders, but believers must not respond by withdrawing into safe sectarian seclusion — for how then could they fulfill the commission outlined in 2:9-10? No, their crucial task is not to hide, conform, or fight back, but to "maintain honorable conduct," that is, to conduct their lives in such a way that there will be no basis for judgment against them, now or at the day when God's judgment is revealed (v. 12).

48. One hears an echo of Abraham's self-description in Gen. 23:4 and the reference to this tradition in Ps. 39:12.

The bulk of the body middle describes these honorable practices in relation to various spheres of life in human society. The section that follows is similar in form and content (though not precisely so) to the "household codes" (German *Haustafeln*) promoted by ancient Greco-Roman moralists, theologians, and philosophers.[49] These codes were set forth as a means to order human power relationships in home and society in the manner that would best promote the security and unity of the Roman state. Christians sometimes mimicked these well-known cultural artifacts (cf. Eph. 5:21–6:9; Col. 3:18–4:1) to provide a platform for describing the distinctiveness of life conducted in Christ in comparison to life in the world.

Two general rules govern the advice that follows: believers are to witness to Christ by submitting to those in authority over them and by suffering like him when they are abused. The call to "submit" repeats throughout this section (2:13, 18; 3:1, 5; 5:5), and the many abuses of this instruction in Christian history require us to move through this material a bit more slowly.

The root verb *tassō* refers to the imposition of order by arranging things in a particular way. The verb *antitassō* means to oppose or resist that order, and the verb here, *hypotassō*, means to bow down "under" that order, that is, to submit to it. Two important points must be made about the distinctive understanding of submission in 1 Peter. First, given the letter's persistent call to inhabit an alternative way of life, this call to "submit" to social power structures cannot be an exhortation for the believers simply to affirm that order or passively to acquiesce to it. Instead, it is best understood as a call *to disarm the power of that order by enacting their submission in imitation of Christ.* Maintaining their identity as strangers in a strange land, they are to bear it in the knowledge that these are temporal, perishable human structures in light of the eternal call of God in Christ. But that call requires them to live differently in the world after the pattern of Christ; thus their "bearing it" *must be accomplished in a manner that will draw attention to the living hope that orders their lives,* thereby drawing the slander and mockery they have been told to expect.

Second, the Christian code outlined here differs strikingly from its

---

49. All the major commentaries include some overview of the ancient *Haustafel* tradition. See especially Elliott, *1 Peter,* pp. 503-11; Michaels, *1 Peter,* pp. 121-23; and the excellent "Excursus 8: the Context of the Exhortation to Subordination" in Feldmeier, *First Letter of Peter,* pp. 152-57, for solid overviews of the ancient sociocultural realities to which the *Haustafeln* point and especially the ways in which this section of 1 Peter both conforms to and departs from this common literary device.

cultural exemplars, which order society by maintaining a careful balance of submission by subordinates and appropriate reciprocity by superiors (that is to say, the codes address emperor *and* citizen, husband *and* wife, master *and* slave). In contrast to this, Peter's code begins and ends with general injunctions to everyone and fills the gap by primarily addressing only subordinates. Joel Green has noted that Peter's code is formed according to an inverted parallelism focused on the example of Christ:

> 2:13-17: instruction for *everyone*
>   2:18-20: instruction for *slaves*
>   2:21-25: the example of *Christ*
>   3:1-7: instruction for *wives* (and briefly to husbands)
> 3:8-12: instruction for *everyone*

The structure suggests that Peter is doing far more than calling for particular powerless Christian subgroups (i.e., wives and slaves) to bow down under the worldly power structure. Instead, first, the call to submit goes out to *all Christians* as the central feature of their reverence to Christ (Eph. 5:21 governs its household code in a similar manner), and, second, the instructions to the already subordinate slaves and wives are meant to be illustrative models of the submission to which all believers are called. This is made plain not only by the framing of the entire section by general instructions to all believers but also by the fact that the instructions to slaves (2:18-20) are modeled directly on the example of Christ, the pattern for all (vv. 21-25), and that the instructions to wives (3:1-6) are echoed later in instructions to all Christians (vv. 14-16). Thus, the powerful call of Christian submission is a means of *engaging the dominant culture by participating in its system in a manner designed to draw the society's attention to what God has done in Christ.* When this happens, some will be converted and others will react by oppressing the believer in a manner akin to the oppression of Christ. In either case, Christ will be reverenced as Lord.

So believers must not resist the governing structures of their day, for if they do they will simply justify the charge that they are evildoers (2:13-15). As servants of God they are technically free in relation to a worldly power that has no authority in and of itself, but this freedom does not allow them to live however they please (v. 16). Still, they cannot follow their culture in serving a human emperor venerated by society as a god incarnate. Instead, a reordering of priority is required: believers should honor everyone, love their fellow believers, and reserve their utmost respect and allegiance for God alone (v. 17a-c). Within this scheme, the emperor falls not in the final category but in the first: believers are to honor him as a human being, no more and no less than they honor anyone else (v. 17d). In cultural context, this structure represents a radical reduction of the emperor's status and authority in light of the rule of God in Christ.

Similarly, servants are to submit to their masters without reference to the kinds of masters they serve (2:18). If they are beaten unjustly and persevere with patience, they are blessed, for in this way they are following the transformative path of Christ (vv. 19-21). The verses that follow make it clear that this call to bear unmerited suffering is not a call to passive, powerless inaction in the face of injustice but active, powerful transformation of victimization into dynamic participation in God's work of healing the world. Viewed through the lens of Isaiah's prophecy, Jesus the suffering Servant "bore our sins in his body" so that "free from sin we might live to righteousness; by his wounds [we] have been healed" (v. 24). In like manner, the suffering Christian servant is to view her situation through the lens of the pattern of redemption made known in Christ. By refusing to respond in kind she breaks the cycle of violence instigated by the oppressor; by absorbing the sin of the other in her suffering body, she manifests the power of Christ in her very self, and in so doing, invites the abuser into the healing realization that self-giving service as revealed in Christ Jesus is a more powerful force than violence and domination.

Likewise, the call for wives to submit to their husbands is specified as a means of evangelizing non-Christian husbands: wives are to be submissive "so that, even if some of them do not obey the word, they may be won over without a word by their wives' conduct" (3:1). Religiously mixed marriages were common in the earliest church (1 Corinthians 7) and posed a significant problem for Christian wives who, viewed as the "weaker sex" in that culture (3:7), were expected to worship the gods of their husbands.[50] Peter

---

50. "Dominant . . . was the notion that the woman was by nature inferior to the man. Because she lacked the capacity for reason that the male had, she was ruled by her emotions, and was as a result given to poor judgment, immorality, intemperance, wickedness, avarice; she was untrustworthy, contentious, and as a result, it was her place to obey. . . . She could not vote or hold office, could not take an oath or plead a case in court, could not be the legal guardian of her own children, and was legally dependent on either her father or a guardian" (Achtemeier, *1 Peter*, pp. 206-7; see also Feldmeier, *First Letter of Peter*, pp. 178-79; both offer helpful reviews of ancient Hellenistic attitudes toward women).

offers two specific words of advice to women in this situation. First, to avoid the charge of evildoing (2:12), they should not resort to the power of words in an attempt to convert or rebel against their husbands (3:1). Likewise they must not attempt to gain power over their husbands by means of seductive dress (v. 3). Instead, they must comport their lives as all Christians should: with purity (cf. 1:22; Jas. 3:17) and reverence (cf. 1:17; 3:16), adorning themselves with the imperishable power of a gentle (cf. 3:15-16; Matt. 5:5; 11:29; 21:5) and quiet spirit (cf. Isa. 53:7; 1 Tim. 2:2; 1 Thess. 4:11; 2 Thess. 3:12). Like all Christians, they are called to live in hope (cf. 1:3), like Sarah who continued to follow Abraham despite the improbability of the promise they had received.[51] The final phrase, "and do not be terrorized," grounds the foregoing advice in an allusion to Prov. 3:21-25:

> keep sound wisdom and prudence, and they will be life for your soul and adornment for your neck . . . do not be terrorized by sudden panic or by the storm that strikes the wicked, for the LORD will be your confidence and will keep your foot from being caught.

Just as the servants who are to fear God and not the emperor (2:17), so also wives are to hold on to their faith despite the potential of intimidation and violence from their unbelieving husbands.

Peter's directives to cultural subordinates imply an assumption that Christians will not be found among the governing and slaveholding elites. But what of Christian women with believing husbands? Christian men are in a predicament of their own in a culture that expects them to subordinate their wives. The one sentence devoted to them begins with "likewise" (3:7), indicating that the logic governing slaves and women rules them as well: they too should consider themselves to be subordinates. They are to live with their wives "according to the knowledge" that they are in fact partners, "joint heirs of the grace of life" (cf. Gal. 3:28). Thus they are to "honor" their wives no differently than they would the emperor or anyone else (cf. 2:17). If they ignore this advice, Peter warns, God will ignore their prayers (cf. 3:12).

The entire code ends with a closing exhortation directed once again to the entire Christian community (3:8-12), with v. 9 providing an apt summary of the logic that undergirds the entire code: "Do not return evil for

---

51. Peter has Gen. 18:1-15 in mind: "Sarah laughed to herself, saying, 'After I have become old, shall I have pleasure, my *lord* being old also?'" (18:12).

evil or abuse for abuse; but on the contrary, repay with a blessing. For to this you have been called, that you may inherit a blessing." In a world where people are ranked according to social, racial, and gender divisions, the Christian community is to be a place of unity and sympathy, a place where tenderness and humility enable true familial love (v. 8). The entire exhortation is then closed with another quotation of Psalm 34 (cf. 2:3) in order to once again ground the entire teaching in Scripture and "place it under a promise"[52]: the one who faithfully endures the temporary trials of this life will find the Lord to be a faithful companion on the journey to salvation (cf. 1:6-7).

The final section of the body middle (3:13–4:11) begins to draw the body of the letter to a close by emphasizing the ultimate vindication of those who follow the advice of the Psalm to "turn away from evil and *do right*" (3:11). Though Peter clearly hopes that believers who do right will be vindicated by their contemporaries (3:13; cf. 2:12, 15), it is often the case that those who do right in a twisted world end up suffering for their actions. So Peter returns to the "suffer now, glory later" theme that has been building throughout the letter (1:6-7, 10-11, 21; 2:12; 3:9). Echoing the Sermon on the Mount, he insists that those who suffer for righteousness' sake will ultimately be blessed by God (3:14a; cf. Matt. 5:10). The point is emphasized by yet another christological reading of Isaiah 8 (3:14b-15; cf. 2:8). After describing Assyria's coming destruction of Israel, Isaiah tells the people of Judah:

> Do not call conspiracy all that this people calls conspiracy, and do not fear what it fears, or be in dread. But the Lord of hosts, him you shall regard as holy; let him be your fear, and let him be your dread. He will become a sanctuary, a stone one strikes against. . . .

Christians who "sanctify" the co-suffering Christ "as Lord" of their whole lives will be able to stand confidently under persecution; when called to account, their good conduct will provide them with a clear conscience, enabling them to calmly defend themselves[53] and clearly articulate the hope that has directed them to a life lived out of step with the rest of society (3:15b-16).

---

52. So Feldmeier, *First Letter of Peter,* p. 187.

53. The ethic of non-retaliation advocated throughout the letter is clearly meant to apply verbally as well (cf. 2:12, 15, 22-23; 3:1, 9-10).

The divine intention behind connecting suffering and redemption is made explicit in the confessional formulation in 3:18-22. Christ's atoning death freed the believers from their sins and brought them to God. Dying to the flesh and rising to new life in the Spirit is associated with baptism, by which the believer participates in the death and resurrection of Christ (3:21; cf. Rom. 6:1-11). The pattern of Christ they follow, then, is not simply in his suffering death but also in the redemption of his resurrection: just as Christ's death brought them to God, so also their spiritually empowered faithful suffering has the capacity to bring others to God.

3:19-20 insists that their capacity to suffer redemptively in this way does not come from their own strength of will, but from the eternal victory of Christ over the powers of sin and death that formerly ruled the world. Christ's "proclamation to the spirits in prison" was traditionally understood to refer to Christ's preaching to the dead in the underworld during his days in the tomb, but scholars now understand the phrase to refer to Christ's declaration of victory over the rebellious angels described in *1 Enoch*, those "who in former times did not obey, when God waited patiently in the days of Noah" (3:20).[54] Because of this victory, all "angels, authorities, and powers are subject" to Christ (v. 22), and the knowledge of this empowers the believer to witness with a clear conscience in the manner described in vv. 14-16.

"Therefore," says Peter, "arm yourselves with the same intention" and live according to the "suffering leads to glory" pattern of Christ (4:1). There is no time for living according to the worldly cravings that dominated their former pagan lives (vv. 2-3), and believers should not be surprised that they are abused for their refusal to participate in the conventional lustful consumption of their culture. Indeed, it is the abusers themselves who will be surprised when they are asked to give account for their lives at the end of time (v. 5). No one will escape this judgment, not even those who have already died, for the gospel was preached to them as well so that all might have a chance to "live in the spirit like God" (v. 6).[55]

---

54. Dalton's *Christ's Proclamation to the Spirits* is the study that has had the greatest impact on scholarly views of this passage. The case against the traditional interpretation is based mostly on the verbal parallels with the *1 Enoch* narrative (see chs. 6-10 and 18-19 and *Jub.* 7:21), but also on the absence of anything here implying a descent and the choice of the verb *kēryssō* ("made proclamation") rather than *euangelizō* ("preached good news").

55. 4:6 is widely recognized as a difficult verse to interpret. Who preached what to whom? Are "the dead" here the same as the imprisoned spirits of 3:19-20? Are they residents

In contrast to the life they left behind, believers must hold tightly to the practices of their new life in Christ. Just as they patiently bear abuse from outsiders in order to bring them to God, so also they must not allow anything to cause their love for one another to falter, for hospitable, ungrudging "love covers a multitude of sins" (4:8-9), the second allusion to Prov. 10:12 in the CE collection (cf. Jas. 5:19-20). The parallel with James is instructive: together they depict a Christian community committed to the kind of mutual correction and unfailing love that has the capacity to save souls from death (Jas. 1:20; 5:20; 1 Pet. 1:9, 22; 2:11). But again, the capacity to save belongs to God: believers must therefore employ their gifts in the knowledge that they come only by God's grace (4:10); they must speak in the knowledge that God is speaking through them and serve knowing that they do so only by God's strength, "so that in everything God may be glorified through Jesus Christ" (v. 11).

Body Closing: The Judgment of God's Household (4:12–5:11)

The doxology in 4:11 and the second direct address to the reader as "beloved" in v. 12 signal the shift to the closing section of the letter, which is itself framed out by a final doxology in 5:11. The sections inside the doxological frame describe the believers' suffering in eschatological terms, and these in turn frame a culminating exhortation to proper conduct in Christian community.

> 4:11: doxological frame
>> 4:12-19: an eschatological view of suffering
>>> 5:1-5: proper conduct in Christian community
>> 5:6-10: an eschatological view of suffering
> 5:11: doxological frame

The structure ends the letter as it began (1:3-9) by "embracing" right Christian conduct in the worship of a powerful God who promises ultimate deliverance from distress.

---

of Hades, the place of the dead, who somehow heard the aforementioned announcement to the disobedient spirits? Are they those who are *spiritually* dead? For an overview of the interpretive options, see, e.g., Achtemeier, *1 Peter*, pp. 286-91, and Michaels, *1 Peter*, 235-41.

Rather than respond with surprise when they find themselves tested by the fire of persecution, by now it should be clear to the readers that suffering is in fact reason to rejoice, because it shows that they are following the pattern of Christ (4:12-13; the echo of 1:6-7 and our earlier reading of Jas. 1:2-4 is hard to miss) prepared for them by the Creator. While suffering as a wrongdoer or a meddler[56] should be unthinkable for a Christian, suffering under the name of Christian is a badge of honor essential for the proper glorification of the triune God (4:14-16). Again, all this is playing out according to the Creator's foreknowledge (cf. 1:2), who uses suffering to perfect believers and is now utilizing the scorn of their neighbors to inaugurate the judgment of the world, which begins with a fiery purification of "the house of God" (4:17).[57] The imaginative shift called for here (and, indeed, throughout the entire letter) functions as both promise and warning; to those tempted to forsake their faith to alleviate suffering *now*, Peter quotes Prov. 11:31 to press home the point that the pain of divine purification is inevitable for everyone (4:18). The truly wise will face that pain now, in the comforting knowledge that "those who suffer according to God's will do right and entrust their souls to a faithful Creator" (v. 19).[58]

Immediately after this call to "do right" Peter turns ("therefore", 5:1) to address the community elders, setting himself forward as an example to those who are themselves examples to others. He has already discussed power relations between Christians and pagan society (2:13–3:12), but how should privilege be negotiated inside the walls of God's house? Peter begins by describing himself not by means of an honorific like "Rock" or

56. The Greek is *allotriepiskopos*, "overseer of other people's affairs" (cf. 2 Thess. 3:11). The word is not used in other NT vice lists or in earlier Greek literature and so is difficult to translate accurately. One option is to read it as a moral vice, in which case Peter is saying it is not the Christian's job to tell pagans how to live their lives — hence the translation "troublesome meddler" (NASB) or even "mischief maker" (NRSV). Given that the prior three examples suggest illegal activity, however, Achtemeier, *1 Peter*, p. 115, suggests "one who defrauds others" (following J. B. Bauer, "Aut maleficus aut alieni speculator (1 Petr 4,15)" *BZ* 22 [1978]).

57. The phrase draws our minds back to the earlier exhortation (2:5) for believers to be built together into a spiritual "house" where sacrifices are offered to God through Christ.

58. While the conviction that God is the Creator of all things pervades early Christian faith and is the central characteristic of the first person of the Trinity in the CE collection, it is only here in 1 Peter in the whole of the NT that God is called *ktistēs*, "Creator." Here Peter insists explicitly what Christian readers infer from Jas. 1:18, that is, the Creator of the entire cosmos is now working for their salvation.

"Apostle" but simply as a "fellow elder." Of course, he is not just *any* elder; his authority is predicated on the fact that he is a "witness to the sufferings of Christ," both in terms of passive observation (cf. Luke 22:28) and active advocacy (as has been made clear throughout the letter). Moreover, he has become a "partaker in the glory that is to be revealed," which is to say that he not only commends the redemptive value of suffering but also lives a life that reflects his participation in that suffering. On this basis he exhorts these elders in a position of power to "tend the flock of God" (recall John 21:15-17) in a manner that comports with the alternative vision set forth thus far: in contrast to "worldly" assertions of human power, elders are to take up their duties willingly, not grudgingly; freely, not greedily;[59] not as lordly power brokers but as examples of powerlessness before the Lord (5:2-3), always keeping in mind that they are themselves sheep in the flock of the Chief Shepherd (v. 4). In the same manner ("likewise," v. 5a) the younger ones are to be subject to their leaders. Indeed, everyone must come dressed in humility toward one another (v. 5b), for as the living and abiding word insists, "God opposes the proud, but gives grace to the humble" (v. 5c, quoting Prov. 3:34). The "suffer now, glory later" rule requires all, leader and led alike, to humble themselves so that in due time God may be the one to do the exalting (v. 6).

James's use of the same sayings in a similar context (Jas. 4:6-10) underscores the unity of the Pillar apostles' message to believers struggling in the Diaspora. But where James calls believers to repentance, Peter brings word of comfort: "Cast all your anxieties upon him, for he cares about you" (5:7). Again, disciplined sobriety is called for (cf. 1:13; 4:7); suffering people easily lose focus, and a loud lion is lurking around the edge of the flock seeking to draw them away from the Shepherd who protects them (5:8). This dangerous adversary is resisted when believers focus their eyes on the suffering of Christ, for in doing so they will recall that trials are intended by God to be accomplished in all believers everywhere (v. 9). These trials will persist for only a brief time (cf. 1:6-7), for it is a God of grace who is ruling all things (5:11), and the path that has been laid leads through suffering to ultimate restoration and strengthening in the glory of Christ (cf. 1:8-9).

---

59. Cf. Matt. 6:24; Luke 16:13; Acts 20:33; 1 Tim. 3:3, 8; Tit. 1:5-9.

Letter Closing: Final Greetings (5:12-14)

With the letter body closed, Peter offers a quick restatement of his purpose for writing this "brief" letter: to encourage his readers to stand firm in his testimony that the exile they suffer is in fact "the true grace of God," that is, a sign of God's fellowship and not a punitive abandonment (5:12). The message comes "through Silvanus," which most likely means he was the one charged with delivering the letter.[60] Readers will quite naturally assume that this person is the Silas[61] known as Paul's missionary partner in Acts 15–18, coauthor of the Thessalonian letters, and cofounder of the church in Corinth (2 Cor. 1:19). That this Silas also carried the apostolic decree to Gentile believers in Antioch (Acts 15:22) solidifies his canonical portrait as one who served the earliest apostles.

The letter also comes joined with greetings from two others (5:13). Good evidence exists for associating "she who is co-elect in Babylon" as the church (cf. 2 John 1) in the city of Rome (cf. Rev. 14:8; 16:19; 17:5; 18:2, 10, 21).[62] That a figurative designation for a church is intended here is confirmed by these verses' design, intended to parallel the letter's opening address:

1 Peter 1:1-2	1 Peter 5:12-14
Written by Peter	"I have written"
to the elect	She who is co-elect
in the Diaspora	in Babylon
Peace to you	Peace to you[63]

Greetings also come from someone called "my son Mark." Like Silvanus, a Mark is also known from Acts as an associate of Paul (Acts 12:25; 13:5, 13; 15:37, 39); his name also comes up periodically in the farewell greetings of

---

60. The issue is still debated, but identification as "the faithful brother" appears to have been a customary designation for the individual charged with delivering letters (Rom. 16:1; Eph. 6:21; Col. 4:7; Ignatius, *Rom.* 10.1; *Smyrn.* 12.1; Polycarp, *Phil.* 14.1).

61. Silvanus is generally believed to have been the Latin form of the Semitic name Silas.

62. While there is no tradition linking Peter with the geographical region of the actual Mesopotamian city, there is a good deal that associates him with Rome. Jews and Christians alike often called Rome "Babylon" (especially after the destruction of Jerusalem by Roman forces, e.g., *2 Bar.* 11.1-2; 67.7; *2 Esdr.* 3:1-2; *Sib. Or.* 5.143; Rev. 14:8; 16:19 and chs. 17–18) and ancient interpreters understood Peter to be referring here to that city (e.g., *H.E.* 2.15.2).

63. So Jobes, *1 Peter*, p. 319.

Paul's letters (Col. 4:10; 2 Tim. 4:11; Phlm. 24). Though the Acts story implies that he may have had a previous association with Peter through the Jerusalem church (12:12-25), his presence here along with Silas has the canonical effect of connecting associates of Paul with Peter, thereby underscoring the unity of the apostles, despite what one might be led to infer from the conflict between Peter and Paul in Gal. 2:11-14.

The closing call to greet one another with "a kiss of love" accentuates this letter's emphasis on the central importance of genuine love in the community (1:22; 2:17; 3:8; 4:8). This greeting, normally reserved in Greco-Roman society for family and close friends, was common in earliest Christianity (Rom. 16:16; 1 Cor. 16:20; 2 Cor. 13:12; 1 Thess. 5:26) as a gesture to demonstrate that believers had been "born anew" into a new family in Christ. The final words, "Peace to all of you who are in Christ," stand in parallel with the opening greeting and have the effect of wrapping the whole letter in the distinctive form of peace described throughout the letter: Christian peace does not derive from the absence of hostility, but from the assurance that "those who suffer according to God's will" and "do right" in relation to others can "entrust their souls to a faithful Creator" with confidence (4:19).

Commentary: 2 Peter

Letter Prescript (1:1-2)

As with 1 Peter, so also 2 Peter begins with an epistolary prescript that conforms to standard expectations of the day. Where 1 Peter identifies its author as "Peter, an apostle of Jesus Christ," 2 Peter is from "*Simeon* Peter, a *servant* and apostle of Jesus Christ" (1:1). The name Simeon is unusual in that people in Jesus' day would have used the Greek name "Simon" (as witnessed throughout the NT) in place of the older Hebrew transliteration "Simeon."[64] While commentators often consider this a deliberate "archaizing" on the part of the pseudonymous author (to make the address seem more solemn and authoritative),[65] and others have used it to build a case

---

64. J. A. Fitzmyer, "The Name Simon," in *Essays on the Semitic Background of the New Testament* (London: Chapman, 1971), 105-12.

65. E.g., J. N. D. Kelly, *The Epistles of Peter and of Jude* (BNTC; London: Black, 1969), p. 296; E. J. Richard, *Reading 1 Peter, Jude, and 2 Peter* (Macon: Smyth and Helwys, 2000), p. 319.

for an early date of composition[66] or for Peter's ongoing association with Jewish Christians in Rome,[67] most also note Acts 15:14, where James calls Peter "Simeon." The effect in that context is to cast James in explicitly Jewish tones as the leader of the Christian mission to Jews. The use of the name here has the same effect insofar as it locates Peter in the symbolic world of the ancient Jewish-Christian mission narrated by the book of Acts. This effect is intensified by the use of the term "servant" in addition to "apostle": within the CE it is James and Jude, the brothers of Jesus, who are identified as "*servants* of Jesus Christ." 1 Peter identifies Peter as an "apostle," but 2 Peter's "servant and apostle" increases the linkage between Peter and the brothers of Jesus. This is yet another example of how the CE collection places Peter within the biblical frame as a Jerusalem Pillar apostle rather than the later monarchical bishop of western tradition.

Though the content of the letter points to a specific audience with specific concerns, the recipient's address is as generalized as any in the NT: this is a letter written to anyone who shares the same "precious" faith as the apostles, on whose behalf Peter speaks in this letter (note the "we" of 1:16-19). "Faith" here appears to refer not simply to the disposition of the believer but also to the content of the faith shared by the apostles (Jude 3; cf., e.g., 1 Tim. 1:2; Tit. 1:4) and indeed all who keep "the way of righteousness" (2:21), like Noah (2:5) and Lot (2:7-8), those who seek after the place "where righteousness dwells" (3:13, in contrast to that of the "unrighteous" false teachers [2:9] who are condemned in the letter). This way of righteousness was opened by Jesus (3:18), who is identified here as both God[68] and Savior.[69] The latter term is used more frequently in 2 Peter than in any other NT text (1:1, 11; 2:20; 3:2, 18). The other dominant title for Jesus in 2 Peter is "Lord" (1:2, 8, 11, 14, 16; 2:20; 3:2, 18; cf. 2:1). The two terms com-

---

66. E.g., C. Bigg, *The Epistles of St. Peter and St. Jude* (ICC; Edinburgh: Clark, 1901), p. 248.

67. So Bauckham, *Jude, 2 Peter,* p. 167: "The form *Symeōn* may reflect the fact that the writer was an associate of Peter's who belonged to Peter's circle in Rome. Because that circle included Jewish Christian leaders (such as Mark and Silvanus) who had known Peter in Palestine, the name *Symeōn*, which was current in Palestinian Christian circles, continued to be used in the Roman Petrine circle."

68. This is one of the few places in NT Scripture where Jesus is referred to as "God" directly (cf. John 1:1-3; 20:28; Heb. 1:8-9).

69. The title "savior" was reserved in Judaism for God (e.g., Pss. 24:5; 25:5; 27:1, 9; 65:5) and in Roman culture for the emperor as divine (e.g., Philo, *In Flacc.* 74; 126; *Leg. ad Gai.* 22; Josephus, *Bell.* 3, 459).

bine to describe Jesus in authoritative terms as the ruler of the kingdom of God who must be submitted to and obeyed.[70]

As we have already noted, the substance of the letter's greeting is shared with 1 Peter and Jude, but 2 Peter adds "in the knowledge of God and of Jesus our Lord" (1:2). The word translated "knowledge" (*epignōsis*, 1:2, 3, 8; 2:20) is often distinguished from a more common term (*gnōsis*, 1:5-6; 3:18) by its "inceptive" quality: it is the initial knowledge that comes from conversion, not the knowledge that is cultivated and deepened over the course of a believer's life.[71] As the next verses will make clear, Peter is concerned for believers whose initial meeting with Jesus is not developed into a deeper knowledge of Jesus as Lord and Master of their lives.

Letter Exordium (1:3-11)

V. 3 launches the letter "exordium," which functions rhetorically as a kind of "solemn decree"[72] or "opening homily"[73] representing the definitive summary of the apostolic testimony to be remembered (1:12-15). A short reflection on the saving act of God (vv. 3-4) is followed by a set of ethical exhortations (vv. 5-10) and a proclamation of the outcome for those who heed the call (v. 11).

Because of Christ's divine power, all things needed for a life of godliness have been provided to believers. "Godliness" is the preferred term in 2 Peter (1:3, 6, 7; 3:11) for the appropriate Christian posture of piety and obedience before God that leads the believer to maturity and, ultimately, to salvation (that is, to Christ's "own glory and excellence"). This gift is bestowed on believers at conversion in the form of knowledge regarding God's "precious and very great promises" (1:4). Though the precise prom-

---

70. So P. H. Davids, *Letters of 2 Peter and Jude* (PNTC; Grand Rapids: Eerdmans, 2006), p. 152. This Christological vision expands the articulation of Christ in 1 Peter, where the focus is on Jesus' *past* exemplary role as suffering Servant. 2 Peter's focus on Jesus as a *present* ruler enlarges and activates 1 Peter's recurring references to Christ's glory (1:11, 21; 4:13; 5:4, 10), thereby enabling the two letters to proclaim Christ as both suffering Servant (1 Peter) and exalted Lord (2 Peter).

71. See R. E. Picirelli, "The Meaning of 'Epignosis,'" *EvQ* 47 (1975), pp. 85-93.

72. So H.-J. Klauck, *Ancient Letters*, p. 410.

73. Bauckham, *Jude, 2 Peter*, p. 132, identifies the opening homily as a component of the testamentary genre.

ises are not listed at this point, later the "promise" will be identified as having to do with Jesus' return (3:4, 9) and establishment of the new creation (3:13; this final occurrence of the word forms an inclusio with 1:4, bracketing the whole letter within this theme). The word will also be used as a point of contrast with the false teachers, who promise people freedom while "they themselves are slaves of corruption" (2:14).

Here in 1:4, the promises are said to enable the believer "to escape the corruption that is in the world because of lust" and to "become participants in the divine nature,"[74] that is, to escape the immorality and corruptibility of this world by entering "the eternal kingdom of our Lord and Savior Jesus Christ" (v. 11). Thus it would seem that a contrast is being made between the promises mediated by the teachers (tainted by corruption) and those mediated by the apostles (which will enable escape from immorality and corruptibility; cf. vv. 16-18). The obscure phrase "participants (literally 'sharers') in the divine nature" is distinctively Hellenistic, but the idea does not seem far from what Paul describes in Rom. 8:18-25 and 1 Cor. 15:42-57. Given that elsewhere "the promise" is associated with the giving of the Spirit (e.g., Luke 24:49; Acts 1:4; 2:33, 38) and the inclusion of the Gentiles as fulfillment of God's promise to Abraham (e.g., Rom. 4:13-20; note especially Gal. 3:14, which brings the two together), Peter seems to be describing the kind of partnership with God made possible by the Spirit's work of bringing pagans into covenant with God.

These promises are associated with the believer's initial, conversional knowledge of God. The chain of virtues that follow (1:5-7) describes the stepping stones the believer must walk if this initial knowledge is to become effective and lead ultimately to salvation. Walking this path will require effort (v. 5); it all begins with faith, of course, but believers have already been told that salvation does not come by faith alone (Jas. 2:24). No, faith is the first of seven virtue-steps that lead the believer to love. The effort of taking these steps is what keeps the believer's conversional knowledge from being ineffective and unfruitful (1:8; cf. Jas. 2:20); failure to take them will leave the believer stumbling back into old sinful ways (1:9). The call and election of Christ that brought about conversion must be con-

---

74. The precise meaning of this phrase, unparalleled as it is in the NT, is widely debated. For a full treatment of the text, see J. M. Starr, *Sharers in the Divine Nature: 2 Peter 1:4 in Its Hellenistic Context* (CBNTS 33; Stockholm: Almquist & Wiksell, 2000). For a shorter yet thorough overview, see Bauckham, *Jude, 2 Peter,* pp. 179-82.

firmed by a right response of godliness (v. 10), for only in that way will entrance to God's kingdom be provided (v. 11).

Body Opening: Peter's Testament (1:12-15)

The purpose of the letter is provided in 1:12-15. That Peter has written primarily to remind believers is made clear by the threefold repetition of "remind" over four short verses (1:12, 13, 15). Though believers have already been "stabilized" in the truth of the apostolic teaching just described (v. 12), constant reminder is required for them to remain in that secure place. Indeed, the coming false teachers will be able to entice "unstable souls" (2:14) because they themselves are "ignorant and unstable" (3:16). To keep believers from losing their own "stability" (3:17), Peter will "always" remind believers of the apostolic word of truth just proclaimed, both while he remains alive (1:13) and after his imminent death (vv. 14-15).

The section is rich with linkages to the canonical Gospels. The reference to Jesus informing Peter of his death (1:14) recalls John 13:36 and 21:18. Peter speaks of his death as his "departure" *(exodos)* and then refers to the Transfiguration (1:16-18), where, in Luke's version, Jesus' death is called "the departure *(exodos)* he was about to accomplish at Jerusalem" (Luke 9:31). Finally, word of Peter's intention to leave behind a means by which believers may always "recall these things" (1:15) may lead the reader to recall "my son Mark," mentioned at the end of 1 Peter (5:13) and the person traditionally remembered as "the disciple and interpreter of Peter" who "after his departure . . . handed down to us in writing what had been preached by Peter" in the form of the Gospel according to Mark.[75] These seemingly intentional references to the gospel tradition have the effect of grounding the content of Peter's opening homily in the teaching of Jesus, whose "precious and very great promises" (1:4) enable the believer to escape worldliness and enter the kingdom he rules (v. 11).

Apostolic Testimony and the Word of Prophecy (1:16-21)

1:16 marks the beginning of the argument that will dominate the remainder of the letter. Evidently someone has suggested that the apostles fol-

---

75. Irenaeus, *Adv. Haer.* 3.1.1.

lowed "cleverly devised myths" when they made known "the power and coming" of the Lord Jesus Christ (1:16), that is, his return in glory (cf. 3:4) to judge the living and the dead (cf. 2:3b-10a; 3:5-10; 1 Pet. 4:5).[76] Peter's first response is to appeal to the authority of eyewitness testimony. What the apostles saw and heard ("and looked upon and touched" with their hands, 1 John 1:1-3) was Jesus' receipt of "honor and glory from God the Father," whose voice they heard speaking from "the majestic glory" when they were with him on the mountain of Transfiguration (1:17-18; cf. Matt. 17:1-8; Mark 9:2-8; Luke 9:28-36). That voice identified Jesus as God's royal son (Ps. 2:7) and transfigured him into a majestic figure shining in divine glory. According to the Psalm alluded to, the kingly Son of God is given authority over all the nations of the earth (Ps. 2:8) to establish justice so that all the earth will serve the Lord (Ps. 2:9-11). Thus the apostolic witness to the Transfiguration appears to establish two key points in the case being argued: first, God does intrude into the world, transforming everyday nature by his powerful word (cf. 3:3-7, where it is clear that the "scoffers" deny that God engages in such interference), and, second, in the Transfiguration God's word unveiled Jesus' identity as Lord and Judge of the whole earth.[77]

In the following sentence about "the prophetic word" (1:19a) it is unclear whether the prophetic message is "more fully confirmed" (NRSV) because of the Transfiguration or is akin to the Transfiguration in being "completely reliable" (NIV) in its support of the doctrine of Christ's return. Either way, the argument involves bringing the prophetic word alongside the Transfiguration. Given the lack of a single prophetic "word" set forth and the appeal to the OT throughout the next chapter, it seems likely that Peter is speaking here of the entire OT, as was common in the Judaism of his day. Readers are exhorted to devote themselves to Scripture as one would cling to a bright lamp when walking in a dark place (cf. Ps. 119:105). But when "the day dawns" (that is, when Christ returns: 3:10, 18) and "the morning star rises" (Rev. 2:28; 22:16), the lamp will no longer be needed.

---

76. The word for "cleverly devised" *(sesophismenoi)* bears the sense of something invented deceitfully out of an inappropriate motive: the story was "concocted." J. Neyrey has argued that the false teachers' accusation resembles that of ancient Epicurean critique; see his "Form and Background of the Polemic in 2 Peter," *JBL* 99 (1980), pp. 407-31, and *2 Peter, Jude* (AB 37C; New York: Doubleday, 1993), pp. 122-28.

77. Indeed, the Synoptic Transfiguration account itself joins that event to the reality of final judgment when it prefaces the scene with references to Jesus' return as judge (Matt. 16:27-28; Mark 8:38–9:1; Luke 9:26-27).

Though 1:20 is commonly translated "no prophecy of Scripture is a matter of one's own interpretation" (NRSV, ESV, NASB), a majority of scholars prefer the translation "no prophecy of Scripture came about by the prophet's own interpretation" (NIV). The communicative intent here is not that no one should attempt to interpret Scripture for himself but that true prophets speak the word of God and not their own words (e.g., Jer. 23:16-22; Ezek. 13:1-7); the prophetic word derives not from the power of a human, but from a human empowered by God (1:21).

To summarize the argument, then: Peter is insisting that the eventual return of Jesus as Lord and Judge is not a message dreamed up by the apostles but something attested to in Jesus' lifetime, when they heard God's word identifying Jesus, and corroborated by the OT witness, which is the reliable record of God's word in history. The apostolic word is trustworthy precisely because it is borne forth by God's word.

Apostolic Prediction of False Teachers and the Certainty of Judgment against Them (2:1-10a)

But just as false prophets arose in the past with false words, so also, Peter predicts, there will be false teachers within the church. Their teachings will involve a denial of "the master who bought them." That is, they will somehow deny Christ's lordship over the conduct of their lives: it is the "way of truth" that will be slandered, not just the teaching of truth (2:2).[78] Just as predictable is the fact that their smooth talk will acquire many followers to join them on their immoral path. The key word here is "destruction": the teachers will bring in *destructive* teachings (*haireseis,* "heresies")[79] which will eventually bring *destruction* on themselves (v. 1), inasmuch as the eventual *destruction* of such people has been an observable reality from ancient times (v. 3). Given what is said later in the letter (3:3-10), it seems that the teachers are suggesting that the delay of Christ's return indicates

78. We find here an echo of Isa. 52:5, where God complains, "because of you my name is continually reviled among the nations." The verse is frequent in early Christian exhortations to avoid pagan immorality because it gives Gentiles cause to revile the truth of God (e.g., Rom. 2:23-24; 1 Tim. 6:1; Tit. 2:5).

79. The warning about the arrival of false teachers is a common feature of the final "testament" genre in the NT: Matt. 24:11, 24; Acts 20:29-30; 1 Tim. 4:1-5; 2 Tim. 3:1-9; 4:3-4; 1 John 4:1-3; Jude.

the falsehood of the doctrine. God's apparent inactivity leads them to conclude mockingly that judgment, if it is real, is idle, slow, or even asleep.

The following section (2:3b-10a) counters that by vividly describing how the destructive power of God's inbreaking judgment has been made manifest in the past. The single, long sentence offers up three examples of those who experienced God's judgment and two corresponding examples of the righteous who were spared that judgment. All three examples of judgment are detailed through the lens of extrabiblical Jewish teaching.

First are the sinning angels whom God "cast into hell and committed to chains of deepest darkness to be kept until the judgment" (v. 4). Readers of the biblical canon might be left wondering about the identity of these angels. Their subsequent connection with the judgment of the world in Noah's day (v. 5) may lead readers to recall the strange section of Genesis just prior to the Noah story, where "sons of God" observe beautiful human women and capture them to be their wives (Gen. 6:1-2). Immediately after this God sees that the wickedness of humanity has become so pervasive that the only thing to do is to blot out humanity with a flood. Jewish tradition made much of this strange scene, eventually coming to teach that these "angels" (later called "the Watchers") were captured by God and imprisoned in the deepest, darkest part of hell to await the final judgment.[80]

The second example follows the Genesis narrative by referring to "the ancient world of the ungodly" where the only ones spared the flood's destruction were Noah and the seven members of his family (2:5; cf. Gen. 7:13; 8:18; 1 Pet. 3:20). Again, the appeal to extrabiblical Jewish teaching tradition is evident in the designation of Noah as a "herald" or "preacher of righteousness"; it was part of the tradition that Noah both acted righteously and proclaimed the way of righteousness to others, whose failure to listen resulted in their annihilation.[81]

Sodom and Gomorrah provide the final example, showing what is appointed for the ungodly (2:6). Jesus also linked the flood and the destruction of Sodom as an example of eschatological destruction (Luke 17:26-32),

---

80. The tradition of the Watchers is related principally in *1 Enoch* 6–10, 15–16, and 21, but it is reflected in a range of writings from the period (e.g., *T. Naph.* 3.5; CD 2.18; 4Q227; *Jub.* 10.5). The Greek word for "hell" here is "Tartarus," known from Greek mythology as the lowest part of the underworld. Hellenistic Jews took up this word to refer to the deepest, darkest part of hell (*Sib. Or.* 2.302; 4.186).

81. Cf. Josephus, *Ant.* 1.3.1

as did others in Jewish tradition.[82] Indeed, the move from water to fire will be underscored again later in the letter (3:5-7). The corresponding example of righteousness is "righteous Lot" (2:7) who was completely distressed by the licentiousness of the wicked people around him (v. 8). Again, Jewish teaching tradition is evident in the emphatic description of Lot's righteousness,[83] for his depiction in Genesis is not quite so unblemished.

2:9 sums up the evidence just presented by echoing key words from the preceding paragraph: clearly "the Lord knows how to rescue the godly (vv. 5-6) from trial, and to keep the unrighteous (vv. 5, 7-8) under punishment until the day of judgment (v. 4)." While Peter is largely focused on punishment at the final judgment, his examples include a kind of preliminary punishment that precedes the end (vv. 4, 9). The reader is left with the sense that if God does not punish the wicked person in this life, the punishment will surely come in the next.

The particular forms of unrighteousness in focus are those who "indulge their flesh in depraved lust" and those "who despise authority" (2:10). Both are examples of a broader category of vice variously described in the letter as "godlessness" (*asebeia*, 2:5, 6; 3:7), "licentiousness" (*aselgeia*, 2:2, 7, 18), or "lawlessness" (2:7; 3:17). All these terms indicate a lack of moral self-restraint in which passions reduce individuals to the state of irrational animals (2:12), which in turn spills out to have a negative effect on the larger community (see, e.g., Rom. 13:13; Gal. 5:19-21; Eph. 4:16-20). This negative characterization of the opponents forms the basis of a long digression that takes the form of an extended, vicious denunciation (2:10b-22).

Denunciation of False Teachers (2:10b-22)

The denunciation begins on a puzzling note. The teachers are described as "bold" (in the sense of claiming power they do not possess) and "willful" (in an arrogant fashion) and going so far as to even slander "the glories" (2:10b), "whereas angels, though greater in might and power, do not bring against them a slanderous judgment from the Lord" (v. 11). Who are "the glorious ones," and against whom do the angels not bring a slanderous judgment, the teachers or the glorious ones?

---

82. Philo, *Mos.* 2.53-65; Wis. 10:1-8.
83. See, e.g., Wis. 10:6; 19:17. The tradition is picked up again later in *1 Clem.* 11:1.

This particular illustration makes little sense by itself, so two interpretive possibilities are typically put forward. One takes its cue from the parallel in Jude 8-9: there the example of the archangel Michael is presented, for when he struggled with the devil over the body of Moses (a story known from the *Testament of Moses*), he "did not presume to pronounce a reviling judgment on him, but said, 'The Lord rebuke you'" (Jude 9). If this is the intended background here in 2 Peter, it suggests that the "glorious ones" are the fallen angels (previously mentioned in 2:4), and the teachers are so arrogant that they are claiming authority even to slander beings only God has the power to condemn. If this is the case, it suggests that the teachers mock evil spiritual forces as being powerless against them. The holy angels, by contrast, do not rebuke "them" (perhaps both the glorious ones and the false teachers) but humbly leave the condemnation to the Lord, who alone has authority to judge.

The second possibility is to understand the "glorious ones" to be holy angels who, though far more powerful than the teachers, nevertheless do not rebuke the teachers but humbly leave that work of condemnation for the Lord. In that case it might be that the teachers are mocking angels, understood to be involved in the final judgment (e.g., Matt. 24:31; Rev. 14:15-16), by denying the reality of that judgment. Either option is possible in the end, though the former seems more likely.[84]

Regardless, the basic point is clear: the teachers are arrogant enough to slander spiritual beings that are more powerful than they are. But "they slander what they do not understand" and so make it clear that they are irrational beings driven only by lustful instincts (2:12). V. 12b is another interpretive quandary: it is literally "in their destruction they also will be destroyed." It is likely that "their destruction" refers back to the final condemnation of the glorious ones, whom the teachers mock; thus Peter is saying, "They are ignorant of those whom they insult, but, when those beings are destroyed, they themselves will also perish in the same destruction."[85]

The teachers are morally degenerate partyers (2:13b). The claim that they are "blots and blemishes" who celebrate their debauchery "while they feast with you," suggests that they bring their improper behavior into a

---

84. Bauckham, *Jude, 2 Peter*, p. 261, and D. F. Watson, "Second Letter of Peter," *NIB* 12 (Nashville: Abingdon, 1998), p. 350, prefer the first; Davids, *Letters of 2 Peter and Jude*, p. 236, prefers the second.

85. So Bauckham, *Jude, 2 Peter*, p. 258.

Christian celebration and thus turn a holy gathering into something impure (cf. 1 Cor. 11:17-34). They have "eyes full of an adulteress" (2:14), meaning perhaps that they are always on the lookout for an opportunity to gratify their sexual desires. They "entice unsteady souls," that is, they lure immature believers who have been insufficiently educated in the faith. They themselves, by contrast, are thoroughly trained in the art of greediness (v. 14). These "accursed children" are Christians in name only and will be rejected by their Parent when the judgment comes.

Once again, Peter returns to Jewish teaching tradition in his appeal to the well-known "two ways" tradition (2:15-16).[86] The false teachers are Christians who have forsaken the "right" or "straight way" and have "wandered," following "the way of Balaam." Balaam "loved the wages of doing wrong," a reference perhaps to his accepting payment for cursing Israel. Of course, the more familiar story of Balaam (Num. 22:25-31) presents him in a good light as one who refused to curse Israel, but the larger canonical portrait depicted him as giving in to bribes (Deut. 23:4; Neh. 13:2; Jude 11; Rev. 2:14) and drawing Israel into idolatry (Num. 31:16). This is how he was remembered in Jewish tradition.[87] Peter's point is to appeal to Balaam as a biblical example of someone seeking wages for wickedness. Furthermore, Balaam's irrational intention to curse Israel was opposed by a donkey, who thus proved to be the more rational one; the point is that the false teachers (already identified as "irrational animals," 2:12) are less rational than donkeys.

Though "the teaching of the wise is a "fountain of life" (Prov. 13:14), these people are springs that offer no water (2:17). They are tossed by the storm of their lusts and will end up where the sinning angels are being held (cf. v. 4). Their over-inflated, boastful speech is empty of content, yet by their smooth talk they lure in believers who are new to the faith (v. 18). Peter's declaration that they promise "freedom" while they are themselves "slaves of corruption" sheds some light on the content of their teaching. Thus far we have picked up on the sense that they claimed freedom from judgment and from the rules of morality. Elsewhere in the NT we find further examples of people who assumed that Christian freedom liberated them for licentiousness (e.g., Rom. 3:8; 6:1; Gal. 5:13; 1 Pet. 2:16), and indeed, given the later reference to Paul's teaching, we cannot help but as-

---

86. E.g., Deut. 30:19-20; Jer. 21:8; Psalm 1; Prov. 28:18; Matt. 7:13-27.
87. E.g., Philo, *Mos.* 1.264-300; Josephus, *Ant.* 4.118.

sume that the distortion of freedom into decadence is part of what these "ignorant and unstable" teachers have "twisted to their own destruction" (3:16).

The next verses (2:20-22) circle the reader back to the opening lines of the letter (1:3-4) by referring to "escape from the world's corruptions" "through the knowledge of" Christ. Where this language was used earlier of the process of participating with God and eventually entering the Lord's kingdom, here it describes the process in reverse: the teachers escaped the world but were later "entangled" in its corruptions and "overpowered." Thus "the last state has become worse for them than the first" (cf. Matt. 12:45; Luke 11:46; as for the impossibility of repentance from post-baptismal sin, see Heb. 6:1-12 and 10:26-31). The point is clear: Christianity is not simply a set of beliefs, but a *way of righteousness* that must be walked faithfully to the end (2:21).[88] The two final proverbs conclude the lengthy denunciation by reiterating the connection between the teachers "turning back" and irrational animals who likewise return to a former state of uncleanness.

Apostolic Prediction of Scoffers (3:1-4)

The long digressive denunciation ended, Peter now returns to the main theme of the letter set out in 1:12-21. Once Peter has departed (1:12-15), how are believers to respond when confronted by divergent moral and theological claims? On what basis will they distinguish between the way of righteousness and the way of error? The cumulative answer of ch. 3 is that believers must cling to the tradition passed down by the apostles (1:16).

Peter begins by commending his own first letter, which canonical readers will not hesitate to identify as 1 Peter.[89] 2 Peter thus insists that both letters are required in order to receive a right "remembrance" of Peter's message (3:1). In them Peter insists that believers must remember the

---

88. One should recall that Christianity is referred to as "the Way" in Acts 9:2; 18:25-26; 19:9, 23; 24:14, 22.

89. J. A. T. Robinson argued that the former letter was in fact the letter of Jude, as an extension of his thesis that Jude was the actual author of 2 Peter (*Redating the New Testament* [Philadelphia: Westminster, 1976]). M. Green argued that the previous letter is not 1 Peter but an unknown text that is now lost to us (*The Second Epistle General of Peter and the General Epistle of Jude* [TNTC; Grand Rapids: Eerdmans, 1987]).

predictions of the holy prophets (likely the whole OT is in view)[90] and the "commandment of the Lord and Savior" (i.e., the ethical teachings of the gospel) as these have been mediated to believers through the teaching of "your apostles" (i.e., those "sent" to bring the message of salvation to them). The advice, in short, is to cling to Scripture.

But the defense against the false teachers is not yet complete. Peter returns to his earlier predictive posture (note the repetition of 1:20 in 3:3), informing readers that "in the last days scoffers will come scoffing," indulging in lusts and mocking "the promise of his coming" (3:3-4). They will do this, presumably, because of the delay of the parousia ("all things continue as they were since the beginning of creation") and because of the assumption, based on experience in an unrighteous world, that sinners appear to flourish and do not seem to be punished by God. Of course, several NT texts do seem to suggest that Jesus would return soon.[91] Others exhort believers to continue to be ready (e.g., 1 Pet. 4:6) and still others reflect anxiety about the delay (e.g., 1 Thess. 4:13-18). The teachers have taken the delay of Christ's return and subsequent judgment as confirmation that it is a "cleverly devised myth" (1:16) and, therefore, that they can "follow their own passions" (3:3).

The Sovereignty of God's Word and the Patience of the Lord (3:5-10)

In response to the claim that nothing has changed since the beginning of creation (3:4) Peter again directs readers back to Scripture. The false teachers "deliberately ignore" the scriptural narrative of a creation that only came into being because of God's word and was subsequently destroyed by God's word with a flood (v. 6). Thus, once again, the word of Scripture aligns with apostolic testimony (cf. 1:16-21) to secure the teaching that God does indeed intervene powerfully in the world and will do so with fire at the day of judgment (3:7).[92]

---

90. Though he may have specific prophecies in mind (e.g., Isa. 5:18-20; Jer. 5:12-24; Ezek. 12:22; Amos 9:10; Zeph. 1:12; especially Mal. 2:17). So A. Vögtle, *Das neue Testament und die Zukunft des Kosmos* (Düsseldorf: Patmos, 1970), pp. 125-26.

91. Matt. 10:23; 16:28; 24:34; Mark 9:1; 13:30; Luke 9:27; 21:32; John 21:22-23.

92. A final destruction of God's enemies by fire is a common feature of OT depictions of God's judgment (Deut. 32:22; Ps. 97:3; Isa. 66:15-16; Zeph. 1:18). Later Jewish tradition began to extend this judgment to a total annihilation of the whole created order (*Sib. Or.* 3.83-

Peter goes on in 3:8 to offer a counter-rationale for the apparent delay of the parousia. According to Scripture, God's accounting of time is different from ours. According to Ps. 90:4, "a thousand years in your sight are like yesterday when it is past, or like a watch in the night." Yes, Christ's return seems delayed, but this is not due to God's disinterest or inability to act. Indeed, the eternal God is not slow but patient. According to Sirach 18:10-11, "Like a drop of water from the sea and a grain of sand, so are a few years among the days of eternity. That is why the Lord is patient with them and pours out his mercy on them."[93] God is the one actively delaying the return of Jesus, and even this is in accordance with Scripture: according to Joel 2:12-13, "Yet even now, says the Lord, return to me with all your heart, with fasting, with weeping, and with mourning; rend your hearts and not your clothing. Return to the Lord, your God, for he is gracious and merciful, slow to anger, and abounding in steadfast love, and relents from punishing."

But there are limits to God's patience. The day will in fact "come like a thief" (3:10; cf. Matt. 24:43-44; Luke 12:39-40; 1 Thess. 5:2; Rev. 3:3; 16:15), without warning for those who are unprepared. The fiery judgment of that day, mentioned at 3:7, is described in v. 10 in language that is powerfully evocative but not always entirely clear. The heavens will "disappear/pass away"; the adverb *rhoizēdon* brings to mind "a whirring sound made by an object going swiftly through the air . . . a noise made by something passing with great force and rapidity,"[94] a "roar" (NIV) or "loud noise" (NRSV).[95]

92; 4.171-82; 5.155-61; *1 En.* 1.6-9; see Kelly, *Commentary on the Epistles of Peter and Jude,* pp. 360-61).

93. Note also *2 Bar.* 48:12-19 — "For in a little time are we born, and in a little time do we return. But with you hours are as a time, and days as generations. Therefore, do not be angry with humanity, for we are nothing; and take not account of our works. For what are we? For lo! by your gift do we come into the world, and we depart not of our own will. For we did not say to our parents, 'Give us birth,' nor did we send to Sheol and say, 'Receive us.' What therefore is our strength that we should bear your wrath, or what are we that we should endure your judgment? Protect us in your compassions, and in your mercy help us. Behold the little ones who are subject to you, and save all that draw themselves unto you; do not destroy the hope of our people, and do not cut short the times of our aid."

94. BDAG, p. 907.

95. Kelly (citing Oecumenius) notes that the sound "could connote the crackling noise of objects being consumed by flames" (*Commentary on the Epistles of Peter and Jude,* p. 364). Bauckham (*Jude, 2 Peter* p. 315) points to *Sib. Or.* 4.175, "the whole world shall hear a rumbling [of thunder] and a mighty roar," and various passages that describe the roar of God's voice on the day of judgment (Ps. 18:13-15; Amos 1:2; Joel 3:16; 1 Thess. 4:16).

"Elements" *(stoicheia)* might refer to the physical things of creation (since a "new heaven and a new earth" is coming, v. 13), but it more likely refers to heavenly bodies and spiritual powers, as it does in the LXX of Isa. 34:4, "And all the powers of the heavens shall melt, and the sky shall be rolled up like a scroll" (cf. Gal. 4:3; Col. 2:8, 20). And what will happen to "the earth and the works that are done on it"? Will they be "burned up" (RSV/NASB) or "laid bare" (NIV) and "disclosed" (NRSV)?[96] Regardless, the point is clear enough. Everything will be "dissolved" or "destroyed" (3:11a), nothing will be left hidden, every rock and hiding place will be overturned, and the deeds of everyone will be revealed to God (cf. Isa. 2:19; Hos. 10:8; Amos 9:1-6; Rev. 6:15-17).

Closing Exhortation (3:11-18)

Given this fact, Peter exhorts believers to live "lives of holiness and godliness" as they wait for (and even speed along)[97] the coming day of the Lord. Conducting one's life in this fashion is a way of living into the inevitable reality of the future, for a "new heavens and a new earth" is coming, "where righteousness is at home" (3:13; cf. Isa. 65:17; Matt. 19:28; Rom. 9:21; Rev. 21:1). Those who wish to dwell in the place where God's will rules will prepare by living according to God's will now.

Thus, while believers wait, they must make every effort to live their lives in the manner they would hope to be found in when God suddenly arrives: at peace, "without spot or blemish" (cf. 2:13),[98] cheerfully acknowledging that the delay of the parousia means salvation for others (3:14). God suffers patiently, so believers can too. Peter then appeals to Pauline authority, and much is communicated in the process. Paul is "our beloved brother" who "also wrote" these things, clearly indicating that Paul is em-

---

96. We are dealing with textual variants here: the reading *heurethēsetai* ("disclosed" or "discovered") enjoys the best manuscript support, but the very early P72 has *lyomena* ("dissolved"). Most scholars seem to prefer the sense of the former over the latter.

97. The logic is, if human sinfulness leads God, in mercy, to be patient, increased human godliness will reduce the number of people requiring patience and thereby "hasten" the day.

98. Animals with blots or blemishes could not be brought forward for sacrifice (Lev. 1:3); priests with blemishes could not serve before the altar (Lev. 21:21). Peter has "ethicized" the ritual laws of Torah, as did most early Christians (Eph. 1:4; 5:27; Phil. 1:10; 2:15; Col. 1:22; 1 Thess. 3:13; 5:23; Jas. 1:27; 4:8).

braced by the other apostles around Peter (despite the fact that some taught otherwise). Paul wrote "with the wisdom God gave him" (v. 15b) just as God gave words to the prophets of old (1:20-21). Peter and his recipients have access to "all his letters," that is, they have a collection of Pauline writings. Some aspects of Paul's message are "hard to understand," which leads certain "ignorant and unstable" individuals to "twist" their meaning, "as they do the *other* Scriptures" (so Paul's letters are considered "Scripture" alongside the sacred texts of Israel).

It seems unavoidable to conclude that the "false teachers" denounced throughout this letter are in some way claiming Paul as their authority. Even in Paul's day some took him to be preaching antinomianism (Rom. 3:8; 6:15; Gal. 5:13) because of certain things he said about Christian freedom and release from the Law through Christ (e.g., Rom. 4:15; 5:20; 8:1; 1 Cor. 6:12). Given the constant appeal to the OT in this letter, it is possible that the teachers took Paul to be rejecting the authority of Jewish Scripture (Acts. 21:20-21; Rom. 2:28-29; 7:1, 4; Eph. 2:15). Regardless, the implication is that Paul's message is easily misunderstood if it is not framed by the larger biblical witness of prophets and apostles.

Believers have received the grace of being properly forewarned against the error of the false teachers (3:17). The only right response is to follow the directives set out in the opening homily (1:3-11), that is, to "grow" (cf. 1 Pet. 2:2) "in the grace and knowledge" (*gnōsis*, 1:5) "of our Lord and Savior Jesus Christ," to whom belongs "glory both now and to the day of eternity" (3:18). Both now *and* to the day of eternity; the whole of Christian life, past and present, must be thought of as a preparation for that future day when eternal life dawns.

Theology

1. The Creator God

The church's theological grammar is theocentric: God is one, the Creator of all things visible and invisible, whose way of ordering reality sets the norm for creaturely existence. 1 Peter is also theocentric and witnesses to God's activity in the world as it relates to a suffering people who live in those places where the presence of a loving, powerful God may not be self-evident. After all, what sort of God allows innocent people to suffer, especially those who consider themselves to be God's children? 1 Peter's theological conception is centered by this hard question of theodicy.

According to 1 Peter, God can be found and worshiped even in that place of suffering because God's real presence is mediated through the resurrected Jesus (1:3, 21; 3:21). By this experience of the living Jesus, the suffering community realizes that God has not abandoned them — despite public appearance to the contrary — and in fact has a filial relationship with them as "Father" in an intimate manner that is not shared by outsiders (1:2-3, 17). As a community of "resident aliens" (1:1; 2:11), believers anticipate and even now experience the hardships of living as a people belonging to God and not to the Caesar of a pervasively pagan culture (1:6; 2:20; 3:14; 4:12). They are God's own people, citizens of a different, "holy nation" (2:9), and this world is not their real home. The Creator's plan to deliver this people from their present suffering and sense of alienation was long ago presaged by Israel's Scripture (1:10-12), most especially in its prophetic narrative of God's suffering Servant-messiah (1:11; cf. 2:22-24). Through his messianic career the Creator has disclosed the design of divine deliverance that is applicable to all (4:19): the resurrection and glorification of the messianic Servant (3:18-22) testifies to the inevitability of the vindication that awaits those who suffer for their faithfulness to their faithful Creator (4:12-19; cf. 2:22-24).

The Creator's good intentions for all of life extend to every human relationship. As witness to this, believers must "submit to every human institution" (2:13–3:7) for the Lord's sake, extending honor to everyone regardless of social rank or moral worthiness (2:17). God is the Holy One who calls a people out of a pagan world (1:1; 2:10) and purifies them from sin (1:18-19) to live as holy people (1:15; 2:9-10) *in* the pagan world. It is this same God who now protects them for eternal life with God (5:10). In response to these actions of providential care, the faith community reveres and worships God (1:17; 4:11). This interplay between the reader's social and spiritual worlds, fraught with so much ambiguity, forges a spirituality of hope that empowers the believer to submit to the social requirements of daily life in a public manner that embodies, for all to see, the purifying changes a holy God fashions within the human soul (1:22-25; 2:11-12).

To this end, believer (1:17; 5:5-6) and non-believer (4:1-6) alike will stand for judgment before an impartial God whose verdict is based entirely on the hard evidence of whether a people obey the Creator's will (1:17). Those who do God's will and are righteous (3:13-17) will follow the risen

Christ into heaven (3:18-22). The evidence of their obedience to God is their public rejection and suffering at the hands of pagan outsiders (2:11-12). God's eventual judgment of these pagans, by contrast, is so certain (4:5) that the faith community need not seek vengeance against those who provoke their suffering (3:8-12). Indeed, it is only by submitting to suffering they can rightly witness to the Creator's suffering Servant.

The question addressed by a canonical approach to biblical theology is how the theological conception of 2 Peter's equally theocentric witness complements that found in 1 Peter. Even as the Christian confession of God as Creator is central to 1 Peter's *moral* vision, so also it is central to 2 Peter's *apocalyptic* vision (3:5-7). Even as the heavens and earth are brought forth by the word of God, so it is by that same powerful word that both apostles and prophets spoke from God (1:19-21; 3:2; cf. 3:15-16) to map out the promise of creation's salvation from the "defilements of the world" (2:20). Ultimately by this word the punishment of God will be executed on the present godless order (3:7). Thus, while 1 Peter concentrates on the *inauguration* of this salvation in the suffering and resurrection of Jesus, 2 Peter emphasizes its *consummation* in the coming triumph at the Lord's parousia and so more fully rounds out a Petrine conception of salvation's history.

2 Peter justifies the delay of creation's purging and renewal on the basis of God's patience (3:9, 15). The topos of divine patience was already employed by 1 Peter (3:20), but there to interpret the cleansing waters of Christian baptism by which believers participate in Christ's passion and its redemptive results (3:18-22): the believer's sin is purged and life renewed as the primary contemporary evidence that God indeed has triumphed over evil and death. Thus, 1 Peter has the risen Jesus journey to Hades to proclaim God's victory over the powers and principalities of the evil one (3:19). 2 Peter in turn expands the space and extends the time of the same theological point. That is, God's plan of salvation is mapped for a different time zone, to the coming "day of God" (3:12).

The Creator counts time differently than does the creation (2 Pet. 3:8; cf. Ps. 90:4; Rev. 20:3), which allows important two qualifications for a human reckoning of salvation's realization. First, the "real-time" delay in the parousia is due to the merciful Creator's interest in the repentance and restoration of those who might otherwise perish (3:9). The Petrine intertext of the Noah tradition suggests an intriguing qualification to this point. According to 1 Pet. 3:20, God's patience is evinced in Noah's case, who was spared God's judgment "through water." Noah is cited again by 2 Pet. 2:5 to illustrate that the exercise of God's patience is predicated on human "righteousness" (*dikaios* in 2:7-9, *dikaiosynē* in 2:5, 21). Indeed, the deeper logic of 2 Peter's entire conception of God is anchored by its programmatic claim concerning God's "righteousness" (*dikaiosynē*, 1:1). According to this theo-logic, then, a righteous God saves righteous humanity from judgment while punishing the unrighteous (2:9). Further, the critical interplay between the righteousness and patience of a God who waits on humanity's salvation suggests that God cannot wait forever. The righteousness of God (self-)imposes a time limit on God's patience.

Thus, a second qualification is this: in God's counting of time, the "day of the Lord" will come "like a thief" and the unrighteous order will pass away with loud noise and fire, which are the necessary preparations for a new heavens and earth where "righteousness is at home" (3:13). This core conviction of Jewish apocalypticism actually subverts the harsh and graphic images of a corrupt creation's judgment: this cosmic purging of every vestige of evil and death is actually focused on the Creator's healing and restoration of all things. A "new heavens and earth" does not mean a "brand new" cosmos. Rather, it is a recovery of a creation that God has always viewed as "good" from its very foundations.

But what is it about this old order that will ultimately pass away that so distresses its Creator? God's displeasure is concentrated by 2 Peter on false teachers (2:1) who work against the redemptive purposes of the Creator in the manner of the false prophets of the Jewish Scriptures (1:19–2:22) and therefore embody all that is wrong with the present state of God's creation. The issues are both theological and moral. The teachers deny (2:1) and distort (3:16) the central beliefs of the apostolic tradition, which is grounded in the apostles' witness to God's revelation through Christ (1:16-18), which has subsequently been codified as the community's Rule of Faith (3:2). They also subvert the community's moral rule by leading impure lives (2:2, 7-14; cf. 2:18-19). Rather than being motivated by pious devotion to God, they exploit the loyalty of the community for selfish monetary gain (2:3), in clear violation of 1 Peter's exhortation to the community's teachers to be humble shepherds content in the circumstances of their lives (1 Pet. 5:1-5; cf. Jas. 4:1-10).

The decisiveness of this final moment of "real time," the just execution of God's righteousness, circumscribes God's patience in 2 Peter in a different manner than in 1 Peter. Scripture's witness holds God's mercy and justice in critical yet uneasy balance; and so it is in its Petrine witness that God is both patient and demanding. In 1 Peter God's revelation in the sufferings of the messianic Servant is one of "great mercy" (1:3) by which a marginal community of resident aliens, who themselves suffer for righteousness' sake, hope for their eternal inheritance in the coming age. In 2 Peter God's revelation in the parousia of the majestic Lord is the apocalypse of justice; the coming age has now arrived as "the day of judgment and destruction of the godless" (3:7), especially for those whose teaching undermines the faithful. To confess allegiance to a holy God who governs creation as Father and Judge is both life-generating and life-threatening.

2. *Christ Jesus*

According to 1 Peter, God is first of all known as "the Father of our Lord Jesus Christ" (1:3), and God calls the church out of the world for salvation in Christ (5:10), by him (2:21-25), and for him (1:2) for a salvation that will be fully revealed at his parousia as Lord. That is, God is principally known and confessed in terms of God's relationship with Christ's work as suffering Servant (2:21-24), by whose costly obedience God has liberated a suffering community for a future heavenly home (1:3-9; 2:25; 5:13-14). While present suffering is a real problem, Jesus' resurrection is the central symbol of a "living hope" by which the temporary suffering of the present is swallowed up in a future "inheritance" that will be "undefiled and imperishable" (1:4).

1 Peter's interpretation of Jesus' suffering is richly textured. While developed against the biblical background of Isaiah 53 (2:21-25), it drafts prophetic typologies from both the exodus story (1:18-19) and temple symbolism (2:4-8). The suffering Servant is also the paschal lamb, unblemished and spotless, whose blood purifies the souls of believers (1:22) and effects in them an imperishable life (1:23). At the same time, his acceptable sacrifice to God establishes the very "cornerstone" for a "spiritual house" which, though marginal from social perspective (2:11-12), is the very dwelling place of the people of God (2:9-10).

In a book layered with christological affirmations, none is more distinctive than 1 Pet. 3:18-22.[99] Without denying the substantial critical prob-

---

99. For the history of interpretation of this passage as a distinctively Petrine contribution to New Testament Christology, see Michaels, *1 Peter*, pp. 194-222.

lems posed by this passage, it does supply a working glossary of the Christ event and a range of beliefs about him that effectively defines Christ's relationship with humanity as God's suffering Servant:

The first confessed is the traditional belief in the reconciling death and resurrection of Christ (3:18). According to 1 Peter, Christ "suffered for sins," a phrase unique in the NT's theology of the cross that almost certainly recalls 2:21-25 with its emphasis on the messianic Servant's obedience to God. That is, Jesus' death redeems not as a *substitute* sacrifice for sin but because of his *obedience* to God's redemptive purposes. This emphasis on Christ's costly obedience is central to 1 Peter's pattern of humanity's salvation, since it is precisely in the community's active and demanding response to God's call that its salvation at the end of the age is made secure (1:6-9). Yet, Christ's unjust, abusive suffering does not conclude his work. Resurrection does. Suffering is a necessary element of it, of course, even as suffering is a necessary element of the Christian's salvation (1:6-7) and vocation (3:8-17); the christological argument of 1 Peter assures its readers that innocent suffering provides the means into a future with God. Christ's suffering does not end humanity's suffering; it establishes a template that opposes any choice to relieve the costs of discipleship at the expense of a holy lifestyle demanded by a holy God.

The second belief confessed is that Christ journeyed first to the netherworld to proclaim God's triumph to the "spirits" imprisoned there (3:19) and then to heaven (3:22). The history of interpretation of this phrase reflects its theological difficulty and possibility.[100] In context, Christ's journey almost certainly picks up 1 Peter's conflict thematic (2:11-12; 3:8-16; 4:1-6) to interpret it under the light of the triumph of the risen and glorified Christ (3:18, 21) who is now cosmic Lord even over these same "spirits" (3:22). Whatever else 1 Peter might mean by this curious mythology, it illustrates the confidence a suffering people might have in a Messiah whose redemptive work has already defeated those invisible agents at work behind the scenes to wreak havoc today as they did in Noah's time (3:20). Surely the keen Petrine interest in Christ's resurrection as the disclosure of a Creator who is the powerful maker of all things, invisible and visible, underscores the ultimate triumph of the gospel as the very foundation of Christian hope in a milieu of social disruption and suffering (so 4:6).

Finally, the assertion that "baptism now saves you" (3:21), however

---

100. Cf. Dalton, *Christ's Proclamation to the Spirits.*

grammatically convoluted, clearly relates Christ's triumphant experience with that of his current followers and their experience of the living Christ (1:18–2:3). The properties of that experience are of inward purification from sin through Christ (1:18-21) to love each other publicly as friends (1:22-25) and to resist moral vice (2:1-3) — the moral effects of the community's "clear conscience" (3:21) by which it also obeys the truth of the gospel (1:22). These properties are the marks of God's good intentions for humanity.

2 Peter, by contrast, shifts emphasis away from Jesus' past messianic death to his present mediatory role as power broker of God's salvation. 2 Peter therefore refers to the Lord Jesus as "the Savior" (1:1, 11; 2:20; 3:2, 18), underscoring his participation with God in the present work of salvation (1:11). It is significant in this regard that 2 Peter's christological confession is vocalized by God (rather than the faith community), who declares that Jesus is the "beloved Son with whom I am well pleased" (1:17). As a result, then, the Lord Jesus Christ is known by his apostolic representatives in terms of his "power and parousia" (1:16) rather than in terms of his obedient suffering and atoning death. Likewise, the heterodoxy 2 Peter addresses is a denial of Jesus' lordship (2:1) and "commandment" (3:2), both of which are linked to a denial of his parousia in power to execute the Creator's final judgment against a corrupt creation.

Modern scholarship, following Käsemann, has typically responded unenthusiastically to 2 Peter's christological sensibility. A canonical approach to 2 Peter affords two responses: (1) If 2 Peter is read *with* 1 Peter, whose christology is as robust as any writing in the NT, there is little need to repeat claims already made. (2) More importantly, however, 2 Peter makes keener mention of two discrete periods of Christ's messianic mission, not only pushing his work as Savior back from his passion to include earlier events from his life (1:16-18; cf. 1:5-8) but then also pushing ahead to posit the importance of his messianic parousia (3:4-13). The rhetorical effect of 2 Peter's christology, then, is to construct an inclusio, bracketing and concentrating 1 Peter's suffering Servant and his messianic death and resurrection by its prophecy on the holy mountain on one side, and by its cosmic and ultimate results at the coming triumphant of the Creator on the other. The Petrine witness as a whole thus not only resists the tendency to isolate Christ's importance in the past and on the cross but carries the cross's results into the future in a way that continues to judge the present moment in salvation's history.

3. The Community of the Spirit

1 Peter admits a seamless continuity between its Christian readers and OT Israel. While other NT witnesses (e.g., Hebrews) seem to support the church's supersession of Israel, which risks reducing its Scripture to no more than a prefix to God's real action begun in Christ, 1 Peter seems to move us in the opposite direction. Now biblical Israel — God's elect community yet exiled in the world — is typological of the Christian community; 1 Peter's pervasive quotation of Israel's Scriptures describes this community's present faith and life with Christ. This point is dramatically underscored in 1:10-12, which claims that the community's Bible practices are guided by the same Spirit that was at work within the OT prophets to make clear what they themselves did not fully understand. 1 Peter admits to a progressive *illumination*, not to a progressive *revelation.*

In this sense, the biblical story of Israel's election, exodus, and exile is not finally "realized" by the church because of Christ; rather, this antecedent story to which the biblical prophets bear witness is now more fully understood by the Spirit of the risen One as typological of God's way of salvation. The Christ event does not disclose an alternative election or occasion a completely different exile. The church's experience is of a piece with God's election and liberation of Israel, and its present exile in Babylon (cf. 5:13) is also of a piece with the experience of exiled Israel's Babylonian captivity.

Accordingly, 1 Peter's idea of church is that of a community of marginal, "exiled" ones — weak and powerless by societal standards — who are called forth out of a world utterly opposed to God's agenda, not only to live at odds with that world's norms and values but thus to participate in its salvation by walking in Christ's steps as God's suffering Servant (2:21-25). The transition to this alternative existence is enabled by God's empowering Spirit (1:2): those who come to Jesus, the living stone, find themselves spiritually transformed into living stones gathered together by the Spirit to be built into a temple of worship where acceptable sacrifices are offered to God (2:5). By this means the Christian community becomes the Israel of God, "a chosen race, a royal priesthood, a holy nation, God's own people, in order that you may proclaim the mighty acts of him who called you out of darkness into his marvelous light" (2:9).

While it retains 1 Peter's interest in the community's vocation as the elect people of a holy God living within a profane world order, 2 Peter's primary interest is to define the community's calling in terms of apostolic authority (1:16-18) and the body of the apostles' writings (3:2, 15-17), which, together with biblical prophecy (1:19-21; 3:2), delineate the community's theological and moral boundaries. According to this apostolic memory, already serving the community as a proto-canon (3:2), the Christian participates in the divine nature of a noble and virtuous Lord (1:3-11), who has revealed the manner of life approved by God. In this light, then, the theological crisis facing a Christian community is any challenge to this apostolic Rule of Faith.

The theological function of 2 Peter, therefore, is no longer to interpret the hostile relations between the elect community and those on the *outside* (so 1 Peter); for 2 Peter, the threat is *internal* and concerns the theological purity of the tradition inherited from the apostles. 2 Peter is written to settle an intramural conflict over false teachers who have departed from this apostolic canon (2:1-2, 10), the results of which are disastrous for Christian discipleship.

4. Christian Discipleship

Current interpreters of 1 Peter do not require certainty about the historical circumstances of its first readers or about whether its canonical version is the composite of earlier compositions in order to agree that its intended audience suffers (or expects to suffer) for its Christian faith, and that 1 Peter's theological conception is decisively shaped by this experience. Christians who are the book's implied readers are called "resident aliens" (1:1; 2:11); they live in a hostile environment (2:12; 3:16) where they suffer simply for trying to live as Christians ought (4:15-16). Although reasons for this conflict are not precisely given, one can surmise that it is the logical result of competing loyalties: the community suffers the result of a life concentrated on serving the interests of a holy God within a profane world.[101] The parenetic function of 1 Peter is not to domesticate an alien group to prevent future oppression but to prescribe the life of a holy people whose vocation within an alien world is to bear witness to God by walking in the steps of God's suffering Christ and by so doing to herald the revelation of his return to earth in glory.

1 Peter empowers this "alien" perspective by normalizing human suffering as the expected character of purified human existence within a pro-

---

101. This is the thesis of Elliott's influential reading of 1 Peter; see now *1 Peter*.

fane world: Christian discipleship is cruciform by nature since believers follow a crucified Lord. The real issue facing the community is the manner of its response to suffering; indeed, its final salvation depends on that response (4:17). Sharply put, the right(-eous) response is firm and steadfast obedience (1:13-14) to God's will (3:17) in a cultural milieu that rewards the opposite. God's will fully encompasses personal ethics (2:11; 3:8-9) and the various arrangements of human life; thus, the community's rule includes loving relations with others (1:22; 2:1-2) and with outsiders (2:12; 3:15-16) as well as with the institutional (2:13-17) and social and familial (2:18-20; 3:1-7) structures of the cultural order. Critical to this moral order is the role of the community's leaders (5:1-5), who must be exemplars of the Christian life (5:2-3), especially for a suffering people (5:1) when the potential for disaffection (5:9-11) or exploitation (5:5-8) is very great.

This Petrine ideal of a holy obedience is complemented by a glossary of hope (1:3, 13, 21; 3:5, 15), the central feature of 1 Peter's practical theology. This seems to follow the calculus of the prophetic model, to which 1 Peter refers (1:10): if divine judgment is the prior experience of divine salvation, then a people's purification depends on this purging of sin. Thus, 1 Peter can speak intelligently of the community's purification as the result of the Messiah's suffering (1:14-18; 2:21-25), but also say that the Creator's purging of a broken creation of its sin is indicated by the community's own suffering (4:17-19), even if suffering is the unjust result (2:19) of living as a Christian rather than the just desert of vice (4:15-16). The result is a sacred text that looks ahead to the future revelation of God's salvation, when the homeless will enter their eternal home (cf. 2 Pet. 3:11-13).

This is precisely why the false teachers' abandonment of the apostolic Rule of Faith is depicted as a nightmare for Christian discipleship in 2 Peter. The teachers deny the essentially ethical nature of faith: discipleship is a "way of righteousness" (2 Pet. 2:21; cf. 1:11; 2:2) and not merely the affirmation or denial of particular beliefs. In this sense, 2 Peter maintains 1 Peter's emphasis on "right(-eous)" living (see 1 Pet. 2:14-15, 20; 3:14; cf. 2:24), although with different terms and to settle a different crisis, by a positive emphasis on virtue as a "complement" *(epichorēgeō)* to faith (1:5-8), as well as by its strong denunciation of the false teachers' ethical abuse of the Pauline "freedom" principle, supposing rather that their "knowledge" of Christian faith (1:2, 3, 5, 6, 8; 2:20; 3:17) liberates the enlightened from any threat of divine punishment at the parousia of Christ. It is not knowledge of God but "godliness" (1:3, 6, 7; 3:11) that will deliver them from eschatological judgment.

Indeed, whereas the Pauline gospel speaks of a "righteousness by faith," the Petrine gospel emphasizes a "righteousness of life": the moral character of a virtuous life marks a people out as belonging to God. According to the deeper logic of the Pauline gospel, this same "righteousness" is a natural result of Christ's death, in which the believer participates as beneficiary by faith; sharply put, Paul does not require the rigors of a spiritual discipline (2 Pet. 1:5; 3:14) that habituates faithful acts of obedience to God's rule (1:9) called for by 2 Peter. Clearly, the deification of believers (1:4) does not result in an inevitable obedience to the commandment of the Lord (2:20-21). The logical result of following Paul at this point, even though perhaps uncritically (cf. 3:15-16), is a self-indulgent lifestyle (2:2, 10, 13, 18) that pursues personal pleasure (2:13) and private property (2:15-16) instead of a rigorous obedience to the "commandment of the Lord" (3:2; 2:21).

5. Consummation in a New Creation

The biblical narrative of God concludes where the Rule of Faith does: with salvation's consummation in God's triumph over evil and death at the Lord's future parousia. The importance of this teaching is introduced in 1 Peter, whose "hope in God" theme (1:21; 3:15) points toward a future heavenly inheritance (1:3-5), predicated on a christological pattern already revealed (so 3:18-22) that moves from the experience of present suffering to one of future glory (1:6-9, 20; cf. 5:1). A community that posits hope at the "revelation of Jesus Christ" (1:7, 13; cf. 4:13; 5:4) has two foci that bracket and so qualify the community's present suffering: Christ's resurrection and subsequent return as exalted Lord. On the one hand, the past resurrection of the suffering Servant discloses the triumph of his steadfast obedience to God (1:3; 3:18); on the other hand, his future return discloses on earth God's final triumph over the hostile forces that continue to provoke the suffering (and death?) of God's holy children. The triumph of the risen Messiah, already revealed in the empty tomb, prefigures the inevitable vindication of those faithful to him — a future revelation when the faithful Creator will restore all things to their pristine order (4:19) that thus satisfies the "living hope" of a suffering community. In this sense, 1 Peter cultivates trust in a God whose best is yet to come.

What does 2 Peter contribute to this core Petrine conviction that salvation's history will consummate at "the revelation of Jesus Christ"? Significantly, the beginning point for 2 Peter is not the resurrection but the Transfiguration of Jesus, which confirms the "power and parousia of our Lord Jesus Christ" (1:16-17) by appeal to the apostle's eyewitness authority (cf. 1 Pet. 5:1). This appeal may well carry more rhetorical clout in the letter's argument against those who scoff at the parousia (3:3-4), who suppose that this article of Christian faith is a clever fiction (1:16) rather than a delayed reality (3:8-13), and so deny that God is capable of either creation's destruction or its new beginning (3:3-4). The heretical teachers suppose on this basis that they can act with impunity, as though the Lord issued no moral command (3:2; cf. 2:21).

Against this backdrop, the principal contribution of 2 Peter to Petrine eschatology is its keen emphasis on the Creator's final judgment — an emphasis that underscores the decisive action of the Creator as purifier of a corrupted creation (2:11-22). The Petrine community lives in a symbolic world mapped from beginning to end by biblical prophecy; thus, even as the community's Scriptures herald the Messiah's suffering as God's Servant (1 Pet. 1:10; 2:22-24), so also they foretell his triumphant parousia as Lord (2 Pet. 3:2-5) in the judgment stories of the flood (2:4-5; 3:5-6) and Sodom and Gomorrah (2:6-8). According to this authorized witness, the Creator is perfectly capable of both the destruction of the ungodly (angels and cities) and the deliverance of the righteous (Noah and Lot).

But destruction comes first and is the condition of deliverance; this seems the eschatological calculus of the Petrine tradition. 1 Peter's belief in God's judgment emphasizes its present force in the Christian community, experienced either as ethical incentive (1:17; 2:12) or as a cipher of its suffering (2:23; 4:17). This core belief is then expanded in 2 Peter with apocalyptic images located at the coming triumph of God as Judge when both "living and dead" provide a moral accounting of their lives (cf. 1 Pet. 4:5). This formative emphasis on ethical Christianity, where God's eschatological verdict is based on the performance of faith and not on its mere profession, is made even more precise by 2 Peter: "the day of the Lord" (3:10) will bring a fiery destruction of all things, both human (2:1; 3:7) and material (3:7, 10-12), followed by "the day of eternity" (3:18) which brings a more complete restoration of all things, both human (3:11) and material (3:13). The community's baptism into a Christian hope because of the Messiah's suffering (1 Peter) will thus be confirmed at the Messiah's parousia (2 Peter).

The Catholic Epistles of John

Introduction

1. The Canonical John

The most obvious problem that faces the interpreter of the three Johannine epistles in their canonical setting is their apparent dissimilarity with the other CE in literary genre, vocabulary, and theological grammar. Although we hope to make a range of connections among the CE to mitigate this perceived problem, especially the thematic importance of the apostolic tradition shared between 1 John and 2 Peter, on the face of it there is little that connects John's epistles with those from the other Jerusalem Pillars. Even scholars sympathetic to the canonical approach are hesitant to consider them integral bits of the CE collection "because of historical-critical sensibilities," as one interpreter recently put it.[1]

Most contemporary introductions to the NT follow the lead of R. E. Brown, who places the letters in close working relationship with the Fourth Gospel, the one correcting dangers latent in the other. In this sense, 1 John in particular provides its first readers with a commentary on the community's controversial Gospel.[2] Whether or not Brown's construction is followed, almost all note the common ground shared by the NT collection of Johannine writings, which includes the three epistles, the Gospel, and sometimes the book of Revelation.

---

1. D. Lockett, *An Introduction to the Study of the Catholic Epistles* (ABS, New York: Clark, 2012), p. 6.

2. R. E. Brown, *The Epistles of John* (AB, New York: Doubleday, 1982), pp. 69-115.

157

This critical practice has an ancient precedent (see "The Canonization of the Johannine Epistles" below). We also agree there are good reasons to follow this ancient practice, if only to raise the volume of John's distinctive witness to God's way of salvation. At the same time, the canonical process left this "Johannine corpus" divided: John's Gospel is placed with three others to form the fourfold whole, and John's Apocalypse is placed at the end of the NT canon to conclude Scripture's story of redemption. The three epistles are gathered together in due time and placed in a second collection of "catholic" letters, so named because of their broad usefulness and their defense of apostolic or "catholic" Christianity.

We will turn shortly to the question of why the church repositioned and fixed John's epistles within a new letter corpus to add to the NT canon. Suffice it to say that the historical record is silent about the church's intentions for subdividing the Johannine corpus. Although surely evident differences of literary genre and practical uses may have led the church to reposition each text with similar others, a canonical approach understands the deep logic of the church's canonical process, including the repositioning of the Johannine epistles with the other CE, in theological terms. The titling of these otherwise anonymous texts as from "John" not only secures their teaching to an authoritative apostolate that is formative of a genuine Christianity (over against non-apostolic Christianities), it does so in a way that safeguards the full cohort of Jerusalem Pillars (cf. Gal 2:7-9). Their collective testimony, reified and recalled by this canonical deposit, is set next to the Pauline testimony within the NT canon to engender a conversation that makes a distinctive contribution to Scripture's pluriform witness to God's salvation.

We should note that Irenaeus claims that the Valentinians, specifically Ptolemy, also accepted John and his Gospel as apostolic (*Adv. Haer.* 1.8.5). While this datum by itself is much too slight to engender a hypothesis, it should remind us again that the canonical process unfolded at a time when apostolic traditions were being contested by rival Christianities. The opening words of 1 John are therefore heard within the bounds of the canonical process as an affirmation of the apostolic tradition against alternate claims. In this same sense, the concluding benediction of 1 Timothy (1 Tim. 6:20-21) and the opening of 2 Timothy (2 Tim. 1:13-14) sound a similar note, which may explain why both letters (along with Titus) were added to complete the Pauline canon at this same time in response to a similar kind of epistemic crisis when the identity of a canonical Paul and his apostolate was up for grabs.

This historical observation is not unimportant for drawing a portrait of this canonical John, the Lord's "beloved disciple," as the implied author of the three Johannine letters.[3] Images of John in the Fourth Gospel and Acts supply the raw materials for constructing a portrait of this canonical John. This portrait should not be confused with a historical construction, but is fashioned within a biblical setting and confirmed in the early reception of John's testimony during the canonical process (see below). While we think this biblical John is grounded in what was remembered about him as a leading disciple, this is also a portrait shaped by a deeply affecting allegiance to John's understanding of Jesus as "the word of life." His angle on Jesus is different from those of the other Pillars or of Paul, who was not one of the Twelve.

According to the Synoptic Gospels, John was among Jesus' first converts and then his constant companion. His name routinely appears at the top of the list of disciples with Peter and James. Especially in Mark's telling of Jesus' story, John is privileged to special revelatory events along with Peter, such as the Lord's Transfiguration (Mark 9:2) and his vigil in Gethsemane (14:33), which may lead the reader to assume a more intimate insight into Jesus' relationship with God and his messianic mission. This personal intimacy with Jesus may have emboldened John to police the activities of others, as indicated by Luke 9:49-50, which is strategically placed before a narrative marker (v. 51) that begins Jesus' farewell journey to Jerusalem and his Passion. And John's assumed authority among the disciples may also have prompted him to ask Jesus for a seat of honor on their arrival in the Holy City, presumably to establish the messianic kingdom (Mark 10:37-40; cf. Matt. 20:20-22). In any case, even a cursory reading of the Synoptic Gospels secures the impression of John's close proximity to Jesus and so a clearer line of sight to "the life that was revealed" than others had, on the basis of which the authority of his apostolate to announce the prospect and conditions of "eternal life" to future generations is defended (so 1 John 1:2-3).

His portrait is elaborated with dramatic effect in the Fourth Gospel,

---

3. While the title "beloved disciple" is nowhere attributed to a particular person in the gospel tradition and remains contested among scholars on historical-critical grounds, his joint appearances with Peter in Acts and the Fourth Gospel make it almost certain that Scripture depicts him as John, son of Zebedee. See B. F. Westcott, *The Epistles of St. John* (reprint Grand Rapids: Eerdmans, 1966), pp. ix-lix. More importantly, this is almost certainly the John the church had in mind in receiving "his" three letters (and Gospel) as Scripture.

where he is not called (we suppose) "John" but "the beloved disciple." Significantly, and in a setting that sounds a somewhat different tone than the Synoptics, this disciple makes his first appearance in the narrative as he reclines in a seat of honor with a distressed Jesus at the Last Supper (John 13:21-23). This occasions Peter to ask John to field a question he wants addressed (the identity of the betrayer) — a gesture that seems to recognize John's influence with Jesus. This tacit rivalry is reflected in the Fourth Gospel's Easter narrative, where John outraces Peter to reach the empty tomb as its first witness (20:3-5). These images of Johannine priority are brought to even sharper focus in the telling of the Passion: rather than abandoning Jesus as Peter did (18:15-18), the beloved disciple joins the Marys beside the cross and Jesus entrusts to him the care of his mother. Hardly a more striking symbol of one's trust for another can be imagined.

The result of this extraordinary layer of narrative not found in the other Gospels is to deepen and secure the reader's sense of a close relationship between John and Jesus. If anyone is in a position to testify to the real truth about Jesus, especially against an opponent of the apostolic tradition, it is the beloved disciple! Of course, one could argue this is special pleading from the Evangelist who claims to have written the narrative in the epilogue (21:24-25). But in canonical setting, these images of a faithful and trusted disciple gloss the opening claims of 1 John in a way that confirms the church's recognition of the epistle's status as inspired Scripture.

The subtext of this observation is how different the idea of an "apostolic tradition" is for the Johannine tradition than for Paul, whose apostolate was not funded by an intimate knowledge of the historical Jesus. The epistemic quality of this collection's appeal to eyewitness testimony when compared to the Pauline witness should not be underestimated. And perhaps this explains some of the distinctive accents of this collection's Christological grammar. These qualities are pressed for in the Johannine collection in particular because their implied source is the "beloved disciple," an intimate insider to the Messiah's life.

Over against the critical consensus on the dissimilarity of the apostolic traditions reflected in the epistles attached to their names we see the adumbration of John's inseparable partnership with Peter in the opening chapters of Acts (1:13; 3:1-4, 11; 4:13, 19; 8:14). In Acts, they speak as one, presenting a unified apostolic presence that suggests — at the very least — solidarity between their two traditions. Together they provide Spirit-filled leadership for the messianic community, even if most scholars agree that

John plays second fiddle to Peter's spiritual virtuosity. The Synoptic Gospels' triad of "Peter, James, and John" is reduced to "Peter and John" until John goes missing when Paul replaces him to initiate the church's mission beyond Jerusalem to the Gentiles (Acts 9–15; but see Gal 2:6-10). Nonetheless, the early pairing of "Peter and John" commends to the Bible's readers the idea of a pluriform apostolic tradition, both in terms of the Spirit-inspired acts the two perform together (Acts 3–4) and the faithfulness with which they lead the community's succession in absence of the risen and now departed Jesus (cf. 4:19-20; 8:25). In fact, their bold response to the warning of Jerusalem's political authority is stated in an idiom that recalls the prologue of 1 John and its claim on the impress of the apostolic word in defining the terms of salvation: "it is impossible for us not to speak about what we have seen and heard" (4:20; cf. 1 John 1:1).

Perhaps even more importantly, this apostolic tradition is based on what Peter and John actually saw and heard of the incarnate One — a point introduced by 2 Peter and elaborated by 1 John, where the reception of the apostolic message funded by this eyewitness is normative of what a community knows and confesses to be truth and how it conducts its moral practices. The Pauline conception of apostleship concentrates on the revelation of the divine word (= gospel) rather than on an eyewitness of the incarnate (and revelatory) word, since Paul did not know Jesus "in the flesh." Moreover, it draws on Jewish and Hellenistic moral traditions (rather than Jesus' life) to draft its moral codes. This difference, which Galatians suggests may have been a source of intramural conflict within earliest Christianity, extends to Christology as well. While there is certainly overlap, the Jerusalem Pillars emphasized a life of Jesus they witnessed as exemplary of covenant faithfulness and embodied truth. The Pauline agreements are more abstract (or "cosmic"), emphasizing Christ's death and resurrection as the signs of God's victory over sin and death.

2. The Composition of the Johannine Epistles

The Composition of 1 John. Scholars agree that there is hardly another NT book whose structure is more difficult to follow than 1 John. In part this is due to the puzzlement that remains over its literary genre, which extends to the overarching design of its argument. 1 John is not really a "letter" in form (even if it is in its pastoral function): it reads more like a pastor's exhortation or "message" (1:5; 3:11) both in written expression and rhetorical exuberance. This said, we take the repeated catchphrase, "this is the message" (*estin hautē hē angelia*, 1:5; 3:11), as cuing the letter's expansive expositions of two core beliefs that clarify Jesus' revelation of the truth about God, witnessed from the beginning by his apostles: God is light (1:5–3:10) and God is love (3:11–5:12).[4]

Regarding its placement in the CE collection, which most scholars now disregard, we consider the transition from 2 Peter into the prologue of 1 John (1:1-4) strategic to the collection's overall coherence. Simply put, both letters respond to an epistemic crisis occasioned by disagreements between rival teachers. Both letters target the apostolic tradition as normative for their readers in settling such disagreements. In this sense, 1 John continues 2 Peter's insistence, although in a different idiom, that the message believers have received from the apostles is revelatory of the truth about God's word (cf. 2 Pet. 3:1-7).

Following on 2 Peter's stunning conclusion, which looks ahead to the future apocalypse of a new creation formed by God's word, 1 John begins by pulling readers back to "the beginning," when the apostles witnessed the "word of life" within history. In continuity with God's preexistent word that formed creation and then predicted a new creation, this incarnate word is revelatory of the truth about God and of the eternal life that is with God. The surety of this word's content is ultimately predicated on its identification with "Jesus Christ," who is God's "Son" (1:3). To see him "in the flesh" from the very beginning of his messianic career is to understand God better, since the Son is in a position to reveal the truth about his Father.

The memory of what the Lord's apostles have personally seen, heard, and handled of the real Jesus is what defines what is true, not only about the past and future of Jesus but also about the precise nature of the eternal life that is with the God who is revealed by the Christ (1:2). The apostolic proclamation, then, which has been received by the community, establishes the authoritative criterion by which anyone comes out of the world and into a covenant-keeping relationship with God and each other.

The initial statement of purpose for writing this message down (1:4) is highly provocative in its canonical setting, since its first phrase clearly al-

---

4. Similarly, Brown divides 1 John into two main parts by the repetition of this same catchphrase, even if he develops each part differently than we do. *Epistles,* pp. 116-29, especially 119-22.

ludes to the conclusion of the Fourth Gospel (21:24-25) — as though 1 John continues from its testimony of Jesus (even if to correct misinterpretation of it) — and its second phrase recalls Paul's words in Philippians (Phil 2:2) that frames an appeal to the incarnation (Phil 2:5-11) to secure an apostolic exhortation for the congregation to love one another self-sacrificially (Phil 2:3-4) — as though 1 John interacts with the Pauline witness on a shared matter central to the Christian gospel.

However, this apostolic message about Jesus continues to divide the church, even as it divided Israel according to the Gospel and Acts. Even if the historical circumstances are uncertain, the letter's plain sense suggests that it is written to help settle this intramural conflict over the source and content of the gospel's truth. Whether a war of words between different teachers or a debate over different theology, this conflict has been provoked, as such divisions often are, by differing accounts of Christian faith and discipleship. Whenever disagreements threaten to split the church, leaders of rival groups typically debate issues of evidence and sources, each claiming superior evidence mined from better sources to confirm their particular version of truth over the falsehoods of others. Similarly, 1 John's response to this religious crisis provides a biblical model for today's church whenever a division within the ranks threatens to break apart the body of Christ.

This said, 1 John has little interest in defining and demonizing this rival Christianity comprised of so-called "antichrists" (1 John 2:18, 22; 4:3; 2 John 7); in fact, an "antichrist" is probably not a person at all but a theological metaphor for anyone who opposes the community's apostolic message (cf. 2:18-19, 22). Even so, modern criticism has tried in vain to build a résumé of the identity and threat of this rival group while 1 John mentions these faceless "antichrists" only in passing. What seems clear from the entire letter is that the apostolic tradition stipulates the theological criterion for eternal life and regards any disagreement with it a death sentence. This internal conflict is a serious matter that threatens the community from within and requires a decisive response about the power of a message delivered by those who have directly heard, seen, and touched "from the beginning" this incarnate word about eternal life (1:1-2). There is an epistemic quality to this claim that ends debates with those whose gospel message does not square with the gospel message received from the church's apostolic tradition.

While the letter refuses to identify these opponents, or the author and his readers for that matter, which gives the letter a kind of timeless (or "catholic") quality,[5] his repeated first person address throughout the letter (2:1, 7, 12-14, 21, 26; 5:13) suggests a mentoring relationship similar to the one found in the Pastoral Epistles between the apostle and faithful members of his apostolic community whose instruction is necessary to secure the faith against all kinds of threats, real and imagined.

We contend, then, that the primary purpose of canonizing this letter is not to recall the theological errors of a particular group, even though that group's departure from the apostolic community evidently required a response. Rather, the reading of this canonical letter is occasioned by the need for the church to clarify its identity as a communion of saints whose fellowship is with the Lord's apostles (1:3a) and who are assured of having "fellowship with God and with God's Son Jesus Christ" on that basis (v. 3b). From antiquity, the church has confessed itself to be "apostolic"; 1 John defends this address as the location where the real truth about God is found.

The letter's vocabulary clearly reflects an epistemic crisis by its variety of relevant dualisms, such as light-darkness, truth-falsehood, knowledge-deception, witness-liar, confess-reveal. This special vocabulary is used here with greater frequency than in any other biblical writing.[6] This is a letter whose very language seeks to draw clear boundary lines between rival Christianities, one apostolic and the other not. The threat is internal and not secularism or paganism. Therefore the pathos is different from that of 1 Peter but of a piece with that of 2 Peter.

Roughly a quarter of all references to "sin" in the NT are found in this letter. While the problem of sin and the promise of salvation from sin's power and destructive effects concern the Pauline witness as well, unlike a Pauline missional narrative of salvation, which begins with and is mostly oriented toward those sinners outside of Christ, 1 John pays attention to the continuing problem of sin in the believer, which threatens fellowship with God and with others in the covenant community. The practical prob-

---

5. See J. M. Lieu, *I, II & III John* (NTL, Louisville: Westminster John Knox, 2008), pp. 6-9.

6. Consider the following three verbal ideas, which in this epistolary setting are each actions taken with respect to the apostolic witness: (1) *Phaneroō* ("reveal"): 1:2; 3:2, 5, 8; 4:9, in each case linked to the incarnation — a word of life in history with and for us. Jesus came to reveal an observable "word of life" (1:2), to take away sin (3:5) and destroy the works of the devil (3:8), and to make known the love of God (4:9); and he will reappear in the future for children of God to see as they will be (3:2). (2) *Ginōskō* ("know by learning"): 2:3, 4, 5, 13, 14, 18, 29; 3:1, 6, 16, 19-20, 24; 4:2, 6, 7, 8, 13, 16; 5:2, 20. (3) *Oida* ("know by perception, interpret"): 2:11, 20, 21, 29; 3:2, 5, 14, 15; 5:13, 15, 18, 19, 20.

lem 1 John considers is different from the Pauline crisis: even though God's truth disclosed via the incarnate Word and received from apostolic tradition (mostly "heard" via "writing") as confirmed by the "anointing of the Holy One" (2:20) intends that believers do not sin (2:1), even though sins are forgiven "for Christ's sake" (2:12; 3:5), even though the Evil One cannot influence the child of God (5:18; cf. 3:8), it is still an error for the believer to claim either the status of having no sin (1:8) or the experience that "we have not sinned" (v. 10). Believers sin. And this sin must be dealt with in order for the believer to be restored into and thus remain in fellowship with God, with whom sin cannot coexist (v. 5). Indeed, "no one reborn of God as a child of God, and in whom God's nature thereby abides, commits sin" (3:9, etc.). If this concept of transformed nature is the central mark of "becoming Christian," it is also the pivotal problem of "staying Christian" for 1 John. The practical concern of 1 John is, then, to underscore the real damage done to one's relations with God and to one another when truth — that is, the "word" the apostles have apprehended "from the beginning" — gets mismanaged, distorted, or denied altogether.

1 John's response to this distortion of the gospel truth is not a species of early Christian apologetics that carefully defends the apostolic faith against pagan outsiders. The source of the problem is a razor-thin Christology that subverts the rigorous moral practices and deep obligation for theological purity that characterizes Christian discipleship. To safeguard the truth is to underwrite a robust Christology predicated on the apostle's trusted witness of the divine word of life, Jesus, in whom the absolute terms of Christian faith and discipleship are revealed. To deny this witness is to deny the truth about the incarnate One; and to deny this divine word is to set aside the normative compass that guides the way toward eternal life (5:13) and moral purity (2:5-6). Simply put, this letter is written so that the readers of the apostolic community might "know him who is true" (5:20).

We have argued that the canonical process that formed and shaped this second collection of NT letters for use within the church had this practical use ever in sight. The persistent attention the final redaction of the CE collection pays to the church's apostolic traditions picks up the same note sounded by the Pastoral Epistles of the Pauline canon, which invites a reader's attentiveness to the constructive (and not adversarial) character of the interplay between these two epistolary collections.

The collection's rubric "catholic" is instructive in this regard, especially in light of the current controversy provoked mostly by skeptics over the seemingly restrictive (and some say arbitrary) nature of the canonical process. Since the referent of canonization is a particular person, Jesus, in whom the word of life is disclosed and to whom the apostles testify, there is some truth to the charge that its course was restrictive, even though hardly arbitrary. That is, writings that did not agree with the apostles' memory of what Jesus said and did were excluded from the biblical canon. The Christianity of the "antichrists" mentioned in 1 John is rejected as non-apostolic precisely because its Jesus does not measure up to the apostolic rule.

To sum up, the crisis that occasions a reading of this canonical letter regards an apostolic conception about sin in the believer. In fact, the community's *koinonia* with God hinges on getting clear on what the apostles witness in the incarnate One about the light and love of God, since this light and love are freighted by the remains of sin. Here are the points clarified by this letter that secure an apostolic take on this matter: (1) Believers must reject any teaching that opposes what the apostles ("we") observed of the word of life "from the beginning" regarding the marks of authentic Christian discipleship. Particularly in mind is any occasion when sin in the believer's life is spiritualized or dematerialized — the claim of a moral docetism that argues that Christians have a nature that makes sinning inherently impossible or spiritually irrelevant, a ramped-up "sola fideism" (faith alone-ism) in which "beliefs alone" saves. The keen emphasis on "confession" in 1 John (*homologeō*, 2:23; 4:15) envisages corrections to what is confessed or denied about Christ that has led to this variety of "Christian perfectionism." (2) Those who promote this teaching are called "antichrists" because they deny the importance of "Christ has come in the flesh" (4:2). Christ has come bodily as humanity's moral exemplar of obedience to God (2:3-6) and as the Holy One who discloses a Word about God, and then as the glorified Paraclete he continues to "anoint" believers into this truth (2:20). As the crucified Christ he repairs the relational/covenantal damage done by their sin (2:1-2; 1:7, 9). That is, he deals with the world's sin (2:2; 3:5), including its ongoing consequence in the believer's life (2:1). (3) If the activity of sinning has become irrelevant for covenant keeping, along with a robust doctrine of Christ that can account for the activity of sinning, then the moral life of the community and especially how believers treat other believers is imperiled. That is, if "doing what is righteous" (2:29; 3:7-10; cf. 1 Peter), which is the very mark of covenant keeping, is no longer a Christian imperative, then loving one another — the essential commandment of God — can no longer be sustained as a rule of life. Purity cannot be maintained (3:3), the community's relations cannot be maintained, and as a result the community's future is jeopardized (3:2, 19-24).

The Composition of 2 John. Unlike 1 John, 2 John is written in the literary form of most Hellenistic personal letters, typically followed by Paul: it opens with a greeting (vv. 1-3), followed by thanksgiving for the recipients with a hint of the spiritual crisis that occasions this pastoral response (v. 4), then a body of instruction and exhortation that attends to this crisis (vv. 5-11), and a concluding benediction (vv. 12-13). Yet the brief letter's special vocabulary (e.g., truth, love, remain, antichrist) and its occasion (a congregation divided by false teaching) follow from 1 John. Only two new words are introduced, including its personal address to the "elect lady," whose identity is otherwise unknown and unimportant to the letter's exegesis. In fact, the literary relationship between 1 and 2 John is quite different from that between the Gospel and 1 John, which is characterized by the letter's creative use of the traditions introduced by the Gospel.[7]

For this reason, the church has generally read 1 and 2 John together since the second century. In canonical setting, when the sequence of compositions suggests a logical relationship, we are inclined to read the second epistle as the "epitomizer" of the first — to borrow St. Augustine's consideration of the relationship between Matthew and Mark — no matter what historians may conclude about their authors or the chronology and occasion of their compositions.[8] That is, within canonical context 2 John is

---

7. See especially Lieu for this comparison, *I, II & III John,* pp. 14-24.

8. This idea that 2 John follows 1 John to supply readers with a condensed or "epitomized" version of its themes borrows from St. Augustine, who took for granted that the sequence of the Gospels in the NT was the order in which they were composed and were to be read as Scripture (though he came to think that Luke was composed before Mark). He thus introduced an interpretive strategy of the fourfold Gospel that dominated study until the influence of early modern biblical criticism in the eithteenth century. Augustine assumed that each writer had read the work of every predecessor. Thus, he argued, Mark not only was dependent on Matthew but actually "epitomized" or condensed Matthew's narration of Jesus' life. In *Consensus of the Evangelists* 1.2.4 he says, "Although each of these [Evangelists] may appear to preserve a certain order of narration proper to himself, this certainly should not be taken as though each individual writer chose to write in ignorance of what his predecessor had done, or left out things, which nonetheless another [Gospel] is discovered to have recorded, as matters about which there was no information. Rather, the fact is that as each of them received the gift of inspiration, they abstained from adding to their distinct works any

read after 1 John as its Reader's Digest version in order to make more emphatic the core themes of the apostolic tradition set out in a more expansive way in 1 John.

For example, the catchphrase "from the beginning" (vv. 5-6) cues the importance of the apostolic testimony of Jesus (cf. 1 John 1:1) and the mention of the "new commandment" cues the prior discussion of the community's spiritual tests (cf. 1 John 2:3-11). Mention of "the antichrist" (v. 7) as a threat to the community's future with God (v. 8) concentrates 1 John's warning about a rival Christianity (cf. 1 John 2:18-27 and 2:28-3:2; 4:1-6 and 3:19-24), which evidently has now spread beyond the Johannine community "into the world" (2 John 7). The admonition to "confess" (v. 7) the "doctrine of Christ" (v. 9a) as the criterion of "abiding in"/"having" God (v. 9b) has the effect of bringing clarity to the community's confession of Jesus (cf. 1 John 4:2; 3:23).

Even more critically, the command to "love one another" as the moral badge of a community's possession of the truth is restated as the practice of hospitality toward those who walk in the truth (vv. 10-11; cf. 1 John 4:11-21; Rev. 18:4). 2 John epitomizes 1 John's moral imperative in two important ways: Clearly, 2 John understands the practice of loving one another by the manner a community receives/greets strangers (missionaries?). Second, the use of *ponēroi* (v. 11, "evil things") continues from its repeated use in 1 John (2:13, 14; 3:12; 5:18-19), where the articular singular form refers to "the Evil One," that is, Satan, who is in charge of the "whole world" (5:19). The point of 1 John is that the mature believer has nothing to worry about regarding this "evil one" (2:13, 14; 5:18). In this sense, then, showing hospitality to any who do not hold to the truth about Jesus is a sign of spiritual immaturity and thus of availability to the inward corruption of the evil one/world (cf. 1 John 2:15-17).

While we think there is much to commend a reading strategy that fol-

---

extra shared compositions. For Matthew is understood to have undertaken to construct the record of the incarnation of the Lord according to the royal lineage, and to give an account of most of His words and deeds as they relate to this present human life. Mark follows him closely, and looks like his assistant and epitomizer. For in his narrative he gives nothing apart from the others that agrees with John. He has little to record distinctly on his own. He has still less in common with Luke that is distinct from the rest. But he has a very great number of passages in common with Matthew. He also narrates much in words almost the same in number and identity as those used by Matthew, where this agreement is either with that evangelist alone, or with him in connection with the rest."

lows the canon logic envisaged by the final placement of collections and even of individual writings within them, we also note in the commentary below that in several important ways the "epitomizer" also elaborates crucial themes introduced by 1 John in ways that enrich the Johannine contribution to the CE collection.[9]

The author identifies himself only as "the elder" (v. 1; cf. 3 John 1), which suggests that he holds a position of leadership within the community (and perhaps the apostolate) of the Lord's beloved disciple, John. The reader should approach 2 John therefore as authored by someone intent to safeguard the apostolic message, especially since it is threatened by a rival Christianity led by "the antichrist" (vv. 7-8; cf. 1 John 2:18-27). The promise of a future visit from the elder (v. 12) is an exercise in spiritual authority, since its implied purpose is to make certain that the letter's warning is heeded (vv. 7-11) and perhaps on this basis to give a "seal of apostolic approval" to the congregation.

The letter is written to warn readers about the potential threat of "deceivers" (v. 7) and one in particular called "the antichrist" (v. 7), whose refusal to confess the apostolic "teaching about Christ" (v. 9; see 1 John 1:1-2) could influence real Christians and undermine the future prospect of their "full reward" (v. 8; cf. 1 John 3:2). In fact, in an effort to curb the influence of this apostate group, the elder now qualifies the community's command to love one another (vv. 5-6) by instructing them not to extend hospitality to anyone who does not affirm this apostolic rule of faith (vv. 10-11). Such inhospitable treatment of teachers whose theology lay outside the apostolic circle suggests a strategy of safeguarding and stabilizing an apostolic tradition at the local level. In any case, the interdependence of truth and love in the Johannine tradition is nowhere better or more practically addressed than in this instruction.

The Composition of 3 John. 3 John, like 2 John, is a brief letter written by an anonymous spiritual leader who calls himself "the elder" (see above); in fact, its literary form and features conform even more closely to the typical Hellenistic personal letter. For example, unlike 2 John, it addresses a recipi-

---

9. The expanded, more formal title for 2 John found in the uncial ms. L (Byzantine, ninth century) is "Second Epistle of the Holy Apostle John the Theologian," which may reflect its canonical role as representing the theology of 1 John (and so the Johannine witness) for a more catholic audience.

ent by name rather than by metaphor, as in 2 John, and concludes with greetings from friends. The letter's recipient, Gaius, is evidently a congregational insider greeted as someone "truly loved" (v. 1; cf. 2 John 1) and as one of the writer's "children" (v. 4). This personal note, then, sounds a close working relationship between the two.

Gaius is elaborately praised as an exemplar of hospitality, the moral signature of any who embrace the gospel's truth and remain faithful to God for eternal life (vv. 3-4). Nothing more is known about him, or of Diotrephes (v. 9), the writer's opponent in an apparent power struggle for congregational leadership. This more practical matter on social manners marks a shift of emphasis from the battle over correct doctrine that marks 1 and 2 John's primary interest in preserving and clarifying the apostolic tradition.

This makes 3 John's reception into the CE collection surprising and perhaps explains why its early use by the church is sparse and separate from the more extensive use of 1 and 2 John well into the third century. What doubt is registered early on about its canonicity stems from this lack of use rather than from its lack of sound doctrine or practical usefulness. This observation, however, along with the lack of parallels between 3 John and 1 John (less so 2 John), raises the question about its fit within the CE collection, and in particular what insight into the Johannine witness might be gained from reading 3 John after 1 and 2 John, which read together more naturally and offer readers more substantive theological exposition.[10]

Although recognized as Scripture after 1 and 2 John, 3 John's similar vocabulary and topics naturally place it with the other two Johannine letters in the CE collection. The letter's enduring use in the church has, in fact, been more practical than theological. First, the elder's commendation of "beloved Gaius" for extending hospitality and support to strangers provides

---

10. Demetrius (v. 12) may have been the courier who delivered 1 and 2 John, and 3 John may have been written in part as a letter of introduction; see L. T. Johnson, *The Writings of the NT: An Interpretation* (revised ed., Philadelphia: Fortress, 1999), pp. 560-61. If so, 3 John's canonization may be approached from the perspective that it was added to the Johannine epistles to "introduce" 1 and 2 John. This raises a question, however: How does 3 John, if read in retrospect, frame or "reintroduce" the church's prior reading of 1 and 2 John as Scripture? Our response to this question concentrates matters on two elements of this tradition, namely, the intramural nature of the conflict addressed and the practice of hospitality as an act of loving one another, which is central to the Johannine epistles' gloss on the apostolic tradition and its claim that "God is love."

a pattern for loving others, especially in caring for traveling missionaries (vv. 5-8). That is, the distinctive timbre of John's love command — which is to love other believers (see 1 John 4:20) — is operative in the elder's relationship with Gaius and in the practice of hospitality toward the community's missionaries. This illustrates a love of "deed and truth" (1 John 3:18).

Second, the elder's admonition of choosing sides in an intramural disagreement with Diotrephes (vv. 9-12), apparently over a particular application of hospitality according to 2 John 10-11, has provided an example of church discipline in settling internal disagreements between church leaders that may otherwise divide a congregation (cf. 1 Tim. 5:17-25).[11] When Diotrephes refuses to "welcome the brothers and sisters" (v. 10), perhaps by appealing to the principle that the elder himself set out in 2 John 9-11, he is sternly rebuked not because he has excluded strangers from his love but because he withholds support and falsely accuses other Christians for self-centered reasons and so betrays Christ's example of self-sacrificial love. Perhaps the admonition is a practical elaboration of a latent concern of 1 and 2 John for church solidarity, brokered by the community's spiritual leaders, to withstand the threat of non-apostolic religions.

3. The Canonization of the Johannine Epistles

Like the Petrines, so also the three Johannine letters experienced an uneven process of reception. While the larger letter of John was known and celebrated in the early church as a letter from the beloved disciple of the Lord,[12] ancient Christians did not share a uniform opinion of what should be done with the shorter letters eventually titled 2 and 3 John.

As we might expect, we possess only echoes of the letters prior to

---

11. See A. Malherbe, "The Inhospitality of Diotrephes," in *God's Christ and His People*, ed. J. Jervell and W. Meeks (Oslo: Universitetsforlaget, 1977), pp. 222-32, who argues that the issue at stake is not theology but the practice of hospitality, which in antiquity carried social significance.

12. Irenaeus identifies the author of the Fourth Gospel and 1 John as "the disciple of the Lord" and then elaborates this attribution by an allusion in the Fourth Gospel that links its narrator, John, with "the beloved disciple" who leaned on the Lord's breast (John 13:23). Irenaeus also recalls that Polycarp knew the apostle John and heard him tell stories of Jesus similar to those in the Fourth Gospel. He learned from Polycarp that it was this "disciple of the Lord" who was with Paul in Ephesus, then the center of earliest Christianity, where he recognized John as a "true witness of the apostolic tradition" (*Adv. Haer.* 3.3.4).

Irenaeus at the end of the second century.[13] Most of these supposed echoes are far too distant to secure as true instances of quotation or allusion,[14] but the best of them comes, once again, from Polycarp. In the midst of comments about "false brethren," Polycarp says, "For everyone who does not confess that Jesus Christ has come in the flesh is antichrist [1 John 4:2-3 and/or 2 John 7]; and whoever does not acknowledge the testimony of the cross is of the devil [possibly 1 John 3:8]" (*Phil.* 7.1). This first clear appeal is consistent with the dominant trend in patristic reception of the Johannine letters as Scripture: John was a prophet who foresaw the coming of second- and third-century heresies.

Indeed, according to Irenaeus, John not only predicted the advent of heretics (*Adv. Haer.* 3.16.5), he also detailed the precise content of their teachings (3.16.8) and offered advance directives for Christian interaction with them (1.16.3). Tertullian joins Irenaeus in this: nearly half of his references to the Johannine letters are to 1 John's "antichrist" passages,[15] specifically identifying Marcion and his followers as antichrists because they deny the incarnation of Christ (*Adv. Marc.* 3.8.1; 5.16.4).

Interestingly, in *Adv. Haer.* 3.16.5-8 Irenaeus fails to differentiate between his citations to the first two Johannine letters, including a reference to 2 John 7-8 in the midst of a series of quotations from 1 John and citing all of them as coming from the same "epistle of John." Tertullian, meanwhile, never quotes from 2 John in his many references to the antichrist. This uneven usage appears typical for the period; while Hill has argued that a "Johannine corpus" existed already in the second century,[16] Lieu has

---

13. Papias is said explicitly by Eusebius to have known and used 1 John (*H.E.* 3.39.16), though of course we do not have Papias's own works to corroborate this claim.

14. For an overview of these echoes, see J. Painter, *1, 2 & 3 John* (SP 18; Collegeville: Liturgical, 2002), pp. 39-41.

15. E.g., *Adv. Prax.* 31.3; *Praescr.* 3.13; 4.4; 33.11.

16. C. E. Hill, *The Johannine Corpus in the Early Church* (Oxford: Oxford University Press, 2004). In fact, Hill explains the inclusion of 2 and 3 John, rarely heard from during the second century, in the canon's CE collection on the basis of the church's awareness of this corpus as a whole — a kind of "canon consciousness" (pp. 470-71). Even if we find Hill's defense of an actual collection of this apostolic testimony unpersuasive, the combined use of these writings by early Christian teachers suggests the clear existence of a "collection consciousness" within the early church at the beginning of the canonizing process. And, of course, we agree with Hill's understanding that a corpus of apostolic writings, whether Pauline or Pillars, is the means by which the spiritual authority of the apostles continues to be mediated to still others (cf. 2 Tim. 2:2).

described how the letters appear to have circulated in different combinations, sometimes 1 John by itself, sometimes 1 and 2 John, and sometimes all three.[17] Painter, meanwhile, takes Irenaeus's blurring of the first two epistles as supporting evidence that 2 John was received as a "cover letter" for 1 John.[18] Our own canonical sense of the relationship between the first two letters is that 2 John "epitomizes" 1 John in order to make more emphatic the core themes of the apostolic tradition set out in a more expansive way in 1 John. We had more to say about this, of course, when we considered the "composition" of each letter.

While the remaining fathers of the second to fourth centuries continue to appeal to the Johannine letters in their various attacks on the heresies of their days, they also apply the letters to other ends. Both Tertullian and Cyprian use them to develop their doctrine of sin and repentance in the midst of penitential controversies.[19] Cyprian himself never quotes 2 John, but it was quoted in his presence at the Council of Carthage in 256 when Bishop Aurelius of Chullabi cited 2 John 10-11 as an apostolic teaching regarding the need for lapsed Christians to be rebaptized.[20] Clement of Alexandria, meanwhile, was most impressed with John's moral exhortation, especially the call to love (*Strom.* 4.16.100.4-6 and *Quis* 37.6-38.2). He refers to 1 John as John's "larger epistle" (*Strom.* 2.15.66) and wrote a short commentary on 1 and 2 John.[21]

It is with Origen in the third century that we finally hear reference to all three letters. The largest collection of references to 1 John is found (unsurprisingly) in his famous commentary on John's Gospel, where passages from the letter blur with those of the Gospel to offer a more robust witness to Johannine Christology. Indeed, in harmony with Tertullian and Cyprian's use of the letters in their doctrine of sin, Origen repeatedly appeals to 1 John 2:1-2 and 3:8 in his explication of Jesus as the atoning Lamb of God who takes away the sin of the world.

Eusebius quotes Origen as saying that the apostle John "also left an

17. J. Lieu, *The 2nd and 3rd Epistles of John: History and Background* (Edinburgh: Clark, 1986), pp. 1-36.

18. Painter, *1, 2 & 3 John*, p. 42.

19. Tertullian, e.g., *Pud.* 19.10, 26-28 (1 John 4:2; 5:16-17); Cyprian, e.g., *Quir.* 3.9.5-6; 3.11.69-75; 3.19.12; *Op.* 3.54; *Ep.* 55.18.1; 58.1.3.

20. *Sent.* 81; cf. Lieu, *2nd and 3rd John*, p. 9.

21. Cassiodorus has preserved fragments of Clement's *Hypotyposes* that include selected comments on 1 and 2 John (*Adum.*).

epistle of a very few lines, and, it may be, a second and third; for not all say that these are genuine" (*H.E.* 6.25.10). It is quite likely that Origen did not in fact accept them; at least, there are no clear references to 2 or 3 John in any of the Greek or Latin manuscripts of Origen's work. Eusebius himself places 2 and 3 John in his list of "disputed" books, no doubt following Origen's opinion. He notes that they "may be the work of the evangelist or of some other with the same name" (3.25.3).

As our "shaping" chapter made clear, eastern canon lists after Eusebius are uniform in placing 1-3 John among the other CE in the order James, Peter, John, Jude. This is the canonical order that prevailed even though several church fathers — especially Irenaeus and Origen — clearly approached these letters as a component of a "Johannine corpus" together with the Gospel and the Apocalypse. Even when the Gospel is separated out early in the process several western lists appear interested in avoiding the separation of 1-3 John and the Apocalypse.[22] Among the factors involved in the ultimate breakup of the Johannine corpus was the undermining of the church's confidence in its common authorship. Early on Papias preserved the memory of another John in Ephesus, called "the presbyter" (Eusebius, *H.E.* 3.39); later Dionysius of Alexandria could examine the writings and conclude that differences in vocabulary and style among them suggest that another John, perhaps this "Presbyter" referred to by Papias, wrote Revelation (*H.E.* 7.25).

Despite this, the ultimate view of the church was that all three epistles were written by the apostle John and that the letters and the Apocalypse should be separated from one another by the letter of Jude. While we have no historical witness accounting for this separation, the ultimate sequence makes sense both thematically and theologically when it is understood that the CE collection was designed to be received as the literary deposit of the Jerusalem Pillars, figures known to readers of the NT from their prior reading of the Acts of the Apostles and Paul's letter to the Galatians. This canon logic, first described in our "shaping" chapter, will be more fully explicated in our final chapter.

---

22. So the Muratorian Fragment (ca. 200), the Mommsen/Cheltenham Canon (mid-late fourth century), Rufinus (404), and Junilius Africanus (ca. 545).

Commentary: 1 John

Prologue: The Apostolic Witness of the "Word of Life" Reveals the Truth (1:1-4)

The major contributions from the Johannine tradition to the NT canon (the Gospel, 1 John, and Revelation) all come with expansive prologues that set the table for their use as Scripture. The verbal and literary independence of these prologues from the compositions suggest in each case a later addition, perhaps by editors of the so-called "Johannine School" who wished to cue a congregational reading of these compositions in worship (see Rev. 1:3). While the parallelism between the Fourth Gospel and 1 John is striking (so R. Brown), the allusion to the Gospel's ending (1:4; cf. John 21:24-25) is even more illuminating of the canonical function of 1 John, which is to continue Scripture's witness to John's Jesus, perhaps to correct the community's misappropriation of him.

The letter's purpose is set out in its prologue: to write down (1:4; cf. John 21:24-25) what is proclaimed by those who were witnesses of the incarnate word "from the beginning"[23] (1:1-2).[24] This revelatory "word of life" witnessed and then proclaimed to the community establishes the criterion by which its members enjoy fellowship not only with its apostolic founders but also with God, with whom there is "eternal life" (1:2-3; cf. 5:13, 20).[25] By this same criterion, then, Christian discipleship is established and

23. The catchphrase "from the beginning" (cf. Acts 1:1; 2 Pet. 3:4) is repeated several times in 1 John in connection with what is written and proclaimed as a reference to apostolic authority and priority. Unlike the Fourth Gospel, which frames "word" in cosmic terms, 1 John frames the word in apostolic terms — from the beginning of the apostolic tradition, when the word was seen, heard, and touched by the apostolic eyewitnesses. It is now a word that is written and proclaimed. This Christoformed word is received from the apostles and believed as the basis fellowship with God, with whom there is eternal life (cf. Acts 4:20).

24. The authority of the implied author of 1 John is underwritten by direct witness of the incarnate word. The arresting and unexpected image of "touching" the word may recall conversations about not only seeing but also "touching" the risen Jesus on Easter narrated only by the Fourth Gospel (John 20:17, 25). In that narrative world, touching the risen One supplies hard evidence that he is human, but also testifies to his full glorification by and solidarity with the Father.

25. "Fellowship" translates *koinōnia*, a widely used NT trope for a covenant relationship in which God enters into a partnership with a people whose life with God is maintained by their covenant-keeping faithfulness. This text reverses the logic of the Pauline tradition according to which *koinōnia* with Christ naturally yields *koinōnia* with other believers. In this

regulated: one is not a real Christian without also affirming that the apostolic message about Jesus is true.[26]

Such an opening makes good sense of a letter that addresses a Christian community divided over rival claims of truth. In fact, no other biblical writing so forcefully underwrites the religious importance of a community's reception of a common apostolic tradition than this letter. Simply put, 1 John is written and so read in response to the question, often raised by Christians during a process of discernment: How does one decide between competing messages of the gospel truth? 1 John's short response is: consider the source! If "no one has ever seen God" (4:12), then the importance of a direct and intimate witness of the "Son of God (who) has come and has given us understanding so that we may know him who is true" (5:20) is of decisive epistemic importance.

First Movement: God Is Light, So True Believers Must Live without Sin or Falsehood (1:5–3:10)

Although difficult to follow, 1 John presents the apostolic testimony of the "word of life" in two sweeping movements, each of which develops the substance and practical application of the tradition's two core theological beliefs. The message received by the community announces that "God is light,"[27] which is then applied to the problem of lingering sin that threatens the community's fellowship with God, in whom there is absolutely no "darkness" (i.e., sin, lies, falsehood, or deception, 1:5). To walk with God in the light (1:7) Christians must forego their lies and confess their sin, which is for-

---

instance, *koinōnia* with those who safeguard the apostolic legacy leads to *koinōnia* with God and God's Son. This subtle reversal would seem to suggest, again, the high purchase of the apostolic witness of the incarnate word of life.

26. If we allow that in Scripture "word" is generally used as a metaphor for revelation, then its use here as a Christological trope may be a reference to either the personification of truth about God in Jesus or the message that is proclaimed about Jesus. Both meanings are implied here. Of the five relative clauses that surround "Word of life" in the opening sentence, the first four involve various acts of knowing someone's life intimately and comprehensively: hearing, seeing, and touching that person "from the beginning" provide intimate details of that person's life. In this sense, what the apostles have learned about "the word of life" is as comprehensive as their intimate knowledge of the particulars of Jesus' life.

27. The word translated "message" is *angelia*, which is used only here and 3:11 in the NT, which provides evidence of its strategic use in this letter.

given and completely cleansed because of Christ's expiatory death (1:6–2:2; 4:9-10). Now freed from sin, the forgiven believer can live in obedience to God's commandments according to the example of Jesus (2:3-6; 3:3-10).

When used as a theological trope in Scripture, "light" typically refers to divine illumination (2:8; cf. Matt. 4:16; 2 Pet. 1:19; Isa. 58:10), while "darkness" refers to minds darkened by ignorance or deception (cf. John 1:1-18). God is the singular source of truth about human existence: all truth is God's truth. The six statements that follow the prologue (1:6, 8, 10; 2:4, 6, 9) function as a catena of false claims, typical, we presume, of those prompted by the rival Christian community of "antichrists" (see 2:18-19). Such people walk in darkness (1:6) and therefore "do not belong to us" (2:19; cf. 1:3). In contrast, truth is made plain to those who have fellowship with God, not only by publication of the apostolic testimony (cf. 2:21, 26) but also by the charismatic experience of "anointing" (cf. 2:19c-20, 27).

1 John's use of the "light" metaphor refers not only to divine illumination but also to the purity of God's covenant-keeping conduct. Logically, then, its application in 1 John not only concerns the truth of the matter but is also an effective response to the Christian's problem with sin: the spiritual crisis to which 1 John responds is lies and deceptions promoted within the Christian community about the nature of sin, especially whether sin continues to threaten a believer's covenant with God. Unlike the Pauline tradition, whose narrative of salvation is plotted as God's response to a universal problem of human sinfulness, 1 John is more narrowly focused on the sin that remains in the believer, which contaminates his or her relationship with God. As in James, if spiritual failure is tolerated as part of Christian discipleship because of theological deception (cf. Jas. 1:13-16), then the community's friendship with God is imperiled (cf. Jas. 2:14-26).

Sin in the Believer (1:5–2:2). The development of the statement that God is "light" and tolerates no "darkness" (1:5) unfolds from three bold statements about sin made by an imaginary interlocutor, each of which examines the practical implication of walking in the light in communion with God (1:7). To so walk, believers must rid themselves of darkness (i.e., falsehood, deception, and sin), and the various actions called for in response to the interlocutor's boasts all enable the community to walk in the light.

Although nothing is said that would help identify this interlocutor, most commentators have assumed he represents a rival Christianity whose teachers oppose the apostolic tradition and its core theological agreements about God and Christ and so ultimately about the nature and demands of Christian discipleship. Implied by this departure from the church's apostolic Rule of Faith is a practical claim, voiced by the interlocutor, that sinning does not subvert a Christian's covenant with God.

Three conditionals are introduced by the rhetorical formula "if we say" (1:6, 8, 10), each followed by a boast about the nature of sin that functions as a foil for clarification of apostolic teaching about Christian existence — a theme central to this letter and to the Pauline tradition as well (cf. Romans 5–6). Each counterclaim helps to fashion a practical Christology, we presume predicated on the direct witness of the incarnate word of life (1:1-2), which enables the community to walk with God in the light. The universal scope and penetrating effect of Christ's expiation for sins is of paramount importance to 1 John (2:1-2): all sins are cleansed (1:7); all unrighteousness is forgiven (1:9), not only the sins of the whole world but "our sins" in particular (2:2). These arresting claims, repeated in short order and without equivocation, show that the apostles' message falsifies any claim that believers no longer need worry about their unconfessed sin or that there is no residue of sin that requires the gracious remedy of a faithful and righteous God.

The initial exchange sets out the general belief about the status of sin in Christian discipleship (1:6-7). The repetition of "walk" (*peripateō*, cf. 2:6, 11) alerts the reader to the letter's interest in a practical theology of not sinning (see below on 2:28–3:10). To "walk in the light" is to move toward God, who exists "in the light." Conversely, those who "walk in darkness" do not "exist" *(poieō)* in the truth and cannot have fellowship with God or the "eternal life" that is with the Father (1:2).

The second exchange issues from the interlocutor's boast that real Christians "have no sin" (1:8). Almost certainly this does not refer to "original sin" or to sins of omission, both of which are postbiblical conceptions. Nor is this a perfectionist belief in a salvation so thorough that sin is no longer possible, or the boast of a *sola fide* Paulinist who wrongly insists that sin no longer counts against him because God has declared him righteous. Against these readings, the decisive clue is retrieved from the Fourth Gospel, where to "have sin" refers to the inward state of guilt carried over from prior sins (John 9:41; 15:22, 24). That is, the interlocutor's boast is "we do not bear the inward guilt of past sin" that requires God's forgiveness.[28]

28. Brown, *Epistles* pp. 205-7; cf. 233-34.

But surely this is self-deception, 1 John contends, since it denies the effect past sin can have on Christian existence. For this reason, Christian worship should include the liturgical practice of "confessing our sins" (cf. Jas. 5:16) in the belief that God (who is light) will forgive the believer's prior spiritual failures in order to restore fellowship. The effect is that the community can then walk with God in the light.

The interlocutor's final boast, "we have not sinned" (1:10), requires a more elaborate response since it addresses head-on the theological crisis that occasions this letter, namely, the question of whether a Christian should tolerate sin that will damage fellowship with God and so the prospect of eternal life. On the face of it, this boast seems to repeat the prior one in v. 8. Yet the verbal idea and aspect are different: in this case, the verb is "sin" rather than "have" and the tense is perfect ("we have not sinned") rather than present ("we have no sin"). The perfect tense suggests that any sinful action that originated in the past continues into the present. The boast, then, is that there is no residual effect in the present from sins committed in the past or on the believer's fellowship with God in the future. A kind of *sola fide*ism on steroids!

The climactic response in 2:1-2 sets out in bold relief the core beliefs of apostolic Christology. For the Christian to contend that he has no need to cleanse away the remains of guilt from past sin or to seek forgiveness for sins committed as though it does not affect his relationship with God is not only deception but a tacit rejection of Christ's role in the narrative of God's salvation. Unlike Paul's version of this narrative, however, 1 John's clarifying response targets *Christians* who wrongly contend their relationship with God is not damaged by unconfessed sins.

1 John's memorable recital of the core agreements of an apostolic Christology is prefaced by a parenthetical comment that interrupts the response to the interlocutor's third and final boast, cued by an abrupt shift to a direct address of Christians: "My little children, I am writing these things to you so that you may not sin" (2:1a). The letter's purpose is clearly stated here, which sets out the principal marker of Christian discipleship developed in this first movement: if God is light and the true Christian walks with God in the light, then "you may not sin." Indeed, the interlocutor's apostolic conversation partner has already declared that "the blood of Jesus cleanses away all sin" (1:7) and a "faithful God forgives all unrighteousness" (1:9). But this address also shifts the focus from what God does to the prospect of the congregation's practice of not sinning, the effect of regen-

eration (see 2:28–3:10). Its introduction here as preface to 1 John's glorious recital of Christ's work would lead the reader to suppose that God's cleansing of sin and the believer's practice of not sinning are both the result of Christ's work (cf. Rom. 6:1-14).

1 John turns back to the interlocutor's final boast (1:10) with the admission that Christians do sin and when they do it must be forgiven as a condition of walking with God in the light (2:1b-2). The recital of Christological agreements clarifies the confidence by which "any (Christian) who does sin" can restore fellowship with God; it therefore undergirds every exhortation and every assumption about Christian discipleship in 1 John and nicely interacts with similar confessions, especially in 1 Peter, to fund the CE collection's Christology.

1. "We (i.e., Christians) have an advocate *(paraklētos)* with the Father" (2:1b). Readers of the Fourth Gospel are prepared for Jesus' identity as *paraklētos:* there he speaks of the Spirit as "another *paraklētos*" (John 14:16-17), which implies that Jesus too is a *paraklētos.* Although its meaning is contested, as reflected in the different English translations, most commentators favor a legal connotation: a "paraclete" is a paralegal who, in this case, helps God settle disputes or argues cases on behalf of Christians (cf. Rev. 12:10-11). In absence of Jesus, however, the Gospel extends the Spirit's role into non-legal matters as well that include teaching and comforting disciples, reminding them of Jesus (John 14:26), leading them into truth (16:13), and glorifying the Son (16:14).

But 1 John's depiction of Jesus' role as the Paraclete is stipulated differently here. Unlike the narrative setting of the Fourth Gospel's "farewell discourse" in which the Spirit's arrival is cued by the Lord's stunning announcement of his absence from his disciples (John 13:33), 1 John indicates that the risen Jesus remains with his disciples: "we have (present active) an advocate with the Father." Moreover, Jesus' legal advocacy regards those disciples whose sin undermines Christian fellowship with other believers and fellowship with God (cf. 1:3).

2. "Jesus Christ, the righteous one *(dikaios)*" (2:1c). The Lord's effective performance as the community's legal counsel instantiates who he is: his successful advocacy for the community is due to its unity with the Father, whose forgiveness is predicated on the nature of one "who is faithful and righteous *(dikaios,* 1:9; cf. 2:29)." Logically, then, God's just and faithful pardon of "all unrighteousness *(adikia)*" must be secured by a righteous counselor. Critically, 1 John's use of the Christological title "righteous one"

in this setting alludes to "the righteous one *(dikaios)*" of Isa 53:7-12, whose unjust sufferings ("he did no sin," 53:9; cf. 1 John 3:5) were recalibrated by God as a sacrifice for sin (53:10) in order to mediate for the transgressors (53:12) and make them righteous (53:11).

3. "Jesus is the sacrifice *(hilasmos)* for our sins" (2:2a). The word translated "sacrifice" is found in the NT only in this letter (also 4:10), but its use in the LXX for the Day of Atonement (Lev. 25:9; cf. LXX Ps. 129:4), especially when glossed by the earlier phrase "the blood of Jesus God's Son" (1:7), commends the sense here of a blood sacrifice as the means of grace in restoring the covenant community to God. The canonical antecedent of "our sins," then, refers to members of the covenant community: Christ's death atones for the sins of Christians and so restores their covenant relationship with God. Further, the congregation's liturgy of confession (1:9) may well reimagine a day of atonement.

4. "(N)ot only for our (sins) alone, but for (the sins) of the whole world" (2:2b). The application of Christ's death as the effective basis for a Christian liturgy of confession is made more clear by the distinction made between "our sins" and "the sins of the whole world." Although commentators have long debated whether Jesus' sacrificial death, and so his mediation of the covenant community, results in the appeasement of an angry God (propitiation) or the cleansing of sin (expiation), the latter sense seems clear from this context. Moreover, the very idea of an angry God who must be appeased before reconciliation is possible seems incompatible with an apostolic tradition centered on the theological belief that God is love (cf. 4:9-10; John 3:16). Nonetheless, the reading of 1 John is occasioned to make certain that Christians know that unconfessed sin unsettles their relationship with God; Christ's atoning death continues in force long after conversion as the means of acquitting guilt and repairing sin's damage.

Three Tests of the True Disciple (2:3-11). Following these signal claims about Jesus in response to the threat sin poses to Christian existence, the interlocutor returns to make another series of three claims about Christian discipleship. In each case, the formula "the one who says" (*ho legōn*, 2:4, 6, 9) introduces a spiritual test or practice that exposes the hard evidence that warrants one's claim of walking with God and each other in the light (cf. 1:7; 2:9).

The passage's arc from theological claim to practiced proof follows the general narrative of salvation found in Second Temple Judaism and also (roughly so) in the Pauline canon. That is, confession of trust and confirmation by practice stand side-by-side, the one yielding to the other. Therefore, if the professing sinner claims that Messiah's self-sacrifice gets him "into" (or "back into") fellowship with God — what we might refer to as a "first justification" — then the right response of the newly redeemed is to obey God's commandments, which keeps the believer in fellowship with God for what might be called a "final justification."[29] According to Paul, the community's obedience is possible because of its partnership with a grace-giving God mediated by the transforming presence of God's Spirit. The works that God requires on the day of judgment (Rom. 2:5-11) are produced only by those believers who are made righteous in union with Christ and who are transformed within the bounds of this new covenant by the power of the Spirit.

While we agree that 1 John shares this general conception of salvation with Paul, especially stressing partnership (or "abiding") with Christ for a life of obedience to God's rule, the expanded role of the Spirit in empowering such a transformed life, so crucial for Pauline soteriology, is lacking in the CE as a collection. Rather, what is found, as in the Johannine letters, is the powerful impress of "the truth," communicated by apostolic instruction, which compels and guides obedience to God's commandments (cf. John 8:31-33). In our mind, this narrative of salvation follows more closely a traditional Jewish conception of covenant-keeping rather than the more radical Pauline innovation of the Spirit-filled life (cf. Tit. 3:5-8a). More will be said on this point in our theological reflections.

The first test of the true disciple seeks to secure the assertion "I know him (i.e., God)" (2:3-5a; cf. 2 John 4b). The verb "know" *(ginōskō)* refers in this case not to special knowledge about God but to affirmation of the apostolic testimony to the revelatory "word of life" just outlined in response to the interlocutor's false boasts (2:1-2; cf. 1:7, 9). In the Pauline circle, "to come to the knowledge of the truth" (1 Tim. 2:4) is conversion-speak, and it probably carries similar freight here: the initial test of covenant-keeping

29. See in particular S. J. Gathercole, *Where Is Boasting? Early Jewish Soteriology and Paul's Response in Romans 1-5* (Grand Rapids: Eerdmans, 2002). Much of the work published in recent years on Pauline soteriology is based on either the "new perspective" of E. P. Sanders or reaction to it. What is striking to us is that hardly any application is made of that current discussion, whether of the "covenantal nomism" of Second Temple Judaism or Pauline soteriology, as it might relate to 1 John, where the issues are strikingly similar.

concerns the integrity of the Christian's conversion to Jesus, whether or not she believes the right things about God as a result.

Hardly a measure merely of one's orthodoxy, 1 John's repeated use of words from an epistemic glossary routinely makes a commonsense connection between belief and behavior. That is, the test of the convert's profession of truth is whether she lives like it. If someone claims to have applied Jesus' expiatory death to "cleanse us from all sin" (1:7; 2:2) but then disobeys Jesus' "commandments" as though he does not really exist, then this functional atheism exposes that person's conversion as a fraud (cf. Jas. 2:14-17). While 1 John is unclear which "commandments" are on the table, the equivalence between "his commandments" and the "new command" to love one another seems clear from 2:7-11. The material evidence that one "knows God" is the practice of love for one another (see below); the two are of a piece, which is nicely epitomized by 2 John's address, where love and truth interplay repeatedly and seamlessly (see 2 John 1-3).

The extraordinary reference to "the love of God" that reaches "perfection" *(telos/teteleiōtai)* in those who obey God can refer either to God's perfect love (subjective genitive, so also 4:9) or to the disciple's perfect love for God (objective genitive, so also 5:3). Although the belief that God's love has priority is never far from the letter's thought world (see 4:19), in this context of spiritual testing the perfection of loving another probably refers to the obedient believer's love for God. This goal is possible only when sin is removed. As in the argument of Jas. 2:21-26, then, friendship with God is not conditioned on what one believes about Jesus but by those works of mercy that "complete" *(teleioō)* an orthodox faith (Jas. 2:22). The perfect tense of "made perfect" also implies that one's love for God and God's friendship with us are organic and realized over time.

The second test of faith regards the believer who claims, "I abide in God" (2:5b-6).[30] This is the first mention of "abiding," a strategic theme in 1 John's understanding of Christian discipleship. Its repeated use (2:24, 27-28; 3:6; 3:24; 4:12-16) shapes the reciprocity of two covenant partners: God "abides" in believers even as believers "abide" in God. The more critical subtext of this covenantal reciprocity is that the community's covenant-

---

30. The "him" of this claim is not specified. If one takes *ekeinos* as introducing another referent (i.e., Jesus), then the claim is likely "I abide in God." Again, however, the fluid interchange between God and God's Son in 1 John makes these kinds of exegetical decisions/ translations difficult to nail down.

keeping practices must therefore reciprocate God's practices; if they do not, then God cannot abide in us or we in God.

This test evaluates the abstraction of those who claim they "abide in Jesus" (2:6a). Lieu correctly observes here an emphasis on the interiority of the Christian life, similar to James, which naturally leads the believer into "spiritual self-examination." The result, she contends, is that the community's test of faith is individualistic and highly subjective.[31] Perhaps alert to this threat of a congregation's theological solidarity (cf. 1:3), 1 John stipulates the test of whether Jesus/God indwells the believer is whether one "walks just as that one (Jesus) walked" (2:6b). Of course the Christian tradition is rooted in eyewitness testimonies of what was "heard, seen, looked at, and touched" of Jesus and so offers a particular rule of life on this basis. The test might be restated, then, this way: if a believer has been cleansed of all sin and truly abides in Jesus, then she will walk just as Jesus walked, which is defined by the apostolic testimony as faithful to God and without sin (so 3:5; cf. Jas. 2:1; 1 Pet. 2:21-25).

The final test regards the claim "I am in the light" (2:9; cf. 1:6). 1 John has already stipulated that fellowship with each other is predicated on walking in the light since God is light (1:7); and knowing God is evinced by obedience to God's commandments (2:4). Beliefs are never far from appropriate actions in this discourse. Passing this test, which requires obedience to a "new commandment," is "from the beginning" — a catchphrase always linked to the apostolic testimony of Jesus in 1 John (see 1:1). Even though not stipulated, then, the "new commandment" to love one another is not brand new but has always been a central demand of discipleship according to the apostolic testimony "from the beginning" (2:7; cf. 1:1). Its restatement in 2:8, however, suggests that walking in God's light is more organic: in the present world, which is "passing away" (v. 17), the victory of God over darkness (sin, falsehood) is becoming increasingly more evident wherever love triumphs over hatred in the community of true disciples.

In this context, "stumbling" (*skandalon*, 2:10, used only here in 1 John; cf. John 6:61; 16:1) refers to failing the test of faith (cf. Jas. 1:13-16), choosing to live in the world's darkness (and so hating one another) rather than in God's light (and so loving one another). The implied "scandal" is not the disaffection of rival Christians who have departed from the apostolic tradition, but a kind of functional atheism that claims to exist "in the light" of

31. Lieu, *I, II & III John*, p. 74.

God but lives "in the darkness" and so in a manner contrary to the nature of God. Axiomatic of apostolic Christianity is a kind of coherence in which what the messianic community confesses to be true about God matches the manner of its internal conduct one toward another.

Discipleship in but Not of the World (2:12-27). The repetition of the letter's purpose, "I am writing to you" (2:12-14), and its address, "little children *(teknia),"* recalls the parenthetical comment of 2:1a and then also the apostolic respondent's application of the community's core beliefs about Christ ("on account of his name," 2:12b) to the interlocutor's boast that real Christians do not really sin (cf. 1:10). The community's forgiveness and the restoration of its covenant relationship with God presume that the interlocutor's boasts have been rejected in favor of the truths received with the apostolic message.

The implication of this opening platitude is then applied to the three different groups within the community as though the prior three tests have been passed (even if with differing levels of maturity), and so the atoning effect of God's perfect love has been secured: the "parents" have known the apostolic testimony of Jesus "from the beginning" (2:13a; cf. 1:1; 2:4), the "young people" have defeated the evil one (2:13b), and the community's young "children" *(paidia)* have known the Father (2:14a). Although unstated, these familial tropes appear to distinguish people according to their spiritual maturity or perhaps their prominence within the Christian household. They probably do not refer to age groups.

The parallelism of literary structure repeats the letter's address to the community's parents (2:14b), young people (v. 14c), and children (v. 18) but with differing exhortations to secure the allegiance of the entire community to the apostolic message about Jesus. For example, the faith of the community's elders is secured by their firm knowledge of the apostolic tradition: they "know him who is from the beginning" (2:13a, 14b; cf. 1:1).[32]

The more expansive exhortations that target the "young people" and "children" may reflect a greater concern for threats that face newer or less mature converts. The "young people," while they have defeated the Evil

---

32. The important catchphrase "from the beginning" recalls the letter's opening phrase, which we take to refer to the scope and therefore integrity of the apostles' witness of the incarnation. Its repetition in 1 John as a trope for the community's apostolic foundation functions as a constant reminder of the epistemic criterion for fellowship with God and with one another (1:3).

One (2:13b), typically struggle to escape "the things in the world" (cf. vv. 14c-17). Although 1 John speaks of "the world" as the object of God's saving love (2:2; 4:9, 14; cf. John 3:16), more often the term is used of a vast network of forces and factors that operate under the Evil One's rule (5:19b). The norms and values of the world order oppose the community's apostolic definition of eternal life. This is not the material creation that 1 John has in mind, as though apostolic Christianity is a world-denying religion like its second-century rivals. The world that is inhospitable to the Creator's ways is rather occupied by false beliefs and theological deceptions, by unconfessed sin, and by hatred and disloyalty for other Christians (cf. Rom. 1:18-32). To abide in God, who is light, is to separate from the ways of the world, which contains everything that is subversive to the community's relationship with God and one another.

Separation from the world is not defined in practical terms but in terms of the individual's inward "desire" (*epithymia;* cf. Jas. 1:14-15). Although interpretation of this text has attempted to nail down the triad of desires listed — flesh, eyes, and wealth — to specific sources (biblical and secular) or practices, the clear impression of 1 John's expansion of worldly love is of the individual's total self-absorption in practices that are contrary to God. Such preoccupation makes it impossible to love God or another; the self-centered individual is also inclined to rely on his peculiar version of the truth rather than submit to the community's apostolic testimony of the incarnate One.

Likewise, while the community's spiritual "children" have come to "know the Father" (2:14a), they are especially vulnerable to the theological errors of the "antichrists" (cf. vv. 18-27) who deny the Father and so the Son (so vv. 22-23). To remain in the knowledge of the Father is to remain in the Son (so v. 24). This more expansive address of the "children" implies a pastor's concern for the faith formation of new converts. According to this typology of Christian formation, a family's young children are the most impressionable, dependent members of a family; they require the most attention and care accordingly. Recent converts are more likely to experience spiritual failure, which distinguishes them from the elders (cf. 1 Tim. 3:6); for this reason, their careful education is especially crucial in establishing their future well-being.

The warning about the arrival of "antichrists," a conventional apocalyptic trope, signals "the last hour" (cf. 2 Thess. 2:3) and anticipates the letter's stunning announcement about the end time in 2:28–3:10 (see below).

There has been considerable speculation about the identity of the antichrist(s) who "went out from us" (2:19a); no detail is provided, however, either because the first readers knew it or, more likely, because the primary intent is pastoral and concerns the spiritual formation of the congregation's "children." The similarity of the words for "antichrist" *(antichristos)* and "anointing" *(chrisma,* vv. 20, 27), both exceedingly rare words paired only here in Scripture, implies a contest over sources from whom to learn knowledge of the truth (especially vv. 20-21). This stands at the center of the epistemic crisis that occasions this letter. On the one hand, the antichrists are apostates: they "went out from us . . . did not belong to us" (v. 19). Presumably they are those who deny that "Jesus is the Christ *(Christos,* v. 22) and so are anti-Christ. One cannot learn the truth about Jesus from them.

On the other hand, even the community's spiritual children "have knowledge" (2:20) and "know the truth" (v. 21) about Christ from the apostles. So secure is this source of truth that this experience of anointing contributes nothing to what they have already received from the apostolic message (v. 27). To what does this "anointing by the Holy One" refer? There are various options. (1) If one understands this experience by the farewell words of John's Jesus, it is likely that 1 John's "Holy One" is the Holy Spirit, who is given by God to mediate Jesus' union with the disciples (cf. 1 John 3:24). In this case, the Spirit's anointing ministry *(charisma=chrisma),* glossed by Jesus' prophecy of the Spirit's future ministry in John 14–16, refers to the charismatic experiences of the indwelling Paraclete ("advocate") in teaching and comforting disciples following the departure of Jesus.[33] (2) However, if one understands 1 John as a corrective to the Gospel's divisive use within the community (so R. E. Brown), perhaps to correct exaggerated dependence on the Spirit's charisma (e.g., Montanism), then "Holy One" may refer to Jesus himself (cf. John 6:69). If so, then 1 John's Christ has taken over the tasks of John's Spirit-*paraklētos* (see 2:1) in order to restore believers to God and not — as in the Gospel — to teach and comfort believers in absence of Jesus. According to 1 John 3:24–4:6, the Spirit has a different role to perform: to enable a congregation to test the content of a teacher's instruction and confession about Jesus. If

---

33. Because John's Gospel glosses our reading of 1 John, the Gospel's connection of the Spirit's post-Easter arrival with the continuation of Jesus' teaching of the truth (so John 14:26; 15:26) may suggest that Jesus is the anointer and the Spirit is the anointing (cf. Tit. 3:5-6).

the Anointer is the abiding Christ, to deny him is to deny his anointing and to deny his anointing is to forego the religious experiences that would enable the community to know the truth about God with surety and so live in a manner pleasing to God (so 3:19-24). (3) Lieu understands the referent of "the anointing" as God's word, which she also applies to God's "seed" in 3:9.[34] (4) Could this "anointing" be a metaphor for catechesis or some other rite of initiation (e.g., baptism) into the covenant community where truth is made known? If an allusion to the OT liturgy of "anointing oil" when consecrating priests for ministry (LXX Exodus), 1 John probably has a material rather than metaphorical meaning in mind, whether a charismatic experience or the community's reception of God's Word.

Even though the dispute between the rival and apostolic communities is unknown, the sense of this passage is plain: the apostolic testimony of the incarnate word (complemented by an anointing) delineates the absolute truth of God's way of salvation. Practically, this definition of truth enables "children" to distinguish truth from error, especially about sin (cf. 1:5-10) and the moral manner of Christian discipleship (2:3-11).

The Future of Sin (2:28–3:10). The repetition of the "passing away" of darkness/world (2:8, 17) suggests the community's active participation in God's victory over sin. The "and now" of 2:28 recalls and elaborates what will happen at the "last hour," which climaxes in an upgraded personal relationship with the living Jesus when he returns to earth to complete his messianic mission (3:2). While typically stated boldly without compromise, the believer's victory over sin is experienced in an organic, unfolding way. The practice of not sinning is the stunning hallmark of a believer's new birth; it heralds publicly for all the world to see God's future and the end of sin. At the same time, the believer's experience of new birth, which enables these extraordinary new competencies, underwrites the believer's confidence that her covenant with God does not come with term limits!

While this concluding section of the letter's first movement continues to clarify the truth about sin against the horizon of the community's confession that God is light, interest shifts from sin's threat to Christian life to its total elimination when Christ arrives to complete his messianic mission to save the world. The believer's present struggle with sin now takes on a

---

34. J. M. Lieu, *The Theology of the Johannine Epistles* (Cambridge: Cambridge University Press, 1991), pp. 34-35.

different cast. The purpose of living in solidarity with Christ during this "last hour," which requires the community to reject false claims about him and to confess sins against him, is now made clear by the purpose clause, "so that *(hina)* when he appears[35] we may have confidence [cf. 3:21; 4:17; see 5:14] and not shrink in shame [cf. 1 Pet. 4:16] at his coming *(parousia)*" (2:28).

The action of this clause is plotted by the parallelism of two aorist passive verbs which express reciprocal acts that complete God's plan of salvation: Christ "appears" and the community "does not shrink in shame." To remain in Christ is to affirm the truth of his future coming and the messianic tasks left for him to do. Among those tasks is the prosecution of God's judgment of sin. The covenant-keeping community that "does not shrink in shame" presents evidence of faithfulness during a time of difficulty (cf. 1 Pet. 4:16; Jas. 2:19) and so secures divine approval rather than judgment.

The important Johannine catchword "confidence" *(parrhēsia,* 2:28; 3:21; 4:17; 5:14) is introduced in connection with Christ's future appearing. In 4:17, the perfection of love for one another forges confidence to face the day of judgment, as in the implied point scored in 3:21: active love for one another forges those inward affections that assure believers of God's devotion to them. For this reason, repeated in 5:14, the community is confident that God will be responsive to its petitions for help. It is crucial to observe that a community's firm assurance of God's covenant loyalty is formed in those whom God indwells, but God's indwelling is conditioned on acts of obedience to God's commandments, especially the commandment to love one another (3:22). Not only, then, is the connection between eschatology and ethics in 1 John substantive, so that the community's moral practices herald the coming age (see 3:2-3), but the community's future participation in the coming victory of God is conditioned on present conformity to God, who is light and love.

The use of "coming" *(parousia),* found only here in the Johannine writings, glosses the similar sounding word for "confidence" *(parrhēsia).* This trope of Jesus' reentry into the world to complete his messianic mis-

---

35. The ambivalence between Father and Son in 1 John 2:18-27 carries over to v. 28, where the antecedent of the "he" who "appears" could be either God who is "righteous" (v. 29) or Jesus who "comes" (v. 28). While we take it that the "he" of this text is the Messiah Son who "comes," this imprecision illustrates the interpenetrating unity of Father and Son in 1 John (cf. 1:2-3). In effect, both Father and Son "come" in victory even as both are "righteous" as are those who abide in both.

sion doubtless intends to recall the letter's earlier reference to the Son's first coming into the world to reveal the truth about the Father (1:2-3). The shape of Johannine eschatology, while cast in a distinctive idiom, follows an apostolic consensus: at day's end, the Messiah's *parousia* will lend *parrhēsia* to the truth disclosed to the apostles "from the beginning," which they have announced to the community (1:1, 4-5).

As has been made clear so far, the central theological crisis that threatens the community's bold confidence for this future day is the question of whether the truth they have received is the real truth about its future with God. The "world" is no help, because it "does not know." What follows, however, injects a new theological element into 1 John's narrative of salvation that carries with it a stunning implication for Christian existence: believers are God's children who are "born of God" (2:29; 3:9) and therefore have the DNA to do what is right. For this reason, God's children, who otherwise are rejected by the world, live in the hope that when Jesus comes again they will "be like him, because we will see him as he is" (3:2; cf. 2 John 8).

What follows in 3:3-10 concludes the letter's theological exposition on the theme "God is light," with a definition of Christian discipleship equal to its hope: "everyone who hopes in (Jesus) purifies himself as he is pure" (v. 3). To elaborate this response, vv. 4-10 presents a series of sharp contrasts that lay bare the radical, transformative nature of a believer's self-purification to become as Christ: sin is contrasted with righteousness (vv. 4-7; cf. 2:29) even as the children of the devil are contrasted with the children of God (vv. 8–9), and each is marked out by contrasting practices of hatred and love (v. 10). The future implication of God's victory through Christ is especially clear in v. 9: those who are born of God have God's "DNA" (CEB) in them and are of a new nature that does not sin.[36] They practice righteousness; they practice love. Those who are of the devil, on the other hand, do not do right: they hate (cf. 3:13).

---

36. The word translated "DNA" is *sperma*, "sperm." But to what does this "sperm" metaphor refer? Most commentators understand this as a metaphor of regeneration: a new kind of human existence has been conceived in faith. But who is the agent of this new birth? The history of interpreting 1 John privileges God's Spirit and links it to the "anointing" experience (2:20, 27). If the central theological crisis addressed by 1 John is epistemological, however, the divine sperm is more likely the apostolic witness to the "word of life" in which the children of God abide (so 2:14). The community's reception and practice of this apostolic word cultivate new habits of life, which include evidently the habits of not sinning and of loving one another.

After calling those who say they do not sin self-deluded liars (see 1:8, 10), it seems like a stunning flip-flop that 1 John now asserts that God's children do not sin. But this same tension is found again in the letter's concluding affirmations about the Christian life: while God forgives the believer's sins in response to the congregation's prayers (5:16-17; cf. 1:8-9), those born of God do not sin (5:18; cf. 3:6, 9). This dynamic tension between sinning and not sinning is characteristic of 1 John's conception of new birth, a realistic experience of those who occupy the in-between time following Jesus' atoning sacrifice for sin but preceding his return, when true believers will become just like him (3:2).

Paul writes of this same experience in Romans 6 when he affirms that believers have been freed from sin because of their union with Christ (6:5-7), but then warns them not to allow sin to creep back into their lives (6:12-14). The different levels of spiritual maturity in the congregation, acknowledged by 1 John (2:12-14a and 14b-27), coupled with the use of present tenses (e.g., "do not sin") in this passage,[37] suggest that this inward tension is resolved progressively during this "in-between time" in those who remain in loving fellowship with a faithful God (3:6, 9; cf. 4:16-21) and with one another (cf. 3:18-24) by cultivating the spiritual discipline of not sinning, until Christ's return when they will "be like him" (3:2) and "cannot sin" (3:9; cf. 3:5).

37. Linguistic theory speaks of verbal tenses no longer in an exclusively temporal sense but also in terms of what tenses "portray" — a verb's "aspect" or frame of reference toward the action depicted. It strikes us that this new development may provide a way forward in resolving the perceived conflict of interests between the claims that Christians sin (1:6–2:2; 5:14-17) and that Christians do not sin (2:28–3:10; 5:18-19). That is, perhaps the "aspect" of the present indicatives in 3:9 portrays an "imperfective" or unfolding action. In this sense, the pair of verbs that depict the full effect of regeneration — that God's children "cannot" and "do not" sin — envisages an imperfective or organic action, unbounded by time constraints (see B. M. Fanning, *Verbal Aspect in New Testament Greek* [Oxford: Clarendon Press, 1990], pp. 221ff.). The shift from the present practice of not sinning to the state of not being able to sin, both present indicatives, projects an experience of regeneration as an unfolding whole that includes a future, envisaged when they will exist in Christlikeness (2:28; 3:2). Thus, even though the temporal sense of this difficult claim is located in the present, its "aspect" suggests that Christians' practice of not sinning heralds the community's future union with the Son as an unfolding but divine inevitability.

Second Movement: God Is Love, So True Believers Must Love One Another (3:11–5:12)

The repetition of "this is the message/gospel that you have heard from the beginning" (3:11; cf. 1:5) signals the beginning of the letter's second movement (3:11–5:12), which elaborates a second core belief of the apostolic community's theological grammar: "God is love" (4:8, 16). This movement, however, is introduced by a moral practice rather than theological confession: "we should love one another." This practice of love is defined by the apostles' authoritative testimony of Jesus' self-sacrifice (4:7-10) by which the "works of the devil," including hatred, are destroyed (3:8). Those born of God, whose nature is love, are prone to love one another (4:7-8); in fact, such Godlike love is the community's final exam of covenant-keeping.

Unlike 1 John's first movement, which proceeds from the firm announcement that "God is light" to a dramatic conclusion that Christians should therefore practice not sinning (which means not hating: so 3:10), the second movement unfolds from the moral practice of loving one another before climaxing in the confession of faith that "God is love." This movement's inductive logic is most clearly expressed by the letter's most famous saying: "We love because God first loved us" (4:19). That is, the letter's definition of Christian discipleship is deeply indebted to the community's prior experience of being loved by God, who forgives and regenerates, and subsequently to the practices of a covenant-keeping community whose members reciprocate God's love by actively loving each other. It is once again Jesus whose atoning death bears witness to the self-sacrificial nature of divine love and whose example is followed by the loving community of his disciples.

The Community That Loves (3:11-24). The first movement's concluding contrast between "children" who engage in the works of the devil, which includes hating one another, and the children of God who herald the apocalypse of God's victory over sin by not sinning, is extended by allusion to the biblical story of Cain (3:12). Cain presents a type similar to Paul's Adam type in Romans 5, 7, and 1 John's logic is roughly the same. According to its absolute dualism "the world" is populated by those like Cain "who was of the evil one" and participated in the "works of the devil" (3:8), including murder, which is the most egregious act of hatred and an assault on a community's mutual love and solidarity.

Clearly, 1 John understands that love targets other members of the faith community — "brothers and sisters" (3:10). Cain's murder of his brother is recalled, then, as the ultimate type of anti-family hatred, of Christians versus Christians. If the terms of eternal life are disclosed by Jesus as testified to by his apostles (1:2), then, in contrast to Cain, "we know" that God's love is disclosed by Jesus' self-sacrifice (3:15-16), so if a brother or sister is in need, "the world's goods" are used to meet it (v. 17). If v. 18 is read as the conclusion of the preceding idea (rather than the thesis statement of the next unit), the emphasis in Jesus' example is placed on its active nature: Jesus' mission is climaxed "not in word or speech" but in the act of self-sacrificial love in which the vital truth of divine love is disclosed.

The letter's use of the formula "by this we will know" (3:19; cf. 2:3, 5; 4:13; 5:2) indicates evidence that supports a claim: self-sacrificial acts of love toward each other assure both the community and God of the covenant relationship. Axiomatic of the surety of this relationship is God's sublime knowledge of all things, such that when the community's assurance of its standing before God is compromised by self-doubt, God overrides that doubt, knowing the community's true destiny (v. 20). This awareness of the triumph of God's faithfulness enables believers to pray boldly, not only because of God's irrepressible faithfulness toward God's "little children" (v. 18), but knowing also that when God finds evidence of a community's covenant-keeping acts of love and confession of faith in Christ (v. 23) God will answer its petitions (see 5:14-17).

The combination of "our hearts" (3:21) and abiding "by the Spirit" (v. 24) suggests an internal moral compass, as in Pauline thought (Rom. 8:2-17), that guides God's children to obey God's commandment — what Paul calls "the law of the Spirit of life" (Rom. 8:2). In this sense, then, obeying God's twofold command to love each other and confess faith in Christ (3:23) is evidence of the Spirit's presence that marks a people out as belonging to God. In fact, abiding in God by the Spirit is the condition by which a people can boldly approach God with petitions and receive from God whatever is asked (vv. 21-22). This ask–receive formula envisages the reciprocity of covenant-keeping.

The Witness of the Spirit (4:1-6). The epistemic crisis provoked by a rival Christianity (cf. 2:12-27, especially vv. 18-19) has prompted this letter's clarification of the apostolic message that sets out the gospel truth about the "word of life." This truth is confirmed by the internal witness of the Spirit

(3:24; cf. 2:20, 27). It is the letter's new claim about the testimony of the in-dwelling Spirit, sent by God, which prompts an extended parenthesis about rival "spirits" and the contrasting communities they indwell.

On the one hand, the community given God's Spirit (3:24) "confesses that Jesus Christ has come in the flesh" and "is from God" (4:2; cf. 2:18; 1 Cor. 12:3; Rom. 10:9); this confession identifies the community as belong-ing to God. This confessed Jesus is the same Jesus received from preachers of the apostolic tradition, whose eyewitness testimony of the "word of life" sets the plumb line between truth and error (4:6; cf. 1:1-2). On the other hand, the community led by "false prophets" (4:1) is indwelled by the "spirit of the antichrist," who rebels against God's command and denies that Jesus is from God (4:3, cf. 3:23). The membership of this rival group is not from God but rather "from the world" (4:4-6; cf. 2:15-17).

The rhetoric of this passage is shaped by a biblical typology that pits true against false prophet (cf. Deut. 13:1-18; Matt. 7:15-23) and perhaps by Judaism's doctrine of two spirits featured in various Qumran writings.[38] The false prophet, led by the spirit of antichrist, preaches apostasy as truth and is portrayed as seditious and so a threat to the community's covenant with God. These two spirits of truth and of error occupy human commu-nities, prompting them to make choices that are either from God ("spirit of truth") or from the world ("spirit of error"). Obviously, the epistemic crisis is resolved in God's favor within the community led by the spirit of truth (= Johannine/apostolic tradition), which cooperates with the apos-tolic message of the true prophets.

God Is Love (4:7-12). Believers are born of God, who by nature is love, and if believers enjoy fellowship with God, they too will love as God loves. The hymnlike repetition of *agapē* ("love") words in this passage produces, in canonical conversation with Paul's 1 Corinthians 13, one of Scripture's seminal definitions of divine love, with vast implications for 1 John's defi-nition of Christian discipleship. Indeed, the implication is that disagree-ments among Christians, which are evident in manner of life, have their source in different ways of thinking about God.

Having now thoroughly established the authority of the apostolic message over its false rivals, 1 John returns to 3:11 to develop the theological

38. See J. R. Levison, *Filled with the Spirit* (Grand Rapids: Eerdmans, 2009), pp. 407-21. Cf. C. G. Kruse, *The Letters of John* (PNTC; Grand Rapids: Eerdmans, 2000), pp. 151-55.

foundation for the letter's principal exhortation for Christians to love each other *(agapōmen allēlous)*. Not only is the source of love "from God" but the natural capacity to do so is "fathered" *(gennaō)* by God (4:7; cf. 3:9; 5:1). Knowledge that "God is love" (4:8) — and so is the source and progenitor of love — is revealed by the "one and only Son," whom God sent as a "sacrifice for our sins" (4:9-10). This revealed definition of divine love is received "among us" *(en hēmin)* — that is, in the Son's incarnation that is seen, heard, and handled by the apostles from the beginning (cf. 1:1-2).

The practical effect of being reborn by God, who is love and whose act of loving others is sending the Son to atone for sins, is to love one another in like manner (cf. John 3:16-17). The letter's emphasis on the community's responsibility for the sins of its members (e.g., the liturgy of confessing sins in 1:9, concern for the "stumbling" of others in 2:10, and prayer for the forgiveness of sins in 5:14-17) applies this teaching to the community's life together.

The odd refrain that "no one has seen God at any time" (4:12; cf. v. 20; John 1:18) seems misplaced immediately after the assertion that we can know God through the Son's incarnation (4:8-10). No one in antiquity would have denied that God is inaccessible to mere mortals, either because God is invisible or because humans lack the ability to see God. In fact, when God does show up (e.g., Genesis 17–18 and Exodus 34), especially in the Son's incarnation, that occurs to make the truth about God accessible to mere mortals. The epistemic upgrade of the incarnation is qualitative, then, not quantitative. In this case, however, the point is commonsensical rather than theological: the transcendent God, who is love, can only be made known to others when divine love is embodied in the practices of God's people. The passive perfect participle "made perfect" (CEB) suggests an action brought to completion by another over time: this love from God, whose love is perfect, will bring to perfection the love one person has for another in the same manner that God loves.

The Community Loves Because God Is Love (4:13–5:4a). The remainder of the letter's second movement elaborates the love of God. The formula "by this" is used fourteen times in 1 John to introduce into evidence those practices or phenomena that confirm the apostolic message. In this case, the primary datum is the reception of God's Spirit (4:13, i.e., the "Spirit of truth": see v. 6), which confirms what is known from the apostolic testimony (= "we," v. 14). The Spirit's confirmation and safeguard of the apostolic tradition is similar to 2 Tim. 1:13-14 (cf. Romans 8), but generally differs from the Pauline tradition, which assigns to God's Spirit the role of either witness to the community's adoption/union with Christ or agent of the community's transformation to be like Christ. More typical is the Spirit's prompting the believer to confess the lordship of Jesus (so 1 Cor. 12:3; Rom. 10:9), which is similar to what we see in 1 John 4:15, even if 1 John substitutes Jesus' divine Sonship (but see 5:1; cf. 1:3) for the Pauline emphasis on his lordship. But the practical effect is exactly the same for both apostolic traditions: the confession of faith in Jesus demonstrates publicly a people's allegiance to God (4:15). In fact, the community's confession of Jesus is focused on God, who as the ultimate source of love and truth is the vital location of Christian existence (v. 16; cf. 1:3).

But what are the experiences of those who reside in God who is love? What follows in 4:17–5:3a catalogs various gains expected for those who confess that Jesus is God's Son and believe that God is perfect love. For example, confidence that their confession of faith in Jesus, even though contested by rival Christians, will be vindicated (rather than rejected) by God "in the day of judgment" (4:17-18). This letter allows no room for uncertainty in one's status with God, present or future; such uncertainty drives fear, which is incompatible with Christian love that is from God. The dualistic idiom draws truth and false claims so sharply and not only clarifies how things stand but cultivates assurance among readers. The apostolic tradition, witnessed to by the Spirit of truth (v. 13; cf. v. 6), establishes the epistemic criterion by which fellowship with God and with God's Son (and so eternal life) is based (so 1:3).

John Wesley for good reason considered 1 John 4:19 "the sum of all religion." The verse recalls the primary exhortation that opens the letter's second movement: the apostolic message exhorts believers to love each other (3:11). Based on the prior theological development of divine love, 1 John now is able to say that Christians are able to love one another because God has loved them first, not only to regenerate them and so give them the capacity to love others (so 5:1-2) but to reveal and so give them knowledge of the right manner of loving others. This, of course, means that one who claims a relationship with God but then hates rather than loves is proved to be a fraud (4:20-21).

Similar to the fearlessness that God's love perfects in Christian existence, obedience to God's commandments (see 3:23-24) is not burdensome (5:3a; cf. Matt. 11:28-30). Although the experience of divine love and Christians' love for one another may well cultivate a glad willingness to obey God's commands, 1 John sustains the contention that new birth gives one the capacity to be like God, whose nature is love. The force of the *hoti* clause, "because everyone who has been fathered *(gennaō)* by God" (4:4a; see 2:29; 3:9; 4:7), implies that covenant-keeping comes naturally and therefore is the birthmark of God's progeny. In 1 John's dualistic universe, the present world order is characterized by everything that those who are born of God are not: hatred rather than love, wickedness rather than sinless perfection, lies rather than truth-telling, and so on. The coming victory of God (2:28) means, of course, that those activities that are "of the world" will be conquered, and everything that impedes the community's relationship with God will be no more on that day when "we will be like him because we will see him just as he is" (3:2). This is possible only when what is of the world is dissolved.

The Triumph of the Apostolic Witness (5:4b-13). The triumphal nature of 1 John's "overcoming" *(nikaō)* idiom (5:4-5) is not unexpected, not only because of its earlier uses in this letter (2:13-14; 4:4) and its dualistic tenor, but also because of its strategic use in John's Revelation in a way that encloses the entire vision (Rev. 2:7, 11, 17, 26; 3:5, 12, 21 and 12:11; 15:2; 17:14; 21:7). What perhaps is surprising in so theocentric a letter, however, is that it is "our faith" that conquers the world (5:4b) rather than God's faithfulness — a claim that provides the thesis for this concluding passage of the letter's second movement.

"Our faith" has the definite article and so is "our Christian faith" — the content of which is doubtless supplied by the apostolic message (cf. 5:5-6). It is the community's unwavering commitment to the announcement that God is light and love, predicated on the apostles' witness of Jesus as God's Son from the beginning (5:5; cf. 1:1-2), that is vindicated. Not only is the world order defeated according to this epiphany (cf. Tit. 2:11-14) but also the works of the Evil One (2:13-14; 3:8; 5:18-19) and every spirit that does not confess Jesus (4:3). This is a complete conquest of all that is opposed to the light and love of the God disclosed by Jesus.

Mention of the testimony of the Spirit to Jesus' revelation of God's truth repeats the point scored in 4:1-6 (cf. Rom. 1:4). "Water and blood" is probably pars pro toto that implicates the Lord's entire mission (i.e., "water" is a metaphor of baptism and "blood" a metaphor of crucifixion). The agreement of the three, Spirit, water, and blood, then, implies that the

Spirit's witness to Jesus (cf. John 1:32-34) confirms the apostles' testimony of Jesus "from the beginning" (so 1:1-3). Later scribes added "Father, Word, and Holy Spirit" (the "Johannine Comma") to the stated three to elaborate the "testimony of God," which is "greater" than (or the measure of) the "testimony of men" (i.e., apostles, 5:9). To this extraordinary collaboration of divine and human witnesses is added a third: the individual's experience of God's inward confirmation that Jesus is God's Son (5:10).

This triad of witnesses returns the reader to the letter's prologue (1:2-3) to recall what is witnessed: eternal life (5:13). The effect of this repetition is to fashion an inclusio that highlights the condition and character of "eternal life" as the letter's central concern: "that you may know that you have eternal life" (5:13). This "eternal life" is with/in/from God because God is eternal (cf. v. 20b); yet because God is unseen (4:12, 20), knowing that "God has given us eternal life" (5:11a) requires acceptance that "this life is in God's Son" (5:11b), whose arrival has "given us insight to know" God (5:20). This holy insight is received by the community with confidence, because it comes from the apostles, who have seen the Son, and by the Spirit, who confirms the trustworthiness of the apostles' witness (vv. 6-9). Presuming that 5:13 is the letter's capstone cues the reader to review the sweep of its argument. 1 John's two grand movements form an integral whole: because God is light and love, God's victory over falsehood and sin is experienced within a community whose practice of truth-telling and not sinning is embodied in acts of love rather than hatred for one another. This, then, is the nature of eternal life that is with/in/from God, and it is the essential message of the apostolic tradition that orders the community's fellowship with God.

Concluding Affirmations (5:14-21). The letter concludes in a series of three bold affirmations predicated on the assurance and experience of eternal life with God: (1) God answers prayers (5:14-17), (2) God's children do not sin (vv. 18-19), and (3) those who know the truth about God and eternal life will abstain from idols (vv. 20-21).

The first affirmation reprises the letter's opening concern about cleansing of sins that may threaten Christian discipleship (see 1:6–2:2). The opening response to the interlocutor stipulated a liturgy of confessing sins that a faithful God will forgive because of Jesus' atoning death. In this case, another worship practice is stipulated: intercessory prayer to restore to God those Christians who sin but in a way that does not result in death —

that is, that does not side with the claims of apostate antichrists against the apostolic message, which is tantamount to a death sentence.

The second affirmation reprises the letter's most arresting claim that those born of God do not sin (so 2:28–3:10). We encounter the same tension provoked by the earlier passage, which seems to reverse the letter's earlier responses to the interlocutor's boasts that "we do not sin" (1:8, 10). In this case, the second affirmation trades on the first, since the community's petitions for its wayward members presume that sinning still goes on among Christians! Perhaps the point of this affirmation is to remind believers that we live before the end time, when "we will be like Jesus" (3:2; cf. 2:28), that both our susceptibility to sin and our practice of not sinning herald the coming day when those fathered by God "will not be able to sin" (3:9). At the moment, we experience both God's forgiving grace that cleanses away all sin and God's regenerating grace that has reformed our very nature with a new capacity for not sinning (see the comments on 2:28–3:10). The repetition of this point suggests that it is a purposeful, even decisive feature of Christian discipleship according to 1 John, presented as a dialectic between the vision of perfect love and not sinning and the hard reality of sinning and theological deception.

What this purposeful tension commends, then, is a definition of Christian discipleship as an unfolding, dialectical process between sinning and not sinning until we are unable to sin (3:9) because "we will be like him and see him just as he is" (3:2). The effects of God's regeneration and abiding presence are experienced dynamically, in an unfolding way, as the community encounters new problems and questions on the ground. There is always the recognition of things "out there" — in this case a group of "antichrists" — that will require new applications of the tradition that expose yet other facets of the whole gospel truth. The abiding presence of God is apprehended with unique power and clarity by the faith community — with an insider's "knowledge" according to 1 John — in a context of its public confession of the apostles' Jesus and its members' self-giving love for one another (3:23).

The dialectic between the confession of the apostolic testimony, fixed for all time, and the ongoing experience of God's abiding presence, which is continually responsive to what is happening on the ground, continually amplifies the community's core commitments. This ontology of experience in which both community and God are participants is not simple but reflects all the complexities of a living covenant relationship that allows for a people's struggle with sin and even a deep ambivalence about their transcendent God. It allows for the community's intramural conflicts over the self-revelation of God that produces mixed messages and epistemic confusion, which can bring an exasperated God to the edge of what God can tolerate (cf. Exodus 32). What seems clear to us is that this biblical dialectic, which 1 John depicts in its theology of sin, always seeks to retain both the visional and the pragmatic, between what manner of life God's regeneration enables (no sin) and what manner of life is actually experienced on the ground (sin). Neither element of this dialectic can be compromised because the truth of the matter is located in the Spirit-led process that continually shapes and reshapes in every new setting the community's identity as a people belonging to God.[39]

The affirmation that "the one born of God keeps herself" (5:18b) is extremely difficult, and how one interprets its syntax is decisive to its meaning and translation. The main verb is the third person singular present indicative active "s/he keeps," a verb repeatedly and strategically used in 1 John of the proven believer who "keeps" the commandments of God (see 2:3, 4, 5; 3:22, 24; 5:3). So what is in view is the believer who has passed the spiritual testing of her faith; this is the one who "keeps" herself from the Evil One. This result is consistent with the earlier claim that the community's "young adults," brought to some maturity in their faith, have "conquered" the Evil One (2:13-14; cf. 5:3-5). In this case the devil's threat is nonexistent (cf. Rev. 12:13-18), and so the affirmation underwrites the very possibility of not sinning, since "the works of the devil" have no access to the faithful who reside in God. This is God's loving work, then, that does not permit "the whole world" to intrude on the community's fellowship with God (see 1:3, 5-6).

Appropriately, the letter's final affirmation reprises its central epistemic claim: the community knows the real truth about God and eternal life because God's Son has revealed it to the apostles. The message received from these eyewitnesses of this revelatory word of life secures the only viable source of knowledge about eternal life. This is the letter's essential polemic against any non-apostolic Christianity and the confusion it may provoke among the faithful.

But the final warning is an odd way to end this affirmation: why this

---

39. This paragraph draws upon the ideas of Paul D. Hanson in *Dynamic Transcendence* (Philadelphia: Fortress, 1978), pp. 46-60.

parting exhortation to "guard against the idols" (5:21), especially since the opening invocative, "little children," appears to frame its importance? We think it is of a piece with the prior theological assertion that God is true and is the source of eternal life. That is, this exhortation against idols would have the same meaning for the apostolic community that God's word on Mount Sinai had for Israel: if God is the one and only God who brings you out of Egypt and points you to a promised land, then it is sheer folly to worship any other than God.[40] Eternal life belongs to God, so live like it!

Commentary: 2 John

Greeting to Those Who Remain in the Truth (vv. 1-3)

The address is a single sentence that combines the author's unusual introduction as "the elder" (but without his name) and his recipient, "an elect lady and her children."[41] Both metaphors locate this communication and its pastoral concerns within any Christian congregation, but in a faceless, timeless social location — a truly "catholic" yet personal letter!

"Elder" could refer to the sender's old age (and so his greater experience and wisdom) or to his senior leadership position within the Johannine apostolate; we think the two are likely related in this case.[42] The use of the adjective "elect" (also v. 13; cf. 1 Pet. 1:1; 2:9) indicates that the letter's address to a "lady" and "her children" is the membership ("children") of any Christian congregation ("lady"). The noun form of the adjective, "the elect," is used in Rev. 17:14 of faithful followers of the Lamb (cf. Rev. 14:1-5) — a vision in which the citizens of the new Jerusalem are personified as a

---

40. The warning against idolatry combines "guard" (Acts 21:25) and "from idols" (Acts 15:20) in a way that recalls the purity code of Acts 15 and 21, which forms a critical piece of the Jerusalem Council's "apostolic decree" in response to the problem of Paul's mission to the Gentiles and Gentile inclusion in Christian fellowship. If this Johannine concluding exhortation (via Gal. 2:9) is indexed by Acts and forms an interesting intertext with its apostolic purity code, then the subtext of the concluding exhortation is similar to 3:3, where hope is predicated on public purity — that is, sinlessness.

41. The expression "elect lady" has no article, which shapes the impression of a letter without a particular address.

42. Cf. Lieu, *1-2-3 John*, pp. 241-43.

woman. The verbal form is frequently used in the Fourth Gospel of those chosen by Christ rather than the world to follow the truth of God (6:70-71; 13:18; 15:16-19), which seems apropos of this letter as well (cf. vv. 4, 6-7).[43]

Apropos of this letter's role as 1 John's epitomizer, the repetition of "truth" is combined with "love" in the salutation (v. 3) to put the reader on notice that a concern for theological orthodoxy cannot be detached from more practical concerns: the community that exists in solidarity with the apostolic tradition (= "in us") and so "loves/knows the truth" will also live "with us forever" (v. 2). 1 John also emphasizes the interdependent relationship of God and the incarnate Son, Jesus Christ (1:3, 7; 4:10, 14-15; 5:1-12): to abide in one is to abide in the other (2:24). The congregation's "children" are greeted as an apostolic community that shares eternal and loving fellowship with God based on a shared understanding of truth. In fact, the arresting impression of this greeting is that God's abiding presence and God's "grace, mercy, and peace" into the future are conditioned on acceptance of this version of the truth.

Thanksgiving for Those Who Remain in the Truth (v. 4)

The elder's expression of joy marks the letter's transition into his response to the crisis that occasioned its writing and so reading. The clause literally translated "that I have found from your children those walking in truth" suggests that only a portion of the congregation, here addressed more directly in the second person, adheres to the elder's apostolic faith.

The use of "walk" instead of a confessional idiom hints at a practical or ethical problem: perhaps the love (i.e., hospitality) shown to traveling teachers of the rival group is considered lending support to "the antichrist" (vv. 9-11). It is clear from 1 John that love for one another according to the command of God extends only to those "of the truth" (1 John 3:23-24; 4:20–5:4) and excludes any who lie outside the apostolic fold (2:18-27). In any case, the inseparability of truth and love — between right theology

---

43. Lieu makes the intriguing suggestion that 2 John is purposefully imitating 1 Peter, which also is addressed to "the elect" (1:1) from an "elder" (5:1). While she allows the relationship is more inspirational than substantive, if "the elder" writes this letter with 1 Peter in hand, perhaps the implication of 1 Peter's use of "elect" (i.e., the community's social alienation as "strangers" in a pagan world) carries over to 2 John, even if with a more intramural application.

and Christian discipleship — is sharply expressed by the key phrase "walking in truth." Obeying the command of God assumes the community's embrace of the apostolic message about God — that God is light and love (so 1 John). To know this about God is to reject all rival notions and to accept the "walk" (= lifestyle) that it obligates.

Main Body of Instruction (vv. 5-11)

The main body of a personal letter responds more fully to the spiritual crisis only hinted at in the thanksgiving. In this case, some members of the congregation apparently remain unconvinced or confused by the apostolic message, presumably because of the influence of a rival Christianity led by "the deceiver" (v. 7). The letter's substantive teaching both "epitomizes" while elaborating several important themes introduced by the first letter (see 1 John 2:18-27; 4:1-6), mostly regarding the effect bad theology may have on a congregation's future with God (see 1 John 2:28; 3:19-24).

God's command to love other believers is obeyed not out of obligation to those other members of the covenant community but to God as a covenant-keeping act (cf. 1 John 5:3). In this sense, loving one another supplies the hard evidence of knowing and believing God (cf. 1 John 3:19-24). The repeated phrase, "had/heard from the beginning" (vv. 5, 6), is also a crucial marker in 1 John of the community's origins at its reception of the apostolic message (1 John 2:24; 3:11; cf. 1:1; 2:7, 13, 14), which centers on the revelation of divine love in the self-sacrifice of Jesus (1 John 4:9-10). To learn of God from the apostles, then, is to know not only the command to love one another but to love one another self-sacrificially.

1 John's presentation of "God's commandment" integrates as though a singular whole the community's confession of Jesus and its members' love for one another (1 John 3:23). 2 John repeats this point in vv. 7-11, but in a different idiom that expands and formalizes its implication in two different ways. First, those who love the truth confess that Jesus' coming "in the flesh" not only includes the apostolic witness to Jesus' first "coming" (i.e., his faithful life and atoning death) but also the expectation of his second coming (cf. 1 John 2:28). The action of the present participle of "coming" extends into the future,[44] then, presumably

---

44. Cf. G. Strecker, *The Johannine Letters* (HC; Minneapolis: Fortress, 1996), p. 232.

not only to include the vindication of those who reside in Christ (1 John 2:28; 3:2) but also to render a negative verdict regarding the works of those who do not (John 3:19).

Accordingly, those who do not confess the (second) coming of a judging Jesus are similar to those who boast that they have no sins to confess (1 John 1:8): both are deceived into thinking that their status or "reward" from God, with whom there is eternal life, is secure, when it is not. 2 John reminds readers that there exists the real possibility of losing the "full reward" *(misthos)* they have earned (v. 8; cf. Rev. 22:12; 1 Cor. 3:14), which is to see and be like Jesus "just as he is" (so 1 John 3:2). The addition of the verb "work," not found in 1 John, may recall John 6:28-29, which defines the work required by God: to "believe in the one whom God sent" (cf. 1 John 3:23) — in this case "the teaching about Christ" (v. 9; cf. 1 John 2:1-2).

While probably not a reference to a particular individual but generic of all who belong to a rival Christianity, "the antichrist" seeks to deceive others into thinking that the apostolic witness is a lie (v. 7; cf. Rev. 12:9; 20:1-3; 1 John 2:26). His instruction "goes on ahead" *(proagōn;* cf. 2 Tim. 3:13) or advances truth beyond what is stipulated as the norm by the apostolic Rule of Faith, here called "the teaching (or doctrine) about Christ" (v. 9). This more formal measure of doctrine, reminiscent of the Pastoral Epistles' notion of "healthy doctrine" (1 Tim. 1:10; 6:3; 2 Tim. 1:13; 4:3; Tit. 1:9), is not found in 1 John but "epitomizes" various creed-like statements about Jesus in the letter.[45] To receive this rendering of Christ as true is to remain in him and in the God whom he reveals.

Second, those who embrace this apostolic rule as the truth will love one another, but in a particular manner. The singularity of truth and love in the Johannine witness is nowhere better captured than in 2 John's negative instruction on hospitality, which is the principal practice of loving another according to 2 and 3 John. Hospitality is not to be extended to the traveling teacher from a rival Christian community who does not remain "in this teaching" (vv. 9b-10). In fact, such a person is to receive the silent treatment since even to greet such a person — the most minimal expression of hospitality in this social world — would be the same as to "share in his evil deeds" (v. 11). The sense of such an exaggerated warning is to fore-

---

45. We take the genitive "of Christ" as objective: teaching about Christ. But it could also be understood as subjective: the teaching from Christ that is heard and observed by his apostles (so Lieu, *I, II & III* John, p. 258).

stall the threat of false teaching, which apparently has influenced some less mature members (the "children") of the congregation (see v. 4; cf. 1 John 2:18-19).

Benediction (vv. 12-13)

The letter's concluding words are typical of other Hellenistic (and NT) letters: a personal letter is often written as a literary substitute for an expected but delayed personal visit from a leader, and also as a vehicle for exchanging greetings between friends. These are missionary congregations, and perhaps the elder is himself a traveling teacher such as the one he warns against in vv. 10-11. The purpose of a congregational visit is to complete "our joy," which recalls the prologue of 1 John, where the same expression responds to the community's solidarity with God based on its reception of the apostolic message (1 John 1:4). This is the endgame of both the elder's letter and his pastoral house-call.

Commentary: 3 John

Greeting Gaius, Who Is Truly Loved (vv. 1-2)

As with 2 John, this letter's opening reflects the conventions of letter writing in antiquity: the sender ("the elder") greets the recipient by name (Gaius) and adds a wish for his good health. The address combines the elder's keenly felt sentiment, "whom I *(egō)* love *(agapaō)* in truth," followed by an endearment, "beloved one *(agapētos)*," both rarely used in Scripture, to underwrite the loyalty shared between them. This depth of intimacy has a political edge to it, as soon will be evident, given the elder's disagreement with Diotrephes.

The distinction between the elder's wish for Gaius's good health and prosperous "soul" (v. 2) is sometimes used to justify programmatic distinctions between spiritual and material prosperity in accounts of divine blessing.[46] Lieu suggests, however, that the point in this distinction is to encourage a holistic understanding of Christian discipleship that goes be-

---

46. See R. W. Yarbrough, *1-3 John* (BECNT; Grand Rapids: Baker, 2008), p. 367.

yond the physical and considers one's prosperity in terms of non-transient things — "walking in the truth." This idea is similar to the idea of "contentment" found in the Pauline witness (1 Tim. 6:3-10).

Thanksgiving for Gaius's Faithfulness to the Truth (vv. 3-4)

The repetition of "walking according to the truth" in characterizing Gaius's Christian life, which accounts for the elder's joy, sounds a key theme of the Johannine correspondence. The elder's impression relies on the repeated testimony of "the brothers" (v. 3), who are unknown to Gaius (v. 5). "The truth" is set out by the apostolic message, which functions as the criterion for a community's fellowship with God. The shift of subjects from Gaius to "my children" (v. 4), all of whom "walk according to the truth," locates Gaius within this community. What follows is an explanatory footnote that describes the manner of life that is of the truth.

Body of Exhortation (vv. 5-12)

The Johannine community is here described as a network of local "churches" or assemblies (v. 6) linked together by itinerant missionaries, called "the brothers" (v. 5). Their identity as those who "go out on behalf of 'the Name'" (v. 7), as well as the strategy of internal financial support (v. 8), may imply some kind of ordination or commissioning. "The Name," a familiar title for Jesus, is used as both the object of a community's faith (John 1:12; cf. Acts 3:16) and the means of God's forgiveness (1 John 2:12; cf. Acts 2:38).

The refusal of the brothers to accept support from non-believers is consistent with the highly sectarian sociology that characterizes this community, where love (i.e., practice of hospitality) is extended only to like-minded Christians (see 2 John 9-11). The "for whom" of hospitality has become a test of loyalty to the apostolic tradition.

Moreover, the text indicates a channel of news reporting: these travelers "came (to the elder) and testified to your (Gaius's) truth" (v. 3). Especially when this report is taken with the pointed exhortation that Gaius would do well to "send them on their way in a manner worthy of God" (v. 6), the brothers' portfolio seems to include more than a ministry of the gospel but perhaps also a political role that seeks to identify and even recruit a "cooperative of coworkers" (v. 8) loyal to the elder in his intramural conflict with Diotrephes.

Nothing more is said about a letter the elder wrote to an unnamed church (v. 9), but clearly its reception and public reading have been blocked by Diotrephes. This hostile act has occasioned the writing of 3 John and its appeal to Gaius for support. Here is the unwritten backstory pieced together from a close reading of vv. 9-11: Diotrephes is doubtless a leader of "the church" the elder is recruiting for his "cooperative of coworkers," since only a leader could exercise the right to censure a letter or withhold hospitality from its sender and carrier (v. 9). Gaius is a member of the receiving church and so is witness to Diotrephes' "wicked" actions. In his capacity as a leader, Diotrephes has made charges against the elder, which the elder now dismisses as baseless, evil, self-centered, and inhospitable (v. 10).

Given the personal terms used in his polemic and the silence about theological matters (unlike 2 John), the elder's countercharge does not seem to target a doctrinal divide (unlike his warning against "the antichrist" in 2 John and its recollection of 1 John's primary concern) but is more like a power struggle between two church leaders. However, if the principle of hospitality set out in 2 John 9-11 is in play, then Diotrephes' refusal of hospitality to the brothers (and by association, the elder himself) and even his excommunication of them (he "throws them out of the church," v. 10), which is a highly provocative signature of his authority, may also have a theological basis (cf. 1 Corinthians 5). What seems clear in reading 3 John as a gloss on 2 John's teaching on hospitality is that that teaching is itself subject to abuse and must be carefully regulated (presumably by the elders of the church) according to the truth — that is, the apostolic Rule of Faith.

The passing mention of Demetrius (v. 12), whom Gaius evidently knows, has occasioned considerable speculation about the history of 3 John. Recent criticism places him among "the brothers" who report to the elder and sees v. 12 as identifying him as the carrier of this postcard to Gaius. More simply, he could be mentioned here as an unimpeachable personification of "what is good" (v. 11) — an exemplar of "the truth itself" (v. 12) — in sharp contrast to Diotrephes, "who does what is wicked" (v. 11). The use of the editorial plural in the concluding phrase, "we testify to (Demetrius)," may function as the apostle John's own imprimatur, which would suggest that Diotrephes is a rival not only to the elder but to the apostolate itself.[47]

L. T. Johnson contends that 3 John is a letter written to commend Demetrius as the messenger of a "three-letter packet from the elder." His highly evocative thesis presumes that 3 John is read first and 2 John next as a cover letter for the main course, the public reading of 1 John.[48] Without speculating on the order of their public reading, the role of 3 John as supplying the framework for the other two is useful in appraising its canonical role. Even though cast in highly personal terms, 3 John frames a reading of the Johannine letters that makes it very difficult to separate out doctrinal from more practical and personal threats to the truth, when a grammar of core beliefs is also embodied in a lifestyle that "walks the truth."

Benediction (vv. 13-15)

The concluding words of 3 John are similar to those of 2 John 12-13. The addition of an exchange of greetings between "friends" (v. 15) is typical of the letter form, as is the "passing of the peace." Again, the prospect of a personal visit (v. 14) suggests that what has been written with "pen and ink" (v. 13) is an inferior but necessary substitute for the pastoral work of the elder on location. The assumption of these closing words, however, implies that the topics raised in the letter will be the subject matter of any visit.

Theology

1. The Creator God

Because 1 John is occasioned by an epistemic crisis (see above), it exhibits a density of "knowing" phrases (e.g., "by this we know") and words (e.g., "truth," "message," "understanding," "stumbling block," "anointing") that target two core beliefs about God: God is light (1:5) and God is love (4:8,

---

47. Cf. Yarbrough, *1-3 John*, p. 384.

48. L. T. Johnson, *The Writings of the New Testament* (3rd ed.; Minneapolis: Fortress, 2010), pp. 499-500.

16).[49] Tertullian reminds us that these two claims have absolute priority over human existence, since they express the nature of the one who alone produced all things through the creative word and also of those fathered by God, in whom God's DNA resides (3:9). These are also the two beliefs announced by the apostolic message as a commentary on all of life. And, indeed, the letter's concluding exhortation, "guard against idols," alludes to the Ten Words of Israel's Sinai contract and so to its decisive statement of God's sovereignty: since God has no real rival in the world, it is sheer folly to place any other gods before Israel's God.

The elemental content of these two beliefs about God is shaped by the apostles' direct and comprehensive witness of God's Son Jesus Christ "from the beginning": they observe him as the incarnate "word of life" (1:1-2) in whom the Creator is disclosed (1:2; cf. John 1:2-3) and by whom all may live (4:9). Acceptance of this apostolic witness is the epistemic criterion by which the community sustains its fellowship *(koinonia)* with God and God's Son Jesus Christ, with whom is eternal life (1:2-3).

The apostolic witness, first of all, proclaims that "God is light and in him there is no darkness at all" (1:5). The polyvalence of "light" serves 1 John well as a theological trope, since the apostolic message that "God is light" carries with it a religious as well as epistemic claim. According to 1:6–2:2, if God is light, truth-telling will ultimately win out over lies and deception (cf. 2:28), and, if God is light, the believer will be cleansed from sin and wrongdoing rather than remain in them.

Second, the apostolic message proclaims that "God is love" (4:8, 16; cf. 3:11). Not only is this an intimate personification of God, unlike the more abstract attribution that God is light, it issues in a sharp contrast with the world characterized by hatred for one another (3:13). God's love is disclosed in the Son's entry into a hostile world (which is "passing away," 2:17) to save its inhabitants from sin for eternal life (4:9-10). Logically, then, those Christians fathered by God will naturally not hate one another but love one another (3:9).

The act of sending God's only Son into a hostile place so that "we might live through him" discloses two essential characteristics of divine

---

49. Significantly, a third core belief of the Johannine community found in the Gospel, "God is spirit" (4:24), is lacking in 1 John. Other "spirit" claims found in the Fourth Gospel are also lacking in 1 John, which leads one to think that the epistle's occasion may include an implicit correction of a misguided pneumatology similar to what was later found among the Montanists.

love: (1) "Not that we have loved God but that God loved us." The act of God sending the Son is at God's own initiative. As in the case of forgiveness, God's initiative to save the world is an operation of God's faithfulness and righteousness. It does not respond to the world's love for God since the world cannot love and is ignorant of God's truth. (2) "As the expiation for our sins." God's costly love gets results. The principal result is that believers love one another publicly and perfectly so that the community, made wakeful to the truth about God by the apostolic proclamation of the word of life, can itself witness to God, whom no one has actually seen (4:11-12).

The concluding affirmation that the Creator God "gives life" in answer to certain prayers (5:14-17) is a fitting touchstone for the letter's most crucial claims about God. The community's confidence in making petition before God is based on the belief that God is love and "hears us" (5:14, 15). The community's "confidence" in this belief is based on its possession of the truth about God — that God is love — which is testified to by the apostolic witness to the Son (4:8-10) and confirmed by the experience of being loved "in deed and truth" (3:18-20). But what is also known by the community is that God is light and cannot tolerate sin. The substance of the community's petitions according to God's will, then, concern ridding its membership of "all unrighteousness" (5:17; cf. 1:8-9). The trenchant loyalty of God toward this community is expressed by the qualification that its petitions for forgiveness will be answered only for those sins "not resulting in death" — that is, not the sins of those whose beliefs about Jesus place them outside God, in whom is eternal life (cf. 3:23-24; 4:13-16).

2. Christ Jesus

Father and Son form an interpenetrating whole in 1 John, and it is often difficult for the reader to distinguish between the two — a purposeful ambiguity since to know the Son is to know his Father. The Son has "come in the flesh" to disclose a definitive "word about (eternal) life" (1:1-2). The Son's revelation of the truth about God is necessary since no one has ever seen God (4:12, 20) and so no one is able to distinguish truth from falsehood. Any who deny the Son — or rather the apostolic witness to him — will inevitably engage in an epistemological error, while those who receive the apostolic witness have a full portfolio of truth to order their lives rightly. That is, if eternal life is with God (1:2) and this life is in God's Son (5:11), then the one who abides in the Son has eternal life from God (5:12-13).

Tertullian's claim that Jesus is "this word called 'God's Son'" captures the essence of Jesus' identity according to these epistles: this "Jesus in the flesh" to whom the Spirit bears witness (5:8; cf. Rom. 1:4; 1 Tim. 3:16) is directly observed as the revelatory "word of life" that the apostles witness (1:1), proclaim (1:3), and write about (1:4; 2:13; 5:13). Sharply stated, the primary purpose of the Son's mission is to make known his Father, who is otherwise unseen and unknown (cf. 4:12, 20).

The apostolic testimony interprets the problem of sin according to the incarnate Word's revelation that God is light in whom no darkness can exist. Not only does he disclose the problem of sin but he provides its remedy by his atoning death. What is distinctive about 1 John's theology of the cross is its particular application for Christians who struggle with spiritual failure and must be cleansed from all unrighteousness to "walk in the light as God is in the light" (1:7). This is not a missionary setting (as typical of the Pauline letters) but one that requires a pastoral response to confusion among Christians as to whether the presence of unconfessed sin can imperil a believer's relationship with God.

Three core beliefs about Christ are set out in response: 1 John speaks obliquely of "that one" (*ekeinos*, 2:6; 3:3, 5, 7, 16; 4:17) in this series of strategic Christological texts. We would suggest that this summary funds whatever 2 John means by "the teaching about Christ" (v. 9).

1. "We (Christians) have an advocate (*paraklētos*) with the Father" (2:1b). The present tense of Jesus' advocacy before God is especially for Christians who sin ("if anyone does sin," 2:1), and whose sinning imperils their relationship with God. His role as the community's legal counsel implies that he remains present with and active for his disciples, presumably through the Spirit (so the use of *paraklētos* for the Spirit in John 14–15).

2. "Jesus Christ is the righteous one (*dikaios*)" (2:1c). The community's confidence in the Lord's advocacy on its behalf is due to his unity with God as God's Son. He is "the righteous one" even as God is "faithful and righteous (*dikaios*)" (1:9; cf. 2:29); legal arguments are made and God's pardon of "all unrighteousness (*adikia*)" is granted on this same basis. 1 John's use of the Christological title "righteous one" in this setting alludes to "the righteous one (*dikaios*)" of Isa 53:7-12 LXX, whose unjust sufferings ("he did no sin," 53:9; cf. 1 John 3:5) were recalibrated by God as a sacrifice

for sin (53:10) to mediate for the transgressors (53:12) and make them righteous (53:11).

3. "Jesus is the sacrifice *(hilasmos)* for our sins" (2:2a; cf. 3:16). This echo of the Day of Atonement (Lev. 25:9; cf. LXX Ps. 129:4) glosses the believers' confession as self-referential: that is, Christ's death atones for *their* sins and restores their covenant relationship with God (cf. 5:14-17). This pastoral emphasis does not mitigate against the universal application of Christ's atoning death, since he died "not only for our sins but also for (the sins of) the whole world" (2:2b; cf. 4:9-10).

Jesus Christ exemplifies the manner of life in which believers ought to live in obedience to "God's word" (2:5; 5:20). Central to the apostolic message is the integration of what is believed about Jesus and a manner of life like his; together, this forms the singular "commandment" of God (cf. 3:23). In fact, the test of claiming to "know" Jesus (2:4) is to live "just as he lived" (2:6). And the evidence of being born again is abiding in "that one" in whom there is no sin (3:5; cf. 2:29). While 1 John is vague about the manner of Jesus' life, grounding it in the way in which he loved in giving his life to cleanse us from our sins (4:12-15), in its wider biblical setting this exhortation is given added depth of meaning by the canonical narrative of Jesus' life in the fourfold Gospel.

Jesus not only "abides" in those who keep his commandments "by the Spirit" (3:24) but enables them to know God's word in order to perform it. While the hallmark of Christian spirituality according to 1 John is "abiding in Jesus," we doubt this is a purely mystical or inward experience of the Lord's spiritual presence (whether by this "anointing" or otherwise), since 2:10, 14 suggest that the disciple "abides" in what 2 John calls the "teaching *(didachē)* about Christ" (see 2 John 9). Compliance with this doctrinal standard measures whether one "has God" (2 John 10; cf. 1 John 2:23). The impression is that the apostolic testimony of the historical Jesus (1 John 1:1-2), initially delivered as a proclaimed message (1:5) or written letter (1:4), has now been refashioned into a fixed curriculum or Rule of Faith.

Finally, Jesus' advent "overcomes" the world (2:28; 3:19-24; 4:17; 5:1-5), which presently is in the firm grip of the evil one (5:19). His final tour as Messiah will complete his mission to destroy the "works of the devil" (3:8) and vindicate those who believe (5:4-5). On that "judgment day" (4:17), when Jesus "comes" again *(parousia,* 2:28), the embarrassment of some Christians will be due to the fact that these "works of the devil" have not yet ceased in their lives. On the other hand, the "confidence" of God's children is predicated on their righteousness (2:28-29), their confession of the apostles' Jesus (4:15), and their experience of perfected love (4:16-19). On that day, God's children "will see him just as he is" — the full and final revelation of Jesus that secures an intimate knowledge of God's truth and so eternal union with God (3:1-2).

3. The Community of the Spirit

Membership in the Johannine community is gained by the cleansing of all sins, and its most distinctive practice is individual self-purification (3:3) and not sinning (3:4-10), which heralds the victory of God over sin and the prospect of Christlikeness at God's coming victory (3:2). While it is a lie or self-deception for God's children to say that they have no need to deal with the remains of sin, it is equally a deception to say that their new birth has no effect on their sinning. This moral determinism is the flipside of unbridled optimism. Not only does the forgiveness of a faithful and righteous God cleanse away *all* sins/wrongdoing, the expiatory death of Jesus (2:2; 4:10) is "for our [i.e., believers'] sins as well as for the sins of the whole world."

And yet there is no other NT writing with a more sustained defense of the apostolic tradition than 1 John. Its reception by the community in the company of the "Spirit of truth" (4:1-6) is the criterion of the community's life and eternal fellowship with God. Because shared belief in a particular version of the truth stipulates what is practiced and who is loved, theology (truth) and ethics (love one another) are of a piece.

The interplay between the addresses of 2 John and 3 John is important to note in this regard. While the purposeful anonymity of the metaphor "elect Lady and her children" (2 John 1) commends a catholic address, unbounded by time or place, the highly personal opening of 3 John and the letter's practical concerns about leadership and hospitality target a local congregation. 3 John reminds us that the catholic address of this collection should not be mistaken for an amorphous, universal church without direct application to particular congregations of believers. The intermingling of truth and love is the project of every community of faith, no matter its size, location, or time.[50]

---

50. See Yarbrough, *1-3 John*, pp. 26-27, whose word for this is "microcosmic."

While the source of the community's knowledge is the apostolic message, its members also experience truth inwardly as an "anointing" (see 1 John 2:20, 27) by the Spirit whom God has given those who abide in God (3:24–4:6). The community's experience that "tests the spirits" (4:1-6) implies that God's Spirit leads in a discernment process that enables true believers to discriminate between "false prophets" (4:1, 3: the "antichrists"; cf. 2:18), who are led by a "spirit of error," and those who teach and write to clarify the apostolic testimony of the word of life and who are authorized by the "Spirit of truth." Tertullian reminds us that this discernment process is conducted under the leadership of God's Spirit, who we assume is 1 John's "Spirit of truth."[51]

The community's solidarity was evinced not only by its doctrinal purity but also by its moral purity. This is made clearer by 2 and 3 John's exhortations regarding the practice of hospitality, which is applied to signal a division between true and false Christianity. That is, the body of Christ must be divided if its doctrinal purity is imperiled by instruction of "antichrists" (2 John 7-11). In this sense, then, community solidarity is built around its confession is that "Jesus Christ is the only Son of God" (1 John 4:15) who has come in the flesh from God (4:2-3) to reveal to the whole world that God is light and love so that "we might live through him" (4:9).

The community's characteristic moral practice is love for one another. Within its own sectarian social world this commandment draws the beloved "other" narrowly, not just as other Christians (4:20-21) but as those Christians who believe that the apostolic testimony of Jesus discloses what is true about God. 2 John epitomizes this point by integrating truth and love (vv. 1, 3) and applying this principle to the community's practice of hospitality. The crisis to which 3 John responds concerns this same application but in this case chastises Diotrephes for misapplying the practice of hospitality to serve his own political interests against the elder. In this regard, 2 John provides a concrete example of mutual love, regu-

---

51. We have found, however, that the CE collection does not emphasize the Spirit's role in the community's life, especially when compared to the Pauline witness or the narrative of the community's origins in Acts. Perhaps this reflects the moment of its canonization when the church was struggling with the "orthodoxy" of charismatic movements, such as Montanism, which influenced Tertullian himself. In any case, the Johannine Epistles seem to move away from the keenly pneumatic nature of the community of disciples in Christ's absence anticipated by the Fourth Gospel. Now the Spirit's role is to lend its witness to the apostolic message, which has authority to communicate truth into the community's life.

lated by the criterion of truth, in the congregation's hospitality extended to itinerant missionaries (see above on 2 John 9-11). The example of Diotrephes, however, warns us how easily the practice of love disclosed by Jesus is trumped by contested notions of truth or by political power struggles.

3 John reminds the reader that the community's moral practices also raise issues of governance since typically they are directed by spiritual leaders, for good or for ill. Diotrephes' disciplinary act of "throwing (members) out of the church" (v. 10) is a heavy-handed expression of his spiritual authority. Even the mention of the elder's prospective visit in his letters' benedictions (2 John 12; 3 John 14) envisages his political role within the community of managing its common life against potential threats. In this sense, the elder understands that he is in the right and that his leading role within the community is as the guardian of its tradition rather than its mentor or innovator.

The community's worship practices include public confession of sins (1 John 1:9) and intercessory prayers to restore wayward believers (5:14-17), which also demonstrate its unity with God and of its members with one another and its conflict with the world order (2:15-17; 3:1, 13; 4:4-5; 5:19). The prayers for the restoration of straying Christians are thematic of the rescue missions encouraged in the conclusions of James and Jude and reflect a congregational concern for the spiritual well-being of its members. In 1 John, much as in Hebrews, God will not cooperate in the rescue of apostates — again, a sharp reflection of the church division that occasions a reading of the Johannine letters.

4. Christian Discipleship

Christians are God's children, born of God, carriers of God's DNA (1 John 3:9), whose new nature enables them to walk in God's "light" (tell the truth and not sin) and to love one another as they have been first loved by God. That is, the community's identity in 1 John is not a status into which they are adopted as God's children (so Romans 8); rather, they are born as God's children and can practice righteousness (2:29) and not sin (3:9). Since one's genetic inheritance is irreversible, 1 John goes on to make the stunning claim that God's children "cannot sin" (3:9), which we take as proleptic of what has not yet been revealed (3:2). The community's confidence before God, which extends from the assurance of its forgiveness to answered prayers (5:14-17), is grounded on its belief in new birth.[52]

The persistence of sin remains a real threat to Christian discipleship, even though the victory of God in Christ offers a firm remedy for it and the prospect of sinlessness is not only desired (2:1) but realistic (3:3-10). The apparent conflict in the letter's interplay between sinful Christians (1:8–2:2; 5:14-17) and sinless Christians (3:3-10; 5:18-19), so often regarded as problematic by commentators, is really not, but is a fair description of the ever-present tension in Christian experience of God's restorative grace that cleanses away all sin and God's regenerating grace that provides believers with divine DNA incapable of sin (3:9). Faithful Christians are all the while becoming, step-by-step, what they have already become in new birth. 1 John captures this tension, especially in its concluding affirmations (see above on 5:14-18), as well as any biblical witness.

An array of formulas are used in 1 John, such as "if we say" (1:6, 8, 10), "the one who says" (2:4, 6, 9), and "by this we know" (2:3, 5; 3:19, 24; 4:13; 5:2; cf. 2:4, 18; 3:10, 16; 4:2, 6, 9, 20) to introduce spiritual tests to distinguish God's true children, who abide in God for eternal life, from those imposters who do not. These tests concern issues of truth and love, the essential markers of Christian discipleship: to abide in God who is light is to know the truth; to abide in God who is love is to love one another. If people confess lies rather than truth or hate rather than love, they flunk their spiritual examination and remain in death rather than eternal life (3:14-15).

Because the spiritual crisis addressed by these letters concerns right knowledge, the examination questions do as well — if only indirectly and in generalities. Real believers publicly "confess" (2:23; 3:23; 4:15) the truth about the person (or "name") of Jesus Christ: that he is the prophesied "righteous one" (2:1), the Son of God (4:15) in the flesh (4:2; cf. 1:1-2) whom God sent into the world as its Savior (4:14) for the expiation of our sins (2:2; 4:10), and is now the community's legal advocate before the Father (2:1). If the community abides in this "word of God" (2:14) rather than succumbing to the "lies" of antichrists/false prophets (2:18-27; 4:1-6), it will not be overcome by the world or its evil ruler (2:14; 5:18-19) or stumble from the truth about God (2:10).

The acts of sinning and hating are of a piece with "the world." Al-

---

52. Cf. Lieu, *Theology,* pp. 33-38.

though no codes of conduct are provided (and in canonical setting, such codes are supplied by other CE, especially James), sin is opposition to the will of God. Loving the things of the world rather than the word of God produces an inner life — human "nature" — that is inclined away from God and susceptible to the spirit of error, which opposes the truth (2:15-17; 4:1-6). On the other hand, those who are children of God, who know and practice righteousness, are fathered by God. They have a new nature that opposes the world (3:1), inclines them toward God, and enables them to practice not sinning (3:3-10). 1 John's arresting ontological claim lies at the center of a Johannine narrative of salvation. But, like the Pauline witness, it suggests that the Christian's radical imitation of Christ is an effect of divine grace: the practice of purifying oneself (3:3) is not an act of self-will but is possible only because of God's forgiveness (1:9; 2:12; 4:9) and new birth (2:29; 3:9).

5. Consummation in a New Creation

The future of God's salvation is an emphatic theme of the Johannine epistles. The pronounced emphasis on the shape of Christian existence has led most commentators to speak of Johannine eschatology as "realized" rather than futuristic. This platitude is more true of the Fourth Gospel than of the letters; especially if the role of 2 John is to epitomize the content of 1 John, the ultimate importance of God's final verdict is clearly drawn by the warning "not to lose the things worked for to receive the full reward" (2 John 8). Those things "worked for" are defined by the letter's repetition of 1 John's catchphrase of the past, "from the beginning" (vv. 5, 6; cf. 1 John 1:1; 2:7, 13-14, 24; 3:8, 11), which refers to the apostolic witness of Jesus' entire ministry from "water" to "blood" (5:8). This interplay between past and future, between the community's reception of the apostolic message and God's future judgment, supplies the dynamic of the conception of salvation's consummation according to the letters of John. In fact, 1 John makes the stunning claim that the Christian faith, defined by the apostolic tradition, will ultimately overcome the world (see above on 5:4).

The arrival of antichrists/false prophets who are "in/from the world" (1 John 4:1-6) signals an indeterminate "last hour" (2:18), which is the time of the community's final examination. The test results will be recorded for the parousia of Jesus (2:28), which is a "day of judgment" (2:17a, 28; 3:19-21;

4:17-18) when those who fail the test are "shamed" (2:28) and "condemned" (3:20), and when those who remain in the truth and pass the test are given their "full reward" (2 John 8).

God's future reward is not the "eternal life" that has been disclosed by Jesus and is presently experienced by those who are "born" of God and remain in God (1 John 2:29; 3:9; 4:7; 5:1, 4, 18). In fact, the future prospect of being blameless and fearless before God is already realized by those who abide in God. Rather this "reward" *(misthos)* is something "worked for" — a wage that is earned and can also be lost (2 John 8). What reward is given goes unmentioned in the Johannine epistles, but they surely imply that the future of salvation includes some divine discrimination of human merit: there is a lesser or greater "enjoyment of everlasting life and of the heavenly promises" for the saints depending on the work they have performed.

A more traditional expression of the community's future with God is mentioned in 2:28 and 4:17. Both texts speak of the Lord's coming and God's day of judgment as a way of expressing the community's "confidence" *(parrēsia;* cf. 3:21; 5:14) of its future vindication. The first introduces the concluding section of the letter's exposition of the statement that God is light. Recognizing that such a God does not tolerate sin or falsehood, the community's confidence is placed in God's coming victory over sin and error. Indeed, Christian discipleship heralds sin's future by telling the truth and doing right in the present.

The second text comes in the letter's exposition of the statement that God is love. Here, the community's fearless confidence that it will not be punished but rather vindicated in God's coming judgment is based on its present experience of divine love and the believers' love for each other. The repetition of the verbal idea "perfect/complete" in the perfect tense (4:17, 18) implies a dynamic unfolding experience of love, which itself anticipates its future completion.

Finally, in both these key passages is found the idea of Christlikeness. The future of sin is finally captured by the hope that God's children "will be just like him, because we will see him just as he is" (3:2). Indeed, this hope motivates the present act of self-purification, by which the believer becomes "pure just as (Jesus) is pure" (3:3).

The Catholic Epistle of Jude

Introduction

While all of the CE have suffered a lack of attention in the church, none has suffered more than the short letter of Jude. Like 2 and 3 John, Jude is not included in any of the contemporary major church lectionaries. The former two are buoyed by their association with 1 John, but Jude is seen by many as an unnecessary addition to the NT letter collection, too short to make a difference theologically and too obscure to provide any meaningful comfort and direction to the faithful.

Our contention in this commentary is that the letter of Jude can only be appreciated rightly when it is read as the culminating letter in the CE collection. It is the anchor, the final statement, the closing flourish. Read on its own, in isolation from the others, it may have little to offer, but when we read it according to its canonical role as the closing book of the collection, Jude's contribution is revealed to be essential.

1. The Canonical Jude

Though his name is literally Judas *(Ioudas),* long-standing tradition has sought to distinguish this Judas from the more famous betrayer by rendering the name "Jude." The figure is almost completely unknown from the canonical narratives and would indeed be impossible to identify were it not for the authorial description provided in the letter, "Jude, a servant of Jesus Christ and brother of James" (v. 1). The letter's placement as the bookend of the CE collection sounds an echo from the collection's open-ing: "James, servant of God and of the Lord Jesus Christ" (Jas. 1:1).

Few in the early church would have been confused about this author's identity. Two of the four Gospels name Jesus' brothers (Matt. 13:55; Mark 6:3), and both a James and a Judas are listed.[1] Though insufficient evidence exists for us to determine the brothers' attitude toward Jesus' earthly min-istry,[2] Acts includes them in the group of believers devoting themselves to prayer in the upper room (1:12-14). These same were evidently present for the spiritual empowerment bestowed on the day of Pentecost (2:1). Acts goes on to portray James as the leader of the Jerusalem church (12:17; 15:13-21; 21:18-25), and by the time of Paul's letters the other "brothers of the Lord" were so well known as traveling missionaries that they did not have to be named (1 Cor. 9:5). Though the evidence is admittedly sparse, what we have provides a clear enough portrait of Jude as a brother of Jesus who was a revered leader in the earliest church.[3]

2. The Composition of Jude

Though it follows the customary structure of ancient Greco-Roman letters, several features encourage us to approach Jude as a literary pastoral letter

---

1. The name *Ioudas* appears forty-five times in the NT. Luke lists a "Judas of James" among the twelve disciples (Luke 6:16; Acts 1:13), but Matt. 10:3 and Mark 3:18 name this per-son "Thaddeus." Concern over Mary's perpetual virginity led Catholic tradition to join these together as the same person (following the so-called "Hieronymian" view that Jesus' "broth-ers" were actually cousins), but Protestants consider them different people (following the so-called "Helvidian" view that Mary and Joseph produced other sons and that James and Jude were Jesus' blood brothers). For an exhaustive study of these and other issues sur-rounding Jesus' family members, including detailed evidence for their ongoing prominence in earliest Christianity, see R. Bauckham, *Jude and the Relatives of Jesus in the Early Church* (Edinburgh: Clark, 1990).

2. The plain sense of the Gospel texts appears to be that Jesus' brothers did not become his disciples prior to his death and resurrection (e.g., Mark 3:21 and especially John 7:5, which plainly states that "not even his brothers believed in him"). Nevertheless several scholars have tried to build a case for the possibility that James, at least, may have been a fol-lower; see Bauckham, *Jude and the Relatives of Jesus*, pp. 45-57; R. Ward, "James of Jerusalem in the First Two Centuries," *ANRW* 2.26.1 (Berlin: de Gruyter, 1988), pp. 786-90; J. Painter, *Just James: The Brother of Jesus in History and Tradition* (Edinburgh: Clark, 1999), pp. 11-41.

3. See also Eusebius, *H.E.*, which preserves some ancient traditions about Jude and the other relatives of Jesus (3.19; 3.20.1).

much like 2 Peter: it has a highly unspecified address, it lacks the thanks-giving and health wishes typical of an opening proem, the body of the letter is made up of a typological midrash followed by a closing parenesis, and instead of a conventional farewell the letter closes with a doxology. It seems best to conclude that Jude is a "real letter" that is rather homiletic in nature.

While Jude is carefully composed and reveals an author well-versed in contemporary Greek language and rhetoric (including a fondness for rhetorical triplets[4] and an unusually high number of *hapax legomena*[5]), the letter is akin to James insofar as it is saturated in the literary world of Judaism. As in James, so also in Jude the author identifies himself as a "servant," a title deeply rooted in Jewish literature as a designation for the heroes of Israel's past who mediated between God and the people.[6] Another example is the commonly Jewish identification of God as "our Savior" in distinction from Jesus, who is the far more common recipient of that title in the NT.[7] The author also makes liberal use of Jewish texts, traditions, and interpretive schemes, expecting his audience to be sufficiently acquainted with them to require no explanation. Chief among these is *1 Enoch* (vv. 6, 12-16), from which he derives the one and only formal scriptural quotation in the letter.

Though earlier critics considered Jude a pseudepigraphic "early Catholic" treatise against second-century Gnosticism,[8] most now recognize that the situation of the letter most directly addresses the sort of antinomian response to the gospel common in the later apostolic era.[9] As in

4. Called, loved, kept (v. 1); grace, mercy, love (v. 2); Israelites, angels, Sodom and Gomorrah (vv. 5-7); defile flesh, reject authority, slander glories (v. 8); Cain, Balaam, Korah (v. 11); ungodly, ungodly, ungodly (v. 15); divisive, worldly, unspiritual (v. 19); pray in the Holy Spirit, keep in the love of God, wait for the mercy of the Lord Jesus Christ (vv. 20-21); be merciful, save some, show mercy (vv. 22-23).

5. R. Bauckham, *Jude, 2 Peter* (WBC 50; Waco: Word, 1983), p. 6, lists fourteen words not found elsewhere in the NT, and three found elsewhere only in 2 Peter, which repeats them from Jude.

6. The appellation *doulos theou* is found in the LXX in reference to Moses (1 Kgs. 8:53; Ps. 104:26, 42; Dan. 9:11; Mal. 4:4), David (2 Sam. 7:5; 1 Kgs. 8:66; 1 Chron. 17:4; Pss. 77:70; 88:3; 131:10; 143:10; Jer. 33:21; Ezek. 34:23; 37:25), and all God's prophets (Jer. 7:25; 26:4ff.; 44:4; Ezek. 38:17; Joel 3:2; Amos 3:7; Jonah 1:9; Zech. 1:6).

7. The LXX title "God of our salvation" (LXX Pss. 64:5; 78:9; 94:1; *Pss. Sol.* 8:33; 17:3) is very rarely carried over into the NT (Luke 1:47; 1 Tim. 1:1; 2:3; 4:10; Tit. 1:3; 2:10; 3:4).

8. E.g. E. M. Sidebottom, *James, Jude and 2 Peter* (CBC; London: Nelson, 1967), p. 75.

9. Watson notes that the antinomianism of Jude's opponents "is akin to that faced by

2 Peter and 1-3 John, so also in Jude the trial facing believers has to do with the crisis occasioned by disagreements between rival forms of Christian teaching and practice. But unlike these earlier letters, Jude does not include concern about particular instances of doctrinal deviance: the crisis is not specifically identified as the result of a denial of apostolic teaching regarding the parousia and judgment (as in 2 Peter) or Christology (as in 1 and 2 John) but is instead revealed to be a species of pneumatic arrogance. The designation of the opponents as "dreamers" (v. 8) most likely identifies them as itinerant teachers or prophets who have "snuck into" the community (v. 4) and have claimed spiritual authority over the leadership. Thus they are causing divisions (v. 19) with novel teachings and practices that bear fruit in a disastrous deviation from the Christian moral practices handed down by apostolic tradition. That very tradition, of course, predicted the coming of such people as a harbinger of the end times (vv. 17-19), so believers are exhorted to hold fast confidently to "the faith that was once for all delivered to the saints" (v. 3).

Jude thus ends the CE as James began it, with an uncompromising assertion of the soteriological significance of right human action: the faith handed down by the apostles requires believers to conceive of themselves not as libertines but as faithful covenant partners with God through obedient service to the "only Master and Lord, Jesus Christ" (v. 4). Indeed, the brothers of Jesus are agreed in making it absolutely clear that the central calling of the church is the task of rescuing errant brothers and sisters from wandering into paths of sinful behavior that lead ultimately to condemnation (Jas. 5:19-20; Jude 22-23).

As we will see, however, Jude extends this exhortation by means of an important culminating corrective that should be extended across the CE as a whole. Believers are exhorted to "keep yourselves in the love of God" (v. 21) in the knowledge that it is God who keeps them safe (v. 1); more than that, God "is able to keep you from falling and to make you stand in the presence of his glory with rejoicing" (v. 24). In this way Jude ends the CE by insisting that the divine-human covenant is not a relationship of equal partners. While readers of the Pauline witness may overemphasize God's initiating covenant grace in a licentious manner that undermines

---

Paul (Rom. 3:8; 6:1, 15; 1 Cor. 5:1-8; 6:12-20; 10:23; Gal. 5:13), but there is no firm support for thinking that the false teachers were of the ilk encountered by Paul." "Letter of Jude," *NIB* 12 (Nashville: Abingdon, 1998), p. 475.

the importance of obedient human response, readers of the Pillars might overemphasize covenant obedience in a legalistic manner that undermines God's sovereign and sustaining grace. Canonically, Jude's powerful doxology stands as a worshipful corrective to this potential misunderstanding.

3. The Canonization of Jude

Given its diminutive size, the letter of Jude is remarkably well-attested in the ancient world. Some time in the early second century it was taken as a source for 2 Peter, which is in itself a testimony to the level of its authority at the time. By the end of that century it was widely acknowledged as authoritative Scripture. Though Irenaeus does not refer to the letter, it is listed without qualification in the western Muratorian Fragment. When the North African theologian Tertullian appealed to *1 Enoch* to support his condemnation of female ornamentation, he justified his use of the questionable text by a series of defenses culminating in what he took to be the decisive argument: "Enoch possesses a testimony in the Apostle Jude."[10] If the apostle Jude used *Enoch,* Tertullian asserts, who would dare condemn its use?

Jude was also known and used in the East. Clement of Alexandria cited Jude 5-6 and 11 to demonstrate how God sets forth the punishment of the licentious as an example for Christians, "that we may be kept from sin out of fear of the penalty."[11] In another place he condemns a variety of heretical views and concludes by saying, "I fancy Jude was speaking prophetically of these and similar sects in his letter."[12] The sixth-century Latin writer Cassiodorus has a work entitled *Adumbrationes in Epistolas Catholicas* which preserves translations of Clement's commentaries on 1 Peter, 1 and 2 John, and Jude. Therein we find Clement joining Tertullian in justifying the use of *1 Enoch* along with the *Testament of Moses* by appeal to Jude's prior use. This commentary is also the first time we find Jude identified as a "Catholic Epistle," though it is impossible for us to know whether the designation comes from Clement himself or from the hand of the sixth-century translator.

10. *Cult.* 1.3.1-3.
11. *Paed.* 3.8.44.3-45.1.
12. *Strom.* 3.2.11.2.

Origen also knew Jude and celebrated it as "a letter of few lines, it is true, but filled with the healthful words of heavenly grace."[13] There are around fourteen references to Jude in Origen's extant works, most of which leave us with a clear sense of his reception of the letter. On one occasion, however, he does suggest that Jude is doubted by some, introducing a quotation with "and if indeed one were to accept the epistle of Jude."[14] This hint of concern is confirmed in the later witness of Eusebius, who in a discussion of the letter of James says,

> it is to be observed that it is disputed; at least, not many of the ancients have mentioned it, as is the case likewise with the epistle that bears the name of Jude, which is also one of the seven so-called catholic epistles. Nevertheless we know that these also, with the rest, have been read publicly in very many churches. (*H.E.* 2.23.25)

Given prior eastern support for the letter by Clement and Origen, Eusebius's declaration that "not many of the ancients have mentioned it" is puzzling. The clearest articulation of concern about the letter comes a century later from the pen of Jerome, who writes,

> Jude, the brother of James, left a short epistle which is reckoned among the seven Catholic Epistles, and because in it he quotes from the apocryphal book of Enoch it is rejected by many. Nevertheless by age and use it has gained authority and is reckoned among the Holy Scriptures. (*Viris* 4).

Jerome's witness leads us to recall the earliest tradents of Jude: the author of 2 Peter, who used it as an honored source but edited out its references to *1 Enoch* and the *Testament of Moses,* and Tertullian, who supported *his* use of *1 Enoch* by appeal to its prior use by Jude. We are left with the strong impression that Jude was received as authoritative early on but subsequently questioned only as the boundaries of the canon solidified to exclude writings like *1 Enoch.*

Though the concerns were real, it remains the case that the vast majority of fourth- and fifth-century canon lists in both the eastern and western

---

13. *Com. Mt.* 10.17.40.
14. *Com. Mt.* 17.30.9-10.

churches include Jude. Our "shaping" chapter noted the consistency of title and sequence in the eastern church, where James is always first and Jude always last. Amphilochius of Iconium, however, noted a dispute: "some say we must receive seven, but others only three" *(Iambi)*. The "others" are almost certainly representatives of the Syrian churches who accepted only James, 1 Peter, and 1 John. The western church received the CE collection from the East, so acceptance of all seven letters only took place gradually; and even after all seven letters were commonly accepted, most did not maintain the eastern order. Nevertheless, though the sequences vary, two features remain consistent: western authorities placed Peter's letters first, and they place the brothers James and Jude side-by-side (Augustine, Filaster, Innocent, the north African councils, Rufinus, and Cassiodorus). Whether the western linking of James and Jude was simply in recognition of their authorial identities or an acknowledgment of a related canonical function is not immediately clear from the historical witness. The final form, however, leads us to affirm both: the witness of Jesus' brothers forms an inclusio within which the CE collection as a whole should be interpreted. This canonical intention was described in our earlier "shape" chapter, and will be explicated in the commentary that follows.

Commentary

Letter Prescript: Jude to the Called, Beloved, and Kept (vv. 1-2)

The letter of Jude begins with a prescript identifying the author and his recipients in a manner that establishes Jude's coherence within the larger CE collection. Two descriptors establish the authority of the writer: he is a "servant of Jesus Christ" and "the brother of James." While the former title is not uncommon in early Christianity (Rom. 1:1; Phil. 1:1; Tit. 1:1; Jas. 1:1; 2 Pet. 1:1) the absence of the attendant designation "apostle" links the letter most directly to the letter of James, which is also written by one identified solely as a "servant." The identification of the author as "brother of James" solidifies the intended connection: the CE collection begins and ends with the witness of the brothers of the Lord, who knew him in the flesh and subsequently served as well-known leaders in the earliest mission.

The recipients are provided a threefold identification: they are "called, beloved in God the Father, and kept safe for Jesus Christ" (v. 1).[15] Bauck-ham has made the case that "called, beloved, and kept" derive from the identification of Israel in Isaiah's Servant Songs.[16] Jude thereby upholds the theme of James and 1 Peter that recognizes believers as the eschatological Israel foretold by the prophets. "Called" *(klētos)* recalls the opening verses of the Petrine letters, which identify the readers as both "chosen" (*eklektos,* 1 Pet. 1:1) and "called" (*kaleō,* 2 Pet. 1:3) by God. Describing them as "beloved *in* God the Father" recalls 1 John's understanding of the covenant relationship with God as a place to abide "in" (e.g., 3:24; 4:16). Insisting that they are "kept safe for Jesus Christ" underscores the earlier claim that God is the protective guardian of our salvation until it is brought to completion at the coming of Jesus (1 Pet. 1:5).

This confession of God as the faithful custodian of salvation forms the rhetorical frame for the letter as a whole: we who are "be*love*d in God and *kept* for Jesus" (v. 1) are exhorted to "*keep* yourselves in the *love* of God" (v. 21), trusting all the while that God is the one "who is able to *keep* you from falling" (v. 24). The letter thus begins with God's graceful initiative (v. 1) and ends by calling forth the kind of human response (v. 21) appropriate for one in covenant relationship with a trustworthy, saving God (v. 24).

This love-keep inclusio draws the reader's attention to the recurrence of these words throughout the letter. Believers are identified as "loved" four times (vv. 1, 3, 17, and 20); they have "love" wished upon them in the greeting (v. 2) and express this loving communion with God and one another in a ritualized "love feast" (v. 12). Likewise, those who are kept for Jesus Christ (v. 1) must keep themselves in the love of God (v. 21) or risk association with those who do not "keep their own position" (v. 6) and are thus either currently "kept in eternal chains" (v. 6) or heading toward a punishment that "has been eternally kept" by God (v. 13). The sense in all of this is that God is not only a sovereign power who orders all things toward an intended conclusion but also a loving Savior (v. 25) who works to keep believers safe within that economy of salvation.

---

15. The dative here could indicate "kept for" (NRSV) or "kept by" (NIV); the latter presents Jesus as the king protecting his people; the former depicts him as a king ready to receive people brought to him by God. P. H. Davids prefers "kept for": "These believers are being guarded (perhaps by the Father) *for* Jesus, so that they remain loyal to Jesus as their ruler." *2 Peter and Jude: A Handbook on the Greek Text* (Waco: Baylor University Press, 2011), p. 2.

16. Bauckham, *Jude, 2 Peter,* p. 25, links "called" to Isa. 41:9; 42:6; 48:12, 15; 49:1; 54:6; "loved" to 42:1; 43:4; cf. 44:2 LXX, and "kept" to 42:6; 49:8.

Appeal: Contend for the Faith! (vv. 3-4)

Jude informs his readers that he was just preparing to write about this salvation when he was alerted to the news that the security of "the faith that was once for all entrusted to the saints" (v. 3) had been put at risk. The Greek verb translated "entrusted" *(paradidōmi)* functions as a kind of *terminus technicus* for the handing down of apostolic traditions of belief and practice (Luke 1:2; Acts 16:4; Rom. 6:17; 1 Cor. 11:2, 23; 15:3; 2 Pet. 2:21). Jude calls his letter an "appeal" for readers to "contend" or "struggle" for this entrusted faith. The fact that the appeal itself is not directly expressed until vv. 20-23 enables readers to receive the typological midrash that dominates the letter (vv. 5-19) as an extended aside designed to emphasize the background reason for the appeal.

But this does not mean the denunciation that follows is somehow incidental to the message of the letter. Indeed, it is imperative that the opponents are provided a detailed description, for their specific actions threaten the "once for all" (v. 3) quality of the apostolic articulation of faith in Christ. Jesus died to sin "once for all" (Rom. 6:10) and "entered once for all into the holy place" as both priest and sacrifice (Heb. 9:12, 28), "suffering for sins, once for all" (1 Pet. 3:18). Accordingly, Christ's apostolic authorities proclaimed this faith "once for all": just as his complete work leaves us without need of another high priest or pure sacrifice, so also the apostolic articulation of faith is complete and requires no modification or improvement by subsequent innovators (recall 1 John 2:26-27).

Yet certain "intruders" (a helpful word provided at v. 4 by the NRSV translation) who have infiltrated the community of faith have brought with them just such an innovation. The verb for "secretly slipped in" *(pareisdyō,* "crept in unnoticed," NASB, ESV) occurs only here in the Scriptures and communicates the sense that the individuals were not original members of the community but have become so over time. In light of the cumulative description they receive in this letter, Bauckham identifies them as "itinerant charismatics,"[17] that is, traveling Christian teachers or prophets proclaiming a revelation that is out of step with the apostolic tradition the addressees received from the original apostolic representatives (v. 17). Such figures were a frequent cause of concern in early Christian

---

17. Bauckham, *Jude, 2 Peter,* p. 12.

churches (e.g., Matt. 7:15; 2 Corinthians 10–11; within the CE see especially 2 Pet. 2:1; 1 John 4:1; 2 John 10).

These intruders have several charges leveled against them in v. 4. The first is that they fit the pattern of individuals condemned in Scripture. While *hoi palai progegrammenoi* could refer to their having been "long ago designated" (NRSV, ESV), perhaps in the heavenly books,[18] the scriptural argument that follows strongly suggests that Jude means their condemnation was "written about long ago" (NIV) and preserved in the scriptural witness for our benefit.[19]

The intruders are described as "ungodly persons who pervert the grace of our God into licentiousness." The words in the "ungodly" group *(asebeis, asebeō, asebeia)* recur so frequently in this short letter (five times in vv. 4, 15, and 18) that it could rightly be received as a one-word summary of Jude's indictment. The term is the opposite of "godly" or "righteous" and describes the moral behavior of one who conducts life as a sinner (1 Pet. 4:18; cf. Rom. 4:5; 5:6). It is paired with a synonym translated "licentiousness" *(aselgeia)*. The latter bore clear sensual connotations in the period (Rom. 13:13; 2 Cor. 12:21; Gal. 5:19; 1 Pet. 4:3; 2 Pet. 2:2, 7, 18) and thus identifies the intruders' moral deviance as at least partly sexual in nature.

The description closely resembles the antinomian response to the Pauline gospel of grace encountered elsewhere in the NT (Rom. 3:8; 6:1, 15; 1 Cor. 5:1-2; 6:12-14; 10:23; Gal. 5:13). Indeed, some have wondered if the otherwise unknown practice of blaspheming angels described in Jude 8-10 is in some way related to the Pauline boast about being liberated from the "elemental spirits of the world" (Gal. 4:3, 8-9; Col. 2:17-19) and of having superiority over angels (Rom. 8:38-39; 1 Cor. 6:3; Col. 2:17-19) who were responsible for mediating God's law to Moses (e.g., Gal. 3:19). On this basis many scholars follow the earliest tradent of the letter, the author of 2 Peter, in identifying the intruders as teachers promulgating a distortion of Paul's gospel (2 Pet. 3:15-16).

Regardless, the end result is that the intruders "deny our only Master and Lord Jesus Christ." Given that they are participants in community life (vv. 4, 12), it is extremely unlikely that their denial is confessional. Rather,

---

18. So, e.g., Clement of Alexandria, *Adum.*, followed by J. N. D. Kelly, *A Commentary on the Epistles of Peter and Jude* (BNTC; London: Black, 1969), pp. 250-51.

19. So, e.g., Bauckham, *Jude, 2 Peter*, p. 35, and L. R. Donelson, *I & II Peter and Jude* (NTL; Louisville: Westminster John Knox, 2010), p. 175.

they confess Christ with their lips but conduct themselves as though Jesus is not the only Master and Lord of their lives. They conceive of grace as warrant for moral libertinism, not empowerment for holy servitude.

Letter Body: The Scriptural Case against the Intruders (vv. 5-19)

The disclosure statement that introduces v. 5 ("Now I desire to remind you") signals the transition to the letter body, a tightly crafted, typological "proof from prophecy" that runs through v. 19 and explains what Jude means by saying the intruders' "condemnation was written about long ago." Jude thus counters innovation with recollection, reminding the readers that they are already "fully informed" (again, recall 1 John 2:26-27). He thus directs believers to the Scriptures they received from the apostles to serve as a lens through which to view the reality of their present situation. His midrash identifies six OT types in two triplets (vv. 5-7, 11), applies them to the intruders (vv. 8-10, 12-13), and culminates in prophecies from *1 Enoch* and from the apostles (vv. 14-16). All this forms the background justification for the appeal introduced in v. 3 and fully articulated in vv. 20-23.

Spitaler has detected a chiastic rhetorical structure for the section leading up to the culminating proof from the prophecy of the Apostles:[20]

> A. (v. 4) *the Lord's judgment*
>   B. (vv. 5-7) examples of negative behavior
>   C. (v. 8) application to the intruders
>   D. (v. 9) *Michael defers judgment to the Lord*
>   C'. (v. 10) application to the intruders
>   B'. (vv. 11-13) examples of negative behavior
> A'. (vv. 14-15) *the Lord's judgment*

The section as a whole is thus held together by references to God's judgment (vv. 4, 9, 14-15). At the center is the appeal to the archangel Michael, the only contrasting positive example in the section, who does not judge

---

20. P. Spitaler, "Doubt or Dispute (Jude 9 and 22-23): Re-Reading a Special New Testament Meaning through the Lens of Internal Evidence," *Bib* 87 (2006), pp. 201-22. Our presentation of the chiasm differs slightly from his.

the devil but leaves condemnation to the Lord. References to Zechariah 3 and the repetition of the verb *diakrinō* link v. 9 with vv. 22-23, strongly suggesting that "Michael's deference of a judgment that constitutes blasphemy functions as the central paradigm for non-judgmental conduct towards the community's infiltrators that Jude expects of his audience."[21]

All six OT types presented in the argument are examples of judgment leveled against the disobedient. The first example (v. 5) is that of unfaithful Israel in the wilderness and refers to either Exodus 32 or Numbers 14.[22] The scene is frequently recalled in Israel's history in terms like "rebellion" (Deut. 9:23-24; Psalm 106; Heb. 3:16-19). Paul makes strikingly similar typological use of the story in 1 Corinthians 10, and the point in all these passages is relatively clear: being a participant in God's initial deliverance does not ensure ultimate reception into salvation, for an ongoing covenantal relationship of trusting obedience is required to avoid falling into destruction. In this one immediately recalls the letter's framing device, wherein readers who are "kept by God" (v. 1) are exhorted to "keep" themselves "in the love of God" (v. 21).

The second example (v. 6) is that of the "disobedient angels" obliquely described in Gen. 6:1-4 but significantly elaborated in Jewish tradition, especially in *1 Enoch* (see especially chs. 6–19), the text which clearly lies behind Jude's reflection here. Like the Israelites in the first example, so also these angels forsook a position of privilege in God's ordering of things; they did not "keep their own position" "but left their proper dwelling" and descended to mate with human women. Given the use of the term *archē* for "position" and the particular emphasis placed on this event in Jewish tradition,[23] it seems likely that what the angels failed to keep was their designated level of authority in their service to God, making them an ideal an-

---

21. Spitaler, "Doubt or Dispute," p. 207.

22. There is an interesting scribal dispute evident in the ms. witnesses to this verse. While the majority of manuscripts say that "the Lord" saved the people, others present "God" as the active agent, several important witnesses (including Alexandrinus, Vaticanus, the Vulgate, several Coptic versions, and Origen) say "Jesus" saved the people. If that is not original, it is likely that the description of Jesus as Lord in v. 4 led scribes to follow through with the identification in v. 5. If it was original, we have another example of the early Christian affirmation that the preexistent Christ was present with Israel in the wilderness (e.g., 1 Cor. 10:4).

23. *Jub.* 2:2; 5:6; *1 En.* 82:10-20; 1QM 10:12; 1QH 1:11; *T. Lev.* 3:8; note also how *archē* is used as a term for cosmic powers in the NT (Rom. 8:38; Eph. 1:21; 3:10; 6:12; Col. 1:16; 2:15).

alogue of the infiltrators, who are claiming authority above their position. According to *1 Enoch*, these angels (called "the watchers") were captured by the archangel Michael, imprisoned in the earth's darkness, and kept there until the day of judgment.[24]

Jude links the third example, the citizens of Sodom and Gomorrah (Genesis 18–19) and the surrounding cities (v. 7), with the previous one. These citizens were judged for literally "departing after different flesh." Though many have read this as a direct condemnation of homosexual acts, others have rightly countered that Jude primarily intends to reverse the previous example: just as the rebellious angels departed from God's proper ordering of things in seeking to have sex with human women, so also the citizens of these cities distorted God's intention by seeking to have sex with angels.

Thus we see that this first set of types coalesces around three primary themes: first, they all describe rebellion against God as violating the boundaries prescribed for creatures by the Creator; second, the focus in each is not on intellectual assent to doctrine but on proper response to God's action; and third, they all describe an in-breaking immediacy of judgment that precedes the final judgment. In all three cases, God acts in history to condemn the ungodly. In the last two, the specific ungodliness has to do with sexual immorality.

Jude provides his own threefold conclusion to the typology in v. 8: those he is opposing (whom he calls "dreamers") "defile the flesh, reject authority, and slander the glorious ones." The designation "dreamers" is extremely significant insofar as it is a common OT epithet for false prophets, who proclaim the dreaming of their own imagination and not the word of the Lord (e.g. Deut. 13:1-5; Jer. 23:23-32; 29:8-9; Zech. 10:2). In this we find strong evidence that the intruders are claiming revelatory authority for their deviation from apostolic norms. Like the citizens of the sinful cities and the angels of the rebellion, they "defile the flesh" with improper sexual relations. Like the rebellious angels and the disobedient Israelites, they "reject authority" (*kyriotēs*, "lordship," linking back to the opening charge in v. 4 that they deny their Master and Lord Jesus Christ).

The charge of "slandering the glorious ones" (or simply "glories") is elaborated by what follows in v. 9's reference to an ancient supernatural

---

24. This angel tradition is reflected in 1 Pet. 3:19-20; 2 Pet. 2:4 and possibly also 1 Cor. 11:10.

struggle over the body of Moses.[25] The scene of Moses' death and burial in Deut. 34:1-12, and especially the line "no one knows his burial place to this day" (v. 6), eventually led to the tradition that Moses was buried by angels. Several church fathers identified this passage from Jude as deriving from a work they called the *Assumption of Moses*;[26] scholars today generally consider this to be the lost ending of the extant *Testament of Moses*. In that story the devil makes a claim for the body of Moses by condemning him as a lawbreaker for murdering the Egyptian (Exod. 2:11-15). The story fits Jude's purposes (hence its placement at the zenith of the "judgment" chiasm) insofar as it provides a significant contrast: while the angels he mentioned in v. 6 broke out in rebellion against the creational order, and the devil presumed the authority to pronounce slanderous judgment, the archangel Michael "did not presume" the task of judgment but left it to the Lord.

As already noted, Michael's declaration "The Lord rebuke you!" appears to derive from the fourth vision of Zechariah (3:1-10) where the High Priest Joshua is the subject of a similar debate between the Angel of the Lord and the Accuser. The importance of Michael's counterexample will be made especially clear when Jude returns to this prophecy again during his appeal at the end of the letter (vv. 22-23). For now, Jude continues his denunciation with a third repetition of the word "slander" or "revile" (*blasphēmia, blasphēmeō*): the intruders "slander the glorious ones" (v. 8) following the lead of the devil, who also pronounced "slanderous judgment" (v. 9), but Jude wants the reader to know that they slander what they do not understand (v. 10). The "dreamers" who claim visionary understanding do not in fact understand anything; they claim to provide revelatory knowledge, but in fact they are driven like animals by the lusts of their impulses.

V. 11 introduces three more OT types in quick succession to continue the scriptural description of the intruders. The opening "woe to them!" recalls the OT prophets who often proclaimed woe over those facing God's imminent judgment (e.g., Isa. 3:9-11; 45:9-10; Jer. 4:13, 31; 10:19; Amos 5:16, 18; 6:1). To say that they "walk in the way of Cain" (note the connection with 1 John 3:11-18) brings to mind OT kings who followed the moral ex-

---

25. See Bauckham's extensive excursus on the background and sources of v. 9 in *Jude, 2 Peter*, pp. 65-77.

26. E.g., Clement of Alexandria, *Adum.*; Origen, *Prin.* 3.2.1.

ample of their ancestors (e.g., 1 Kgs. 15:26, 34; 16:2, 19, 26; 2 Kgs. 8:18, 27; 16:3) instead of the way of God's commandments (e.g., 1 Kgs. 2:3-4) and thereby led God's people into sin and judgment.[27] Though the story in the book of Numbers has Balaam refuse Balak's temptation to curse God for money (Numbers 22–24), he was nevertheless remembered as a false prophet who practiced divination (Josh. 13:22) and enticed God's people into sexual immorality and idolatry for the sake of profit (Num. 31:16, recalling 25:1-3).[28] Korah led a rebellion against Moses' administration of God's law and was swallowed up alive into Sheol (Numbers 16; 26:9-10). Jewish tradition remembered him as the first schismatic and heretic.[29] Like these three, the intruders follow a way of error and rebellion for the sake of gain that will end in their destruction.

The real danger is revealed in v. 12: these are not outsiders to the community, but participants in the church's communal meals. Jude calls them *spilas*, literally "rocks" or "reefs" on which ships wreck; he may be intending wordplay with *spilos*, "blemishes," which defile the gathering in God's sight.[30] They celebrate "without fear" or "reverence," suggesting that their immoral behavior is carried on in the presence of the worshipping community. They are, literally, "shepherding themselves," a reference to the condemnation in Ezekiel 34 of the faithless shepherds of Israel who devour God's sheep instead of protecting them. Their egocentric leadership results in the scattering of the sheep, who become prey for wild beasts (Ezek. 34:5-8); so also Jude will condemn the intruders for introducing divisiveness (v. 19) that threatens the commonality of their salvation (v. 3; note the important contrast of these "shepherds" with the exhortation to the elders in 1 Pet. 5:1-3).

Vv. 12b-13 continue with a series of images describing a distorted and unproductive created order: the intruders are like dramatic, windblown clouds that offer no gift of water to enable growth (Prov. 25:14); they are like fruitless, dead trees (e.g., Matt. 7:15-20) or wild waves that simply leave the beach covered in wispy, friable foam (Isa. 57:20; cf. Jas. 1:6-8). The image of

---

27. Later tradition remembered Cain as one who taught others to sin (Josephus, *Ant.* 1.52-62; Philo, *Post.* 38-39).

28. Josephus, *Ant.* 4.126-30; Philo, *Mos.* 1.266-68, 292-99; *b. Sanh.* 106a; Rev. 2:14.

29. Bauckham, *Jude, 2 Peter,* p. 83, notes that the targums say that Korah and his company "made a schism" (*Neof.* Num. 16:1; 26:9; *Ps.-J.* Num. 26:9) and that this characterization of them as schismatic is reflected in *1 Clem.* 51:1-4.

30. Davids, *2 Peter and Jude,* p. 69.

"wandering stars for whom the deepest darkness has been reserved forever" comes from *1 Enoch's* description of the fallen angels who rebelled against God (18:15; 21:6; 86:1; 88:1-3) and prepares us for the prophecy from that text that follows in vv. 14-15. The quotation chosen (*1 En.* 1:9), coming from a book purportedly written within seven generations of Adam, confirms that this "condemnation was written about long ago" (Jude 4); it draws the previous references to judgment (vv. 4, 6, 9) against the ungodly (v. 4) into a dramatic crescendo as it describes a final judgment in which the Lord will come to convict "*ungodly* sinners" for "all the deeds of *ungodliness* that they have committed in such an *ungodly* way." The prophecy specifies ungodliness of both deed and speech, so the closing scriptural description in v. 16 emphasizes dangerous word-acts that recall the previous OT types: They are "grumblers and complainers" like the generation delivered from Egypt but barred from the promised land (cf. v. 5) and the rebellious Korah (v. 11); they "indulge their own lusts" like the fallen angels (v. 6) and the citizens of Sodom and Gomorrah (v. 7); their mouths are full of overinflated speech like Balaam (v. 11) and the devil himself (v. 9). They use this speech to flatter people, literally to "show partiality for the sake of favor." The language recalls Jas. 2:1-7 and may reflect a similar situation, one in which partiality is shown to those who might return material benefit.

The return to the direct address "beloved" in v. 17 (as in v. 3) indicates Jude is transitioning toward an emphatic conclusion to the case he has been building. Davids has noted that vv. 3-5 and 17 form a parallel inclusio for the letter body:[31]

beloved (v. 3)	beloved
I want to remind you (v. 5)	remember
the faith that was once for all entrusted to the saints (v. 3),	the apostles of our Lord Jesus Christ foretold
deny our Lord Jesus Christ (v. 4)	

One can also discern a pattern by simply attending to the repetitions of "beloved," "faith," and "holy":

---

31. Adapted from Davids, *2 Peter and Jude*, p. 85.

Beloved, . . . I find it necessary to write and appeal to you to
contend for the *faith* that was once for all entrusted to the *saints
(hagios)* (v. 3).

> But you, *beloved,* must remember the predictions of the apostles
> of our Lord Jesus Christ (v. 17).

But you, *beloved,* build yourselves up on your most *holy (hagios)
faith* (v. 20).

The emphasis placed on this apostolic tradition makes it clear that Jude
considers this the decisive prophecy to end the argument. Though there
are many parallels to the apostolic message presented here,[32] none that we
have are close enough to be identified directly with the words of v. 18. Since
wisdom literature commonly referred to people who mock those who live
righteously as "scoffers" or "mockers" (e.g. Ps. 1:1; Prov. 1:22; 9:7-8; 13:1;
15:12; 21:24), it is implied that the intruders take a superior, haughty attitude toward those who criticize their libertinism. These "follow their own
ungodly lusts," indicating once again (vv. 11, 16, and in clear concert with
the CE as a whole) that conduct, a way of "walking," is being criticized
here.

The final verse of the letter body sums up the critique with a closing
descriptive triplet. These individuals are either "causing divisions" within
the community or are "separating themselves": the rare Greek verb here,
apodiorizō, was used by Aristotle to describe making distinctions in the
process of classification.[33] These people cannot be schismatics, since they
continue to participate in the communal meal (v. 12), but we have already
heard that they are self-seeking in that gathering and that they "show partiality for the sake of favor" (v. 16). Whether they are classifying Christians
into different ranks or distinguishing themselves as spiritual elites, their
actions are communally divisive. Though they clearly think of themselves
as spiritual, Jude insists they are in fact *psychikoi,* "natural" or "worldly,"
following the wisdom "from below" as articulated in Jas. 3:15. Indeed, they
are not just unspiritual; they are entirely "devoid of the spirit," guided by
animal instinct (v. 10) and not by divine revelation.

---

32. Matt. 7:15-20; 24:11; Mark 13:22; Acts 20:29-30; 1 Tim. 4:1-3; 2 Tim. 3:1; 4:3-4; 1 John
2:18; 4:1-3.

33. Bauckham, *Jude, 2 Peter,* p. 105.

Body Closing: The Appeal (vv. 20-23)

A final direct address ("But you, beloved") introduces the conclusion of the letter body, which finally articulates the appeal first introduced at v. 3. Jude's readers were called to "contend for the faith" at the beginning of the letter: What does that struggle actually entail? It cannot involve verbal denunciation, for then they would not be following the pattern of the archangel Michael, the one positive example in the case from Scripture, who "did not presume to pronounce a reviling judgment" but left condemnation to the Lord (v. 9). It also cannot involve shunning the intruders, for that would make the readers guilty of the same divisiveness (v. 19).

The only appropriate response is to "build yourselves up *(oikodomeō)* on your most holy faith," a common exhortation in early Christianity rooted in the metaphor of the church as the eschatological temple of God (cf. 1 Pet. 2:5). The charge, in effect, is for the readers to respond by being the church, the covenant-partnered ecclesia of God, the ones called out of the world in order to witness to God's salvation in word and deed. This "building up" is articulated by means of yet another triad: they are to pray in the Holy Spirit, keep themselves in the love of God, and wait for the mercy of the Lord Jesus Christ. Combined, the four exhortations are built on two significant patterns: the second, third, and fourth are Trinitarian, and the first, third, and fourth suggest the three theological virtues of 1 Cor. 13:13: build up in *faith*, keep in God's *love*, and look forward to (or *hope for*) the mercy of Jesus.

To "pray in the Holy Spirit" suggests being "under the inspiration of the Spirit"[34] in sharp contrast to the intruders, who are inspired by their lusts. The call to "keep yourselves in the love of God" begins the inclusio with v. 1: believers who are "loved in God and kept for Jesus" are now reminded that they must strive to "keep themselves" in that privileged position by maintaining covenant obedience (echoing 1 John 3:24, which insists that "all who keep his commandments abide in him, and he in them"). They are to pray and obey in eager expectation as they "wait for the mercy of our Lord Jesus Christ that leads to eternal life." The language here recalls the opening description of those who deny the Lord Jesus Christ with their licentiousness (v. 4) and will therefore be convicted by him as ungodly when he comes "with his holy myriads to execute judgment on all" (v. 15).

But how should believers relate to the intruders and those affected by

---

34. Matt. 22:43; Mark 12:36; Luke 2:27; 4:1; Acts 19:21; Rom. 8:9; 1 Cor. 12:3; Rev. 1:10; 4:2.

their influence? For beloved ones (vv. 1, 2, 3, 17, 20), inspired by the Spirit (v. 20), seeking peace (v. 2) and living their lives in expectation of God's mercy (vv. 2 and 21), the only appropriate response is to extend that same mercy to others. Though the textual history of these verses is profoundly complex,[35] it appears that three different recipients of mercy are described in vv. 22-23. The first are either those who are "wavering/doubting," that is, believers struggling to find their footing amidst the conflict of authorities) or those who are "disputing," that is, the intruders themselves; the verb *diakrinō* can mean both, but the latter is the more common meaning. Since its only other appearance is in v. 9's contrast between the non-judgmental model of Michael and the arrogant disputation set forth by the devil, it makes the most sense on internal grounds to conclude that the call is to extend mercy to the disputing intruders and their ilk.[36]

This gracious act of rescuing the ungodly, of "saving *(sōzō)* others by snatching them out of the fire," draws our minds back to the similar call that ends the letter of James. There believers were reminded "that whoever brings a sinner back from the error of his way" — *plane hodou autou*, like the intruders who are described in Jude 11 as those who "follow the way *(hodos)* of Cain and abandon themselves to Balaam's error *(planē)*" — that rescuer "will save *(sōzō)* the sinner's soul from death and will cover a multitude of sins" (Jas. 5:20). According to the brothers of Jesus, the saints are called to an ongoing rescue operation that seeks the merciful restoration of all those who walk in error.

But real mercy is not be confused with thin tolerance: believers must express loving mercy to the offender while hating the defilement that has been brought onto the community (v. 23). The imagery of these latter phrases is inspired by Zechariah 3, a text quoted earlier in the positive example of the archangel Michael:

> Then he showed me the high priest Joshua standing before the angel of the LORD, and Satan standing at his right hand to accuse him. And the LORD said to Satan, "The Lord rebuke you, O Satan! . . . Is

---

35. Vv. 22-23 have numerous textual variants, each describing either two or three parties of people deserving mercy. For analysis, see S. Kubo, "Jude 22-23: Two-Division Form or Three?" in *New Testament Textual Criticism*, ed. E. J. Epp and G. D. Fee (Oxford: Clarendon, 1981), pp. 239-53; S. C. Winter, "Jude 22-23: A Note on the Text and Translation," *HTR* 87 (1994), pp. 215-22.

36. So Spitaler, "Doubt or Dispute," and Bauckham, *Jude, 2 Peter*, p. 115.

not this man a brand *plucked from the fire?*" Now Joshua was dressed with *filthy clothes* as he stood before the angel. The angel said to those who were standing before him, "Take off his filthy clothes." And to him he said, "See, I have taken your guilt [LXX *anomia*, 'lawlessness'] away from you, and I will clothe you with festal apparel." (Zech 3:1-4, NRSV)

Christians are to respond to lawlessness not with accusation and condemnation, for that is God's job. The task laid on the church is the merciful rescue and restoration of humans distorted by a disordered creation. Indeed, given the advent of God's mercy in sending the Messiah to extend mercy and love to all, what other action could possibly be appropriate?

Letter Closing: Benediction (vv. 24-25)

The angel's words to Joshua go on to describe what is to come with the coming Messiah:

Now listen, Joshua, high priest, you and your colleagues who sit before you! For they are an omen of things to come: I am going to bring my servant the Branch. For on the stone that I have set before Joshua, on a single stone with seven eyes, I will engrave its inscription, says the LORD of hosts, and I will remove the guilt of this land in a single day. On that day, says the LORD of hosts, you shall invite each other to come under your vine and fig tree. (Zech 3:8-10, NRSV)

Messiah Jesus came to remove guilt and invite all into obedient covenant relationship with the merciful God of Israel. Jude ends with this prophecy in mind: those who are kept by God (v. 1) can be at peace as they strive to keep themselves in the love of God (v. 21) because they know that ultimately God is the one who is able to keep them from falling (v. 24).[37] Indeed, God is a savior, a deliverer (v. 25); through Jesus, God's desire is revealed to be not condemnation but empowerment to "stand without blemish in the presence of his glory with rejoicing."

---

37. The prayer to be *"kept from stumbling"* appears frequently in the Psalms: 38:16; 56:13; 66:9; 73:2; 91:12; 94:18; 116:8; 121:3.

In this way, the strident call to obedience that characterizes the CE collection as a whole is concluded with a strong note of worshipful confidence before judgment (cf. 1 John 4:13-18). Like the living stone with seven eyes described in Zechariah's prophecy, the seven letters of the CE are set before us inscribed by God with the promise that one day the Creator's work through the Christ will remove our guilt and establish us as the worshipful covenant community we were created to be for the sake of the world.

Theology

1. The Creator God

Despite its brevity, the letter of Jude offers up a robust conception of God. This God has been revealed through the history and literature of Israel to be a loving Father, powerful Creator, merciful Savior, and eternal Judge.

The God of Israel is best conceived of as a loving "Father" who expresses this love by protecting believers as they respond to the call of covenant relationship (v. 1). Participants in this relationship are recipients of divine grace (v. 4) and become "beloved ones" (vv. 1, 3, 17, 20, 21) as a result. These beloved are protected in a variety of ways: they are saved from forces that enslave them (v. 5), shielded from human and non-human threats (vv. 5-7), and will ultimately be kept from stumbling on the long journey to stand in worship before God's presence (v. 24).

This covenant-keeping "Father" is in fact the powerful Progenitor of creation itself. God's creation is characterized by carefully ordered relationships in which animals, humans, and angels are all called to maintain an appointed position in relation to the Creator. Paradoxically, however, this ordered creation is also characterized by creaturely freedom: those saved from slavery are still free to disbelieve (v. 5), angels are capable of breaking out in rebellion (v. 6), and even believing covenant partners are free to distort rightly-ordered loving relationship into the slavery of lustful licentiousness (v. 4). The fruit of this rebellion is an animalistic irrationality (v. 10) that results in a kind of creational chaos (vv. 12-13). But the creature is not equal to the Creator; though creation is characterized by freedom, creation is never free of the Creator's hand — indeed, creaturely rebellion itself is revealed to be an aspect of the Creator's plan. Because

God is love (1 John 4:16), room must be made within the economy of creation for creatures to reject the Creator's ordering.

God's covenant partners have been clued in to the relation between Creator and creation because it was "written about long ago" in the holy Scriptures of Israel (v. 4). These Scriptures reveal that God is not only a loving Father and a powerful Creator but also a merciful Savior (v. 25) who rescued a people out of slavery in Egypt (v. 5), captured the angels who rebelled (v. 6), and sacked the cities of Sodom and Gomorrah when they perpetrated injustice against the vulnerable strangers in their midst (v. 7).

The Scriptures reveal that this saving God also intervenes in creation as eternal Judge to punish those who pervert grace into licentiousness (v. 4; cf. Rom. 2:1-11) and deform God's creation with ungodliness (vv. 14-15). Those delivered from slavery may afterward be destroyed for not trusting (v. 5); the loving giver of eternal life (v. 21) is also a Savior who punishes with eternal fire (v. 7). Nevertheless, mercy triumphs over judgment (Jas. 2:13); this Savior desires not punishment but rescue (Jas. 5:19-20; 2 Pet. 3:9; Jude 24). On this basis, believers can entrust themselves to this faithful Creator (1 Pet. 4:19). Indeed, God's identity as Savior is ultimately put into operation through Jesus Christ (v. 25), whose words and work as Master and Lord (v. 4) most clearly reveal the saving intention of the Father-Creator.

2. Christ Jesus

Jude's portrayal of Jesus parallels that of the Creator. Jude joins his brother James in servitude to their earthly brother Jesus (v. 1). But this very human brother of theirs is, simultaneously, the divinely appointed Sovereign Master and Lord of creation (v. 4) before whom all humanity must bow down. It is he who acts as God's authoritative agent in creation, the one through whom God mediates the mercy (v. 21) of eternal salvation (vv. 24-25).

Indeed, Jesus is himself the Lord (vv. 4, 5, 9, 14, 17, 21, 25) who long ago saved a people from Egypt (v. 5) and now works side-by-side with the Creator God (vv. 1, 21, 25) in advance of his triumphant return as Judge of the world (vv. 14-15). This Sovereign Lord must be respected; the only right creaturely response to God's mercy is obedience to the Master appointed by God (v. 4). In this manner those who are beloved by God strive to keep themselves in the love of God; in so doing they are, in turn, kept by God for the day of the Lord's salvation (vv. 1, 21).

The details of life lived in obedience to this Master are not ambiguous, uncertain, or up for debate, for he has already sent his emissary-apostles into the world to mediate his will and his way (vv. 3, 17-18). These ambassadors of the king were sent out to call forth communities of faith, entrusting them with the preservation of a historic body of teaching that communicates the truth about God and the manner in which God's human covenant partners are to keep themselves in God's merciful, saving embrace.

3. The Community of the Spirit

Of course, there are those who do not accept the "once-for-all" (v. 3) nature of the apostolic tradition handed down to the churches. Indeed, the apostles themselves prophesied before their communities, saying that the last times will see the advent of "scoffers" who will practice a way of Christian faith that is foreign to what was originally communicated (vv. 17-18). Though these intruders will base their novel claims on the authority of direct spiritual revelation (v. 8), they are in fact devoid of the Spirit (v. 19); their deeds are animated by an animalistic spirit of lust (vv. 8, 10, 16, 18) that they have confused with the empowering Spirit of God.

The solution Jude provides is in no way intended to stamp out the spirit of prophecy in the community. It is not prophets or teachers who are condemned (as in 2 Peter) but scoffers, those who mock the godly morality of others on the basis of their supposedly superior experience of the Spirit's revelation; it is pneumatic arrogance that is condemned, not pneumatic experience per se. The focal issue is the epistemic crisis that is always created when individuals in the community of faith claim authority based on an experience of God, but fail to test the veracity of that experience against the testimony of the Creator's deeds as recorded in Scripture (vv. 4-16) and the historic deposit of those apostolic leaders who were eyewitnesses to the earthly advent of creation's Master and Lord, Jesus Christ (vv. 3, 17).

4. Christian Discipleship

Appropriately, then, Jude's remedy for disciples of the Lord is fully Trinitarian in its formulation (vv. 20-21). The only thing for believers to do in the face of such divisive conflict is to build themselves up in the content and practices of their most holy faith. While the opponents reject the Lord's authority and use their faith as a cover for the pursuit of their lustful desires (v. 7), believers "contend for the faith" they received (v. 3) and thereby "keep" it. They pray under the inspiration and guidance of the Holy Spirit as a corrective to the spirit of their lustful desires. They are to keep their appointed place in the love of God as it is made known in the testimony of Scripture and avoid emulating the many counter-examples found there of those who wandered away and suffered judgment as a result. They are to orient their words and deeds now according to their inherited apostolic hope that one day the Lord Jesus will come again to extend mercy to his obedient servants and bring judgment to those who turn that mercy into a license for ungodly living.

Central to this practice of "keeping the faith" is the call to "remember" (vv. 5, 17). Disciples accomplish this remembrance by returning again and again to the Scriptures, which faithfully communicate God's identity and purpose. Indeed, by interpreting their experiences through a scriptural lens, believers will be enabled to unmask the forces in the world that cause them to stumble as they journey in worship toward their final union with God. This deposit of authoritative texts includes not only the Scriptures of Israel (vv. 5, 7, 11) and the testimony of the apostles of Jesus (v. 17) but also useful writings that would later be deemed noncanonical (vv. 6, 9, 14-15). All these texts are able to communicate the means by which the beloved of God might keep themselves in a state of godliness.

Jude leaves no room for a thin, verbal discipleship of mere doctrinal confession. No, godliness is expressed as an appropriate way of walking in the world created by God. Disciples keep their appointed place in the divine economy by maintaining pure and honorable sexual practices, practicing loving and hospitable impartiality, and engaging in humble mutual service. Perhaps most importantly, they follow the example of the archangel Michael, who refused to express words of slander and judgment against his opponent, knowing that judgment is the prerogative of the Lord alone (v. 9). Believers therefore seek unity and avoid schism, even extending this reconciling concern to those who dispute the faith instead of keeping it. Of course, while expressing loving concern for the wayward they must carefully avoid being led astray by their ungodly practices (vv. 22-23), but even in the face of this danger they can act in confident faith, knowing that their ongoing faithfulness to God is not simply a matter of their own strenuous efforts. A key component of keeping oneself in the love of God is constantly bearing in mind that God is the one who ultimately keeps believers from falling as they make their way to the glorious consummation God has planned for all of creation.

5. Consummation in a New Creation

The message of Jude is propelled by "a vital eschatological expectation."[38] All history is unfolding according to an eternal plan for creation written about long ago (v. 4). Through the work of Jesus, the saving God in love and mercy is leading believers to an eternal life that as yet exists as a future reality (v. 21). That future deliverance is near, given the presence of false believers predicted by the apostles (vv. 17-18). Indeed, the Creator has been "keeping" things all along, "before all time and now and forever" (v. 25): condemnation is kept for those who reject their status as servants working under a Master; mercy, protection, and deliverance are kept for those who remember the way and walk accordingly.

Though the threat is very real, believers are not to be overwhelmed by the impending danger of divine judgment. Though they are assaulted on all sides by an ungodly world that even winds its way into the very center of the worship assembly (v. 12), they nevertheless walk in trusting and "re-membering" faith, recalling that the one they follow is powerful enough to keep them from falling and will ultimately guide them directly into the heavenly throne room (v. 24). There they will stand without blemish in a vast, holy congregation of saints, rejoicing together and ascribing glory, majesty, power, and authority to the God who saved them (v. 25). In confidence of this, believers must spend their days dwelling in abundant mercy, peace, and love (v. 2) in the hope that every wandering sinner they meet along the way (Jas. 5:19-20) might be persuaded to cast off their defiling habits (Jude 23) and join them as holy companions on the way that leads to God.

---

38. Watson, "Letter of Jude," p. 479.

PART 3

Conclusion

The Unifying Theology of the
Catholic Epistle Collection

The formation of Scripture's canonical collections was not based on the church's recognition of a theological uniformity without internal disagreement. Rather, selected writings were gathered together in collections to fix the scope and depth of the apostolic witness to God's gospel, and the internal diversity of a canonical collection, when it adds depth and extends the scope of a textual witness, better serves those continuing roles performed by Scripture. The history of interpretation suggests that any single writing or singular collection is "too small to serve as a source for any significant doctrinal material."[1] Sharply put, then, the theological deposit of the different CE, when taken up and used as a canonical whole, articulates a more fluent and influential word that more effectively forms the Christian faith and witness of its readers than does their use as individual documents.

And yet any claim for a center of theological gravity that holds together a collection of such evident diversity seems counterintuitive to most modern readers. Biology has taught us to suppose that selection processes form kinship groups from a common gene pool. Such an intuition more than any other has shaped a way of thinking about the CE collection as a hodge-podge grouping of individual writings that really do not belong together but someplace else within the biblical canon. For example, since the Johannine letters share "common genes" with the Fourth Gospel (and even the Apocalypse), most scholars gather them into a noncanonical collection of Johannine "kin." Of course, this move also strips the Gospels

---

1. J. Ashton, "History and Theology in New Testament Studies," in *The Nature of New Testament Theology,* ed. C. Rowland and C. Tuckett (Oxford: Blackwell, 2007), p. 4.

collection of its fourth member, again on the presumption that the first three, the "Synoptic" Gospels, form their own kinship group of agreements about Jesus' life story. And so on. The problem with this kind of interpretive model, even though commonplace among contemporary scholars, is that it does not fit the evidence! Sometimes groups with a diverse membership form cooperatives simply because they work well together to produce a better result. Sharply put, it is the long résumé of sacred performances that secures the CE as a collection for the church's biblical canon.[2]

We trust our studies of each of the CE in the preceding chapters have helped readers envision the rich theological texture of this canonical collection and have prepared them for this final chapter, which will offer a sense of this collection's theological coherence. It will thus demonstrate that a collection well known for its internal diversity is bound together during the canonical process precisely because the church recognized that its internal diversity, like that of every other canonical collection, adds potential to its formative power when taken and used as an integral whole. That is, this collection is a whole best envisaged not by stockpiling its bits and pieces but by engaging them as integral parts of the collection's dynamic, unfolding, and mutually enriching intratextuality.

The Internal Grammar of the CE Collection

Since critical orthodoxy assumes that the theological and literary diversity of the CE marks out their material independence from one other, even those rare interpreters who admit to common themes among them (e.g., Lockett, Jobes) do so without any sense of their integral, interpenetrating wholeness. In this concluding chapter we seek to illustrate this wholeness as a quality of this collection's "aesthetic excellence." Our contention is

---

2. The eminent social biologist E. O. Wilson makes a similar argument against the widely held view in evolutionary theory that "eusociality" (social order) evolved through the formation of kinship groups, since this best explains the pivotal role altruism performs in species survival. That is, we are more likely to sacrifice our good for the future good of a family member than for a complete stranger. The problem, Wilson notes, is that a relationship between genetic success and altruism is not supported by the evidence, at least not in every species. As with canonical collections, teamwork and performance, rather than a common gene pool, often insure the future of a group; see *The Social Conquest of Earth* (New York: Liveright, 2012), especially pp. 183-90.

that the sequence of the sevenfold collection is not arbitrary or mechanical; that is, it is not based on a chronology of their composition or canonization or arranged by mechanical means. Their dates of composition are indeterminate, and both 1 Peter and 1 John were received as Scripture very early, perhaps already in the first century and long before either 2 Peter or James. Further, while 2 John was added to 1 John and put into circulation in the second century, 3 John was added to the first two much later. Nor, evidently, is this collection ordered by descending length as was, evidently, the Pauline collection. Finally, readers, ancient and modern, have surmised that the sequence is a matter of convenience, simply following the biblical ordering of the Jerusalem Pillars in Gal. 2:9, "James, Cephas, and John."[3] Even though we find this explanation appealing (and even appeal to it on occasion!), the "Pillars" metaphor cannot be applied neatly to a collection that also includes Jude.

In any case, our contention all along is that the seven CE are bound together in a sequence that recommends an order of reading for maximal benefit when "teaching, reproving, correcting, and training" a congregation of faithful readers. The precise placement of the individual writings within the sevenfold collection thereby secures a kind of internal "canon logic" that relates the theological goods retrieved from each letter to the other letters in a way that facilitates their collected use. (As noted earlier, we have retained the five theological rubrics of the apostolic Rule of Faith to facilitate potential interactions both within the collection and between this collection and Scripture's other collections, whose theological materials can be organized and engaged by this same analogy of the faith.)

The elevated importance we grant to the sequence of writings within a canonical collection does not envisage a linear progression of thought that only looks forward, one epistle to the next. Rather a collection's witness to God's word unfolds in a more dynamic way, reading its witness both forward and backward. Not only do successive letters elaborate prior points (reading forward), but the reader will also be prompted by the repetition of these points to recall their antecedent iterations in ways that expand their meaning in earlier settings (reading backward).

We have hypothesized a crucial element of the church's decision that a collection of sacred writings was complete and fixed for canonization must have been recognition of the completed collection's aesthetic excel-

---

3. D. Lührmann, "Gal. 2:9 und die katholischen Briefe," *ZNW* 72 (1981), pp. 65-87.

lence — that its different parts were now properly placed, working well together when performing their roles. The consistency of a particular sequence of Catholic Epistles in both manuscripts and canon lists at the point of canonization in the East secures our point: it suggests that the church recognized that each letter, while making its own distinctive contribution, is materially linked to the others in a precise and deliberate way. Themes introduced by James are elaborated by 1 Peter, a witness which is then completed by 2 Peter, even as 2 Peter is linked to 1 John, which is epitomized by 2 John, qualified by 3 John, and concluded by Jude; this logic apprehends a collection held together like links of a chain. *We commend an interpretive approach to these seven CE, therefore, that approaches the aesthetic of the whole collection as envisaging a working grammar or logic that aids the reader in bringing to full potential the contribution it makes to Scripture's witness of God's word.*

From Paul to Pillars

In his programmatic study of Scripture's Pauline canon, B. Childs contends that the church's theological reflection should begin with a Pauline definition of apostleship.[4] This contention is based on his observation that a collection's apostolicity was an essential category of the early church's recognition of authority, designating the earliest witnesses of Jesus who were appointed to receive and transmit God's word disclosed in him.[5] The apostolic origin of the church's authoritative tradition, then, is an encounter — a "witness" — of Jesus Christ, which was then applied to a variety of settings in a variety of ways, including epistolary.

Childs readily observes the contested nature of Paul's claims to his apostolic office, evident in several of his letters (see Galatians 1–2), and rightly argues that Paul's apologetic use of "apostle" intends to secure his calling to proclaim God's word about Jesus to the nations. But he makes nothing of this controversy that swirled around Paul's claim, which seems over the nature or phenomenology of his "witness" of Jesus. And yet this is a crucial subtext of the Acts of the Apostles, whose canonical performance

---

4. B. S. Childs, *The Church's Guide for Reading Paul: The Canonical Shaping of the Pauline Corpus* (Grand Rapids: Eerdmans, 2008), pp. 81-83.

5. Childs, *Church's Guide*, pp. 21-22.

supplies the narrative setting that frames a reading of the two corpora of letters that follow. Clearly the Paul of Acts, his message and mission, is important to the church's future; and yet, just as clearly, he does not have the résumé required for membership in the church's apostolate (see Acts 1:21-22). Paul's most robust defense of his apostolic appointment, found in Galatians, is against those in the earliest community who apparently argued that his is a pseudo-apostleship, derived secondhand from the Jerusalem Pillars, who schooled him in the gospel since they knew the historical Jesus and Paul did not (cf. Gal. 1:1, 16b-24). He grounds his credibility in revelation (vv. 11-12) and prophetic ecstasy (vv. 15-16a) rather than in an eyewitness encounter with the historical Jesus.

This, then, is the epistemic nub of the issue: What is the real source of the church's apostolic tradition? The reader of Acts recognizes that the source of Paul's authority and by extension of his message is different from that of the Twelve, who were eyewitnesses of the historical Jesus (Acts 1:21-22). Paul's religious authority is rather grounded in his vision of the resurrected Jesus on the Damascus Road and, according to his canonical letters, a transformative experience of participation by faith in Jesus' messianic death. While Luke's triadic formulation of this event (Acts 9:1-19; 22:6-16; 26:12-18) is surely a trope of his narrative's emphasis on an experienced resurrection, it also suggests that Paul's message about Jesus is ex post facto. That is, the content of his gospel, its announcement of the apocalypse of God's salvation and its promise of a transforming experience with Christ, is logically contingent on Christ's death and resurrection. Every gospel claim, every pastoral exhortation, every missionary act, every appeal to Scripture Paul makes in his letters — the epistemic substance of his theological grammar — is commentary on the effects that follow from Jesus' dying and rising. Everything prior to that messianic moment, even though Paul is certainly aware of Jesus' biography (cf. Gal. 4:4), is not a condition of the new creation; every promise God has made to Israel and now realizes in partnership with Jesus Christ follows from Jesus' cross and empty tomb.

We have made much of the importance of the CE collection's appeal to the apostolic tradition in order to locate the origins of its theological conception in a different place from Paul's: its critical source is an eyewitness encounter with the historical Jesus "from the beginning" (1 John 1:1). What logically shapes the epistemology of the CE theological (and especially Christological) conception, then, is an ipso facto experience of the historical Jesus rather than an ex post facto experience of the exalted Lord.

The result is more than rhetorical — the "canonical" use of what was heard and seen in close proximity to the real Jesus to settle disputes or define orthodox faith — but lends material substance to how God's word is articulated, especially in relationship with the Pauline witness.

James: The Collection's Frontispiece

As Wall has argued,[6] James is especially well suited to function as the collection's frontispiece; it is a structurally important piece because it not only frames the pastoral tone of the entire collection but also introduces its core theological elements. These agreements target a community of believers whose covenant-keeping practices, following the example of Christ, maintain its loving relationship with God, from whom it receives the "crown of (eternal) life" (Jas. 1:12).

The "priority" of James is, to a significant extent, the semiosis of its placement at the front of the final edition of a canonical collection. It is the first of the CE read, if they are read in sequence, and so sets into play a range of orienting concerns that are glossed by the succession of epistles. In fact, according to Nienhuis,[7] James was composed for and added to a still inchoate CE collection to introduce a Pillars collection. The letter's strategic role is already cued by the James of Acts, who moderates the second council (Acts 15) to stipulate the church's working relationship with Paul's mission to the nations and Jerusalem's mission to Israel. By analogy, the letter of James stipulates Scripture's working relationship between the Pauline corpus and that of the Pillars.

From James to 1 Peter

We have already discussed the preeminence of Peter in the ancient church. This preeminence was especially present in the western church, which consistently ranked Peter alongside Paul as the two most glorious apostles. It is

6. See especially R. W. Wall, "The Priority of James," in *The Catholic Epistles and Apostolic Tradition,* ed. K.-W. Niebuhr and R. W. Wall (Waco: Baylor University Press, 2009), pp. 153-60.

7. *Not by Paul Alone: The Formation of the Catholic Epistle Collection and the Christian Canon* (Waco: Baylor University Press, 2007).

unsurprising therefore that we frequently find western writers prioritizing Peter's letters in the ranking of the NT letters.[8] But the final ordering of the CE, which emerged out of the eastern church, placed Peter's epistles after the letter of James, a sequence which is significant for a canonical reading of the collection.

James refers to himself as "the servant of God and the Lord Jesus Christ," a title which is deeply rooted in Jewish literature as a designation for the heroes of Israel's past who mediated between God and the people. This authoritative Jewish leader writes from a center (presumably Jerusalem) to readers cast abroad in the Jewish Diaspora (Jas. 1:1). Peter, by contrast, writes as an apostle ("one sent") to readers suffering a dispersion in which he is himself a participant (1 Pet. 1:1; 5:13). He resides in "Babylon," most likely a thinly-veiled reference to Rome, but he is an elder among elders (5:1) and not the later monarchical bishop of church tradition. This symbolic world created by the literary association of James and 1 Peter provides a particular narrative context for reading their letters. Though later western leaders would honor Peter as the first pope and Paul as the apostle par excellence (both martyred in Rome), the content and sequence of the CE remind readers that James and Peter shared an earlier connection through their relationship with the earthly Jesus and their service in the mother church in Jerusalem. In that context, James was the bishop, and Peter was the one sent. The narrative world of the CE, therefore, is that of the two-sided apostolic mission described in Acts and Galatians.

Of course, Galatians describes a conflict involving James, Peter, and Paul, one that has been interpreted to pit James against Paul with Peter caught in the middle (so Marcion in the ancient church and Baur more recently). The close linking of James and 1 Peter helps to alleviate this potential misunderstanding. We note, first of all, that James and 1 Peter often "speak" in the same voice — especially in the opening sections of each letter. Each bears a prescript locating recipients in a Diaspora (Jas. 1:1; 1 Pet. 1:1) and then immediately calls believers to rejoice in "various trials" (*poikilois peirasmois*) because of the role testing plays in producing genuine faith (*to dokimion hymōn tēs pisteōs*, Jas. 1:2-3; 1 Pet. 1:6-9). Soon thereafter James quotes, and 1 Peter alludes to, Isaiah 40 (Jas. 1:10-11; 1 Pet. 1:24-

---

8. Such is the case with the canon lists of Augustine, Filaster of Brescia, the north African canons, Rufinus, Junilius Africanus, and Cassiodorus. See the discussion in the "Shaping" chapter, p. 33 above.

25), and then each speaks of the believer's birth by a word from God (Jas. 1:18; 1 Pet. 1:23). Subsequent close parallels (compare Jas. 4:6-10 with 1 Pet. 5:5-9 and Jas. 5:20 with 1 Pet. 4:8) clearly indicate that James and Peter are in theological agreement.

1 Peter, in turn, ends by referring to the apostle's close association with Mark and Silvanus (1 Pet. 5:12-13), figures presented in the Acts narrative as coworkers of Paul (Acts 12 and 15–18). When 2 Peter then speaks glowingly of "our beloved brother Paul" and describes his letters as occasionally "hard to understand" (2 Pet. 3:15-16), a bulwark is established against a reading of Galatians that might leave readers with a vision of apostles in disagreement: we are not to follow "the ignorant and unstable" who understand James, Peter, and Paul to be in conflict.

Clearly the opening designation of readers in a Diaspora struggling under trials of faith should be taken to underscore the central orientation of the CE as a whole. Between them, James writes from Jerusalem to readers in the Diaspora, warning them against the *external* threat of worldly seductions that enflame the passions that give birth to sin and death. James thus *afflicts the comfortable* with a call to repentance. 1 Peter is also written to believers in the Diaspora, but now the external threat comes in the form of hostile neighbors whose harassment produces suffering and tests the patience of those called to love without retaliation. 1 Peter thus *comforts the afflicted* with a call to entrust their souls to a faithful Creator.

From 1 to 2 Peter

Despite the many substantial differences between them, the two letters of Peter are clearly marked by a series of intertextual linkages securing the intent that they be read together.[9] Each is addressed from Peter, and they share similar greetings (1 Pet. 1:2; 2 Pet. 1:2) and closing doxologies (1 Pet. 4:11; 2 Pet. 3:18). 1 Peter is written to readers designated "the elect" (1:1), and 2 Peter follows this up by exhorting readers to "confirm their call and election" (1:10). They also seem to be linked by a shared purpose: in the first letter Peter says, "I have written this short letter to encourage you and to testify that this is the true grace of God" (5:12); in the second Peter says,

---

9. For a full accounting of the lexical agreements between 1 and 2 Peter, see J. H. Elliott, *1 Peter* (AB 37B, New York: Doubleday, 2000), pp. 27 and 141.

"This is now, beloved, the second letter I have written to you; in them I am trying to arouse your sincere intention by reminding you" (3:1-2). Indeed, 2 Peter continues the "trials" thread established by James, reminding readers of OT stories that assure believers that "the Lord knows how to rescue the godly from trial" (2:9). Even more can be said: each letter bears a strikingly similar reference to the traditions of the disobedient angels (1 Pet. 3:19-20; 2 Pet. 2:4) and the flood (1 Pet. 3:20; 2 Pet. 2:5; 3:6), and each speaks of prophecy in relation to Scripture (1 Pet. 1:10-12; 2 Pet. 1:20-21; 3:2).

Other conspicuous parallels help stake out the different orientations of the two letters. Where 1 Peter is written to marginalized Christians whose trial comes in the form of an *external* threat of social harassment, 2 Peter is written to middle-class Christians who suffer an *internal threat* coming from false believers. Accordingly, 1 Peter says, "As servants of God *(douloi theou)*, live as free people *(eleutheroi)*, yet do not use your freedom *(eleutheria)* as a pretext for evil" (2:16). 2 Peter in turn condemns the false teachers because "they promise them freedom *(eleutheria)* but they themselves are slaves of corruption *(douloi . . . tēs phthoras)*" (2:19). Likewise, where 1 Peter calls readers to imitate the Christ who is "like a lamb without defect or blemish" *(amōmos kai aspilos,* 1:19), 2 Peter condemns the false teachers as "blots and blemishes" *(spiloi kai mōmoi,* 2:13) and reminds readers to hold fast so that they may be found by Christ "without spot or blemish" *(aspiloi kai amōmētos,* 3:14).

From 2 Peter to 1 John

While it is a commonplace to extract the Johannine epistles from the collection by appeal to their dissimilarity to the other CE and similarity to the Fourth Gospel, in fact there are clear verbal and thematic linkages between 1 John and 2 Peter. 1 Peter ended with a reference to Peter as a "witness to the sufferings of Christ" (5:1). 2 Peter makes this the centerpiece of its claims to authority: the apostles "did not follow cleverly devised myths" when they proclaimed the parousia of the Lord, "for we were eyewitnesses of his majesty" (1:16) who "heard" *(ēkousamen)* the voice of God on the holy mountain (1:18). So also 1 John begins by grounding the declaration of the author in his eyewitness status, proclaiming "that which we have heard *(akēkoamen)*, which we have seen with our eyes, which we have looked upon and touched with our hands" (1:1).

Both letters also share a similar occasion for writing. 2 Peter was written to readers/auditors of 1 Peter (3:1) to warn against scoffers who will come saying "where is the promise *(epangelia)* of his coming? For ever since our ancestors died, all things continue as they were from the beginning *(ap' archēs)* of creation" (3:3-4). Peter's reply directs readers to the "word of God" through which all things were created and by which judgment will soon come (3:5-7). Soon after these words 1 John opens by "declaring" *(apangellomen)* "that which was from the beginning" *(ap' archēs)* "concerning the word of life" (1:1). The opponents may think they know what is from the beginning, but Peter and John agree that only the apostles of Christ can speak to these things with authority.

Reading on, we find that 1 John describes opposing leaders or a rival Christianity using precisely the same language as 2 Peter. As in 2 Peter, so also in the Johannine communities the trial involves an internal threat from the presence of apostate Christians, though a progression of sorts is detected: in 2 Peter the apostates are still in church promoting moral laxity (2 Pet. 2:13); in 1 John the apostates have left the community (1 John 2:19), leaving the church struggling with the reality of schism. Nevertheless, in both letters the opponents are called false prophets (2 Pet. 2:1; 1 John 4:1); these are the only two instances of the word *pseudoprophētēs* in all the NT letters. These false prophets are identified as teachers (2 Pet. 2:1; 1 John 2:27) who "deny" *(arneomai)* a key Christological claim (2 Pet. 2:1; 1 John 2:22-23). They are deceivers who have strayed from the truth into error (repeated use of *planē* and *planaō,* 2 Pet. 2:15, 18; 3:17; 1 John 2:26; 3:7; 4:6; 2 John 7). They are associated with "the world" (2 Pet. 2:18-20; 1 John 4:1-6) and are therefore corrupted by the desires of the flesh (2 Pet. 2:9-10; 3:3; 1 John 2:15-17).

From 1 John through 3 John

Earlier in this book we made a case for how the three Johannine letters are related to each other within the collection. The prologue to 1 John picks up this same theme (and implied theological crisis) to frame its distinctive contribution to the CE collection. 2 John then "epitomizes" 1 John, not only to clarify the core themes but to elaborate them in practical ways.

In particular, 3 John is read after 2 John to help readers better understand the practice and administration of hospitality as the principal instantiation of the command to love other believers, forcefully made and elaborated in 1 John (4:16-21). It is this moral practice of loving other members of the community that ultimately tests its allegiance to the truth of the apostolic witness. 3 John also adds the haunting note that it is in the practice of the faith that the community's governance is also tested.

Jude: The Collection's Conclusion

The reader's ready recognition of the idiomatic similarity of Jude and 2 Peter, which is clearly linked to 1 John, should also lead one to recognize that Jude continues the interests and idiom of the Johannine letters. As in the Johannine letters, readers are addressed as "beloved in God" (v. 1), and emphasis is also placed on a threat within the community from those who oppose the apostolic message.

Among other things, the addition of Jude to the three Pillars in the final shape of the collection commends the reader's awareness that it is not only the analogy of Galatians 2 that glosses the sequence of the CE collection but the narrative of Acts as well, since the Lord's brothers (James and Jude) join the Pillars (Peter and John) to lead the community's witness to the risen Jesus in Jerusalem (so Acts 1:12-14). Read in the canonical setting of Acts and Galatians 2, Jerusalem thus becomes a kind of theological trope and not merely a geographical location. That is, even though these letters were sent as encyclicals to catholic addresses, their titles place the origins of each in an apostolic tradition shaped by the theological agreements of "the gospel for the circumcised" (Gal. 2:7) as preached in Jerusalem.

Finally, the reader picks up Jude to continue a thread initiated by 2 Peter, especially the importance of "building yourselves up in your most holy [i.e., apostolic] faith" (v. 20), while also recalling the message of James, especially the church's vocation to rescue its wandering membership (cf. Jas. 5:19-20; Jude 22-23), to ensure the coherence of the collection as a whole. The reader hears the closing words of Jude's famous doxology as a reminder that God is a gracious covenant partner, perhaps to moderate the collection's persistent call to holiness as a condition of eternal life with God. This concluding note not only corrects a potentially legalistic reading of the CE collection but also encourages faithful discipleship predicated on a loving God's capacity "to protect (believers) from falling, and to present (believers) blameless and rejoicing before God's glorious presence" (v. 24).

The Unifying Theology of the CE Collection

1. THE CREATOR GOD Is One God, Who Produced All Things Out of Nothing through His Own Word Sent Forth

James supplies the working theological grammar of the collection's conception of the one God (2:19) who is Creator of all things (1:17), a "Father" (1:17, 27; 3:9) who has birthed (1:18) humanity in God's own likeness (3:9). This generous Father gives only good and perfect gifts (1:5, 17), especially the "word of truth" (1:18) sent forth to provide the wisdom required to pass the spiritual tests of life in a world of seduction and conflict (1:1-5; 4:1-4). This wise word reveals the Creator's plan of salvation and guides redeemed humanity into the age to come (1:12). This word is disclosed in the biblical Torah of Israel and functions as the community's Rule of Faith (1:22-25; 2:8-13). That rule indicates that God is more than willing to give grace to the humble (4:6b) who love their neighbors as they love themselves (2:8, 12-13). The Creator's eyes are therefore especially on the poor (1:9; 2:5) who will be vindicated and will have their material fortunes reversed (1:9-11) on that day when God comes as Judge (4:11-12). Since God is preeminently giving, God denounces those who are *not* giving, that is, the arrogant, worldly rich who have oppressed their fellow creatures (2:6-7; 4:1-4; 5:5-6). The only way to be exalted before this God is to repent (4:7-9; 5:19-20) and walk the way of humility (4:10) and good deeds that ultimately results in salvation (1:12; 2:14-26).

Readers should anticipate that Peter's conception of the Creator is closely aligned with that of co-Pillar James. In 1 Peter, God is both the trustworthy Creator (4:19) and the loving Father (1:2-3, 17) revealed in the Scripture of Israel, one whose eyes are focused on those who suffer trials (1:6-7; 2:11–3:7) in an alien, Diaspora land that operates according to pagan values (1:1; 2:11; 5:13). As in James so also 1 Peter insists that God will come to judge humanity, vindicating only those who have lived their lives in accordance with the Creator's will (1:17; 4:1-6, 17-18; 5:4-6).

1 Peter's key elaboration of James comes in the form of a shift in the perspective of those addressed: where James offered a word of warning to those tempted by the seductions of the Diaspora, 1 Peter is written from the consoling perspective of a co-sufferer *within* that Diaspora. 1 Peter therefore insists that, despite possible appearances to the contrary, the Creator is trustworthy and faithful (4:19; compare Jas. 1:13-16). Far from being

a sign of the Creator's *indifference,* suffering is in fact a demonstration of God's great mercy in the believer's life, for it is a sign that one has been oriented away from the transitory hopes of the world and reoriented to the "living hope" of the eternal inheritance God has provided through the resurrection to life (1:3-5). Far from being a sign of the Creator's *powerlessness,* suffering is in fact an aspect of God's ancient plan of salvation, made known through the history and literature of Israel (1:10-12, 23-25; 2:6-8, 22-25) and most preeminently in the suffering death and glorious resurrection of God's Son Jesus Christ (1:2-3, 20; 3:18; 4:1-2). Far from being a sign of the Creator's *rejection,* the pain and harassment believers experience in the world are not meaningless miseries but indicators that one is an active participant in the covenant community called and chosen by God (1:1-2). Indeed, this deliverance is simply the fulfillment of God's providential exodus that draws people out of a pagan world to be reborn (1:3) by the power of God's word (1:23) into a new people group, "a chosen race, a royal priesthood, a holy nation, God's own people" (2:9).

2 Peter, in turn, extends this vision in an apocalyptic direction in order to ground it more securely in the coming day of God's final victory (3:12). 1 Peter concentrates on the *inauguration* of the Creator's salvation in the suffering and resurrection of God's Messiah Jesus: "He himself bore our sins in his body on the cross, so that, free from sins, we might live for righteousness" (1 Pet. 2:24). 2 Peter focuses on its *consummation* at the Creator's triumph on the day of the Lord's return: "in accordance with his promise, we wait for new heavens and a new earth, where righteousness is at home" (2 Pet. 3:13). The Creator, it turns out, intends to re-create by purifying creation of its many contaminants (3:10-13). This will be a new heavens and new earth that more closely mirrors its Creator; because God is preeminently "righteous" (1:1), creation must ultimately be a place where righteousness is at home (3:13) and ungodliness is banished (1 Pet. 4:8; 2 Pet. 2:5-6). Yet even here, the Creator and Judge of the world is revealed to be a merciful Father (1:17): the delay of the consuming purification is not due to indifference or impotence but the result of merciful patience as God holds the door open for those who might yet repent (3:9) and take up the path that leads to the kingdom (1:5-11).

This "way of righteousness" (2:21) that invites humans to actually participate in the divine nature (1:3-11) and pass through the judgment that will come at the Lord's parousia has been made fully known through the exclusive witness of the authoritative apostles that God has sent (1 Pet. 5:1; 2 Pet. 1:12-18; 3:1-2, 15-18). Here we find the key link between 2 Peter and the

Johannine letters: according to 1 John, knowledge of the Creator is disclosed in an incarnate "word of life" mediated to believers by the apostolic witness (1:1-2) so that all who hear and respond in faith will "abide" therein (2:24) and ultimately gain victory over the world (5:4).

That witness discloses two core beliefs about the Creator: God is light (1 John 1:5) and God is love (4:8, 16). The revelation of these two central features of the Creator's identity is designed to produce a transformation within the creation. Since God is light, creaturely truth-telling will ultimately win out over lies and deception (1:6–2:2). Since God is love, those who abide in God will not hate but will love one another (3:7). All this comes from the Creator's loving desire to "forgive" (1:9; 2:12), an action of reconciliation that is initiated by God (4:10) so that creatures will be healed of their sins (1:7, 9; 2:2; 4:10) and will keep the divine commandments (2:3-5; 3:22-24; 5:2-3) in order to thereby inherit "eternal life" (1:2; 2:25; 5:13).

Jude links up with the previous CE collection's witness to the Creator God by underscoring its key characteristics. As before, so also here God is a loving "Father" who protects believers as they respond to the call of covenant relationship (v. 1), dispensing divine grace (v. 4) to creatures who become God's "beloved ones" (vv. 2, 3, 17, 20, 21) and thereby abide "in" that protective love (vv. 1, 21; cf., e.g., 1 John 4:16). This loving Creator has brought an ordered creation into being, the nature and logic of which are disclosed in the ancient and holy Scriptures of Israel (vv. 5-16) and the witness of the apostles, who have entrusted this tradition of faith to believers (vv. 3, 17). Through these witnesses we learn of a God whose past, present, and future involve the rescue of those who keep the faith (vv. 3, 20) and the punishment of the ungodly, who pervert the grace of God into licentiousness (vv. 4, 14-15).

Though the Creator's judgment is real, punishment is not God's ultimate aim (cf. 2 Pet. 3:9). No, God's mercy is put into operation through the work of Jesus Christ (v. 25), whose words and work as Master and Lord (v. 4) most clearly reveal the Creator's saving intention, thus forming an inclusio with Jas. 5:19-20 and linking up with 2 Pet. 3:9, thus concentrating this notion as a core theme of the CE collection. Thus Jude's final words land the letter group's conception of God on its proper ground by means of a doxological and benedictory conclusion: "the only God" is a "Savior" who "is able to keep you from falling" and is therefore deserving of "glory, majesty, power, and authority before all time and now and forever" (vv. 24-25). Amen and amen.

2. CHRIST JESUS Is This Word Sent Forth into the World to Redeem God's Creation, Disclose God's Truth, and Exemplify God's Love

James describes God as "Father" who has sent the "word of truth" into the world (1:17-18) to save people (1:21) from sin (1:13-16) and death (5:19-20). This word "comes down from heaven" as a revelation of divine wisdom (1:5; 3:17) that enables believers to pass spiritual tests, rendering them perfect and complete, lacking in nothing (1:2-4). This word is "implanted" within those who are receptive (1:21) and pure (1:27); they do what the word requires (1:22-25) and are saved as a result (2:14-26). In doing so they become servants of "the glorious Lord Jesus Christ" (2:1; cf. 1:1) who both taught and lived God's word, Torah's royal law (2:8), by loving his poor neighbors without prejudice and resisting their mistreatment by the rich (2:1-5; 5:1-6).

Though James never explicitly connects "the word" and "the Lord," the reception and placement of James within the CE collection form the reader's intuition that this "word of truth" is instantiated in Jesus, whom Peter and John saw and heard in the flesh. Within a wider canonical setting, James is read with Matthew's Gospel, which depicts Jesus as a messianic teacher of wisdom, and the Pauline witness, which calls Jesus the "wisdom from God" (1 Cor. 1:30) and refers to the gospel as "the word of truth" (2 Tim. 2:15). In fact, the words "God" and "Lord" are used almost interchangeably in this letter, such that at certain points it is difficult to tell whether we are reading about the Creator or the Christ (e.g., 1:7; 3:9; 4:10, 15; 5:4, 7, 8, 10, 11, 14, 15). Whether this high Christology is described as "implicit"[10] or just plain ambiguous, the ultimate effect for a reading of James as Scripture is the same: in the terminology of Tertullian, the Word who was seen in diverse manners by the patriarchs and heard at all times in the prophets was at last brought down by the power of the Father in Jesus the Christ.

The Petrine letters fill out the Christological grammar of James with exceedingly rich detail, making explicit what was implied there. In 1 Peter, God is "the Father of our Lord Jesus Christ" (1:3) who sent him into the world as both atoning sacrifice (1:2, 18-21; 2:22-25; 3:18) and exemplar of faith (2:13, 21; 3:13-18; 4:1, 13-16). In his work and witness on God's behalf,

---

10. E.g., F. Mussner, *Der Jakobusbrief* (Freiburg: Herder, 1964), pp. 250-54; R. Bauckham, "James and Jesus," in *The Brother of Jesus: James the Just and His Mission*, ed. B. Chilton and J. Neusner (Louisville: Westminster John Knox, 2001), pp. 131-35.

Jesus shepherds God's people (2:25; 5:4), guarding their souls (1:5; 2:25) through the hope of the resurrection (1:3, 21) until their salvation is complete (1:7-9, 13). This work and witness is focused most particularly in his role as God's Suffering Servant (2:21-25) whose costly obedience liberates suffering believers, enabling them to abandon their pagan citizenship to become God's resident aliens, living according to the cultural habits and mores of their future heavenly home (1:3-9; 5:13-14). This transfer of hope (1:3, 13), the effect of their "new birth," is brought about by the power of "the living and abiding word of God" (1:23) preached by the apostles of the Lord (1:25).

2 Peter in turn expands the Christological vision further, widening the lens beyond Jesus' past suffering death to include the earthly revelation of his power and glory in the Transfiguration (2 Pet. 1:16-18), his *present* role as the Master (2:1) who provides empowering knowledge of salvation (1:3-11; 2:20; 3:18), and his *future* advent as Lord and Judge of creation (3:10-14). As in 1 Peter so also here it is emphasized that this salvation is mediated to believers through the word of Christ's apostles (1:16-18), who proclaimed this good news in the past and established the epistolary means by which future believers would be continually reminded of their saving proclamation (1:12-15). Those who attend to this apostolic word are protected against the ignorant and unstable who would lead them astray (3:15-18).

The Johannine epistles extend the Christological claims of the previous three letters. As in James, so also here: Jesus is "the righteous one" (Jas. 5:6; 1 John 2:1). As in 1 Peter, so also here: Jesus is the atoning "expiation *(hilasmōs)* for our sins" (1 Pet. 3:18; 1 John 2:2) even though "he committed no sin" (1 Pet. 2:22; 1 John 3:5). As in 2 Peter, so also here: the "word of life" (1:1-2) has come in the flesh and is witnessed to (1:1), proclaimed (1:3), and first witnessed then written about (1:4; 2:13; 5:13) by the Lord's apostles. Right apprehension of this apostolic word is necessary to know the truth about God: since "no one has ever seen God" (4:12, 20), anyone who denies the witness of those who encountered him in the flesh will inevitably end up in epistemological error, while those who receive the apostolic witness will be properly informed in order to live their lives rightly before God. In fact, those who do not abide in this apostolic "doctrine about Christ" do not have God (2 John 9). Those who do remain in the tradition will be vindicated by the Lord when he "comes" again (1 John 2:28) on judgment day (4:17) to destroy the works of the devil (3:8) and vindicate those whose righteous lives evidence their right faith in Jesus (2:28-29; 5:4-5; cf. 2 Pet. 3:1-7).

The letter of Jude rounds out the collection's Christology with a resounding emphasis on Christ as Master and Lord of creation before whom all owe obedience (v. 4). Jude's concluding emphasis repeats the collection's insistence on right action and the need to protect the apostolic tradition to ensure right teaching about Christ as Lord. Jude forms an inclusio for the CE collection on this same theme by speaking of Jesus in the same voice as that of his brother James: because the Christ is the word sent forth by the Creator, each of them blurs Christ and Creator under the title "Lord" (vv. 4, 5, 9, 14, 17, 21, 25; e.g., Jas. 5:4, 7, 8, 10, 11, 14, 15).

3. THE COMMUNITY OF THE SPIRIT Forms Loving Fellowship with God by Following God's Word

James puts into play the collection's principal conception of the church as a Diaspora community, constituted by a poor and powerless membership, who, though tested by many trials (1:2), wisely befriend God rather than the world. God has chosen them to be rich in faith (2:5) and recipients of future blessings promised to those who demonstrably love God (1:12). The community's steady faith, when proved by spiritual testing, is formed and guided by its humble reception of God's "word of truth" (1:21), which is instantiated by various prophetic exemplars, especially the Lord Jesus Christ (2:1). This word provides the compass that guides the community's covenant-keeping practices apropos of friendship with God (2:23; 1:22-27; cf. 4:4). This same compass directs the community's mission to rescue lapsed believers who have departed from God's word and whose future with God is thereby imperiled (5:19-20).

But a "world" of hostile forces resides within individuals (1:13-15; 3:7, 14-16; 4:1-5) and surrounds this powerless community (4:4; 2:2-4, 6-7; 5:1-6) generating difficult tests of faith in God's word (1:2-8). The community's covenant with God is maintained only by a firm rejection of these worldly forces, evinced by its care of needy members (1:22–2:26), by the members' edifying speech toward each other (3:1-18), and by their steady pursuit of spiritual wisdom rather than material possessions (4:1–5:6).

Although the Spirit goes unmentioned in James, the reader's intuition, honed by, for example, a prior reading of the Pauline contrast between "flesh" and "Spirit," will readily recognize similar contrasts in James between, for instance, earthly and heavenly wisdom (3:13-18) and the two rival mindsets (4:4-10). In the first, the reader's intuition may suppose that heavenly wisdom is actually a "word of truth" (1:18) carried by God's Spirit to form a fruitful community (3:17-18; cf. Gal. 5:21-23); in the second, this same Spirit may be insinuated on the purified community to help it resist envy and friendship with the world and draw near to God's Torah instead (4:4-12).

The opening of 1 Peter repeats and elaborates the community's address introduced by James, but in a more optimistic idiom: yes, the church is a Diaspora community (1:1), constituted by resident "aliens and exiles" (2:11; 1:1-2) who "suffer various trials" (1:6) at the hands of a hostile public (4:4, 12-17). But this same community is "sanctified by the Spirit for obedience to Jesus Christ" (1:2) so that the believers may prove their allegiance to a holy God and so secure the salvation of their souls (1:6-9; 4:14).

The community's faith and moral purity are also conceived and formed by attentiveness to God's word (1:23). But 1 Peter elaborates this foundational conception by rooting it in two antecedent stories: first is the story of OT Israel, in which Spirit-led prophets witness the community's participation in election, exodus, and exile (1:12; 2:4-10). The second story plots the Messiah Jesus' footsteps in which the community now treads (2:21) and by whom it now experiences God's promised salvation (3:18-22). The community's suffering, then, is a public marker of its partnership with Christ in the salvation of the world. The hostile world that marginalizes and ridicules this community does so because it is ignorant of God's word and so of the destiny of God's people.

2 Peter repeats 1 Peter's exhortation that the community obey God's word so that God may rescue its members from their trials (2:9) and confirm their election and calling (1:10). Yet 2 Peter understands these trials less in terms of the community's marginal status in the world (as in James and 1 Peter) and rather locates the crisis within the community, where teachers are denying the truth of the apostolic word. In principle, God's word, whether in biblical prophecy (1:20; cf. 1 Pet. 1:10-12) or in apostolic pronouncement (1:16-19), is received and understood in the company of the Holy Spirit (1:21). To deny this word is to deny the powerful impress of God's Spirit in guiding the community's formation and, indeed, its destiny with God forever.

The "trial" faced by 2 Peter, then, is more epistemic: rival claims to truth confuse believers, resulting in their disaffection from the faith (2:1-

3). This theological crisis is also of a piece with the biblical story of unfaithful Israel, which ends in divine judgment rather than promised blessing (2:4-22).

Not only does 2 Peter understand God's word as constitutive of the apostolic tradition, 1 John continues to develop this foundation. As with 2 Peter, the crisis facing 1 John is the community's epistemic confusion stemming from a rival interpretation that subverts the "word of life" received from the apostles (1:1-2). 1 John elaborates the dangers of accepting a non-apostolic version of truth by calling it a lie, a deception, a falsehood, the effect of which is to subvert fellowship with God and among believers. In particular, without a definitive apostolic witness of Jesus that only eyewitnesses can provide, there is no effective remedy for sin and no example of the Christian practice of loving one another.

Again, as with 2 Peter, God's Spirit is given to the community (3:24) to lead its members to distinguish error and truth, false prophets and those whose teaching agrees with the apostles (4:1-6). The members of a community who embrace the truth (2:12-28) and experience new birth (2:29–3:1) purify themselves of sin to practice not sinning (3:3-10). The transformation of moral life and formation of a confident faith herald God's victory over sin and death (2:28; 5:1-5).

The community's characteristic moral practice is self-sacrificial, active love between members who share the same gospel truth (3:11-23; 4:7-21). 2 John, which epitomizes 1 John, applies this moral practice to the community's hospitable treatment of its itinerant missionaries. 3 John glosses this moral norm by warning how easily this practice can devolve into a power struggle between rival leaders more interested in self-love than in practicing selfless love for other believers. Faithful leaders are necessary to govern the community in a way that facilitates the teaching of truth consistent with the apostolic witness and the practice of selfless love for other believers, especially those who depend on the community's support for the ministry of the gospel.

Jude concludes by sounding notes that nicely summarize the collection's witness to the church. The church is "beloved in God" (vv. 1-2), so God's Spirit keeps its company (vv. 19-20). Its membership is marked out as those who adhere to the "most holy faith" (v. 20), "delivered to the saints" (v. 3), and practice love as God loves (vv. 22-23), prays as the Spirit leads (v. 20), and rescues wayward believers to keep them from falling in expectation of a future in God's glorious presence (v. 24; cf. Jas. 5:19-20).

4. CHRISTIAN DISCIPLES Follow God's Word When Responding to Various Trials, Thus Purifying Themselves of Sin and Proving Their Love for God

The members of James's church "in the Diaspora" (1:1) encounter various trials. Their faithful response to God's work forms the steadfast character (1:2-4) that will obtain "the crown of life which God has promised to those who love him" (1:12). Such a response requires humble reception of (1:21) and obedience to the "word of truth" (1:18). This word sets out those practices of "pure and undefiled" behavior (1:26-27) that witness to the believers' friendship with God (2:23).

While there are rich and powerful outsiders who undermine the community's trust in God (2:1-7; 5:1-6), the primary trial is a "spirit of envy" (4:5) that seduces believers, inclining their hearts away from friendship with God toward an impure and adulterous friendship with the world (4:4). That path of "passion for pleasure" (4:1-2) leads to sin, "and sin when it is full-grown brings forth death" (1:15). Only "the wisdom from above" (3:17) will enable the community to resist the deceptions of life in a foreign land. James calls disciples to a set of key purity practices. Principally, they must inhabit the faith of their Lord Jesus (2:1), extending hospitality to their needy neighbors in accordance with God's "perfect law of liberty" (1:27; 2:1-17). Such a practice replaces the world's preoccupation with material goods with a heartfelt devotion to God (4:1–5:6; cf. 1 John 2:15-17). Pure speech is a corollary with this aim insofar as it edifies the community and strengthens its solidarity (1:26; 3:1-12; 5:12-17). Disciples must also demonstrate a commitment to rescuing wayward believers from theological and moral error, both to preserve doctrinal purity and to ensure their end-time salvation (5:19-20). All this is enabled by an unbending commitment to the practice of patiently attending to the word of God, a long obedience of abiding that requires disciples both to hear the word plainly and to embody its teaching in a wise and righteous life (1:22-25).

1 Peter elaborates James's conception of Christian discipleship by shifting the focus to a different social setting. Where James calls believers (especially their leaders) in the Diaspora to keep their eyes on the poor who suffer in their midst, 1 Peter sounds this same exhortation from the perspective of the poor, scattered sufferers themselves. Once again Christ Jesus is the model of faith (Jas. 2:1), but here it is his example of righteous suffering that is to be emulated (1 Pet. 2:21). The question is not whether believers will suf-

fer, but how they will respond to the suffering they should expect as God's alien people in the Diaspora. The only right response is to maintain steadfast obedience to God's will (1:13-17; 3:17) despite the opposition of their cultural milieu. As in James, so also in 1 Peter: obedience to God's word is instantiated by purity practices (Jas. 3:17; 1 Pet. 3:2; cf. Jas. 1:27 and 1 Pet. 2:2), in which believers imitate their Lord (1:18-19). These practices are focused on loving and hospitable relations with each other (1:22; 2:1-2; 4:8-10; 5:5) and with outsiders (2:12; 3:15-16) both within pagan social institutions (2:13-17) and extended families (2:18-20; 3:1-6). If Christians are to be known for anything, it is for their "good conduct" (1:14-17; 2:12; 3:1-2, 16). As in James so also in 1 Peter we find a particular emphasis on pure speech as a requirement for anyone who wants to "inherit a blessing" from the Lord (3:9-12, 15-16; 4:11). As in James so also in 1 Peter the word of God is set forward as the means by which this new life is both attained (1:23-25) and sustained (2:2; 3:9-12) as the believers grow into salvation.

One of 1 Peter's key contributions is its emphasis on "hope" in the future apocalypse of God's salvation, which has already been disclosed proleptically in the Lord's resurrection. The exiles' hope for their unfading inheritance is secured by the apostolic witness of the risen one, and it empowers the letter's practical theology (1:3, 13, 21; 3:5, 15). Herein we find the central link to 2 Peter: the false teachers condemned there embody an impure ethics precisely because they deny the Lord's parousia as a "cleverly devised myth" (1:16). They are thus able to deviate from the "way of righteousness" (2:21), resting content in a knowledge of faith without the accompanying virtues that enable participation in the divine nature (1:3-8) and ensure a warm reception "into the eternal kingdom of our Lord and Savior Jesus Christ" (1:11). Replacing virtue with "freedom" (2:19), these teachers practice a fideism of "knowledge" (1:2, 3, 5, 6, 8; 2:20; 3:17) that results in a life of poor conduct (2:7, 18) — precisely the opposite of that called for in 1 Peter (3:1, 11). Against this, 2 Peter insists that it is in fact not knowledge of God but "godliness" (1:3, 6, 7, 3:11) that will deliver those who have it at the end of time. Indeed, "the Lord knows how to rescue the godly from trial" (2:9); had the false teachers attended rightly to the word of God (2:4-10a, 15-16; 3:5-10) as it was handed on to them from the apostles (1:12-21; 3:1-2, 15-18) they would not have fallen into such error.

Turning to the Johannine witness, readers encounter Christians who have not only fallen into error (as in 2 Peter) but broken off their membership with the apostolic community — and with catastrophic results. The prior epistles have already sternly warned readers about the staining defilements of the world (Jas. 1:27; 4:4; 2 Pet. 1:4; 2:20); this same warning is sounded by 1 John (2:15-16; 5:19) against a backdrop of these ex-members who now show themselves to be "of the world" (4:1-6; 2 John 7). Not to take anyone's profession of fidelity, spiritual tests are given that discriminate who is of God and who is of the world (e.g. 1:6-10; 2:3-6, 9-11; 3:24; 4:2-3, 9-20). Those who are born of God (2:29; 3:9; 4:7; 5:1) demonstrate it by their right confession (2:22-23; 3:23; 4:1-3, 14; 5:1) and right action. Those who are not of the world do not sin (2:1, 29; 3:4-10; 5:18) but rather imitate God's love (2:15; 3:1, 14-18; 4:7-21) and walk in God's light/truth (1:5-7; 2:9-10). This combination of love and truth is especially owned in the practice of hospitality toward those who love the truth (1 John 3:17-20a; 2 John 9-11; 3 John 5-8; cf. Jas. 2:14-17; 1 Pet. 1:22; 4:9-11; Jude 22-23). As before, one maintains this proper state of abiding in God by abiding in the word (2:14), keeping the commandments heard "from the beginning" (2:7, 24; 3:11; 2 John 5-6) from the apostolic leaders (1:1-4; 2:12-14).

Jude rounds off the collection's witness to Christian discipleship as we would expect: the only thing for believers to do in the face of such divisive conflict (v. 19) is to build themselves up in the content and practices of their most holy Trinitarian faith (vv. 20-21). While their opponents deny the apostolic witness to Christ's lordship and use faith as a cover for the pursuit of lustful desires (vv. 7-8, 12, 16), licentious ungodliness (vv. 4, 15, 18), and inappropriate speech (vv. 9-10, 16), believers "contend for the faith" they received (v. 3). They pray under the inspiration and guidance of the Holy Spirit (v. 20). They keep their appointed place in the love of God (vv. 1, 21, 24) as it is clearly revealed in the testimony of Scripture (vv. 5-7, 9, 11, 14-15) and avoid emulating the many counterexamples of discipleship found there of those who refused God's word and wandered away, multiplying sin instead of mercy, peace, and love (v. 2).

Disciples are to orient their words and deeds now according to the inherited apostolic hope (vv. 3, 17) they have been called to remember (vv. 5, 17), that one day the Lord Jesus will come again to extend mercy to his obedient servants and bring judgment to those who turn that mercy into a license for ungodly living (vv. 14-15). As they await this end they uphold the call first set forth by Jude's brother James (Jas. 5:19-20), extending the hope of restoration to those who dispute the faith instead of keeping it (Jude 22-23). Of course, while expressing loving concern for the wayward they must carefully avoid being led astray by their ungodly practices (vv. 22-23) —

but even in the face of this danger they can act in confident faith, knowing that their ongoing faithfulness to God is not simply a matter of their own strenuous efforts (vv. 24-25). They must prove their love for God, of course, but in the end it is God who will prove God's love for them by keeping them safe in the salvation they seek.

5. THE CONSUMMATION of God's Promised Salvation at Christ's Coming Will Restore God's Creation, Reveal God's Victory over Death, and Reward the Community's Obedience to God's Word

According to James, the community's future participation in the revelation of God's salvation will exchange present suffering (1:2) for a "crown of life" that lacks in nothing (1:4, 12). Present choices, especially when occasioned by trials of various kinds, have future consequences that will be revealed at the Lord's coming. On the one hand, God will vindicate those who demonstrate their love for God by the humble reception and steady obedience of "the word of truth" (1:21-27; 5:7-11). On the other hand, God will judge without mercy those who disobey God's word/law and befriend the world instead (2:12-13; 4:4-5, 11-12; 5:4-6). Because God's end-time judgment is imminent (5:7-9), the time for repentance is urgent and immediate (5:19-20).

This core belief is amplified by 1 Peter, which clarifies that the community's present suffering should be expected by its faithful members, who are resident aliens and exiles in a world that is passing away (1:1-7; 2:11-12; cf. Jas. 1:1-4). Their struggle is not internal within the soul and between members as in James, but external with a hostile social world that marginalizes the community (4:12; 5:9) and publicly ridicules its faith in God (2:12; 3:14-17; 4:4). More positively than James allows (so 1 Pet. 5:12), 1 Peter describes the salutary effect of these trials in producing and honing a "genuine faith" (1:6-9; cf. Jas. 1:2-3), birthed in the reception of God's word (1:23; cf. Jas. 1:18) and baptized into "a living hope" (1:3, 21; 3:15). This "living hope" targets a future inheritance that awaits the community's heavenly homecoming (1:4-5) at the Lord's revelation (1:7, 13; 4:13; 5:4). And it is for this inheritance that the community rescues the wandering saint from a multitude of sins (Jas. 5:19-20; cf. 1 Pet. 4:8).

The community's hope that enables it to regard its suffering joyfully (1 Pet. 1:6; cf. Jas. 1:2) has two foci. First, the past resurrection of the Suffering Servant discloses the triumph of his steadfast obedience to God (1:3;

3:18). Second, his future return will disclose on earth God's final triumph over the hostile forces that continue to provoke the suffering of God's holy children. The triumph of the risen Messiah, already revealed in the empty tomb, prefigures the inevitable vindication of those faithful to him — a future revelation when the faithful Creator will restore all things to their pristine order (4:19) and so satisfy the "living hope" of a suffering community. In this sense, 1 Peter cultivates trust in a God whose best is yet to come.

2 Peter completes the Petrine witness, especially its eschatology, by rooting it in an apostolic tradition that has a direct line-of-sight to the Messiah (2 Pet. 1:16-18; cf. 1 Pet. 5:1). Significantly, then, the beginning point for 2 Peter's contribution to Petrine eschatology is the transfiguration of Jesus, witnessed by the apostle, which confirms the "power and parousia of our Lord Jesus Christ" (1:16-17). This appeal to the Petrine apostolate secures the epistle's principal argument against those false teachers who scoff at the community's "living hope" in the Lord's coming (3:3-4), who suppose that it is just a clever fiction (1:16) rather than a delayed reality (3:8-13) and so believe that God is incapable of either creation's destruction or its new beginning (3:3-4). On this basis the scoffers act with impunity as though there is no end-time accounting of works done or not done (3:2; cf. 2:21; Jas. 2:12-13). By ignoring the word of God, they imperil their eternal destiny (3:5; cf. Jas. 1:18).

Against this backdrop of internal conflict, 2 Peter completes 1 Peter's vision of the future with a vivid description of a faithful Creator's final victory. The formative impress of this revelation of divine judgment, when justice is dispensed according to the performance of faith and not mere profession (cf. Jas. 2:14-26 as an expansion of 2:12-13), is made even more precise by 2 Peter: "the day of the Lord" (3:10) will bring a fiery purification of all things, both human (2:1; 3:7) and material (3:7, 10-12), followed by "the day of eternity" (3:18) which will bring a more complete restoration of all things, both human (3:11) and material (3:13). The suffering community's baptism into a "living hope" is finally for a newly restored creation in which holiness is no longer alien but feels right at home (3:11-13).

The link between 2 Peter and 1 John within the collection continues in their conception of God's future triumph, especially as it relates to so-called "false prophets" (1 John 4:1; cf. 2 Pet. 2:1). The arrival of "antichrists" who are "in/from the world" (1 John 4:1-6) signals an indeterminate "last hour" (2:18), which is the time of the community's final examination. Since the presence of these false teachers within the community has provoked an epistemic crisis, the test of faith is whether the apostolic witness of Jesus is believed rather than foolishly replaced by an inferior rival (2:22-25; cf. 2 Pet. 2:1-3). The test results will be posted at the Lord's coming (1 John 2:28), which is a "day of judgment" (2:17a, 28; 3:19-21; 4:17-18) when those who fail the test will be "shamed" (2:28) and "condemned" (3:21) and those who remain in the truth and pass it will given their "full reward" (2 John 8).

This conception of eschatological reward expands the readers' understanding of the community's end-time vindication. Their reward is not merely "eternal life," which is already experienced by those "born" of God who now abide in God (2:29; 3:9; 4:7; 5:1, 4, 18). 2 John epitomizes 1 John's original claim by saying that a reward is in the offing that believers "work for" — a wage *(misthos)* that is earned but that can also be lost by rejecting the apostolic "teaching about Christ" (2 John 8-9).

This idea of reward glosses 1 Peter's "living hope" of a heavenly inheritance (1 Pet. 1:3-4). The inheritance, which is the gift of a loving God (1 John 4:17), is embellished to include this "reward" granted by God to those who persevere through their trials by obeying God's apostolic word (1 Pet. 1:25); it is an element of the "salvation of souls" (1:9) that cannot therefore be detached from the community's confession or moral practices. Salvation is a covenant-keeping matter of faith in "the faith" and also of moral performances in agreement with the apostolic teaching about Christ. Because the community knows the truth, it is "confident" in its hope of future vindication (1 John 2:28; 4:17); further, it will avoid God's judgment because of its present experience of God's love and the believers' love for each other.

Finally, in both these key passages is found the idea of Christlikeness. The future of sin is finally captured by the hope that God's children "will be just like him, because we will see him just as he is" (1 John 3:2). Indeed, this hope motivates the present act of self-purification (3:3) when the believer becomes "pure just as (Jesus) is pure" (3:3).

Jude culminates the collection by encouraging the community to participate with the Creator by "building up" its members in "the holy faith" (v. 20; cf. v. 3) delivered by the apostles (v. 17). In doing so, the community "keeps" its members from falling into end-time judgment, the destiny of those who deny the faith (vv. 4, 7, 13, 15) and fail to learn from the examples of condemnation written about long ago in God's word (v. 4). Their sin is a participation in a distorted, unproductive, and broken creation (vv. 12-13) that divides God's people (v. 19) instead of multiplying the mercy, peace, and love (v. 2) characteristic of those who keep themselves in the love of God.

These latter are believers who know they reside as aliens and exiles in the Diaspora. They refuse to be friends with the world. Therefore they suffer trials as they wait for the revelation of eternal life (v. 21) in merciful and hospitable hope (vv. 22-23), purifying themselves as their Lord is pure, and entrusting themselves to a faithful Creator, knowing that their loving God is able to keep them from falling and, one day, to welcome them into a new heavens and a new earth where righteousness is at home.

A Brief Epilogue

This is a book of introductions written to help readers engage an important but neglected collection of sacred writings, the NT's "Catholic Epistles." At the same time, we have also attempted to introduce and illustrate an approach to these epistles, both individually and collectively, that takes seriously the semiotics of the collection's sevenfold aesthetic as well as those interpretive cues mined from the historical phenomenon of its canonization as an interpenetrating whole greater than the sum of its seven diverse parts.

In working out our approach to the shaping and final shape of a canonical collection, we drink from a well we did not dig and snip fruit from a vine we did not plant. And no one has nourished our thinking more so than Brevard Childs, with whom we share, for instance, a more dynamic conception of a canon of sacred texts that supplies an important (but surely not the only) context for the study of Scripture. That is, rather than attempting to reconstruct the social world of the biblical authors to determine what first readers must have understood by what was written to them, then to establish this past meaning as the present norm, the angle of our interpretive approach to the CE is inclined toward a later historical moment, when these seven epistles, however and whenever composed, were collected together, fixed purposefully into a final sequence, and then recognized as a completed whole and received as such as a strategic member of the church's biblical canon. In this sense the social world of canonization (rather than composition) is soil into which canonical collections are earthed to guide future generations of faithful readers. While biblical texts surely come to us with the particular social worlds of their authors

273

and first audiences, these same occasional texts were received by subsequent audiences "in the fullness of time" as biblical texts, reshaped and resized by the social world of the canonical process for use by subsequent generations of Christians as witness to the word of the Lord God Almighty.

Without paying much attention to the phenomenology of collection-building as a crucial feature in the shaping and shape of the biblical canon, Childs argues that Scripture's final literary form stipulates a critical context, which supplies a sacred place where faithful readers go to find trusted guides for the church's quest for theological understanding. This is not to exclude other readings of this same biblical canon, predicated by different convictions about its ontology and aimed at different interpretive ends. But the very idea of a single biblical canon — one book formed by the church in order to form one church — commends not only the importance of Scripture as a sacred place where God's word is heard, but privileges the importance of those interpretive practices that enable this word to be proclaimed, practiced, and paraded faithfully among God's people.

Toward this end, we have argued that a canonical collection, framed by the history of its formation and the aesthetics of its final form, envisages a particular internal logic that orders its effective and ongoing articulation of God's word; every canonical collection is in this sense "hermeneutical." Moreover, the placement of a collection within the whole biblical canon is highly suggestive of ways that readers can relate these collections together to fashion mutually glossing dialogues. Although Childs nowhere imagines how the corpora of Pauline and Catholic epistles are partners in such a conversation (with Acts serving as the canonical moderator), we have attempted to show how such a conversation was purposed from the very beginning. When the CE collection was formed into its final shape, the church already had started to build a NT canon that included a thirteen-letter Pauline deposit, by the end of the second century. Teachers had already begun to use this canon to catechize the church into the Christian faith. At least in part, then, it is with this experience in mind, perhaps to check-and-balance the church's myopic appeal to Paul to secure non-apostolic versions of the gospel, that the CE collection was added to the church's emergent biblical canon. We argue that the CE collection continues to perform this same role today, especially suitable for those communities who subscribe to a Pauline canon within the canon.

One example of this dynamic dialectic between the NT's letter collections must suffice, even if a fuller study is required to examine and apply this interpretive model to every theological agreement of the apostolic Rule of Faith. At the center of the church's traditional proclamation of the "mystery of faith," recited as part of the eucharistic liturgy, is the Christological affirmation "Christ has died, Christ has risen, Christ will come again." But this affirmation is indebted to Paul's apocalyptic Christology (cf. 1 Tim. 3:16). While the sources of Pauline Christology remain contested, it is surely not grounded in the apostle's witness of the historical Jesus, but rather in his vision of the risen Jesus and the personal transformation he experienced as a result. The tendency of a Pauline account of the church's "mystery of faith" is to detach the material goods of the historical Jesus (e.g., his teaching and moral example) from the Christ of faith, which reduces the content of the Christian gospel and apocalypse of God's salvation to the Lord's passion and parousia — as though the four-fold Gospel's narrative of the Messiah's life does not matter. The practical effect of this Pauline reductionism, evinced throughout the church's history, is to displace the ethics of a holy life, examined and exemplified by Jesus, for glib professions of saving faith.

In response, the Christological agreement of the CE collection (see above), deeply rooted in the apostolic eyewitness of the historical Jesus, concentrates the reader on his faithful life — what was seen and heard of the incarnate Word. That is, without setting aside his messianic death, resurrection, and return, Jesus' lordship is also evinced in his ministry among the poor (James), his costly service to God (1 and 2 Peter), and his self-sacrificial love (1-3 John). The result of this orienting concern is to supply a messianic model of Godlikeness that the church is called to imitate. In this sense, then, the addition of the CE collection to Paul expands the church's understanding of the "mystery of faith" to include the saving life of Christ: "*Christ has lived*, Christ has died, Christ has risen, Christ will come again."

Another feature of our introductions to each epistle is the critical distinction we make between the historical and canonical persons (or "Pillars") of the apostolic tradition. While also pointing out recent reconstructions of the "real" apostles as interpretive cues to their particular witnesses of God's word, we recognize that the canonical profiles of the implied authors of the CE are later, theologically-invested constructions. Even though deeply rooted in the church's memory, traditions of the apostles as witnesses and exemplars (found especially in Acts but also in other early Christian writings) provide readers with a range of interpretive prompts for reading the CE. In distancing ourselves from modern criticism's claims about the authorship of these writings (and generally about theories of their composition and "authenticity"), we have attempted to reposition the "truth question," as Childs calls it, to the sacred writings themselves, framed by the church's reception of them as inspiring carriers of God's word.

Finally, we have taken seriously the final sequence of the CE as suggestive of the collection's deep logic that facilitates a theological reading of its different parts as the bits and pieces of a greater whole. The theological reflections of this final chapter, indexed by the theological agreements of the apostolic Rule of Faith, intend to help readers catch glimpses of this "greater whole." The prior chapters, which provide introductions to and commentary on each CE in turn, intend to help readers understand the decisive contribution each makes to the greater whole. We understand that the stark diversity found among the CE presents a challenge somewhat different than that facing the interpreter of the Pauline canon. But rather than supposing this diversity confers an independence one from the other, our study of this canonical collection demonstrates Karl Popper's notion of a "mutual criticism" that different voices enter and participate in to complement the others and enrich the whole. We pray that our study of the CE collection will encourage such a holy practice in order to form a holy people for the worship of and service to our holy God.

Bibliography

Select Modern Commentaries

The Catholic Epistles

Chester, A., and R. P. Martin. *The Theology of the Letters of James, Peter, and Jude.* Cambridge: Cambridge University Press, 1994.

Donelson, L. *From Hebrews to Revelation.* Louisville: Westminster John Knox, 2001.

Guthrie, D. *New Testament Introduction: Hebrews to Revelation.* London: Tyndale, 1964.

Jobes, K. H. *Letters to the Church: A Survey of Hebrews and the General Epistles.* Grand Rapids: Zondervan, 2011.

Krodel, G. *The General Letters: Hebrews, James, 1-2 Peter, Jude, 1-3 John.* Philadelphia: Fortress, 1995.

Lockett, D. *An Introduction to the Catholic Epistles.* New York: Clark, 2012.

Moffatt, J. *The General Epistles of James, Peter and Jude.* MNTC. London: Hodder & Stoughton, 1928.

Perkins, P. *First and Second Peter, James, and Jude.* Interpretation. Louisville: John Knox, 1995.

Reicke, B. *The Epistles of James, Peter, and Jude.* AB 37. New York: Doubleday, 1964.

Sidebottom, E. M. *James, Jude and 2 Peter.* CBC. London: Nelson, 1967.

Wilder, T. L., J. D. Charles, and K. Easley. *Faithful to the End: An Introduction to Hebrews through Revelation.* Nashville: Broadman and Holman, 2007.

Young, F. "The Non-Pauline Letters." *The Cambridge Companion to Biblical Interpretation,* ed. John Barton. Cambridge: Cambridge University Press, 1998, pp. 290-304.

James

Adamson, J. B. *The Epistle of James.* NICNT. Grand Rapids: Eerdmans, 1976.
————. *James: The Man and His Message.* Grand Rapids: Eerdmans, 1989.
Bauckham, R. *James: Wisdom of James, Disciple of Jesus the Sage.* London: Routledge, 1999.
Blackman, E. C. *The Epistle of James.* London: SCM, 1957.
Brosend, W. F. *James and Jude.* CBC. Cambridge: Cambridge University Press, 2004.
Davids, P. H. *The Epistle of James.* NIGTC. Grand Rapids: Eerdmans, 1982.
Dibelius, M. *James.* Rev. ed. Ed. H. Greeven. Philadelphia: Fortress, 1976.
Hartin, P. J. *James.* SP 14. Collegeville: Liturgical, 2003.
Johnson, L. T. *The Letter of James.* AB 37A. New York: Doubleday, 1995.
Laws, S. *The Epistle of James.* BNTC. Peabody: Hendrickson, 1980.
Martin, R. P. *James.* WBC 48. Waco: Word, 1988.
Mayor, J. B. *The Epistle of St. James.* 2nd ed. London: Macmillan, 1897.
McKnight, S. *The Letter of James.* NICNT. Grand Rapids: Eerdmans, 2011.
Mitton, C. L. *The Epistle of James.* London: Marshall, Morgan & Scott, 1966.
Moo, D. J. *The Letter of James.* PNTC. Grand Rapids: Eerdmans, 2000.
Mussner, F. *Der Jakobusbrief.* Freiburg: Herder, 1964.
Ropes, J. *The Epistle of St. James.* ICC. Edinburgh: Clark, 1916.
Tasker, R. *The General Epistle of James.* London: Tyndale, 1956.
Townsend, M. J. *The Epistle of James.* London: Epworth, 1994.
Wall, R. W. *Community of the Wise: The Letter of James.* Valley Forge: Trinity, 1997.
Williams, R. R. *The Letters of John and James.* CBC. Cambridge: Cambridge University Press, 1965.

1 and 2 Peter and Jude

Achtemeier, P. *1 Peter.* HC. Philadelphia: Fortress, 1996.
Bauckham, R. *Jude, 2 Peter.* WBC 50. Waco: Word, 1983.
Beare, F. W. *The First Epistle of Peter.* Oxford: Blackwell, 1961.
Best, E. *1 Peter.* NCBC. Grand Rapids: Eerdmans, 1971.
Bigg, C. *The Epistles of St. Peter and St. Jude.* ICC. Edinburgh: Clark, 1901.
Cranfield, C. E. B. *The First Epistle of Peter.* London: SCM, 1954.
Davids, P. H. *The First Epistle of Peter.* NICNT. Grand Rapids: Eerdmans, 1990.
————. *The Letters of 2 Peter and Jude.* PNTC. Grand Rapids: Eerdmans, 2006.
Donelson, L. *I & II Peter and Jude: A Commentary.* NTL. Louisville: Westminster John Knox, 2010.
Elliott, J. H. *1 Peter.* AB 37B. New York: Doubleday, 2000.

Feldmeier, P. *The First Letter of Peter: A Commentary on the Greek Text*. Waco: Baylor University Press, 2008.

Goppelt, L. *A Commentary on 1 Peter*. Ed. F. Hahn. Grand Rapids: Eerdmans, 1993.

Green, G. L. *Jude and 2 Peter*. BECNT. Grand Rapids: Baker, 2008.

Green, J. B. *1 Peter*. THNTC. Grand Rapids: Eerdmans, 2007.

Green, M. *The Second Epistle General of Peter and the General Epistle of Jude*. TNTC. Grand Rapids: Eerdmans, 1987.

Horrell, D. G. *The Epistles of Peter and Jude*. London: Epworth, 1998.

————. *1 Peter*. New York: Clark, 2008.

Jobes, K. H. *1 Peter*. BECNT. Grand Rapids: Baker, 2005.

Kelly, J. N. D. *A Commentary on the Epistles of Peter and Jude*. BNTC. London: Black, 1969.

Marshall, I. H. *1 Peter*. IVPNTC. Downers Grove: InterVarsity, 1991.

Michaels, J. R. *1 Peter*. WBC 49. Waco: Word, 1988.

Neyrey, J. H. *2 Peter, Jude: A New Translation with Introduction and Commentary*. AB 37C. New York: Doubleday, 1993.

Reese, R. A. *2 Peter and Jude*. THNTC. Grand Rapids: Eerdmans, 2007.

Richard, E. J. *Reading 1 Peter, Jude, and 2 Peter*. Macon: Smyth and Helwys, 2000.

Selwyn, E. G. *The First Epistle of St. Peter*. London: Macmillan, 1947.

Senior, D. P., and D. J. Harrington. *1 Peter, Jude and 2 Peter*. SP. Collegeville: Liturgical, 2008.

Watson, D. F. "The Second Letter of Peter." *NIB* 12. Nashville: Abingdon, 1998, pp. 321-61.

————. "The Letter of Jude." *NIB* 12. Nashville: Abingdon, 1998, pp. 471-500.

1-3 *John*

Black, C. C. "The First, Second, and Third Letters of John." *NIB* 12. Nashville: Abingdon, 1998, pp. 363-469.

Brooke, A. E. *A Critical and Exegetical Commentary on the Johannine Epistles*. ICC. London: Clark, 1912.

Brown, R. *The Epistles of John*. AB 30. New York: Doubleday, 1982.

Bultmann, R. *A Commentary on the Johannine Epistles*. HC. Philadelphia: Fortress, 1973.

Dodd, C. H. *The Johannine Epistles*. MNTC. London: Hodder and Stoughton, 1946.

Kruse, C. G. *The Letters of John*. PNTC. Grand Rapids: Eerdmans, 2000.

Lieu, J. M. *I, II, & III John*. NTL. Louisville: Westminster John Knox, 2008.

Marshall, I. H. *The Epistles of John*. NICNT. Grand Rapids: Eerdmans, 1978.

Painter, J. *1, 2, and 3 John*. SP 18. Collegeville: Liturgical, 2002.

Schnackenburg, R. *The Johannine Epistles: A Commentary.* Kent: Burns & Oates, 1992.

Smalley, S. *1, 2, 3 John.* WBC 51. Dallas: Word, 2002.

Smith, D. M. *First, Second, and Third John.* Interpretation. Louisville: John Knox, 1991.

Strecker, G. *The Johannine Letters.* HC. Minneapolis: Fortress, 1996.

Westcott, B. F. *Epistles of St. John: The Greek Text.* Reprint, Grand Rapids: Eerdmans, 1966.

Williams, R. R. *The Letters of John and James.* CBC. Cambridge: Cambridge University Press, 1965.

Yarbrough, R. W. *1-3 John.* BECNT. Grand Rapids: Baker, 2008.

Select Studies Related to the Catholic Epistles

Adam, A. K. M. *James: A Handbook on the Greek Text.* Waco: Baylor University Press, 2012.

Balch, D. L. *Let Wives Be Submissive: The Domestic Code in 1 Peter.* SBLMS 26. Atlanta: Scholars, 1981.

Barrett, C. K. "Paul and the 'Pillar' Apostles." In *Studia Paulina,* ed. J. N. Sevenster and W. C. van Unnik. Haarlem: Bohn, 1953, pp. 1-19.

Bauckham, R. "2 Peter: An Account of Research." *ANRW* 2.25.5. Berlin: de Gruyter, 1988, pp. 3713-52.

————. *Jude and the Relatives of Jesus in the Early Church.* Edinburgh: Clark, 1990.

————. "James and the Jerusalem Church." In *The Book of Acts in Its Palestinian Setting,* ed. R. Bauckham. Grand Rapids: Eerdmans, 1995, pp. 415-80.

————. "James and the Gentiles (Acts 15:13-21)." In *History, Literature, and Society in the Book of Acts,* ed. B. Witherington. Cambridge: Cambridge University Press, 1995, pp. 154-84.

————. "James and Jesus." In *The Brother of Jesus: James the Just and His Mission,* ed. B. Chilton and J. Neusner. Louisville: Westminster John Knox, 2001, pp. 100-137.

Bauer, W. "Aut maleficus aut alieni speculator (1 Petr 4,15)." *BZ* 22 (1978), pp. 109-15.

Boobyer, G. H. "The Indebtedness of 2 Peter to 1 Peter." In *New Testament Essays: Studies in Memory of T. W. Manson,* ed. A. Higgins. Manchester: Manchester University Press, 1959, pp. 34-53.

Bray, G. L., and T. Oden, eds. *James, 1-2 Peter, 1-3 John, Jude.* ACCS New Testament 11. Downers Grove: InterVarsity, 2000.

Brown, R. E., K. P. Donfried, and J. Reumann, eds. *Peter in the New Testament.* Minneapolis: Augsburg Fortress, 1973.

Chilton, B., and C. A. Evans, eds. *James the Just and Christian Origins.* Leiden: Brill, 1999.

Chilton, B., and J. Neusner, eds. *The Brother of Jesus: James the Just and His Mission.* Louisville: Westminster John Knox, 2001.

Cross, F. L. *I Peter: A Paschal Liturgy.* London: Mowbray, 1954.

Cullmann, O. *Peter: Apostle, Disciple, Martyr.* London: SCM, 1953.

Culy, M. *1, 2, 3 John: A Handbook on the Greek Text.* Waco: Baylor University Press, 2004.

Dalton, W. J. *Christ's Proclamation to the Spirits: A Study of 1 Peter 3:18–4:6.* AnBib 23. Rome: Pontifical Biblical Institute, 1989.

Danker, F. W. "1 Peter 1:24–2:17: A Consolatory Pericope." *ZNW* 58 (1967), pp. 93-102.

Davids, P. H. "The Epistle of James in Modern Discussion." *ANRW* 2.25.5. Berlin: de Gruyter, 1988, pp. 3621-45.

————. *II Peter and Jude: A Handbook on the Greek Text.* Waco: Baylor University Press, 2011.

Doering, L. "First Peter as Early Christian Diaspora Letter." In *The Catholic Epistles and Apostolic Tradition,* ed. K.-W. Niebuhr and R. W. Wall. Waco: Baylor University Press, 2009, pp. 215-38.

Dubis, M. "Research on 1 Peter: A Survey of Scholarly Literature Since 1985." *CBQ* 4 (2006), pp. 199-239.

————. *I Peter: A Handbook on the Greek Text.* Waco: Baylor University Press, 2010.

Edgar, D. H. *"Has God Not Chosen the Poor?" The Social Setting of the Epistle of James.* JSNTSS 206. Sheffield: Sheffield Academic, 2001.

Elliott, J. H. "The Rehabilitation of an Exegetical Step-Child: 1 Peter in Recent Research." *JBL* 95 (1976), pp. 243-54.

————. *A Home for the Homeless: A Sociological Exegesis of 1 Peter, Its Situation and Strategy.* Philadelphia: Fortress, 1981.

Farkasfalvy, D. M. "The Ecclesial Setting of Pseudepigraphy in Second Peter and Its Role in the Formation of the Canon." *SecCent* 5 (1985), pp. 3-29.

Farmer, W. R. "Some Critical Reflections on Second Peter: A Response to a Paper on Second Peter by Dennis Farkasfalvy." *SecCent* 5 (1985), pp. 30-46.

Francis, F. O. "The Form and Function of the Opening and Closing Paragraphs of James and 1 John." *ZNW* 61 (1970), pp. 110-26.

Francis, J. "'Like Newborn Babes' — The Image of the Child in 1 Peter 2:2-3." *StudBib* 3 (1978), pp. 111-17.

Green, G. L. "The Use of the Old Testament for Christian Ethics in 1 Peter." *TynB* 41 (1990), pp. 276-89.

Grünstäudl, W. *Petrus Alexandrinus. Studien zum historischen und theologischen Ort des Zweiten Petrusbriefes* (WUNT; Tübingen: Mohr, 2013).

Hartin, P. J. *James and the "Q" Sayings of Jesus.* JSNTSS 47. Sheffield: Sheffield Academic, 1991.

―――. *James of Jerusalem: Heir to Jesus of Nazareth.* Collegeville: Liturgical, 2004.

Hengel, M. *Saint Peter: The Underestimated Apostle.* Grand Rapids: Eerdmans, 2010.

Hiebert, D. E. "Designation of Readers in 1 Peter 1:1-2." *BibSac* 137 (1980), pp. 64-75.

Hills, J. "Little Children, Keep Yourselves from Idols: 1 John 5:21 Reconsidered." *CBQ* 51 (1989), pp. 285-310.

Jackson-McCabe, M. A. *Logos and Law in the Letter of James: The Law of Nature, the Law of Moses, and the Law of Freedom.* NovTSup 100. Leiden: Brill, 2001.

Johnson, L. T. *Brother of Jesus, Friend of God: Studies in the Letter of James.* Grand Rapids: Eerdmans, 2004.

Kubo, S. "Jude 22-23: Two-Division Form or Three?" In *New Testament Textual Criticism,* ed. E. J. Epp and G. D. Fee. Oxford: Clarendon, 1981, pp. 239-53.

Lapham, F. *Peter: The Myth, the Man and the Writings.* JSNTSS 239. Sheffield: Sheffield Academic, 2003.

Lieu, J. *The 2nd and 3rd Epistles of John: History and Background.* Edinburgh: Clark, 1986.

―――. *The Theology of the Johannine Epistles.* Cambridge: Cambridge University Press, 1991.

Lohse, E., "Parenesis and Kerygma in 1 Peter." In *Perspectives on First Peter,* ed. C. Talbert. Macon: Mercer University Press, 1986, pp. 37-59.

Love, J. P. "The First Epistle of Peter." *Interpretation* 8 (1954), pp. 63-87.

Lührmann, D. "Gal. 2:9 und die katholischen Briefe." *ZNW* 72 (1981), pp. 65-87.

Malherbe, A. "The Inhospitality of Diotrephes." In *God's Christ and His People,* ed. J. Jervell and W. Meeks. Oslo: Universitetsforlaget, 1977, pp. 222-32.

Martin, T. W. *Metaphor and Composition in 1 Peter.* SBLDS 131. Atlanta: Scholars, 1992.

McKnight, S. "A Parting within the Way: Jesus and James on Israel and Purity." In *James the Just and Christian Origins,* ed. B. Chilton and C. A. Evans. Leiden: Brill, 1999, pp. 83-129.

Neyrey, J. H. "The Form and Background of the Polemic in 2 Peter." *JBL* 99 (1980), pp. 407-31.

Niebuhr, K.-W. "Der Jakobusbrief im Licht frühjudischer Diasporabriefe." *NTS* 44 (1998), pp. 420-43.

―――. "A New Perspective on James? Neuere Forschungen zum Jakobusbrief." *TLZ* 129 (2004), pp. 1019-44.

―――. "James in the Minds of the Recipients." In *The Catholic Epistles and Apostolic Tradition,* ed. K.-W. Niebuhr and R. W. Wall. Waco: Baylor University Press, 2009, pp. 43-54.

Painter, J. *Just James: The Brother of Jesus in History and Tradition.* Edinburgh: Clark, 1999.

———. "The Johannine Epistles as Catholic Epistles." In *The Catholic Epistles and Apostolic Tradition,* ed. K.-W. Niebuhr and R. W. Wall. Waco: Baylor University Press, 2009, pp. 239-305.

Penner, T. C. *The Epistle of James and Eschatology: Re-Reading an Ancient Christian Letter.* JSNTSS 121. Sheffield: Sheffield Academic, 1996.

———. "The Epistle of James in Current Research." *CRBS* 7 (1999), pp. 257-308.

Perdelwitz, R. *Die Mysterienreligion und das Problem des I. Petrusbriefes. Ein literarischer und religionsgeschichtlicher Versuch.* RVV 11.3. Giessen: Töpelmann, 1911.

Picirelli, R. E. "The Meaning of 'Epignosis.'" *EvQ* 47 (1975), pp. 85-93.

Popkes, W. "James and Scripture: An Exercise in Intertextuality." *NTS* 45 (1999), pp. 213-29.

Schutter, W. L. *Hermeneutic and Composition in 1 Peter.* WUNT. Tübingen: Mohr, 1989.

Seitz, O. J. F. "Relationship of the Shepherd of Hermas to the Epistle of James." *JBL* 63 (1944), pp. 131-40.

Snodgrass, K. "1 Peter 2:1-10: Its Formation and Literary Affinities." *NTS* 24 (1977), pp. 97-106.

Soards, M. L. "1 Peter, 2 Peter, and Jude as Evidence for a Petrine School." *ANRW* 2.25.5. Berlin: de Gruyter, 1988, pp. 3827-49.

Spitaler, P. "Doubt or Dispute (Jude 9 and 22-23). Re-Reading a Special New Testament Meaning through the Lens of Internal Evidence." *Bib* 87 (2006), pp. 201-22.

Starr, J. M. *Sharers in the Divine Nature: 2 Peter 1:4 in Its Hellenistic Context.* CBNTS 33. Stockholm: Almquist & Wiksell, 2000.

Talbert, C. H., ed. *Perspectives on First Peter.* Macon: Mercer University Press, 1986.

———. "Once Again: The Plan of 1 Peter." In *Perspectives on First Peter,* ed. C. H. Talbert. Macon: Mercer, 1986, pp. 141-51.

Volf, M. "Soft Difference: Theological Reflections on the Relation between Church and Culture in 1 Peter." *ExAud* 10 (1994), pp. 15-30.

Wall, R. W. "Acts and James." In *The Catholic Epistles and Apostolic Tradition,* ed. K.-W. Niebuhr and R. W. Wall. Waco: Baylor University Press, 2009, pp. 127-52.

———. "The Priority of James." In *The Catholic Epistles and Apostolic Tradition,* ed. K.-W. Niebuhr and R. W. Wall. Waco: Baylor University Press, 2009, pp. 153-60.

Ward, R. "James of Jerusalem in the First Two Centuries." *ANRW* 2.26.1. Berlin: de Gruyter, 1988, pp. 779-812.

Watson, D. F. "James 2 in Light of Greco-Roman Schemes of Argumentation." *NTS* 39 (1993), pp. 94-121.

Webb, R. L. "Catholic Epistles." *ABD*, ed. D. N. Freedman. New York: Doubleday, 1992, 2:569-70.

Webb, R. L., and P. H. Davids, eds. *Reading Jude with New Eyes: Methodological Reassessments of the Letter of Jude.* London: Clark, 2008.

Webb, R. L., and J. S. Kloppenborg, eds. *Reading James with New Eyes: Methodological Reassessments of the Letter of James.* London: Clark, 2007.

Webb, R. L., and B. Martin-Bauman, eds. *Reading First Peter with New Eyes: Methodological Reassessments of the Letter of First Peter.* London: Clark, 2007.

Webb, R. L., and D. F. Watson, eds. *Reading Second Peter with New Eyes: Methodological Reassessments of the Letter of Second Peter.* London: Clark, 2010.

Winter, S. C. "Jude 22-23: A Note on the Text and Translation." *HTR* 87 (1994), pp. 215-22.

Yates, J. P. "The Reception of the Epistle of James in the Latin West: Did Athanasius Play a Role?" In *The Catholic Epistles and the Tradition,* ed. J. Schlosser. BETL 176. Leuven: Leuven University Press, 2004, pp. 273-88.

Select Studies in Text and Canon

Aland, K. *The Problem of the New Testament Canon.* London: Mowbray, 1962.

Barton, J. *Holy Writings, Sacred Text: The Canon in Early Christianity.* Louisville: Westminster John Knox, 1997.

Boring, M. E. "Interpreting 1 Peter as a Letter (Not) Written to Us." *QR* 13 (1993), pp. 89-111.

Brewer, J. A. "The History of the New Testament Canon in the Syrian Church II: The Acts of the Apostles and the Epistles." *AJT* 4 (1900), pp. 345-63.

Brooks, J. A. "The Place of James in the New Testament Canon." *SJT* 12 (1969), pp. 41-51.

———. "Clement of Alexandria as a Witness to the Development of the New Testament Canon." *SecCent* 9 (1992), pp. 41-51.

Bruce, F. F. *The Canon of Scripture.* Downers Grove: InterVarsity, 1988.

Campenhausen, H. von. *The Formation of the Christian Bible.* Philadelphia: Fortress, 1972.

Childs, B. S. *The New Testament as Canon: An Introduction.* Valley Forge: Trinity, 1985.

———. *The Church's Guide for Reading Paul: The Canonical Shaping of the Pauline Corpus.* Grand Rapids: Eerdmans, 2008.

Epp, E. J. "Issues in the Interrelation of New Testament Textual Criticism and

Canon." In *The Canon Debate,* ed. L. M. McDonald and J. A. Sanders. Peabody: Hendrickson, 2002, pp. 503-5.

Farmer, W. R., and D. M. Farkasfalvy. *The Formation of the New Testament Canon.* New York: Paulist, 1983.

Ferguson, E. "Factors Leading to the Selection and Closure of the New Testament Canon." In *The Canon Debate,* ed. L. M. McDonald and J. A. Sanders. Peabody: Hendrickson, 2002, pp. 295-320.

Gamble, H. *The New Testament Canon: Its Making and Meaning.* Philadelphia: Fortress, 1985.

————. "The New Testament Canon: Recent Research and the Status Quaestionis." In *The Canon Debate,* ed. L. M. McDonald and J. A. Sanders. Peabody: Hendrickson, 2002, pp. 267-94.

Gregory, A. *The Reception of Luke and Acts in the Period before Irenaeus: Looking for Luke in the Second Century.* Tübingen: Mohr, 2003.

Hahnemann, G. *The Muratorian Fragment and the Development of the Canon.* Oxford: Clarendon, 1992.

Harnack, A. von. *The Origin of the New Testament and the Most Important Consequences of the New Creation.* New York: Macmillan, 1925.

Hill, C. E. *The Johannine Corpus in the Early Church,* Oxford: Oxford University Press, 2004.

Kalin, E. "Re-Examining New Testament Canon History: 1) The Canon of Origen." *CurTM* 17 (1990), pp. 274-82.

————. "The New Testament Canon of Eusebius." In *The Canon Debate,* ed. L. M. McDonald and J. A. Sanders. Peabody: Hendrickson, 2002, pp. 386-404.

Kruger, M. J. *Canon Revisited: Establishing the Origins and Authority of the New Testament Books.* Wheaton: Crossway, 2012.

McDonald, L. M. *The Formation of the Christian Biblical Canon.* Rev. ed., Peabody: Hendrickson, 1995.

McDonald, L. M., and J. A. Sanders, eds. *The Canon Debate.* Peabody: Hendrickson, 2002.

Metzger, B. *The Early Versions of the New Testament.* Oxford: Clarendon, 1977.

————. *The Canon of the New Testament.* Oxford: Clarendon, 1987.

————. *The Text of the New Testament.* Oxford: Clarendon, 1992.

Moroziuk, R. P. "The Meaning of *katholikē* in the Greek Fathers and Its Implications for Ecclesiology and Ecumenism." *PBR* 4 (1985), pp. 90-104.

Niebuhr, K.-W., and R. W. Wall, eds. *The Catholic Epistles and Apostolic Tradition.* Waco: Baylor University Press, 2009.

Nienhuis, D. R. *Not by Paul Alone: The Formation of the Catholic Epistle Collection and the Christian Canon.* Waco: Baylor University Press, 2007.

————. "The Letter of James as a Canon-Conscious Pseudepigraph." In *The Cath-*

olic Epistles and Apostolic Tradition, ed. K.-W. Niebuhr and R. W. Wall. Waco: Baylor University Press, 2009, pp. 183-200.

Sanders, J. A. *Torah and Canon*. Philadelphia: Fortress, 1972.

————. "Adaptable for Life: the Nature and Function of Canon." In *Magnalia Dei — The Mighty Acts of God: Essays on the Bible and Archaeology in Memory of G. Ernest Wright*, ed. F. M. J. Cross, et al. Garden City: Doubleday, 1976, pp. 531-60.

————. "Torah and Paul." In *God's Christ and His People: Studies in Honour of Niles Alstrup Dahl*, ed. Jacob Jervel and Wayne A. Meeks. Oslo: Universitets forlaget, 1977, pp. 132-40.

————. *Canon and Community: A Guide to Canonical Criticism*. Philadelphia: Fortress, 1984.

Schlosser, J., ed. *The Catholic Epistles and the Tradition*. BETL 176. Leuven: Leuven University Press, 2004.

Seitz, C. "Canonical Approach." In *DTIB*, ed. K. J. VanHoozer. Grand Rapids: Baker, 2005, pp. 100-102.

Sheppard, G. T. "Canonical Criticism." *ABD*, ed. D. N. Freedman. New York: Doubleday, 1992, 1:861-66.

————. "Canon." In *Encyclopedia of Religion*, ed. M. Eliade. New York: Macmillan, 2005, 3:1405-11.

Siker, J. "The Canonical Status of the Catholic Epistles in the Syriac New Testament." *JTS* 38 (1987), pp. 311-40.

Smith, D. M. "When Did the Gospels First Become Scripture?" *JBL* 119 (2000), pp. 3-20.

Spina, F. "Canonical Criticism: Childs versus Sanders." In *Interpreting God's Word for Today: An Inquiry into Hermeneutics from a Biblical Theological Perspective*, ed. W. McCown and J. E. Massey. Anderson: Warner, 1982, pp. 165-94.

Sundberg, A. C. "Towards a Revised History of the New Testament Canon." *SE* 4 (= *TU* 102, 1968), pp. 452-61.

————. "The Making of the New Testament Canon." In *Interpreter's One Volume Commentary on the Bible*, ed. C. M. Laymon. London: Collins, 1971, pp. 1216-20.

————. "Canon Muratori: A Fourth-Century List." *HTR* 66 (1973), pp. 1-41.

Trobisch, D. *Paul's Letter Collection: Tracing the Origins*. Minneapolis: Fortress, 1994.

————. *Die Endredaktion des Neuen Testaments. Eine Untersuchung zur Entstehung Der Christlichen Bibel*. NTOA 31. Göttingen: Vandenhoeck & Ruprecht, 1996. Translated into English as *The First Edition of the New Testament*. Oxford: Oxford University Press, 2000.

————. "The Book of Acts as a Narrative Commentary on the Letters of the New Testament: A Programmatic Essay." In *Rethinking the Unity and Reception of*

Luke and Acts, ed. A. F. Gregory and C. K. Rowe. Columbia: University of South Carolina Press, 2010, pp. 119-27.

Wall, R. W. "The Acts of the Apostles in the Context of the New Testament Canon." *BTB* 18 (1988), pp. 15-23.

————. "The Problem of the Multiple Letter Canon of the New Testament." In *The New Testament as Canon: A Reader in Canonical Criticism,* ed. E. E. Lemcio and R. W. Wall. JSNTSS 76. Sheffield: Sheffield Academic, 1992, pp. 161-83.

————. "Ecumenicity and Ecclesiology: The Promise of the Multiple Letter Canon of the New Testament." In *The New Testament as Canon: A Reader in Canonical Criticism,* ed. E. E. Lemcio and R. W. Wall. JSNTSS 76. Sheffield: Sheffield Academic, 1992, pp. 184-207.

————. "The Canonical Function of 2 Peter." *BibInt* 9 (2001), pp. 64-81.

————. "Introduction to the Epistolary Literature of the NT." In *NIB* 10. Nashville: Abingdon, 2002, pp. 369-91.

————. "A Unifying Theology of the Catholic Epistles: A Canonical Approach." In *The Catholic Epistles and the Tradition,* ed. J. Schlosser. BETL 176. Leuven: Leuven University Press, 2004, pp. 43-71.

————. "The Function of the Pastoral Epistles within the Pauline Canon of the New Testament: A Canonical Approach." In *The Pauline Canon.* ed. S. E. Porter. Leiden: Brill, 2004, pp. 27-44.

Wall, R. W., and Lemcio, E. E. *The New Testament as Canon: A Reader in Canonical Criticism.* JSNTSS 76. Sheffield: Sheffield Academic, 1992.

Westcott, B. F. *A General Survey of the History of the Canon of the New Testament.* 6th ed. Grand Rapids: Baker, 1980.

Other Works Cited

Achtemeier, P. J., J. Green, and M. M. Thompson. *Introducing the New Testament: Its Literature and Theology.* Grand Rapids: Eerdmans, 2001.

Anderson, P. N. *The Christology of the Fourth Gospel.* Norcross: Trinity, 1996.

Ashton, J. "History and Theology in New Testament Studies." In *The Nature of New Testament Theology,* ed. C. Rowland and C. Tuckett. Oxford: Blackwell, 2007, pp. 1-17.

Barton, J. "Historical-Critical Approaches." In *The Cambridge Companion to Biblical Interpretation,* ed. J. Barton. Cambridge: Cambridge University Press, 1998, pp. 9-20.

Barton, J., ed. *The Cambridge Companion to Biblical Interpretation.* Cambridge: Cambridge University Press, 1998.

Bassler, J. *1 & 2 Timothy and Titus.* ANTC. Nashville: Abingdon, 1996.

Bauer, W. *Orthodoxy and Heresy in Earliest Christianity.* London: SCM, 1971.

Brooks, J. A. *An Introduction to the New Testament.* ABRL. New York: Doubleday, 1997.

Davidson, R. "The Imagery of Isaiah 40:6-8 in Tradition and Interpretation." In *The Quest for Context and Meaning: Studies in Biblical Intertextuality in Honor of James A. Sanders.* Leiden: Brill, 1997, pp. 37-55.

Davies, S. L. *The New Testament: A Contemporary Introduction.* San Francisco: Harper & Row, 1988.

deSilva, D. *An Introduction to the New Testament: Contexts, Methods and Ministry Formation.* Downers Grove: Intervarsity, 2004.

Drane, J. W. *Introducing the New Testament.* Oxford: Lion, 2000.

Dunn, J. D. G. *Unity and Diversity in the New Testament.* London: SCM, 1977.

Dunnett, W. M. *Exploring the New Testament.* Wheaton: Crossway, 2001.

Ehrman, B. *A Brief Introduction to the New Testament.* Oxford: Oxford University Press, 2004.

———. *The New Testament: A Historical Introduction to the Early Christian Writings.* 4th ed. Oxford: Oxford University Press, 2007.

Fahey, M. *Cyprian and the Bible: A Study in Third-Century Exegesis.* Tübingen: Mohr, 1971.

Fanning, B. M. *Verbal Aspect in New Testament Greek.* Oxford: Clarendon, 1990.

Fiensy, D. A. *New Testament Introduction.* CPNC. Joplin: College, 1997.

Fitzmyer, J. A. "The Name Simon." In *Essays on the Semitic Background of the New Testament.* London: Geoffrey Chapman, 1971, pp. 105-12.

Gathercole, S. J. *Where Is Boasting? Early Jewish Soteriology and Paul's Response in Romans 1–5.* Grand Rapids: Eerdmans, 2002.

Grant, R. M. *Eusebius as Church Historian.* Oxford: Clarendon, 1980.

———. *Irenaeus of Lyons.* London: Routledge, 1997.

Gundry, R. *A Survey of the New Testament.* 4th ed. Grand Rapids: Zondervan, 2003.

Gustafsson, B. "Eusebius' Principles in Handling His Sources as Found in His Church History, Books I-VII." *TU* 79 (1961), pp. 429-41.

Guthrie, D. *New Testament Introduction.* Rev. ed. Downers Grove: InterVarsity, 1990.

Hanson P. D. *Dynamic Transcendence: The Correlation of Confessional Heritage and Contemporary Experience in a Biblical Model of Divine Activity.* Philadelphia: Fortress, 1978.

Harnack, A. *History of Dogma.* Vol. 2. Boston: Little, Brown, 1901.

———. *Marcion: The Gospel of the Alien God.* Durham: Labyrinth, 1990.

Hengel, M. *Judaism and Hellenism.* Vol. 1. London: SCM, 1974.

Jackson-McCabe, M. A., ed. *Jewish Christianity Reconsidered: Rethinking Ancient Groups and Texts.* Minneapolis: Augsburg Fortress, 2007.

Johnson, L. T. *The Writings of the New Testament: An Interpretation.* Rev. ed. Philadelphia: Fortress, 1999.

Klauck, H.-J. *Ancient Letters and the New Testament.* Waco: Baylor University Press, 2006.

Legaspi, M. C. *The Death of Scripture and the Rise of Biblical Studies.* Oxford: Oxford University Press, 2010.

Levison, J. R. *Filled with the Spirit.* Grand Rapids: Eerdmans, 2009.

Lieu, J. *Neither Jew Nor Greek: Constructing Early Christianity.* New York: Clark, 2002.

Lightfoot, J. B. *The Apostolic Fathers.* 5 vols. London: Macmillan, 1890. Reprint Grand Rapids: Baker, 1981.

Lüdemann, G. *Opposition to Paul in Jewish Christianity.* Minneapolis: Fortress, 1989.

————. *Heretics: The Other Side of Christianity.* London: SCM, 1996.

McDonald, L. M., and S. Porter. *Early Christianity and Its Sacred Literature.* Peabody: Hendrickson, 2000.

Nogalski, J. D., and M. A. Sweeney, eds. *Reading and Hearing the Book of the Twelve.* SBLSS 15. Atlanta: SBL, 2000.

Pervo, R. I. *Dating Acts: Between the Evangelists and the Apologists.* Santa Rosa: Polebridge, 2006.

Pregeant, R. *Engaging the New Testament: An Interdisciplinary Approach.* Minneapolis: Fortress, 1997.

Quinn, J. D. "Notes on the Text of P72." *CBQ* 27 (1965), pp. 241-49.

Räisänen, H. *Neutestamentliche Theologie? Eine religionswissenschaftliche Alternative.* SBS 186. Stuttgart: Katholisches Bibelwerk, 2000.

Robinson, J. A. T. *Redating the New Testament.* Philadelphia: Westminster, 1976.

Spivey, R. A., D. M. Smith, and C. Black. *Anatomy of the New Testament.* 5th ed. Upper Saddle River: Prentice-Hall, 2006.

Theissen, G. *The New Testament.* London: Clark, 2003.

Thielman, F. *Theology of the New Testament: A Canonical and Synthetic Approach.* Grand Rapids: Zondervan, 2005.

Tyson, J. B. *Marcion and Luke-Acts: A Defining Struggle.* Columbia: University of South Carolina Press, 2006.

van Unnik, W. C. "Solitude and Community in the New Testament." *Sparsa Collectica 2: The Collected Essays of W. C. Unnik.* NovTSup 30. Leiden: Brill, 1980, pp. 241-47.

————. "'Diaspora' and 'Church' in the First Centuries of Christian History." In *Sparsa Collectica 3: The Collected Essays of W. C. Unnik.* NovTSup 31. Leiden: Brill, 1983, pp. 95-103.

Vögtle, A. *Das neue Testament und die Zukunft des Kosmos.* Düsseldorf: Patmos, 1970.

Wall, R. W. "Rule of Faith in Theological Hermeneutics." In *Between Two Horizons: Spanning New Testament Studies and Systematic Theology,* ed. J. B Green and M. Turner. Grand Rapids: Eerdmans, 2000, pp. 88-107.

―――. *Acts. NIB* 10. Nashville: Abingdon, 2002.

Wall, R. W., with R. B. Steele. *1-2 Timothy and Titus.* THNTC. Grand Rapids: Eerdmans, 2012.

Williams, M. A. *Rethinking "Gnosticism": An Argument for Dismantling a Dubious Category.* Princeton: Princeton University Press, 1996.

Wilson, E. O. *The Social Conquest of Earth.* New York: Liveright, 2012.

Wolterstorff, N. *Art in Action.* Grand Rapids: Eerdmans, 1980.

Young, F. *The Theology of the Pastoral Letters.* Cambridge: Cambridge University Press, 1994.

Index of Modern Authors

Index of Subjects and Ancient Names and Texts

Abraham, 25-26, 82-83, 88-92, 119n.48, 123, 133

Acts of Peter, 24-25, 112

Acts of the Apostles: brokering the relationship between Paul and Pillars, 20-21, 30, 34-35, 47-48, 53, 60-68, 174, 214n.51, 253, 257, 274; in canon lists, 28, 30-32, 34, 63; Irenaeus's strategic use of, 20-21; as Luke-Acts, 4, 11; narrative character portraits of NT persons, 30, 43n.7, 49-50, 56, 59-68, 75, 79, 93, 99-103, 129-31, 159-61, 220, 250-54, 275; in relation to the CE (the "Apostolos"), 29-30, 32, 34-35, 40, 44, 47, 53, 60-68, 115, 163, 250-51, 257

Adam, 192, 234

Aliens, Christians as, 103, 104n.21, 119, 146, 148, 153, 202n.43, 258, 262, 264, 267, 269-72

Amphilochius of Iconium: on CE sequence, 30; *Iambics for Seleucus,* 37n.39, 113n.37, 225; on James as the first CE, 78; on the number seven, 29, 37; witness to dispute over number of CE, 225

Angels: 23, 37, 240, 242, 255; in 1 Peter, 125; in 2 Peter, 137-40, 156; in Jude, 221n.4, 228-32, 234, 236-39

Antioch, 22, 31, 38, 67, 99, 129

Apocalypse: of God's victory/salvation, 88, 93, 192, 251; in James, 86; in 1 Peter, 267; in 2 Peter, 147-49, 156, 162, 259; in 1 John, 186; in Paul, 275

Apocalypse of Baruch, 107

Apocalypse of John: associated with, but ultimately separated from Johannine letters, 47, 158, 174, 247; canonical placement in scholarly reconstruction, 4, 7; inclusion of seven letters, 37; use of OT in, 102

Apocalypse of Peter, 23, 24n.19, 112

Architecture, ethics of, 14-15

Athanasius of Alexandria: on Hebrews, 59; on James, 78; witness to the CE, 29-30, 32

Augustine of Hippo: on 1-2 John, 167n.8; on James, 78-79, 225; on Jude, 225; on the priority of Peter, 253n.8; witness to CE collection, 33-35, 78-79. Works: *De Trin. (De Trinitate),* 79n.6; *Doc. (On Christian Doctrine),* 33n.32; *Fide. (On Faith and Works),* 34-35, 79nn.6-7

Authority: *passim, but see:* apostolic, 24, 65, 99, 227, 255-56, 259; biblical, 13, 152-53; canonical, despite authorship questions, 32-33, 47-48, 97-98; of collections rather than individual texts, 48;

conflict over, 138-39, 215, 221n.4, 222, 230-32, 237, 241-42; of eyewitnesses, 46, 57, 60-61, 102, 135, 156, 160-61, 175n.23, 184, 194, 200, 241, 251, 255, 265, 275; of James, 25, 47-50, 62, 75; of John, 158-59, 169, 175n.24, 207; of Jude, 36, 47-48; of Paul, 20, 21, 34, 57, 144-45, 250-52; of Peter, 97-103, 128, 135, 156; of Pillars, 22, 40, 47, 99, 158, 250-52. *For the individual CE, see the introductions to each letter. See also* Rule of Faith

Authorities, civil, cultural, and celestial, 120-22, 125

Babylon: as cipher for Rome, 96, 129, 152, 253; as location of exile, 104, 118, 152

Balaam, 140, 221n.4, 234, 237

Baptism: as anointing, 188; homilies as proposed source behind 1 Peter, 103; into hope, 156, 269-70; as participation in Christ's death and resurrection, 125, 147, 150-51, 197; and post-baptismal sin, 141, 173

Barnabas, 25

Barnabas, Letter of, 27-28

2 Baruch, 109n.31

Biblical scholarship, modern: approach to Hebrews, 58-60; approach to James, 74-75; approach to 1-3 John, 163, 167n.8; approach to 1-2 Peter, 95-97, 151; commitments of, 3-12; in distinction from canonical approach, 40-42, 71, 74, 247, 275-76; forced distinction between *Historie* and *Geschichte,* 18-19

Canon: aesthetic excellence of, 11-15, 39, 43-45, 48, 59, 248-50, 273-74; authority of, despite authorship questions, 32-33, 47-48, 97-98; categories of, 28; catholic tendencies reflected, 9-10, 38-39, 42, 45, 53, 106, 163, 165-66; determined by utility, 13-15, 17, 29, 42,

113, 158; epistemology, Pauline and Pillars, 57-58, 60-62, 160, 251; scholarly reconstruction of, 3-8; self-correcting and internally informing, 41, 48n.14, 53, 62; shape as indicative of function, 11-15, 43, 52n.22, 53, 64, 73, 225, 252; shape of, in relation to the CE, 40-69; shaping of, in relation to the CE, 17-39

Canonical approach: *demonstrated throughout, but see* 5, 9-16, 58-60, 63n.33, 68-69, 97, 147, 151, 158, 273-76

Canonization: catholic tendencies of, 9-10, 38-39, 42, 45, 53, 106, 163, 165-66; of collections, 10-16; as ecclesial deceit, 3-4; ethics of, 14-15; from above and below, 12, 18-19; point of vs. point of composition, 4-5, 9-11, 40-43, 53-54, 61-62, 71-72, 76, 104, 250, 273, 275-76

Cassiodorus, 33, 173n.21, 223, 225, 253n.8

Catholic: the ancient tradition, 10-12, 20, 20n.8, 27-28, 37-39, 42, 47, 60, 158, 169n.9, 220n.1; "early catholicism," 61-62, 221; tendencies, reflected in the canon, 9-10, 38-39, 42, 45, 53, 106, 163, 165-66

Catholic Epistles: *passim, but see:* in dialogue with the PE, 52-58; epistemology of, 57-58, 60-62, 160, 251; historical emergence, 19-35; in modern biblical scholarship, 3-8; in relation to Acts (the "Apostolos"), 29-30, 32, 34-35, 40, 44, 47, 53, 60-68, 115, 163, 250-51, 257

Christians: as aliens, 103, 104n.21, 119, 146, 148, 153, 202n.43, 258, 262, 264, 267, 269-72; as "born" again, anew, of God, 115, 118-19, 130, 165, 190-92, 194-95, 197, 199-200, 212, 215, 218, 259, 268, 271; as exiles, 100, 105, 114, 117, 119, 129, 152, 264, 267, 269

Circumcision, 26, 66-67, 76; as euphemism for Jews, 21-22, 75, 257

Index of Scripture References